# Windows NT®
# TCP/IP

**New Riders**

201 West 103rd Street,
Indianapolis, Indiana 46290

Karanjit S. Siyan, Ph.D.

# Windows NT® TCP/IP

Karanjit S. Siyan, Ph.D.

International Standard Book Number: 1-56205-887-8

Library of Congress Catalog Card Number: 98-84884

Printed in the United States of America

First Printing: *August, 1998*

00   99   98            4   3   2   1

Interpretation of the printing code: The rightmost double-digit number is the year of the book's printing; the rightmost single-digit, the number of the book's printing. For example, the printing code 98-1 shows that the first printing of the book occurred in 1998.

*Composed in Bembo and MCPdigital by Macmillan Computer Publishing*

**Executive Editor**
Al Valvano

**Acquisitions Editor**
Stephanie Layton

**Development Editor**
Robin Drake

**Managing Editor**
Sarah Kearns

**Project Editor**
Christopher Morris

**Copy Editor**
Daryl Kessler

**Indexer**
Craig Small

**Technical Reviewers**
John Baker
Roneil Icatar
Lance Skok
Bob Wells

**Production**
Lisa England
Chris Livengood
Eric S. Miller
Heather Shephenson

# About the Author

**Karanjit S. Siyan** is president of Kinetics Corporation. He has authored international seminars on Solaris & SunOS, TCP/IP networks, PC network integration, Windows NT, Novell networks, and Expert Systems using Fuzzy Logic. He teaches advanced technology seminars in the United States, Canada, Europe and the Far East. Dr. Siyan has published articles in *Dr. Dobbs Journal, The C Users Journal, Database Advisor,* and is actively involved in Internet research. Karanjit has worked with computer networks for UNIX, NetWare, Windows NT, OS/2, and computer languages such as C/C++, Pascal, LISP, Algol, Ada, MSL, Jovial, Java for many years. He has written compilers for a number of these languages. Karanjit holds a Ph.D in Computer Science, a Masters degree in Electrical Engineering and Computer Science, and a Bachelor's degree in Electronics and Electrical Communication Engineering. He is a member of IEEE, and ACM, and his career achievements are recorded in *Marquis' Who's Who in the World, Who is Who in America, Who's Who in Finance and Industry,* and *Who's Who in Science and Engineering.*

Before working as an independent consultant, Karanjit worked as a senior member of the technical staff at ROLM Corporation, and as a software developer and technical manager on numerous projects. As part of his consulting work, Karanjit has written a number of custom compiler and operating system development tools. His interests include UNIX-based, NetWare-based, Windows NT-based, and OS/2- based networks. He is actively involved in the application of many computer science disciplines such as networks, operating systems, programming languages, databases, expert systems and computer security. Dr. Siyan holds certification credentials for a number of commercial operating system products, and has written numerous books.

# About the Technical Reviewers

These reviewers contributed their considerable practical, hands-on expertise to the entire development process for *Windows NT TCP/IP.* As the book was being written, these individuals reviewed all the material for technical content, organization, and usability. Their feedback was critical to ensuring that *Windows NT TCP/IP* fits your need for the highest quality technical information.

**Roneil Icatar** is an MCSE who has worked with Windows NT and TCP/IP for over five years. He is currently employed by GE Capital IT Solutions as a Senior Systems Engineer designing and developing BackOffice Solutions for Fortune 500 companies and government and educational institutions. He has installed and configured TCP/IP-based systems in all different types and sizes of environments. He has also written a couple of articles for *Windows NT Magazine* and is an avid participant in the Microsoft Windows NT Newsgroups on the Internet.

**Lance Skok** is a LAN/WAN Support-Process Specialist with Southwestern Bell Telephone Company in San Antonio, TX. Before coming to work for Southwestern Bell Telephone, he held a position of Senior Systems Engineer at Inacom Information Systems for four years. He holds numerous industry certifications including Microsoft Certified Systems Engineer (MCSE), Novell Master CNE and a Cisco Certified Network Professional (CCNP). He has been heavily involved with PCs since 1980 and has skills in programming, networking, and systems integration. He is currently working toward becoming a Cisco Certified Internetwork Engineer (CCIE). You can reach him at lskok@netfix.com.

# Contents

# Acknowledgments

One of the more pleasurable tasks of being an author is to thank the people responsible for the success of a book. I wish to thank all those close to me: Ahal Singh, Tejinder Kaur, Harjeet, Jagjit, Kookie and Dolly. Special thanks to Mother, Saint Germain, El Morya Khan, Djwal Kul, Kuthumi Lal Singh, Kuan-Yin, Bhagwan Krishna and Babaji. Without their spiritual support, this book would not have been possible.

I want to thank Bob Sanregret and Anders Amundson, who initially got me interested in writing teaching materials about computers. I also wish to thank the many people at Learning Tree for their help and support on various projects. In particular I would like to thank Professor John Moriarty, Rick Adamson, Dr. David Collins, Eric Garen, Marti Sanregret, Nancy Harrison, Richard Beaumont, David O'Neil, Robin Johnston and Tom Spurling.

I wish to thank Robin Drake, the development editor, for her experience and professionalism, Stephanie Layton for her numerous phone calls to see if I was on track and her encouragement and cheerful attitude, and Chris Morris and Daryl Kessler for their help in developing this book.

I also wish to thank Drew and Blythe Heywood for their friendship, support and encouragement throughout the many years it has been my pleasure to know them.

# Introduction

There are a number of books in the marketplace about TCP/IP technologies in general, and in recent years there have been even more books written about TCP/IP technologies for the Windows NT and Windows 9x platforms. With the availability of such a diverse range of books on this topic, you might wonder what this book, *Windows NT TCP/IP*, offers.

This book is unique in several respects. While the book covers the features of TCP/IP as it relates to Windows NT 4, beta 1 of NT 5.0, and the Windows 9x platforms, it provides many architectural details of how TCP/IP is implemented on these platforms not found in a single source. This book provides a discussion of the step-by-step procedure to perform administration tasks related to TCP/IP configuration and administration. The decision to provide step-by-step instructions was made to make this book as complete a reference as possible. In many instances, rather than simply provide a step-by-step procedure, which in many cases can be figured out by the advanced reader, there is also an explanation about the concepts behind the decisions made. For example, Chapter 7, "Routing with Microsoft TCP/IP," explains the concepts of OSPF areas and creating virtual links between OSPF areas while presenting the step-by-step instructions to configure OSPF routing. This same chapter also outlines concepts of supernetting, VLSMs (Variable-Length Subnet Masks) and CIDR (Classless Internet Domain Routing), which are not covered in the standard Microsoft documentation and books that are introductory discussions or are focused on the MCSE exams for TCP/IP.

The book also details advanced configuration of TCP/IP parameters through the Registry and the use of Perl5 scripting language to perform these tasks. The Perl5 script examples are addressed line-by-line, so that even though you may not be familiar with Perl5 you can be well on your way to learning this language through the included examples.

There is also a review of TCP/IP traces generated when performing various tasks on a Windows network. These protocol traces are discussed in detail with a complete breakdown of the different fields and actions performed by packets at the Data Link layer, IP layer, TCP layer, NBT (NetBIOS over TCP/IP), SMB (Server Message Block), MSRPC (Microsoft Remote Procedure Call). These protocol traces provide valuable insight into the workings of a TCP/IP network.

## Who Should Read This Book?

This book is for the networking professional who is responsible for administering and managing a Windows NT network that is configured to use the TCP/IP protocol. If you have worked with TCP/IP using other operating systems, you will gain insight and understanding on how TCP/IP is implemented in Windows NT. If you have not worked with Windows NT before, this book will still be of value to you; it exposes you to the architecture of Windows NT and how the TCP/IP protocol and application services work.

# What Is Covered in This Book?

The following is a brief overview on the chapters in this book.

## Chapter 1: TCP/IP Architecture for Windows

Chapter 1 introduces the protocol layering concepts for Windows NT and Windows 9x networks. The OSI layer concepts as they apply to Windows TCP/IP networks are discussed in detail.

## Chapter 2: TCP/IP Protocols Infrastructure for Windows Networks

Chapter 2 discusses the protocols used in Windows TCP/IP networks. The packet structure for the TCP/IP, NBF, and SMB protocols is explained.

## Chapter 3: Installing the TCP/IP Protocol and Services

Chapter 3 details how the network components and TCP/IP protocols are installed on Windows workstations. The installation procedure and issues associated with Windows NT and Windows 98 workstations are discussed.

## Chapter 4: Configuring TCP/IP

Chapter 4 discusses considerations in performing additional configuration for TCP/IP. Name resolution configuration, FTP, and Internet printer services are covered.

## Chapter 5: Advanced TCP/IP Configuration Using the Registry and Perl

Chapter 5 discusses changes to TCP/IP configuration by directly changing the Registry. This chapter also addresses the use of advanced scripting tools such as the Perl5 scripting language in configuring TCP/IP parameters.

## Chapter 6: TCP/IP Protocol Traces

Chapter 6 presents TCP/IP protocol traces for some sample sessions and tasks on a Windows TCP/IP network. The packet headers of several protocol traces are discussed in detail.

## Chapter 7: Routing with Microsoft TCP/IP

Chapter 7 covers IP routing concepts, subnetting, supernetting, VLSMs, and CIDR. This chapter reviews RIP and OSPF and the configuration of Windows NT as a router with RIP and OSPF routing protocols.

## Chapter 8: DHCP Configuration and Management

Chapter 8 discusses the DHCP protocol and mechanism in considerable detail. The procedure for configuring DHCP on a Windows NT server and the DHCP client configuration is outlined.

## Chapter 9: TCP/IP Name Resolution Using WINS

Chapter 9 focuses on name resolution using Microsoft's implementation of a NetBIOS Name Server, called *Windows Internet Name Service (WINS)*. This chapter also discusses the other name resolution methods, such as LMHOSTS and broadcasts, used in Windows NT networks in general, with a special emphasis on how you can install and configure WINS name resolution on a Windows NT network.

## Chapter 10: TCP/IP Name Resolution Using DNS

Chapter 10 discusses the *Domain Name System (DNS)*, a hierarchical, distributed naming system that is commonly used in most TCP/IP networks. This chapter also discusses configuring a Windows NT server as a DNS server. Topics covered include creating name servers, delegating subdomains, integrating DNS and WINS, troubleshooting name services, and configuring security issues.

## Chapter 11: Network Management for Microsoft Networks Using SNMP

Chapter 11 explains the use of the TCP/IP management protocol Simple Network Management Protocol (SNMP). The concepts underlying SNMP operation are presented along with the configuration of SNMP agents on Windows workstations.

## Chapter 12: Accessing the Internet Using RAS and PPTP

Chapter 12 discusses RAS dial in/dial out access services from a Windows TCP/IP network. Also emphasized are IP routing capabilities of the RAS server, and configuration of PPTP and the L2P (Layer 2 Protocol) used for building Virtual Private Networks (VPNs).

## Chapter 13: Network File System Protocol Support for Microsoft Networks

Chapter 13 outlines the *Network File System (NFS)*, a file service protocol originally developed by SUN Microsystems and licensed to a large number of vendors. This chapter teaches you about the different components of the NFS protocol and discusses the configuration of NFS services for Windows NT.

### Chapter 14: TCP/IP Mail Services for Microsoft Networks

Chapter 14 discusses the use of SMTP, POP3, and IMAP4 to provide Internet mail services in a Windows TCP/IP network.

### Chapter 15: Diagnostic Tools for Microsoft TCP/IP Networks

Chapter 15 presents the diagnostic tools that ship with Windows platforms that can be used for troubleshooting and finding out statistical information on the behavior of TCP/IP networks.

# Conventions Used in this Book

Use of the version abbreviation *Windows 9x* indicates that the topic of discussion applies to both Windows 95 and Windows 98. In cases where the topic specifically involves one version or the other, the appropriate version number is indicated. Code and output examples presented separately from regular paragraphs appear in a monospaced computer typeface. Here's an example:

```
134.21.22.13    NTK           #PRE
#INCLUDE    \\NTKS\ETC\LMHOSTS
```

Occasionally, syntax lines include placeholders such as *name*; the italics indicate that *name* is to be replaced with the appropriate value (a filename, in this case).

# 1

# TCP/IP Architecture for Windows

T HE TCP/IP PROTOCOL HAS BEEN IMPLEMENTED on almost all major operating systems and computers ranging from microcomputers and embedded systems to main frame computers and supercomputers. In this section the implementation of the TCP/IP protocol in the Windows operating system is examined. Specifically, you learn about Microsoft's Windows 9x (Windows 95 and Windows 98) and Windows NT operating system implementations. Differences in Windows 95 and Windows 98 implementations are pointed out.

## Protocol Layering for Windows NT and Windows 9x

Although both the Windows NT and Windows 9x operating systems have a similar user interface, their internal architecture is quite different. As a result of differences in this internal architecture, there are differences in the TCP/IP implementation.

Protocol layering concepts for computer systems are traditionally discussed in terms of the Open Systems Interconnection (OSI) model. This model was developed in 1978 by the International Organization of Standards (ISO) and provides a model for developing and describing communication between different communication systems. This chapter uses this time-honored model for describing the different components of the TCP/IP protocol.

## Understanding Protocol Layering in Terms of the OSI Model

Figure 1.1 shows the OSI model and where the TCP/IP protocol fits within this model. The OSI model is an abstract model and serves as a yardstick to describe the different communication functions. When you understand the different communication functions in the model, and see how this corresponds to an actual protocol implementation, you gain immediate knowledge and insight into what that protocol does.

In Figure 1.1, the Internet Protocol (IP) corresponds to layer 3 of the OSI model. Layer 3 of the OSI model is the Network layer and includes the function of network address naming and routing. The network address naming enables nodes in two physically dissimilar networks to have a uniform address format. This uniform address enables the interconnected system to be treated as a single logical system or network by upper layers of the protocol. The routing function of the Network layer enables chunks of data, called *packets*, to be delivered to the correct destination. The routing function is typically performed by Intermediate System (IS) devices called *routers* (see Figure 1.2) that operate at the Network layer of the OSI model. Routers examine the destination address in a packet and forward the packet to the next destination, which brings the packet closer to its ultimate destination.

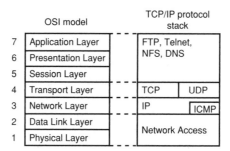

**Figure 1.1** The OSI model and TCP/IP.

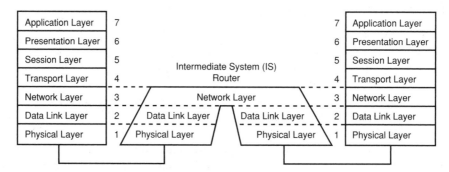

**Figure 1.2** Intermediate Systems (Routers).

Because the Internet Protocol corresponds to layer 3 of the OSI model we can, based on the earlier discussion, deduce the following properties of the Internet Protocol on Windows network:

- The Internet Protocol on a Windows computer provides uniform address naming. The uniform address consists of a 32-bit number called the IP address. The IP address should generally be different for each IP node. That is, each Windows computer must have a unique IP address. If you connect to the Internet, these IP address assignments are obtained from a global or regional INTERNIC or your Internet Service Provider (ISP).

- The Internet Protocol on a Windows computer provides routing functions. The routing function enables the Windows computer to forward IP packets, called IP *datagrams*, to the next destination. A Windows NT computer can perform routing. In large networks, routers are used to perform the routing functions to speed the forwarding of IP datagrams and avoid delays in the router caused by heavy network traffic. Special routing protocols such as RIP (Routing Information Protocol) and OSPF (Open Shortest Path First) that interact with Internet Protocol are used to calculate the best path to a particular destination. These routing protocols are discussed in Chapter 7, "Routing with Microsoft TCP/IP."

Figure 1.1 shows that the Internet Protocol runs on top of the Data Link layer (layer 2), which in turn rests on the Physical layer (layer 1) of the OSI model. An OSI layer makes use of the services immediately below that layer and adds to the services provided by the lower layer. The Data Link layer of the OSI model corresponds to network hardware such as Ethernet Network Interface Cards (NICs) and Token Ring NICs. Therefore, the OSI layer 3, which corresponds to the Internet Protocol, makes use of the network hardware such as Ethernet and Token Ring NICs in sending and receiving IP datagrams. The Internet Protocol can run on a variety of Data Link layer network hardware such as Ethernet, Token Ring, Frame Relay, X.25, ATM, ISDN, and so on. This is an important point to note because the use of the Internet Protocol provides independence from the variety of network hardware that you can choose to build a network. Protocols located above the Internet Protocol on the OSI model, such as the Transmission Control Protocol (TCP), do not have to be concerned about the details and differences in network hardware on a physical network.

All IP implementations are required to implement an auxiliary protocol called the Internet Control Message Protocol (ICMP) that is used for diagnostic purposes and for reporting problems with IP datagrams at different points of transit on a network. For example, the PING tool used that is commonly used in TCP/IP networks to test if a TCP/IP node is reachable uses the ICMP echo request/echo reply packets to accomplish this.

Figure 1.1 shows that TCP corresponds to layer 4 of the OSI model. Layer 4 of the OSI model is the Transport layer and includes the function of reliable delivery, or end-to-end data integrity.

The Transport layer in the OSI model provides enhancements to the services of the Network layer. These enhancements include reliable data delivery over the network and process multiplexing/demultiplexing. To ensure reliable delivery, the Transport layer builds on the error-control mechanisms provided by the lower layers. If the lower layers do a less than adequate job, the Transport layer must work harder. This layer is the last chance for error recovery. In fact, when it comes to providing error-free delivery, you could say, "the buck stops here," at the Transport layer. The Transport layer also may be responsible for creating several logical connections over the same network connection, a process called multiplexing.

*Multiplexing* (or time sharing) occurs when a number of transport connections share the same network connection. The Transport layer is the middle layer of the OSI model. The three lower layers constitute the *subnet* (portion of the network model), and the three upper layers are usually implemented by networking software on the node. The Transport layer is usually implemented on the node also; its job is to convert an unreliable subnet into a more reliable network.

Because of multiplexing, several software elements (OSI terminology uses the term *protocol entities*) share the same Network layer address. To uniquely identify the software elements within the Transport layer, a more general form of addressing is necessary. These addresses, called *transport addresses*, usually are a combination of the Network layer address and a transport *Service Access Point* (SAP) number. Sometimes the names *sockets* or *port numbers* are used to identify transport addresses. In the TCP protocol, the SAP addresses are called port numbers, which can be 16-bit numerical values. For example, the FTP protocol uses TCP port number 21, the Telnet protocol uses TCP port number 23 and the HTTP protocol uses TCP port number 80.

Knowing what the Transport layer does, and also knowing that TCP corresponds to layer 4 of the OSI model we can, based on the earlier discussion of the Transport layer, deduce the following properties for TCP on Windows network:

- The Transmission Control Protocol on a Windows computer provides reliable end-to-end data delivery. The TCP has built-in error checking to compensate for errors that may be caused by lower layers. The reliable delivery is achieved by creating separate logical connections and ensuring that data that is sent is delivered reliably to the upper layers in the order in which it is sent.

- The Transmission Control Protocol on a Windows computer provides software addressing of each end of the network connection. These software addresses or transport addresses are called TCP port numbers.

- The Transmission Control Protocol on a Windows computer provides multiplexing of several logical connections on the same network interface.

All TCP/IP implementations are also required to implement a simpler transport protocol called User Datagram Protocol (UDP) for applications in which the robustness and reliability of TCP/IP are not needed and may be an extra overhead. Therefore, all Windows TCP/IP implementations also implement UDP. UDP is useful in applications that are request-reply oriented. These are applications where a request is sent and a reply is expected, and there is no need to maintain an open logical connection. For example, both DNS and SNMP use UDP as the transport protocol because they are request-reply oriented. UDP is also useful when the nature of the network traffic is broadcast- or multicast-oriented. This is true in Windows networks where many of the browsing and service advertising functions require a broadcast or multicast protocol.

The TCP/IP applications such as Domain Name System (DNS), Telnet, File Transfer Protocol (FTP), Network File System (NFS) interface directly with the TCP or UDP protocols. These TCP/IP applications correspond to the Application layer (layer 7) in the OSI model. Interestingly enough, there are few TCP/IP applications that use protocols that correspond to the Session and Presentation layers of the OSI model. A notable exception to this is NFS, which uses protocols such as Remote Procedure Call (RPC) and External Data Representation (XDR) that correspond to the Session and Presentation layers of the OSI model, respectively.

The reason why few TCP/IP applications use protocols that correspond to the Session and Presentation layers in the OSI model is that these layers provide services and functions that are not needed by a majority of the TCP/IP applications. The Session layer in the OSI model provides enhanced session services such as dialog control, token control, and activity management. The Presentation layer in the OSI model manages how data is represented. The Presentation layer takes into account differences in number and character representation and whether the natural data representation on a computer is little endian or big endian. *Little endian* and *big endian* are terms used to describe how numbers are stored on the computer. The little endian format stores the least significant portion of the number in the lower memory address, whereas the big endian format stores the most significant portion of the number in the lower address. Differences in number format can result in confusion especially when these number values are received by a computer that uses a different format than the sender. The NFS application protocol needs services from OSI layers 6 and 7, and this is the reason why NFS uses the Presentation and Session layer services.

There are several excellent textbooks in the marketplace that describe the details of the TCP/IP protocol headers, including the book *Inside TCP/IP* from New Riders Publishing, written by the author of this book.

## Understanding the Windows NT Architecture

The TCP/IP protocol for Windows NT is implemented as a driver in the Windows NT Input/Output component of the Windows NT Executive. As a first step to understanding the TCP/IP protocol, you should understand what the Windows NT Input/Output subsystem is and the general architecture of Windows NT. This will help you understand how TCP/IP fits inside the Windows NT system.

Figure 1.3 shows the components of a Windows NT system. The general architectural features shown in this figure apply to both the Windows NT Workstation and Windows NT Server products.

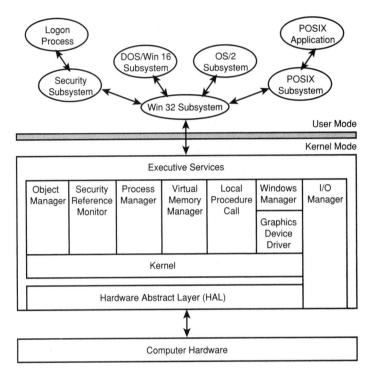

**Figure 1.3** Windows NT Architecture.

Windows NT was designed using a modular approach. The different modules (also called *components*) of Windows NT are shown in Figure 1.3. The Windows NT Server product is optimized for server performance and provides support for the Windows NT domain, Active Directory architecture, and server-specific tools and applications that are not available on Windows NT Workstation.

The Windows NT operating system components can run in two modes: user mode and kernel mode (refer to Figure 1.3). When an operating system component runs in the *kernel mode*, it has access to the full range of machine instructions for that processor and can generally access all resources on the computer system. In Windows NT the Executive Services, the kernel, and the HAL (Hardware Abstraction Layer) run in the kernel mode. The Win32 subsystem and other environmental subsystems such as DOS/Win16, OS/2 and POSIX subsystems run in the *user mode*. By placing these subsystems in the user mode, the Windows NT designers can modify them more easily without changing components that are designed to run in the kernel mode. Another advantage of the kernel mode is that the operating system code is protected from non-friendly programs that may deliberately or inadvertently try to modify the behavior of the operating system.

The Hardware Abstraction Layer virtualizes the computer hardware, so that the kernel can be written to the hardware virtual interface, instead of the actual machine hardware. For the most part, the kernel uses the HAL to access computer resources. This means that the kernel and all other components that depend on the kernel can be easily ported by Microsoft to other hardware platforms. A small portion of the kernel, as well as the I/O Manager, accesses the computer hardware directly without involving HAL.

The Kernel layer (refer to Figure 1.3) provides the basic operating system functions used by other executive components. The kernel component is relatively small and provides core operating system functions. The kernel is primarily responsible for thread scheduling, hardware exception handling, and multiprocessor synchronization.

The Executive components are kernel-mode operating system components that implement services such as managing objects (Object Manager), security (Security Reference Monitor), process management (Process Manager), memory management (Virtual Memory Manager), a local procedure call facility, and I/O Management (I/O Manager).

The subsystems, also called *environmental subsystems*, are user-mode servers that create and support an operating system environment such as for DOS/Win16 applications, OS/2 subsystems, POSIX subsystems, and security subsystems.

The Hardware Abstraction Layer interfaces directly with the computer hardware and provides a machine-independent interface to the Windows NT Kernel layer (see Figure 1.4). This machine-independent interface allows the kernel to be written in a machine-independent manner, and this promotes the portability of the operating system. The HAL routines can be called by the base operating system and from device drivers.

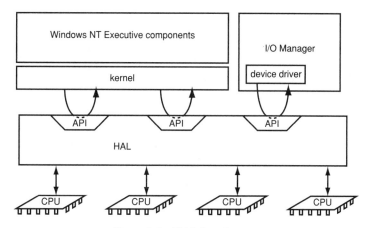

Figure 1.4    HAL Interface.

For computer hardware that uses Symmetric Multi-Processing (SMP), HAL provides a number of virtual processors that can be used by the operating system kernel.

HAL can be used to provide a single device driver interface for the same device on different hardware platforms. Because HAL provides a virtual layer to the computer hardware, the same operating system image can support a large number of variations for a computer based on a specific processor.

The kernel component is responsible for scheduling tasks for the computer hardware. If the computer hardware consists of multiple processors, the kernel uses the virtual processors interface provided by the HAL to synchronize activity among the processors.

The unit of activity that the kernel schedules is called a thread. The *thread* is the smallest unit that can be scheduled. A thread consists of a sequence of instructions executed by a processor within the context of a process. A process can have multiple threads, and must have at least one thread.

The kernel dispatches threads on the next available processor. Each thread has a priority associated with it. There are 32 priority levels divided into a real-time class that has priority levels from 16 to 31, and a variable (also called *dynamic*) class that has priority levels from 0 to 15. Higher priority level numbers imply higher priorities for the thread. Threads that have a higher priority level are executed first, and can preempt lower priority level threads.

The kernel is non-pageable, which means that the pages (fixed units of 4KB memory) that belong to the kernel component are not *paged out* from memory (not saved temporarily to the page file PAGEFILE.SYS). The software code within the kernel itself is not preemptive (cannot be interrupted), but the software outside the kernel component such as that used in the Windows NT Executive is preemptive.

The kernel can run simultaneously on all processors in a computer with multiprocessing hardware, and synchronize access to its critical regions in memory.

The policy decisions about how resources are used are removed from the kernel component and implemented by the Windows NT Executive components. This keeps the kernel simple, and unchangeable if the operating system policy decisions are changed in future releases of the operating system. The kernel does, however, make certain policy decisions about when to remove a process from memory.

The kernel manages two classes of objects: dispatcher objects and control objects. *Dispatcher objects* are used for synchronization and dispatching operations and include objects such as events, semaphores, mutants, mutexes, timers, and threads. Table 1.1 provides a summary definition of the dispatcher objects. *Control objects* are used for controlling the kernel operation and do not have an effect on dispatching functions. kernel control objects include interrupts, processes, profiles, and asynchronous procedure calls. Table 1.2 provides a summary definition of the control objects.

Table 1.1  **Dispatcher Objects**

| Object | Description |
| --- | --- |
| Event | An event is used to record the occurrence of an event and associate an action that must be performed. |
| Semaphore | A semaphore is used to control access to a resource. A number associated with a semaphore controls how many simultaneous accesses to the resource are allowed. When a thread accesses the resource, the semaphore number is decremented, and when it becomes zero, no other threads are permitted to access the resource. As threads release the resource, they increment the semaphore number. If the semaphore number is set to 1, only one thread at a time can access the resource. |
| Mutant | A mutant is used to control mutual exclusive access to a resource. Mutants can be used in the user mode as well as the kernel mode, although typically they are designed for use in the user mode. |
| Mutex | Like a mutant, a mutex also is used to control mutual exclusive access to a resource. However, a mutex can be used only by kernel-mode components, and are not in the user mode. |
| Timer | A timer is used to trigger events and actions at specific times. Timer objects record the passage of time. |
| Thread | A thread is the entity that executes the program code, and is dispatched by the kernel to run on an available processor. Threads are owned by a process object, and are used to provide concurrent execution behavior for a program. |

**Table 1.2  Control objects**

| Object | Description |
| --- | --- |
| Interrupt | An interrupt associates an interrupt source with an interrupt service routine through an Interrupt Dispatch Table (IDT). |
| Process | A process provides a virtual address space and environment under which the threads run. A process object must be initialized before any of its thread objects can run. |
| Profile | A profile is used to record how much time is spent by threads in a block of system program code. |
| Asynchronous procedure call | This object is used to break into the execution of a specified thread and cause a procedure to be called. |

## Protocol Layering for Windows NT

The Windows NT network protocols are implemented as part of the I/O Manager. Figure 1.5 shows how the different OSI layers are implemented within the I/O Manager. The different protocol elements are implemented as a layered list of drivers that interact with each other. For example, the driver that implements the transport protocols interacts with the NIC drivers by using the services provided by the Network Driver Interface Specification (NDIS) interface. Upper-layer protocol functions such as redirectors and servers interact with the transport protocols by using the services provided by the Transport Driver Interface (TDI).

The OSI layers 2 (Data Link layer) through 5 (Session layer) are implemented within the I/O Manager and run in the kernel mode of the Windows NT operating system. The Physical layer deals with networking hardware and is therefore shown to be outside the I/O Manager. All of the protocol components such as NIC drivers, NDIS interface, transport protocol drivers, transport driver interface, redirector, and servers are implemented as a layered list of drivers that run in the kernel mode. Running in the kernel mode gives these drivers full access to the network and machine hardware. It also results in an efficient implementation of the protocols: Context switches between user and kernel modes of the Windows NT computer are not required for the processing of network packets that traverse the protocol stack. In general, excessive context switches are not desirable because they degrade system performance.

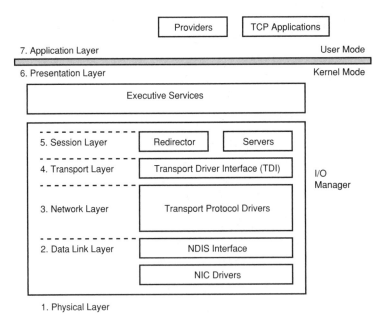

**Figure 1.5**  Windows NT networking model.

The NIC drivers (refer to Figure 1.5) implement the Media Access Control (MAC) sublayer of the IEEE 802 model. The IEEE 802 model is widely used to describe the function of many LAN/WAN network architectures. This model views the Data Link layer of the OSI model as consisting of two sublayers: the Media Access Control sublayer and the Logical Link Control (LLC) sublayer (see Figure 1.6).

The MAC layer communicates directly with the Physical layer and is responsible for using the mechanism of the network hardware to communicate between two computers on the same physical network. For example, in Ethernet networks, the MAC layer uses the Carrier Sense Multiple Access with Collision Detect (CSMA/CD) of the Ethernet hardware to ensure that the physical channel is free of network activity before transmitting a packet. And in Token Ring and Fiber Distributed Data Interface (FDDI) networks, the MAC layer waits for a free token frame before transmitting a packet. The LLC layer provides a common sublayer that runs on top of the MAC layer and provides independence from MAC layer differences to upper-layer protocols. The NDIS interface driver can be seen to implement the function of the LLC layer, although the NDIS interface does considerably more than this.

The NDIS interface provides a method for the transport protocols to use the services of the NIC drivers without knowing the details of the NIC driver implementation. The NDIS interface, in essence, provides to the transport protocols an idealized virtual NIC, with well-defined entry points and services. The transport protocols interact with the network hardware through this idealized interface. The NDIS interface takes care of mapping the interface to the appropriate NIC driver. The NDIS interface maintains protocol bindings between the transport protocols and the NIC drivers.

The transport protocol's module refers to OSI layers 3 and 4 and should not be confused with the use of the OSI Transport layer. Windows NT comes with a variety of transport protocols such as the following:

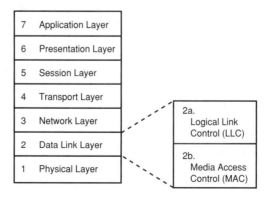

**Figure 1.6**  MAC and LLC sublayers in the IEEE 802 model.

- NBF. The NetBIOS Frame protocol is a transport protocol derived from NetBEUI (Net Basic Input Output System Extended User Interface) and provides protocol compatibility with existing NetBIOS (Net Basic Input Output System) networks such as LAN Manager, LAN server, and many MS-DOS LANs.

- NWLink. This is an NDIS–compliant version of the Internet Packet Exchange/Sequence Packet Exchange (IPX/SPX) protocol used in Novell networks. NWLink can be used to set up peer-to-peer connections with Windows computers and legacy MS-DOS, or OS/2 nodes that use this protocol. NWlink is a routable protocol and can be used to build internetworks.

- DLC. This is the Data Link Control protocol used to access mainframe computers and network-attached computers.

- AppleTalk. AppleTalk is a suite of protocols used by Macintosh clients to talk to an AppleTalk server. The AppleTalk server can be another Macintosh computer or a Windows NT server emulating an AppleTalk server. AppleTalk normally installs on the Windows NT server. Developers can obtain software from Microsoft that enables them to install AppleTalk on a Windows NT Workstation.

- TCP/IP. This is an open protocol implemented on diverse systems and the Internet and is the preferred protocol for practical interoperability. TCP/IP is a routable protocol and can be used to build internetworks such as the existing Internet.

The NBF protocol provides two modes of services: unreliable connectionless services and reliable connection-oriented services. Unreliable connectionless services, also called *datagram* services, are used in request-reply applications and many broadcast-oriented protocols. For example, NBF uses broadcasts to advertise names and these broadcasts can be sent without the overhead of opening a separate connection to each of the nodes to receive the message. Ordinarily, broadcasts are not transmitted across router boundaries because to do so would add to the volume of network traffic on the network. The connection-oriented services, also called *virtual circuit*, are used to ensure reliable delivery of data across the network.

The NBF protocol is used by a variety of Windows services. Unfortunately the NBF protocol is non-routable because it was conceived as a monolithic protocol to run on a single physical network segment. The NBF protocol does not have a separate Network layer and does not have any provision to distinguish one network from another, which makes the protocol non-routable. However, there is a provision to run the NBF protocol over TCP/IP. Because TCP/IP is a routable protocol, using NBF over TCP/IP makes NBF routable. On TCP/IP networks, where applications require NBF, NBF over TCP/IP is invariably used.

The Transport Driver Interface sits on top of the transport protocol modules and provides a standard set of services to upper-layer protocols such as the Session layer services. In Figure 1.5 the redirector and servers are shown as part of the Session layer services. The redirector "redirects" local requests for network services across the network, and the servers are software modules that respond to service requests either locally or from across the network. Because the Transport Driver Interface is a common layer for Session layer services, these services can be written to use the Transport Driver Interface, which then directs the service request to the appropriate transport protocol module.

Although the OSI layer Presentation layer function is shown just above the Executive services (refer to Figure 1.5), in actual practice, this is a null layer for most protocol stacks. The Application layer of the OSI model can be seen to run in the user mode.

The Provider module is a network vendor-provided Dynamic Link Library (DLL) that connects with the appropriate redirector. Windows NT allows for multiple redirectors that enable vendors to provide their own network client software. A Multiple Provider Router (MPR) component is used to link the Provider module with the appropriate redirector module.

Whereas Figure 1.5 shows the Windows NT networking model for any protocol, Figure 1.7 shows the Windows NT networking model specific to the TCP/IP protocol.

Figure 1.7 shows that the IP, TCP, and UDP protocols are implemented as layered drivers in the I/O Manager. The IP layer corresponds to OSI's Network layer (3), and the TCP and UDP layer correspond to OSI's Transport layer (4).

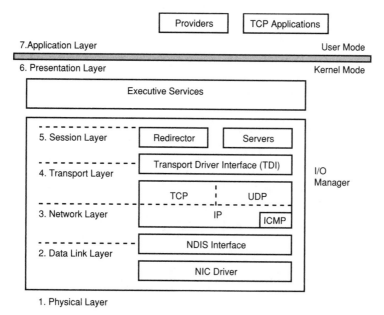

**Figure 1.7**   Windows NT TCP/IP networking model.

## Protocol Layering for Windows 9x

The Windows 9x operating systems lack the sophistication of the protected architecture of Windows NT. The drivers and protocol stacks for Windows 95 provide similar function to that of the corresponding Windows NT drivers but these protocol components are not interchangeable with that of Windows NT.

Figure 1.8 shows the Windows 9x networking model. The NIC drivers provide access to the network hardware described by the Physical layer. The NDIS interface is architecturally the same as that used in Windows NT. It is different from that of Windows NT in the sense that it is written specifically for the Windows 9x platform.

The TCP/IP module is written as a driver. Usually, the Winsock interface is used to interface with the TCP/IP driver. The Winsock interface is based on the Berkeley Sockets interface that is used on many UNIX systems for writing programs that access the TCP/IP protocol. The Winsock interface is implemented as a Dynamic Link Library and provides applications with a standard programming interface. The Winsock interface is also available on Windows NT platforms, and sits above the Transport Driver Interface.

The redirector redirects local requests for network services across the network, and the servers are software modules that respond to service requests either locally or from across the network.

Figure 1.9 shows the Windows 9x network components that implement the architecture shown in Figure 1.8. Windows 9x supports several network protocols simultaneously. These protocols are implemented as 16-bit or 32-bit Virtual Mode Drivers (VxD).

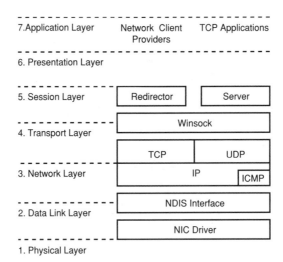

**Figure 1.8**   Windows 9x TCP/IP networking model.

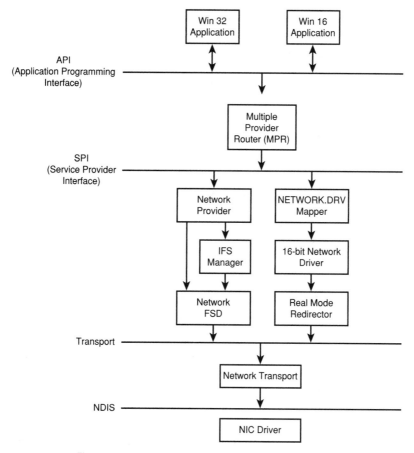

**Figure 1.9**  Windows 9x TCP/IP network components.

The API layer in Figure 1.9 can use either the Win32 or 16-bit Windows Application Programming Interface. The API provides access to shared resources on other computers such as file systems, printers, and so on.

The Multiple Provider Router (MPR) handles routing of all network operations, and implements basic network functions that are common to all networks.

The Network Provider component implements the network service provider interface. The MPR communicates directly with the network provider.

The Installable File System (IFS) Manager handles the routing of file system requests to the appropriate file system driver (FSD). The IFS Manager can handle multiple file systems concurrently and supports loadable file system drivers.

The Network File System Driver (FSD) implements the characteristics of a remote file system on the local Windows 9x computer. An FSD is specific to a type of network and is associated with the network client software from network software vendors.

The network transport implements the transport protocol that is used. Windows 9x supports the simultaneous use of multiple protocols such as NetBEUI, IPX/SPX, and TCP/IP. The Network FSD interfaces with the network transport.

The *Network Driver Interface Specification* (NDIS) is an interface specification that defines the interaction between the network transport protocol and the device driver. The device driver and the network transport protocols must be written to conform to the NDIS specification. NDIS used for Windows 9x consists of the Protocol Manager, the Media Access Control (MAC) driver, a mini-port, and mini-port wrapper drivers. The Protocol Manager includes support for plug-and-play devices. The mini-port drivers include functions that are common to all network adapters and reduce the amount of code that must be written to support the network adapter hardware. The architecture of NDIS is discussed in greater detail in the later section "NDIS for Windows."

The NIC driver is the network adapter driver that interfaces directly with network adapter hardware and controls it. The NDIS interface enables the network transport protocols to communicate with the network adapter hardware.

# Windows NT TCP/IP Protocol Elements

In the earlier section "Protocol Layering for Windows NT," you learned about the general architecture of a Windows NT system. In the following sections you will learn about the details of the protocol elements.

## NDIS for Windows

Prior to the late 1980s, most implementations of transport protocols were written to a proprietary implementation of a MAC-layer interface. This MAC-proprietary MAC-layer interface defined how the protocol would communicate with the NIC. Because of the proprietary nature of this interface, it was difficult for network interface card vendors to support the different network operating systems available on the market. Each NIC vendor had to create proprietary interface drivers to support a variety of protocol implementations for use with network operating system environments. In 1989, Microsoft and 3COM jointly developed a standard defining an interface for communication between the MAC layer and protocol drivers higher in the OSI model. This standard is known as the Network Device Interface Specification (NDIS).

NDIS allows for a standard for data exchange between transport protocols and the NIC driver. NDIS defines the software interface used by transport protocols to communicate with the NIC driver. Any NDIS-conformant protocol can pass data to any NDIS-compliant NIC driver, and vice versa. A process called binding is used to establish the initial communication channel between the protocol driver and the network interface card driver.

Windows NT and Windows 9x currently support device drivers and transport protocols written to NDIS version 3.0. NDIS allows multiple NICs on a single computer. Each NIC can support multiple transport protocols (see Figure 1.10). The advantage of supporting multiple protocol drivers on a single network card is that Windows NT computers can have simultaneous access to different types of network servers, each using a different transport protocol, through the same network interface. For example, a computer can have simultaneous access to both a NetWare Server using IPX and a UNIX server via TCP/IP. The TCP/IP protocol could also be used to access Windows NT Server.

The NDIS 3.0 implementation in Windows NT does not need a Protocol Manager module to link the various components at each layer together. Instead, Windows NT uses the information in the *Registry* (an internal hierarchical database of control and system information) and a small piece of code called the NDIS wrapper that surrounds the network interface card driver.

NDIS for Windows NT is implemented by the NDIS.SYS driver, which acts as an interface wrapper around the NDIS driver (see Figure 1.11). The NDIS interface wrapper communicates with the protocol stack driver and the Windows NT executive components.

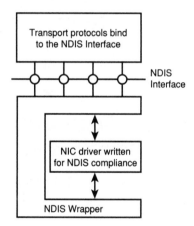

**Figure 1.10**   NDIS interface with wrappers.

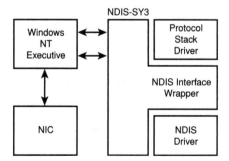

**Figure 1.11**   Windows NT NDIS components.

## Transport Driver Interface

Between the Session and Transport layers of the OSI model, the Windows NT networking model defines a standard interface, called the *Transport Driver Interface*, to communicate with the transport protocols. This is very similar in concept to the NDIS interface that was defined between the Network and Data Link layers of the OSI model.

The Transport Driver Interface (TDI) is not a single program module, but a specification to which the upper boundary of the transport protocols are written (see Figure 1.12). The TDI enables upper-layer protocol programs such as the redirector and the servers to be written to this specification. The standard specification allows communication between upper-layer protocol services and the transport protocols.

## Windows Providers

Providers are network components that enable the client computer to access resources on the network. Providers are commonly network clients (such as the Microsoft client software) that enable Windows 9x and NT computers to communicate with Windows NT Server. Each network software vendor can have its separate clients or providers that access resources on that vendor's network.

On a Windows NT computer, the Provider layer spans the boundary between the Kernel and user modes and manages the commands that access network resources and cause network traffic. Applications can access network resources using the Uniform Naming Convention (UNC) commands or the WNet (Windows Network) API.

The UNC commands identify a shared network resource such as a directory, file name, or network printer. The UNC name has the following general syntax:

```
\\ServerName\ShareName\SubDirectoryPath\FileName
```

The ServerName is the name of the server on which the network resource resides. The ShareName is the name by which the network resource is known and shared on the network. The SubDirectoryPath is an optional subdirectory pathname under that

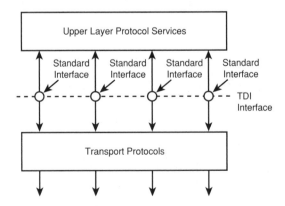

**Figure 1.12**  Transport Driver Interface.

shared name. The `FileName` specifies the name of the file if it is the shared resource. The UNC name enables commands to be written that can assign local drive letters to network resources. For example, suppose you wanted to assign the local drive letter to the network resource \\NTS\Docs. You can do this by using the following command:

```
NET USE E: \\NTS\Docs
```

After issuing the previous command, the local drive letter E: can be used to access the network resource \\NTS\Docs.

The WNet API is part of the Win32 API and enables Windows NT computers to connect to multiple networks, browse network resources, and transfer data between networked computers.

The Provider layer includes two components to route UNC and WNet requests to the appropriate provider: the Multiple UNC Provider (MUP) and the Multiple Provider Router (MPR). The MUP is used for routing UNC requests and the MPR is used for routing WNet requests. When the MUP receives an UNC name command, it locates the appropriate redirector for processing the request. When the MPR receives the WNet commands it passes the request to each redirector in turn until one is found that can satisfy the request.

## Multiple UNC Provider (MUP)

The multiple UNC provider (see Figure 1.13) is so called because on a Windows NT computer there could be a number of UNC providers dealing with each type of vendor-specific network client software. The function of the multiple UNC provider is to locate network resources that are described by their UNC names. On receiving an UNC name, MUP routes the UNC name to one of the registered UNC providers. When a provider indicates that it can locate the resource, MUP sends the remainder of the command to that provider. If applications make calls that include UNC names, MUP routes the request to the appropriate redirector file system driver.

## Multiple Provider Router (MPR)

The MPR (see Figure 1.14) provides an open interface that permits applications to use WNet API system calls to access network resources regardless of the type of vendor specific network resource. The function of the MPR is to ensure that the WNet request is routed to the appropriate file system driver. Requests for local resources are sent to the local file system. Requests for network resources are sent to the appropriate network client.

## Programming Interfaces: Winsock and NetBIOS

Winsock and NetBIOS are alternate programming interfaces for Windows computers. Each of these programming interfaces are implemented as separate DLLs (see Figures 1.15 and 1.16).

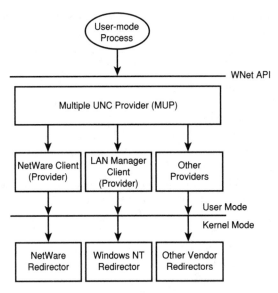

**Figure 1.13**    Multiple UNC Provider (MUP).

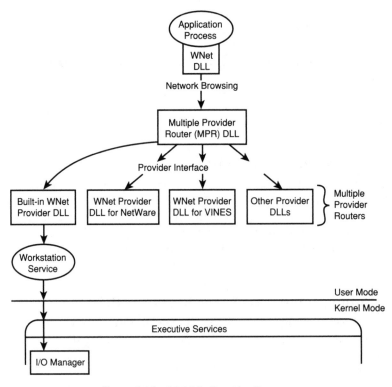

**Figure 1.14**    Multiple Provider Router.

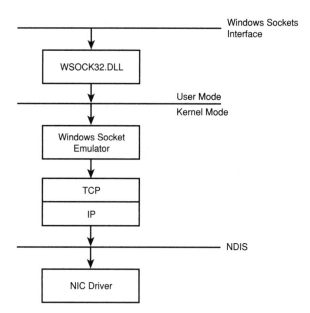

**Figure 1.15**   Winsock interface.

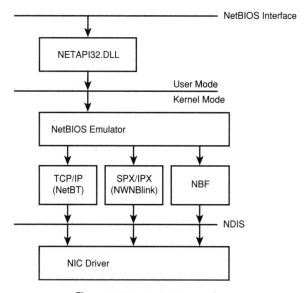

**Figure 1.16**   NetBIOS interface.

Winsock provides a file system model for the TCP/IP protocol stack that is based on the Berkeley Software Distribution (BSD) UNIX Sockets interface. Use of Winsock makes it easier to port existing UNIX-based network software to the Windows environment.

NetBIOS can run directly on the NBF protocol stack or can run on top of TCP/IP. The details of how NetBIOS can run on top of TCP/IP are supplied in the documents RFC 1001 and RFC 1002. RFC documents can be obtained through the INTERNIC at their Web site of **ds.internic.net** or FTP site of **ftp.internic.net**. NetBIOS is a Session layer interface designed for establishing logical names on a network, and setting up network sessions over which data can be transferred reliably.

# TCP/IP Protocols Infrastructure for Windows Networks

M ICROSOFT WINDOWS NETWORKS PROVIDE A VARIETY of choices for network transport protocols such as TCP/IP, SPX/IPX, NBF, and AppleTalk. Regardless of the network transport protocols used, native Windows services use the NetBIOS interface and the SMB protocol. Other standard Internet services such as FTP, Telnet, DNS, SNMP, HTTP, and so on, do not use NetBIOS and SMB; instead, they run on the TCP/IP protocol directly.

On a Windows TCP/IP network, the primary protocols that you see are TCP/IP at the Transport and Network layers of the OSI model, NetBIOS at the Session layer, and SMB at the Application layer. This chapter provides details of the primary protocols on a Windows network.

## Windows Protocols

The NetBIOS interface can be run on a variety of protocols such as IPX, NBF, and TCP/IP. When NetBIOS is run on TCP/IP it is called NetBT or NBT. The mechanism for running NetBIOS on TCP/IP is described in RFC 1001 and RFC 1002. The SMB protocol, as discussed in Chapter 1, "TCP/IP Architecture for Windows," is used for resource sharing on the network. The SMB protocol uses the NetBIOS interface, and the NetBIOS interface can run on TCP/IP. The hierarchy of the protocols on a Windows TCP/IP network is illustrated in Figure 2.1. When you troubleshoot

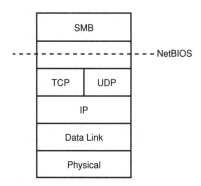

**Figure 2.1**   Windows TCP/IP protocols.

Windows TCP/IP networks, knowledge of TCP/IP will help you troubleshoot only transport protocol-related problems. In order to troubleshoot Session and Application layer-related problems, you must understand NetBIOS and SMB.

The remaining sections in this chapter discuss the details of SMB, NetBIOS, and TCP/IP, starting with the highest layers and proceeding to the lowest layers.

## The SMB Protocol

*SMB (Server Message Block)* is a resource-sharing protocol that has evolved from work done by Xerox, 3Com, and, most recently, Microsoft. Resource sharing with SMB includes sharing files, printers, serial ports, and communications abstractions such as named pipes and mail slots between computers.

The SMB protocol is an Application layer protocol that has been associated with networking products such as LAN Manager and Microsoft Networking. Parts of the specification have been made public through X/Open document. No SMB specification releases were made between 1992 and 1996, and during that period Microsoft became the SMB implementor with the largest market share. With the introduction of Windows NT, Microsoft developed the SMB specification further.

Because of market forces, SMB with some modifications was submitted as an Internet Draft for the Common Internet Filesystem (CIFS). The CIFS is not yet an Internet standard but because of its initiative, the SMB protocol specification is in the public domain and ongoing discussions concerning its specification take place according to the rules of the Internet Engineering Task Force (IETF). Microsoft, Digital Equipment Corporation (now part of Compaq), Data General, SCO, Network Appliance Corp, and others are involved in developing CIFS. It is expected that CIFS 1.0 will be essentially the protocol called NT LM (LAN Manager) 0.12 with some modifications for easier use over the Internet.

According to Microsoft, CIFS defines a standard remote file system access protocol for use over the Internet, enabling groups of users to work together and share documents across the Internet or within their corporate intranets. CIFS is based on the native file-sharing protocols built into Microsoft Windows and other popular PC operating systems, and supported on other platforms, including UNIX (via the *samba* product). CIFS users can open and share remote files on CIFS or SMB servers on the Internet without having to install new software or change the way they work.

## The Nature of SMB

SMB is a client/server protocol (see Figure 2.2). Server computers make file systems and other resources such as printers, mailslots, named pipes, and APIs available to clients on the network. Client computers may have their own local storage, such as hard disks, but may need access to the shared file systems and printers on the servers.

In its typical operation, SMB consists of clients sending requests, and a server responding to these requests. Figure 2.2 illustrates the way in which SMB works. The only exception to the request-response nature of SMB is when the client has requested opportunistic locks, called *oplocks*, and the server subsequently has to break an already granted oplock because another client has requested a file open with a mode that is incompatible with the granted oplock. In this case, the server sends an unsolicited message to the client signaling the oplock break.

SMB Clients connect to servers using TCP/IP, NetBEUI, or IPX/SPX (see Figure 2.3). When TCP/IP is used, it is actually NetBIOS over TCP/IP as specified in RFC 1001 and RFC 1002 that is used. NetBIOS over TCP/IP, as mentioned earlier, is sometimes called NBT, and sometimes NetBT; at other times it is called RFCNB, a reference to the RFC version of NetBIOS.

If SMB is used over TCP/IP or NetBEUI, then NetBIOS names must be used to refer to computer names. Computer names are NetBIOS names and are up to 15 characters long. Microsoft, and some other SMB implementors, insist that NetBIOS names be uppercased.

After a client establishes a connection, it can then send SMB commands to the server that enables the client to access shares, open files, read and write files, and so on. The main SMB clients are from Microsoft, and are included in Windows for Workgroups 3.x, Windows 9x, and Windows NT.

The SMB clients come into play when you use the File Manager or the Windows 95 Explorer, which allow you to connect to servers across the network. The SMB clients are also used when you open files using an *UNC (universal naming convention)*.

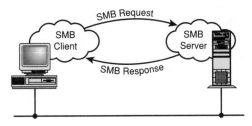

**Figure 2.2**   SMB clients and servers.

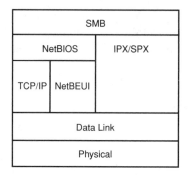

**Figure 2.3** SMB transport protocols.

SMB clients for UNIX include the smbclient from samba, smbfs for Linux, and SMBlib client library. There are many SMB server implementations, including the following:

- Samba
- Microsoft Windows for Workgroups 3.x
- Microsoft Windows 95
- Microsoft Windows NT
- The PATHWORKS family of servers from Digital
- LAN Manager for OS/2, SCO, and so on
- VisionFS from SCO
- TotalNET Advanced Server from Syntax
- Advanced Server for UNIX from AT&T
- LAN Server for OS/2 from IBM

## SMB Protocol Variants

There are many variations of the SMB protocol to handle the increasing complexity of the environments in which it has been employed. Because of this, the actual protocol variant a client and server will use is negotiated using the SMB `negprot` command, which must be the first SMB sent on a connection.

The first protocol variant is referred to as the *Core protocol*. It is also known as the PC NETWORK PROGRAM 1.0. The SMB Core protocol can handle a fairly basic set of operations that include the following:

- Connecting to and disconnecting from file and print shares
- Opening and closing files
- Opening and closing print files
- Reading and writing files

- Creating and deleting files and directories

- Searching directories

- Getting and setting file attributes

- Locking and unlocking byte ranges in files

As vendors discovered a need for greater functionality, SMB was enhanced. A list of the different variants of SMB compiled from a list by Richard Sharpe is shown in Table 2.1. Some variants introduced new SMB commands. Others simply changed the format of existing SMBs or responses, while others added new commands and formats for SMB.

Table 2.1   **SMB Variants**

| SMB Protocol Variant | Protocol Name | Comments |
|---|---|---|
| PC Network Program 1.0 | Core Protocol | Some versions were called PCLAN1.0 |
| Microsoft Networks 1.03 | CorePlus Protocol | Included Lock&Read and Write&Unlock SMBs with different versions of raw read and raw write SMBs |
| Microsoft Networks 3.0 | DOS LAN Manager 1.0 | The same as LANMAN1.0, but OS/2 errors must be translated to DOS errors |
| LANMAN1.0 | LAN Manager 1.0 | The complete LANMAN1.0 protocol |
| DOS LM1.2X002 | LAN Manager 2.0 | The same as LM1.2X002, but errors must be translated to DOS errors |
| LM1.2X002 | LAN Manager 2.0 | The complete LANMAN2.0 protocol |
| DOS LANMAN2.1 | LAN Manager 2.1 | The same as LANMAN2.1, but errors must be translated to DOS errors |
| LANMAN2.1 | LAN Manager 2.1 | The full LANMAN2.1 protocol |
| Windows for Workgroups 3.1a | LAN Manager 2.1x | Windows Workgroups 1.0x |
| NT LM 0.12 | NT LAN Manager 1.0x | Contains special SMBs for NT |
| Samba | NT LAN Manager 1.0x | Samba's version of NT LM 0.12 |
| CIFS 1.0 | NT LAN Manager 1.0 | NT LM 0.12 with additional functions |

## SMB Security Model

The SMB model defines two levels of security:

- Share level
- User level

In the *share level* security model, protection is applied at the share level on a server. Each share can have a password, and a client only needs that password to access all files under that share. This was the first security model that SMB had and is the only security model available in the Core and CorePlus protocols. Windows for Workgroups' vserver.exe implements share level security by default, as does Windows 9x. Windows 9x clients, when logged on to a Windows NT domain, are not restricted to share level security; they can use user level security.

In the *user level* security model, protection is applied to individual files in each share and is based on user access rights. Each user (client) must log on to the server and be authenticated by the server. When it is authenticated, the client is given a user identifier (UID), which it must present on all subsequent accesses to the server. This model has been available since LAN Manager 1.0 and is used in Windows NT.

## An Example of an SMB Exchange

The requests and responses that SMB clients and servers exchange are called *SMB commands* or *SMBs*. SMB commands have a specific format that is similar for both requests and responses. The format consists of a fixed-size header portion, followed by a variable-sized parameter and data portion.

After connecting at the NetBIOS level, either via NBF or NetBT, the client is ready to request services from the server. However, the client and server must first identify which SMB protocol variant they each understand. The client does this by sending the SMB negprot command to the server (see Figure 2.4), listing the protocol dialects that it understands. The server responds with the index of the dialect that it wants to use, or 0xFFFF if none of the dialects was acceptable. Dialects that are more recent than the Core and CorePlus protocols supply information in the negprot response to indicate their capabilities, such as maximum buffer size, canonical file names, and so on.

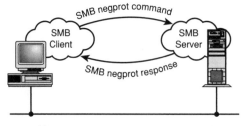

**Figure 2.4**   SMB *negprot* command.

After the SMB protocol variant has been established, the client can proceed to log on to the server. This is done using the SMB *SesssetupX* command (see Figure 2.5). The response to this command indicates whether or not the client has supplied a valid username password pair and additional information. After the client user has authenticated, the server returns the UID of the logged on user. This UID must be submitted with all subsequent SMBs on that connection to the server. Note that in older SMB protocols such as the Core and CorePlus you cannot log on. This is because these protocols provide only a share level security and not a user level security.

After the client has logged on, the client can proceed to connect to a share. The shared resource is also called a *tree* because in the case of a file system directory it has a tree structure. The client sends a *tcon* or *tconX* SMB command specifying the network name of the share that they want to connect to. If the server determines that access to the share name is permitted, the server responds with a tree identifier (TID) that the client will use in all future SMBs relating to that share.

After connecting to a share, the client can open a file with an open SMB, followed by reading it with read SMBs, writing it with write SMBs, and closing it with close SMBs.

## SMB Browsing

In the Windows Explorer it is possible to see a "Network Neighborhood" of computers in the same workgroup name. The workgroup name is actually the name of an SMB workgroup. When you click on the name of one of these computers you see a list of file and printer resources shared by the computer that you can connect to. This process is called *browsing*. By browsing you can navigate the network, seeing what resources are available. The browsing function is implemented by the SMB/CIFS protocol, which allows for resource discovery.

Each SMB server broadcasts information about its presence. Clients listen for these broadcasts and build up browse lists. On a NetBEUI environment limited to a single LAN, this is satisfactory, but in a subnetted TCP/IP environment, a number of problems arise because of the broadcasts. The problems arise because TCP/IP broadcasts are not usually sent outside the subnet in which they originate, even though routers can be configured to selectively transport broadcasts to other subnets. Because of this reason, Microsoft has introduced special browse servers and the Windows Internet Name

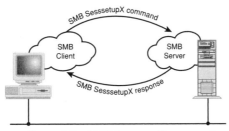

**Figure 2.5**   SMB SesssetupX command.

Service (WINS) to help overcome these problems. WINS is discussed in detail in Chapter 9, "TCP/IP Name Resolution Using WINS."

## SMB Packet Structure

All SMB messages consist of a fixed part of the SMB structure sometimes referred to as the SMB header. The SMB header is followed by a variable number of fields. Figure 2.6 shows the SMB packet structure with fixed and variable parts. Figures 2.7 and 2.8 show the fixed SMB header and the variable fields that follow. Because of the many versions of SMB, alternate formats for SMB commands and responses can be negotiated between the communicating parties.

Fields that are two octets long are ordered such that the low byte precedes the high byte from left to right. This is called the *little endian* order. The fields in Figures 2.7 and

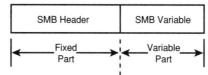

**Figure 2.6**   SMB fixed and variable parts.

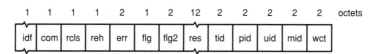

**Figure 2.7**   SMB header.

**Figure 2.8**   SMB variable part.

2.8 have the following meanings:

- idf. This contains the SMB identifier code.

- com. This is the SMB command code. See the later section "SMB Commands in the com Field" for details.

- rcls. This is the error class.

- reh. This is reserved for future use.

- err. This is the error code returned.

- flg. This is the first flags field. See the later section "flg Field Values" for details.

- flg2. This is the second flags field. See the later section "flg2 Field Values" for details.

- res. This is reserved for future use.

- tid. This is used by the server to identify a resource such as a disk subtree. In the LANMAN 1.2 extended protocol environment the TID represents an instance of an authenticated use. This is the result of a successful NET USE to a server using a valid netname and password. If the server is executing in a share level security mode, the TID is the only information used to allow access to the shared resource. Thus if the user is able to perform a successful NET USE to the server specifying the appropriate share name and password the resource may be accessed according to the access rights associated with the shared resource. If, however, the server is executing in user level security mode, access to the resource is based on the UID value validated on the Session Setup protocol and the TID is not associated with access control but rather merely defines the resource such as the shared directory tree. In most SMB protocols, the tid field must contain a valid TID value. Exceptions to this include the state prior to getting a TID established including NEGOTIATE, TREE CONNECT, SESS_SETUPandX, and TREE_CONNandX protocols. Other exceptions include QUERY_SRV_INFO, some forms of the TRANSACTION protocol, and ECHO. A NULL TID is defined as 0xFFFF. The server is responsible for enforcing the use of a valid TID where appropriate.

- pid. This is the caller's process identifier. It is generated by the consumer (redirector) to uniquely identify a process within the consumer's system. A response message always contains the same value in pid as in the corresponding request message.

- uid. This is the UID value of the authenticated process. It is used by the LANMAN 1.0 extended protocol when the server is executing in the user level security mode to validate access on protocols that reference symbolically named resources such as *file open*. Thus different users accessing the same TID may be granted different access to the resources defined by the TID based on the UID. The UID is returned by the server via the Session Set Up command. This UID must be used in all SMBs following Session Set Up and X.

- `mid`. This is used for multiplexing multiple messages on a single Virtual Circuit (VC) when normally multiple requests are from the same process. The `pid` and the `mid` fields uniquely identify a request and are used by the consumer to correlate incoming responses to previously sent requests.

- `wct`. This is the number of 16-bit words that follow this field. It indicates the size of the variable portion of the SMB command.

- `vwv`. This is a variable number of 16-bit words. The size of this field is indicated by the previous field, `wct`.

- `bcc`. This is a count of the bytes that follow.

- `buf`. This is a variable number of bytes. The size of this field is indicated by the previous field, `bcc`.

## *flg* Field Values

The `flg` field can have the following values:

- `bit0`. When set by the server in the Negotiate response protocol, this bit indicates that the server supports the *subdialect*, consisting of the LockandRead and WriteandUnlock protocols defined in the SMB File Sharing Protocol Extension version 2.0, document version 3.2.

- `bit1`. When set to 1 on a protocol request being sent to the server, the consumer guarantees that there is a receive buffer posted such that a "Send.No.Ack" can be used by the server to respond to the consumer's request. The LANMAN 1.2 Redirector for OS/2 does not set this bit.

- `bit2`. This is reserved and must be 0.

- `bit3`. When on, all pathnames in the protocol must be treated as caseless. When off, the pathnames are case sensitive. This allows forwarding of the protocol message on various extended VCs in which caseless may not be the norm. The LANMAN 1.2 Redirector for OS/2 always has this bit on to indicate caseless pathnames.

- `bit4`. When on the Session Setup and the X protocol, all paths sent to the server by the consumer are already in the canonicalized format used by OS/2 and NT. This means that file/directory names are in uppercase and are valid characters, and backslashes are used as separators.

- `bit5`. When on Core protocol Open, Create, and Make New, this indicates that the consumer is requesting that the file be "opportunistically" locked if this process is the only process that has the file open at the time of the open request. If the server "grants" this oplock request, then this bit should remain set in the corresponding response protocol to indicate to the consumer that the oplock request was granted.

- `bit6`. When on Core protocols Open, Create, and Make New, this indicates that the server should notify the consumer on any action that can modify the file delete, setattrib, rename, and so on. If not set, the server need only notify the consumer on another open request.

- `bit7`. When on, this protocol is being sent from the server in response to a consumer request. The `com` field usually contains the same value in a protocol request from the consumer to the server as in the matching response from the server to the consumer. This bit unambiguously distinguishes the command request from the command response. On a multiplexed VC on a node in which both server and consumer are active, this bit can be used by the node's SMB delivery system to help identify whether this protocol should be routed to a waiting consumer process or to the server.

## *flg2* Field Values

The `flg2` field can have the following values:

- `bit0`. When set by the consumer, the running application understands OS/2 and NT style file names.

- `bit1`. When set by the consumer, the running application understands extended attributes.

- `bit2` through `bit15`. These bits are reserved and must be set to 0.

## SMB Commands in the *com* Field

In the SMB Core protocol the SMB commands field, `com`, contains code values that can be grouped into the following four categories:

- **Session Control commands.** Session commands are responsible for starting and ending the communication between a redirector and a server. They also verify the SMB version number between the two communicating entities.

- **File commands.** File commands enable access to directories and files on the server. These commands are issued after the session has been established.

- **Print commands.** Print commands enable the redirector to send files to the server's printer and query the server's print queue for status information.

- **Message commands.** Message commands enable an application program to send individual or broadcast queries.

Table 2.2 shows a list of some of the codes for the core SMB commands.

Table 2.2  **SMB Core Commands**

| Command | Code | Description |
| --- | --- | --- |
| SMBmkdir | 0x00 | Create directory |
| SMBrmdir | 0x01 | Delete directory |
| SMBopen | 0x02 | Open file |
| SMBcreate | 0x03 | Create file |
| SMBclose | 0x04 | Close file |
| SMBflush | 0x05 | Flush file |
| SMBunlink | 0x06 | Delete file |
| SMBmv | 0x07 | Rename file |
| SMBgetatr | 0x08 | Get file attributes |
| SMBsetatr | 0x09 | Set file attributes |
| SMBread | 0x0A | Read from file |
| SMBwrite | 0x0B | Write to file |
| SMBlock | 0x0C | Lock byte range |
| SMBunlock | 0x0D | Unlock byte range |
| SMBctemp | 0x0E | Create temporary file |
| SMBmknew | 0x0F | Make new file |
| SMBchkpth | 0x10 | Check directory path |
| SMBexit | 0x11 | Process exit |
| SMBlseek | 0x12 | File seek |
| SMBtcon | 0x70 | Tree connect |
| SMBtdis | 0x71 | Tree disconnect |
| SMBnegprot | 0x72 | Negotiate protocol |
| SMBdskattr | 0x80 | Get disk attributes |
| SMBsearch | 0x81 | Search directory |
| SMBsplopen | 0xC0 | Open print spool file |
| SMBsplwr | 0xC1 | Write to print spool file |
| SMBsplclose | 0xC2 | Close print spool file |
| SMBsplretq | 0xC3 | Return print queue |
| SMBsends | 0xD0 | Send single block message |
| SMBsendb | 0xD1 | Send broadcast message |
| SMBfwdname | 0xD2 | Forward user name |
| SMBcancelf | 0xD3 | Cancel forward |
| SMBgetmac | 0xD4 | Get machine name |
| SMBsendstrt | 0xD5 | Send start of multiblock message |
| SMBsendend | 0xD6 | Send end of multiblock message |
| SMBsendtxt | 0xD7 | Send text of multiblock message |

Table 2.3 lists the SMB commands that were added by the LANMAN 1.0 Extended File Sharing Protocol.

Table 2.3    **Extended SMB LANMAN 1.0 File Sharing Commands**

| Command | Code | Description |
|---|---|---|
| SMBlockread | 0x13 | Lock then read data |
| SMBwriteunlock | 0x14 | Write then unlock data |
| SMBreadBraw | 0x1A | Read block raw |
| SMBreadBmpx | 0x1B | Read block multiplexed |
| SMBreadBs | 0x1C | Read block (secondary response) |
| SMBwriteBraw | 0x1D | Write block raw |
| SMBwriteBmpx | 0x1E | Write block multiplexed |
| SMBwriteBs | 0x1F | Write block (secondary request) |
| SMBwriteC | 0x20 | Write complete response |
| SMBsetattrE | 0x22 | Set file attributes expanded |
| SMBgetattrE | 0x23 | Get file attributes expanded |
| SMBlockingX | 0x24 | Lock/unlock byte ranges and X |
| SMBtrans | 0x25 | Transaction (name, bytes in/out) |
| SMBtranss | 0x26 | Transaction (secondary request/response) |
| SMBioctl | 0x27 | Passes the IOCTL to the server |
| SMBioctls | 0x28 | IOCTL (secondary request/response) |
| SMBcopy | 0x29 | Copy |
| SMBmove | 0x2A | Move |
| SMBecho | 0x2B | Echo |
| SMBwriteclose | 0x2C | Write and Close |
| SMBopenX | 0x2D | Open and X |
| SMBreadX | 0x2E | Read and X |
| SMBwriteX | 0x2F | Write and X |
| SMBsesssetup | 0x73 | Session Set Up & X (including User Logon) |
| SMBtconX | 0x75 | Tree connect and X |
| SMBffirst | 0x82 | Find first |
| SMBfunique | 0x83 | Find unique |
| SMBfclose | 0x84 | Find close |
| SMBinvalid | 0xFE | Invalid command |

The commands added by the LANMAN 1.2 Extended File Sharing Protocol have the command codes shown in Table 2.4.

Table 2.4    **Extended SMB LANMAN 1.2 File Sharing Commands**

| Command | Code | Description |
|---|---|---|
| SMBtrans2 | 0x32 | Transaction2 (function, byte in/out) |
| SMBtranss2 | 0x33 | Transaction2 (secondary request/response) |
| SMBfindclose | 0x34 | Find close |
| SMBfindnclose | 0x35 | Find notify close |
| SMBuloggoffX | 0x74 | User logoff and X |

# NetBIOS, NetBEUI, and NBF

When NetBEUI was developed in 1985, it was assumed that LANs would be segmented into workgroups of 20 to 200 computers and that gateways would be used to connect that LAN segment to other LAN segments or a mainframe computer. Therefore, NetBEUI was optimized for departmental LANs or LAN segments and no provision was made to make the protocol routable. Microsoft claims that for traffic within a LAN segment, NetBEUI is the fastest of the protocols shipped with Windows NT.

The NetBEUI protocol provides flow control and tuning parameters plus error detection. Microsoft has supported the NetBEUI protocol in all of its networking products since Microsoft's first networking product, MS-Net, was introduced in the mid-1980s.

NetBEUI is the precursor to the NetBIOS Frame (NBF) protocol included with Windows NT. NBF provides compatibility with existing LAN Manager and MS-Net installations, and with IBM LAN Server installations. On Windows NT, the NetBIOS interface is supported under MS-DOS, 16-bit Windows, and Win32 subsystem environments.

NetBEUI is an enhanced version of the NetBIOS protocol used by network operating systems such as LAN Manager, LAN Server, Windows for Workgroups, Windows 95, and Windows NT. The version of NetBEUI used in Windows NT is called *NBF (NetBios Frame Protocol)*. NetBEUI formalizes the transport frame that was never standardized in NetBIOS and adds additional functions to the original NetBIOS protocol implementation. NetBEUI uses the OSI Logical Link Control Class 2 (LLC2) protocol for framing at the Data Link layer.

The NetBEUI protocol is specified in the "IBM Local Area Network Technical Reference Manual" and runs over the standard 802.2 data-link protocol layer using LLC2 framing. Because the 802.2 data-link protocol is not routable, neither is NetBEUI. This was a major limitation in early NetBIOS LANs such as LAN Manager and was a primary reason why it was never a major force in the PC networking world.

In the early '90s Novell recognized that Windows for Workgroups and LAN Manager networks would need to coexist with NetWare and developed NetBIOS over IPX. This allowed NetBIOS–based software to run over routed networks because IPX was a routable protocol. Microsoft adopted this method of running NetBIOS over IPX for Windows for Workgroups and Windows NT. Windows 9x also supports NetBIOS over IPX. Later on, RFCs 1001 and 1002 were published; these describe how to run NetBIOS over TCP/IP. Microsoft Windows network for the enterprise environment typically runs NetBIOS over TCP/IP.

The actual version of NetBEUI shipping with Windows NT is NetBEUI 3.0. NetBEUI 3.0 corrects some limitations in previous versions of NetBEUI.

NetBEUI 3.0, along with the Transport Driver Interface (TDI) layer, eliminates the previous limitation of 254 sessions to a server on one network adapter card. NetBEUI 3.0 is self-tuning and does not require any adjustment of communication parameters.

NetBEUI 3.0 provides much better performance over slow links than did previous versions of NetBEUI due to superior sliding window and timing mechanisms for handling latency in transmission.

Strictly speaking, NetBEUI 3.0 is not truly NetBEUI. Instead, it is an NBF format protocol. NetBEUI uses the NetBIOS interface as its upper-level interface, but NBF conforms to TDI instead. NBF is compatible and interoperable with the NetBEUI shipped with past Microsoft networking products.

NetBEUI does not have the type of addressing that allows packet forwarding on routed networks, but the NetBIOS interface is adaptable to other protocols that are, such as IPX and TCP/IP. The specification for implementing the NetBIOS interface to TCP/IP is defined by RFCs 1001 and 1002.

NetBEUI is considered an efficient protocol for small LANs consisting of a dozen PCs or so. However, NetBEUI provides poorer performance for WAN communications. Although NetBEUI is not a routable protocol, WAN links can be formed by using remote bridges. Therefore, one recommended method for setting up a network is to use both NetBEUI and another protocol, such as TCP/IP, on each computer that may need to access computers across a router or on a WAN. When you install both protocols on each computer and set NetBEUI as the first protocol to be used, Windows NT uses NetBEUI for the communication between Windows NT computers within each LAN segment and TCP/IP for communication across routers and to other parts of your WAN.

Table 2.5 lists the most common network operating systems that use the NetBIOS interface.

## NetBEUI Packet Structure

NetBIOS commands act as a Session layer interface to the transport protocols. The native protocol used to send NetBIOS commands is NetBEUI. NetBEUI is directly encapsulated in the Data Link layer frame. NetBEUI has two packet formats. The first packet format uses the Unnumbered Information (UI) frame of the IEEE 802.2 data link control protocol and provides connectionless or datagram service. The second packet format uses the Information (I) frame of the IEEE 802.2 Logical Link Control (LLC) protocol and provides connection-oriented or virtual circuit service. The datagram service is "best efforts" service and cannot be relied upon to deliver NetBEUI packets. The virtual circuit service, on the other hand, guarantees reliable delivery of data.

Table 2.5  **NetBIOS LANs**

| Vendor | Network Operating System |
| --- | --- |
| Microsoft | MS LAN Manager, Windows for Workgroups, Win9x, and Windows NT |
| Hewlett-Packard | HP LAN Manager and Resource Sharing |
| IBM | LAN Server |
| Digital | Pathworks |

Figure 2.9 shows the NetBEUI frame structure. The NetBEUI frame is encapsulated by the IEEE 802.2 LLC frame. The LLC frame (see Figure 2.10) has a Destination Service Access Point (DSAP) value of F0 (hex) and a Source Service Access Point (SSAP) value of F0 (hex). The Control field indicates the frame type—whether this is a UI frame or an I frame.

The command field in the original NetBEUI frame describes 22 different commands. NetBIOS command codes are 00 hex to 13 hex for Unnumbered Information frames and 14 hex to 1F hex for I frames.

Table 2.6 lists common NetBIOS commands.

## NBF Performance Issues

NBF uses two techniques to improve performance for connection-oriented traffic:

- Adaptive sliding windows
- Link timers

These techniques are described in the following sections.

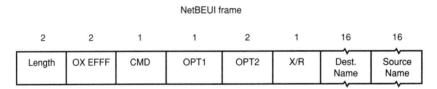

**Figure 2.9** NetBEUI frame structure.

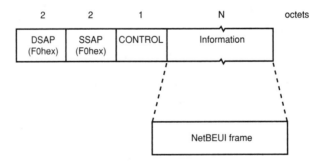

**Figure 2.10** LLC encapsulation of a NetBEUI frame.

Table 2.6  **NetBIOS Commands**

| Frame Name | Frame Code | Function |
|---|---|---|
| `ADD_GROUP_NAME_QUERY` | 0x00 | Checks for duplicate group names on network |
| `ADD_NAME_QUERY` | 0x01 | Checks for duplicate names on network |
| `NAME_IN_CONFLICT` | 0x02 | Duplicate names detected |
| `ADD_NAME_RESPONSE` | 0x0D | Negative response—Indicates that added name is duplicate |
| `NAME_QUERY` | 0x0A | Requests location of a name on a network |
| `NAME_RECOGNIZED` | 0x0E | Name recognized in answer to `NAME_QUERY` |
| `SESSION_ALIVE` | 0x1F | Verifies that session is still active |
| `SESSSION_CONFIRM` | 0x17 | `SESSION_INITIALIZE` acknowledgment |
| `SESSION_END` | 0x18 | Session termination |
| `SESSION_INITIALIZE` | 0x19 | Sets up a session |
| `DATA_ACK` | 0x14 | `DATA_ONLY_LAST` acknowledgment |
| `DATA_FIRST_MIDDLE` | 0x15 | Session data message (first or middle frame) |
| `DATAGRAM` | 0x08 | Application-generated datagram |
| `DATAGRAM_BROADCAST` | 0x09 | Application-generated broadcast datagram |
| `DATA_ONLY_LAST` | 0x16 | Session data message (only or last frame) |
| `NO_RECEIVE` | 0x1A | No receive command to hold received data |
| `RECEIVE_CONTINUE` | 0x1C | Indicates receive outstanding |
| `RECEIVE_OUTSTANDING` | 0x1B | Retransmits last data |
| `STATUS_QUERY` | 0x03 | Requests remote node status |
| `STATUS_RESPONSE` | 0x0F | Remote node status information |
| `TERMINATE_TRACE_REMOTE` | 0x07 | Terminates traces at remote nodes |
| `TERMINATE_TRACE_LOCAL_REMOTE` | 0x13 | Terminates traces at local and remote nodes |

## Adaptive Sliding Window Protocol

NBF uses an adaptive sliding window algorithm to improve performance while reducing network congestion and providing flow control. A *sliding window algorithm* allows a sender to dynamically tune the number of LLC frames sent before an acknowledgment is requested. Figure 2.11 shows frames traveling through a two-way pipe. This figure shows five frames in transit from the sender to the receiver. The receiver can send a single acknowledgment (ACK) for frame 5, and this acknowledges all the previous frames 1 to 4. The sliding window can then move up to the right to indicate that another five frames can be sent.

If the sender sends only one frame into the communications pipe and then has to wait for an acknowledgment, the sender's pipe is underused. If the sender can send multiple frames before an acknowledgment is returned, the sender can keep the pipe

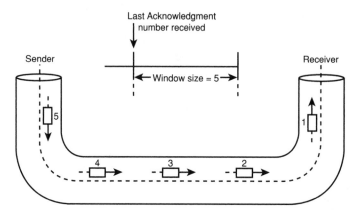

**Figure 2.11** Adaptive Sliding Window.

full, thereby using the full bandwidth of the pipe. The frames travel forward, and then acknowledgments for the received frames travel back. The number of frames that the sender is allowed to send before it must wait for an acknowledgment is referred to as the *send window*.

Normally, NBF does not set a receive window unless it detects that the remote is a version of IBM LAN Server, which never polls. In this case, NBF uses a receive window based on the value of MaximumIncomingFrames in the Registry. The adaptive sliding window protocol tries to determine the best sizes for the send window for the current network conditions. Ideally, the windows should be big enough so that maximum throughput can be realized. However, if the window gets too big, the receiver could get overloaded and drop frames. For big windows, dropped frames cause significant network traffic because more frames must be retransmitted.

Lost frames can be a problem on slow links or when frames have to pass over multiple hops to find the receiving station. Lost frames coupled with large send windows can generate multiple retransmissions. This traffic overhead might make an already-congested network worse. By limiting the send window size, traffic is throttled, and congestion control is exercised.

### Link Timers

NBF uses three timers: the response timer (T1), the acknowledgment timer (T2), and the inactivity timer (Ti). These timers help regulate network traffic and are controlled by the values of the DefaultT1Timeout, DefaultT2Timeout, and DefaultTiTimeout Registry entries, respectively. The following relationship exists with the timer values:

T2 <= T1 <= Ti

The *response timer* (T1) is used to determine how long the sender should wait before it assumes the Information frame (I-frame) is lost. After T1 milliseconds, NBF sends a Receiver Ready (RR) frame that has not been acknowledged and doubles the value for T1. If the RR frame is not acknowledged after the number of retries defined by the value of LLCRetries, the link is dropped.

Where the return traffic does not allow the receiver to send an I-frame within a legitimate time period, the *acknowledgment timer* (T2) begins, and then the ACK is sent. The value for this timer is set by the T2 variable, with a default value of 150 milliseconds. If the sender has to wait until the T2 timer starts in order to receive a response, the link might be underused while the sender waits for the ACK. This rare situation can occur over slow links. On the other hand, if the timer value is too low, the timer starts and sends unnecessary ACKs, generating excess traffic. NBF is optimized so that the last frame the sender wants to send is sent with the POLL bit turned on. This forces the receiver to send an ACK immediately.

The *inactivity timer* (Ti) is used to detect whether the link has gone down. The default value for Ti is 30 seconds. If Ti milliseconds pass without activity on the link, NBF sends an I-frame for polling. This is then ACKed, and the link is maintained.

## NetBIOS Session Limits

Standard NetBIOS has a 254-session limit. This limit arises from the size of a key variable in the NetBIOS architecture called the Local Session Number (LSN). The LSN size is a one-byte number. This limits the LSN values to a range from 0 to 255 with several numbers reserved for system use.

When two computers establish a session via NBF, there is an exchange of LSNs. The LSNs on the two computers might be different. They do not have to match, but a computer always uses the same LSN for a given session. This number is assigned when a program issues a CALL NCB (Network Control Block) command. The number is actually shared between the two computers in the initial frame sent from the calling computer to the listening computer. Figure 2.12 shows this session-creation frame exchange.

The initial frame is a NameQuery frame. In previous implementations of NetBIOS, this frame was broadcast onto the network. All computers read the frame and check whether they have the name in their name space and there is a LISTEN NCB pending on the name. If there is a LISTEN NCB pending, the computer assigns a new LSN (Logical Session Number) for itself, adding it to the response frame and satisfying the LISTEN NCB, which now contains just the LSN used on that computer. Although both computers know the LSN of the other, the information is not used. The more important information for the two computers is the network addresses that are part of the frames. As the frames are exchanged, each partner picks up the address of the other in the source address component of the frame received. This is a form of address resolution in which the address of the sending party is determined by examining its source network address. The NBF protocol keeps the network address of the remote partner so that subsequent frames can be addressed directly.

Windows NT has to use the same NameQuery frame to establish connections with remote computers via NBF; otherwise, it would not be able to talk to existing

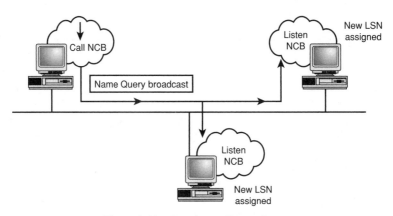

**Figure 2.12**  Broadcast of NameQuery.

workstations and servers. The NameQuery frame transmitted must contain the one-byte-wide LSN to be used. However, each process within Windows NT that uses NetBIOS can communicate with up to 254 different computers. Prior implementations of NetBIOS had the 254-session limit for the entire computer, including the workstation and server components. The 254-session limit does not apply to the default Windows NT workstation or server components. The workstation and server services avoid the problem by writing directly to the TDI rather than calling NetBIOS directly. Calls to the TDI are via a 32-bit handle-based interface.

NBF also has a unique method of handling resources to create an unlimited number of connections, as described in the next section.

## How NBF Breaks the 254-Session Limit

NBF breaks the 254-session barrier by using a combination of two matrices, one maintained by NBF, and one maintained by NetBIOS.

The NBF system maintains a two-dimensional matrix, as shown in Figure 2.13. Along the side of this matrix are the LSN numbers 1 to 254. Across the top are the network addresses for the different computers that it has sessions with. In the cell defined by the LSN and network address is the TDI handle, which relates back to the process that established the connection (either the CALL or LISTEN).

Note that the matrix concept and its contents are for illustration purposes only. The actual implementation uses a more efficient physical storage algorithm such as that used in hash tables.

> **NBF Connections Only**
>
> This process applies for NBF connections. NetBIOS connections established via TCP/IP and RFCs 1001 and 1002 or NBP are handled differently.

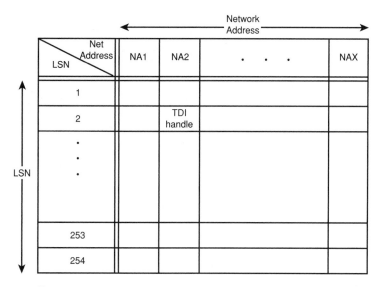

**Figure 2.13**  Implementation consideration for NBF matrix table.

The NameQuery frame from Windows NT contains the LSN number associated with the TDI handle that satisfies either the NCB CALL or the LISTEN. In the case of a CALL, it is not broadcast but is addressed directly to the recipient.

NBF gets the MAC address of the recipient to add to its matrix when doing the CALL by looking up the address of the NameQuery frame received on the LISTEN side.

As shown in Figure 2.14, NBF uses two NameQuery frames.

The following items correspond to the numbered items in Figure 2.14:

1.  The first frame is the FindName format of the NameQuery. However, an LSN of 0 is special because it indicates that it is a FindName. The FindName is broadcast. When the remote computer responds to the frame, NBF has the network address it needs to add an entry to the table.

2.  The second NameQuery is then sent directly to the remote station, with the LSN filled in as a CALL command. The FindName is successfully returned by the remote computer, even if no LISTEN NCB is posted against the name.

3.  If no LISTEN NCB is posted against the name, frame (3) is sent.

NBF must also address another problem, which is that the LSN from the NBF table cannot be the one returned to the process issuing the CALL or LISTEN commands. NBF may have established connections with multiple remote computers with a specific LSN value. Windows NT must return to each process an LSN number that uniquely defines its session.

NBF uses the TDI handle to determine which LSN and network address to send frames to, and each process has its own set of LSNs available to it. Therefore, there

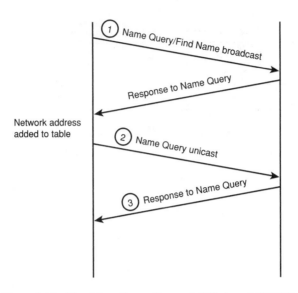

**Figure 2.14** Two NameQuery Frames in Windows NT NBF.

must be a component between the originating process and the TDI interface of NBF that translates a process ID and an LSN into a TDI handle. The component in the middle is called NETBIOS.SYS. This concept is illustrated in Figure 2.15. The table maintained by NETBIOS.SYS is actually 254 LSNs per LANA number per process. In Windows NT, each binding path is represented by a LANA number. In reality, each process can have up to 254 sessions per LANA number, not just a total of 254 sessions.

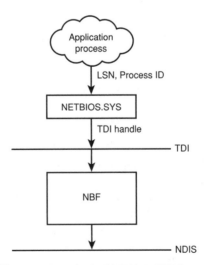

**Figure 2.15** NETBIOS.SYS and TDI.

NETBIOS.SYS builds a matrix that has LSNs down the side, process IDs along the top, and TDI handles in the cells (see Figure 2.16). It is the LSN from this table that is passed back to the originating process.

As an example, suppose a process needs to establish a session with a remote computer. Before the process can issue the CALL NCB, it must issue a RESET NCB. This command signals NETBIOS.SYS to allocate space in its TDI handle table, among other things. Once the RESET is satisfied, the process issues a CALL NCB to make a connection with a specific remote computer. This NCB is directed down to the NETBIOS.SYS device driver. The driver opens a new TDI handle to NBF and sends the command to NBF.

NBF issues the first NAME_QUERY with LSN=0 to find the remote computer. When the remote computer responds, the network address is extracted from the frame, and a column in the NBF table is created. The second NAME_QUERY with an LSN is sent directly to the remote computer. When that frame is returned successfully, NBF returns from the TDI call to the NETBIOS.SYS driver with a successful status code. NETBIOS.SYS then fills in the LSN from its table into the NCB and satisfies it back to the calling process.

## NetBIOS Connectionless Traffic

Three types of NetBIOS commands generate connectionless traffic: name claim and resolution, datagrams, and miscellaneous commands. These commands are sent as UI (Unnumbered Information) frames at the LLC sublayer.

For connectionless network traffic that requires a response from a remote computer, NBF sends out a certain number of frames, depending on the command. The total

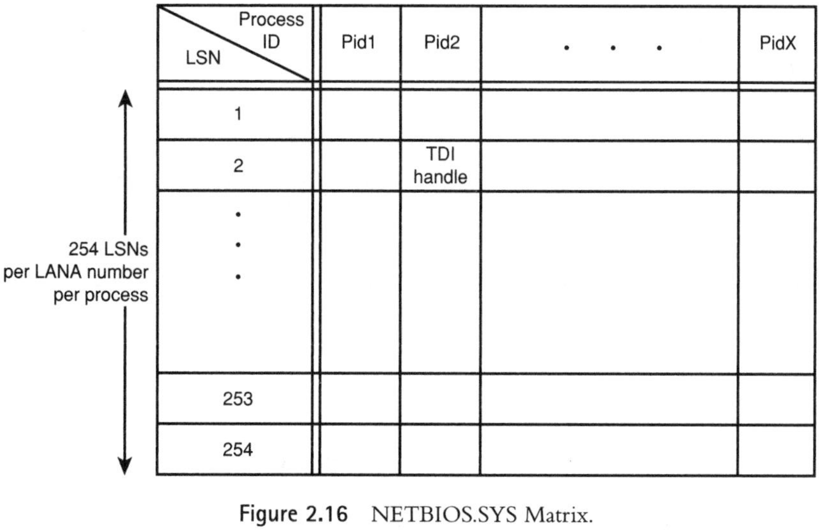

**Figure 2.16**  NETBIOS.SYS Matrix.

number is based on retry Registry value entries, such as `NameQueryRetries`. The time between sending each frame is determined by timeout Registry entries, such as `NameQueryTimeout`.

As an example of how Windows NT uses retry and timeout values from the Registry, consider what happens when Windows NT registers computernames via NBF using the NetBIOS Add.Name command. When NBF receives the Add.Name command, it broadcasts `ADD_NAME_QUERY` frames a total of `AddNameQueryRetries` times and sends these broadcasts at a time interval of `AddNameQueryTimeout`. This allows computers on the network enough time to inform the sending computer whether the name is already registered as a unique name on another computer or a group name on the network.

The following section discusses Windows NT Registry values associated with NBF. These Registry values are found under the following Registry path:

`HKEY_LOCAL_MACHINE\SYSTEM\CurrentControlSet\Services\Nbf`

## NBF Transport Registry Entries

The startup parameters for the NBF transport are found under the following subkey:

`HKEY_LOCAL_MACHINE\SYSTEM\Services\NBF\Parameters`

The Initxxx entries for NBF define the initial allocation and the size of free memory for items. The Maxxxx entries define the upper limits. Within these ranges, the system autotunes performance. By default, the NBF service uses all the resources necessary to handle client requests, and when it is not actively working, it doesn't use many resources. Set Initxxx values to control initial allocation, which can make the system a little faster when you know a server will be busy. Set the Maxxxx values to control limits when you don't want the server to be too busy or to use too much memory for networking.

With Registry Editor, you can modify the following startup parameters for the NBF transport.

### *AddNameQueryRetries*

This parameter specifies the number of times that NBF will retry sending `ADD_NAME_QUERY` and `ADD_GROUP_NAME_QUERY` frames. Adjust this parameter only if NBF is registering addresses on a network that drops many packets. The default value of this parameter is 3 and it is of type `REG_DWORD`. In Windows NT each Registry value entry has a type associated with it. For example, the `REG_DWORD` type is a 32-bit unsigned number.

### *AddNameQueryTimeout*

`AddNameQueryTimeout` specifies the time-out between NBF sending successive `ADD_NAME_QUERY` and `ADD_GROUP_NAME_QUERY` frames. Adjust this parameter only if NBF is registering addresses on a network with slow computers or over a slow network.

The default value is 5000000 (500 milliseconds). The parameter is of `REG_DWORD` type and is measured in 100-nanosecond units.

### DefaultT1Timeout

This parameter specifies the initial value for the T1 timeout. T1 controls the time that NBF waits for a response after sending a logical link control (LLC) poll packet before resending it. Adjust this parameter only if NBF will be connecting over slow networks or to slow remote computers, although NBF is expected to adapt to changes in time-out value. The default value is 6000000 (600 milliseconds). The parameter is of `REG_DWORD` type and is measured in 100-nanosecond units.

### DefaultT2Timeout

This parameter specifies the initial value for the T2 timeout. T2 controls the time that NBF can wait after receiving an LLC poll packet before responding. The value must be much less than that of T1. About one-half or less is a good general rule. Adjust this parameter only if NBF will be connecting over slow networks or to slow remote computers. The default value is 1500000 (150 milliseconds). The parameter is of `REG_DWORD` type and is measured in 100-nanosecond units.

### DefaultTiTimeout

`DefaultTiTimeout` specifies the initial value for the Ti timeout. Ti is the inactivity timer. When it expires, NBF sends an LLC poll packet to ensure that the link is still active. Adjust this parameter only if NBF is connecting over networks with unusual reliability characteristics, or over slow networks or to slow computers. The default value is 300000000 (30 seconds). The parameter is of `REG_DWORD` type and is measured in 100-nanosecond units.

### GeneralRetries

The `GeneralRetries` parameter specifies the number of times that NBF will retry sending `STATUS_QUERY` and `FIND_NAME` frames. Adjust this parameter only if NBF is operating on a network that drops many packets. The default value is 3. The parameter is of `REG_DWORD` type.

### GeneralTimeout

`GeneralTimeout` specifies the time-out between NBF sending successive `STATUS_QUERY` and `FIND_NAME` requests. Adjust this parameter only if NBF is operating on a network with slow computers or over a slow network. The default value is 5000000 (500 milliseconds). The parameter is of `REG_DWORD` type and is measured in 100-nanosecond units.

### InitAddresses

This parameter specifies the number of initial addresses to allocate within any memory limits that might be imposed on NBF. Addresses correspond to NetBIOS names. An *address* is for the actual name, and an *address file* is for a TDI client using that name. Usually you have the same number for the address and address file, but if two users open the same address, there are two address files but only one address. Set this parameter if you know that a large number of addresses are needed. Otherwise, the system automatically allocates space for addresses as needed. The default value is 0, which implies no limit. You can set this parameter to 1 or higher. The parameter is of type `REG_DWORD`.

### InitAddressFiles

This parameter specifies the number of initial address files to allocate within any memory limits that might be imposed on NBF. Set this parameter if you know that a large number of address files are needed. Otherwise, the system automatically allocates space for address files as needed. The default value is 0, which implies no limit. You can set this parameter to 1 or higher. The parameter is of type `REG_DWORD`.

### InitConnections

`InitConnections` specifies the number of initial connections (NetBIOS sessions) to allocate within any memory limits that might be imposed on NBF. Set this parameter if you know that a large number of connections are needed. Otherwise, the system automatically allocates space for connections as needed. The default value is 1. You can set this parameter to 0, which implies no limit, or higher. The parameter is of type `REG_DWORD`.

### InitLinks

The `InitLinks` parameter specifies the number of initial LLC links to allocate within any memory limits that might be imposed on NBF. Typically, you have one connection per LLC link to another network adapter card, because the redirector puts all links to a computer into one connection. However, you may have more if two computers are communicating with each other or if a NetBIOS application is running. Set this parameter if you know that a large number of links is needed. Otherwise, the system automatically allocates space for links as needed. The default value is 2. You can set this parameter to 0, which implies no limit, or higher. The parameter is of type `REG_DWORD`.

### InitReceiveBuffers

The `InitReceiveBuffers` parameter specifies the number of initial receive buffers to allocate. Receive buffers are used by NBF when it calls NDIS TransferData for received datagrams. Usually, this value is allocated as needed, but you can use this parameter to preallocate memory if you know a large number of datagram frames will be received. The default value is 5. You can set this parameter to 0, which implies no limit, or higher. The parameter is of type `REG_DWORD`.

### InitReceivePackets

This parameter specifies the number of initial receive packets to allocate. Receive packets are used by NBF when it calls NDIS TransferData for received data. Usually, this value is allocated as needed, but you can use this parameter to preallocate memory if you know a large number of UI frames will be received. The default value is 10. You can set this parameter to 0, which implies no limit, or higher. The parameter is of type `REG_DWORD`.

### InitRequests

`InitRequests` specifies the number of initial requests to allocate within any memory limits that might be imposed on NBF. Requests are used for in-progress connect requests, remote adapter status requests, find name requests, and so on. Set this parameter if you know that a large number of requests are needed. Otherwise, the system automatically allocates space for requests as needed. The default value is 5. You can set this parameter to 0, which implies no limit, or higher. The parameter is of type `REG_DWORD`.

### InitSendPackets

`InitSendPackets` specifies the number of initial send packets to allocate. Send packets are used by NBF whenever it sends connection-oriented data on behalf of a client. Usually, this value is allocated as needed, but you can use this parameter to preallocate memory if you know a large number of data frames are needed or if you see a lot of "send packets exhausted" messages when using Performance Monitor. The default value is 30. You can set this parameter to 0, which implies no limit, or higher. The parameter is of type `REG_DWORD`.

### InitUIFrames

This parameter specifies the number of initial UI frames to allocate. UI frames are used by NBF to establish connections and for connectionless services such as datagrams. Usually, this value is allocated as needed, but you can use this parameter to preallocate memory if you know a large number of UI frames are needed. The default value is 30. You can set this parameter to 5, which implies no limit, or higher. The parameter is of type `REG_DWORD`.

### LLCMaxWindowSize

The `LLCMaxWindowSize` parameter specifies the number of LLC I-frames that NBF can send before polling and waiting for a response from the remote. Adjust this parameter only if NBF is communicating over a network whose reliability often changes suddenly. The default value is 10. You can set this parameter to 0, which implies no limit, or higher. The parameter is of type `REG_DWORD`.

### LLCRetries

The `LLCRetries` parameter specifies the number of times that NBF will retry polling a remote workstation after receiving a T1 timeout. After this many retries, NBF closes the link. Adjust this parameter only if NBF is connecting over networks with unusual reliability characteristics. The default value is 8. You can set this parameter to 0, which implies no limit, or higher. The parameter is of type `REG_DWORD`.

### MaxAddresses

This parameter specifies the maximum number of addresses that NBF allocates within any memory limits that might be imposed on NBF. Addresses are NetBIOS names that are registered on the network by NBF. An address is for the actual name, and an address file is for a TDI client using that name. Use this optional parameter to fine-tune use of NBF memory. Typically this parameter is used to control address resources with an unlimited NBF. The default value is 0, which implies no limit. You can set this parameter to 1 or higher. The parameter is of type `REG_DWORD`.

### MaxAddressFiles

`MaxAddressFiles` specifies the maximum number of address files that NBF allocates within any memory limits that might be imposed on NBF. Each address file corresponds to a client opening an address. Use this optional parameter to fine-tune use of NBF memory. Typically this parameter is used to control address files with an unlimited NBF. The default value is 0, which implies no limit. You can set this parameter to 1 or higher. The parameter is of type `REG_DWORD`.

### MaxConnections

This parameter specifies the maximum number of connections that NBF allocates within any memory limits that might be imposed on NBF. Connections are established between NBF clients and similar entities on remote computers. Use this optional parameter to fine-tune use of NBF memory. Typically this parameter is used to control connection resources with an unlimited NBF. The default value is 0, which implies no limit. You can set this parameter to 1 or higher. The parameter is of type `REG_DWORD`.

### MaximumIncomingFrames

`MaximumIncomingFrames` is used in some cases to control how many incoming frames NBF will receive before it sends an acknowledgment to a remote machine. In general, NBF automatically senses when to send acknowledgments; however, when communicating with some Microsoft LAN Manager or IBM LAN Server remote computers configured with a very low value for maxout, this parameter can be set to an equal or lower value to improve network performance. This parameter corresponds roughly to the Microsoft LAN Manager maxin parameter. A value of 0 turns off this hint, causing NBF to revert to usual behavior. For communication with most remotes, this parameter isn't used. The default value is 2. You can set this parameter to 1 or higher. The parameter is of type `REG_DWORD`.

### MaxLinks

`MaxLinks` specifies the maximum number of links that NBF allocates within any memory limits that might be imposed on NBF. Links are established for every remote adapter to which NBF communicates. Use this optional parameter to fine-tune use of NBF memory. Typically this parameter is used to control link resources with an unlimited NBF. The default value is 0, which implies no limit. You can set this parameter to 1 or higher. The parameter is of type `REG_DWORD`.

### MaxRequests

This parameter specifies the maximum number of requests that NBF allocates within any memory limits that might be imposed on NBF. Requests are used by NBF to control send, receive, connect, and listen operations. Use this optional parameter to fine-tune use of NBF memory. Typically this parameter is used to control request resources with an unlimited NBF. The default value is 0, which implies no limit. You can set this parameter to 1 or higher. The parameter is of type `REG_DWORD`.

### NameQueryRetries

The `NameQueryRetries` parameter specifies the number of times that NBF will retry sending `NAME_QUERY` frames. Adjust this parameter only if NBF is connecting to computers over a network that drops many packets. The default value is 3. The parameter is of type `REG_DWORD`.

### NameQueryTimeout

This parameter specifies the time-out between NBF sending successive `NAME_QUERY` frames. Adjust this parameter only if NBF is connecting to slow computers or over a slow network. The default value is 5000000 (500 milliseconds). The parameter is of `REG_DWORD` type and is measured in 100-nanosecond units.

### QueryWithoutSourceRouting

When you are using NBF over a Token Ring driver, this parameter instructs NBF to send the queries without including source routing information when connecting to a remote computer. This supports bridging hardware that cannot forward frames containing source routing information. The default value is 0 (false). The parameter can be enabled by setting its value to 1 (true). The parameter is of type `REG_DWORD`.

### WanNameQueryRetries

The `WanNameQueryRetries` parameter specifies the number of times that NBF will retry sending `NAME_QUERY` frames when connecting with RAS. Adjust this parameter only if NBF is connecting to computers over a network that drops many packets. The default value of the parameter is 5. The parameter is of type `REG_DWORD`. RAS is covered in Chapter 12, "Accessing the Internet Using RAS and PPTP."

# The TCP/IP Protocol

The TCP/IP protocol consists of the following main protocol components: IP, TCP, and UDP.

Beta one of Windows NT version 5 has several enhancements to TCP/IP over previous versions of the operating system. These include larger window size, use of selective acknowledgments, and better round trip time estimates.

Large window size enables Windows NT to send large amounts of data without requiring acknowledgments. Flow control is implemented by the receiver advertising dynamically varying window sizes.

Selective acknowledgment enables the receiver to notify the sender about any missing pieces of data.

Round trip time (RTT) estimates are calculated so that the sender knows when to assume that a data segment was not received properly, and to transmit that segment again.

The following sections briefly discuss IP, TCP, and UDP.

## The IP Protocol

The IP protocol is a Network layer protocol that provides connectionless datagram services on top of many data link protocols (see Figure 2.17).

IP does not guarantee delivery of datagrams; it makes the best effort it can to deliver data. Upper-layer protocols such as TCP can be used to build guaranteed delivery services on top of IP. IP provides a number of interesting services that have become the basis of design for other protocols.

IP provides the notion of a logical network address independent of the underlying network. It makes use of an Address Resolution Protocol (ARP) to provide the binding between this logical address (called the IP address) and the physical address of a node.

IP datagrams can be fragmented into smaller units to accommodate the Maximum Transmission Unit (MTU) of the underlying network. If fragmentation takes place, the fragments are created with sufficient information so that they can be reassembled. Reassembly of fragments to make up the original datagram is done at the destination node. Problems with IP, such as unreachable destinations and reassembly time-outs, are reported to the sender by the Internet Control Message Protocol (ICMP).

IP addresses are represented by a 32-bit number. Each network interface in a node that supports an IP stack must have a unique IP address assigned to it. The IP address is a two-part address consisting of a network ID and a host ID, as shown in Figure

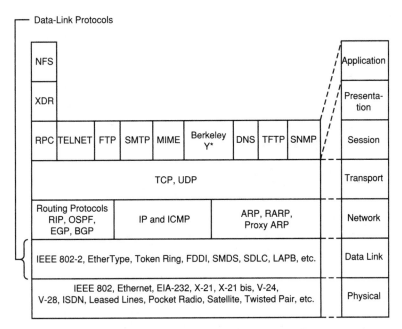

**Figure 2.17**    Example of TCP/IP on different Data Link layer protocols.

2.18. The most significant bits are used to determine how many bits are used for the netid and the hostid. Five address classes currently are defined: A, B, C, D, and E. Of these, class A, B, and C addresses are assignable. Class D is reserved for multicasting and is used by special protocols to transmit messages to a select group of nodes. Class E is reserved for future use.

The netid portion of the IP address is similar to the network number used in IPX protocols. It identifies the network uniquely. All NICs on a subnet should have the same netid. Interconnected networks must have unique netids.

The different types of IP address classes are defined to address the needs of networks of different sizes. Table 2.7 shows the number of networks and nodes per network possible with each address class.

A class A network is suited for very large networks, but because its netid field (see Figure 2.18) is only 7 bits, there can be only 127 such networks. The original

Table 2.7    **Reasons for Using Specific Address Class**

| Address Class | Number of Networks | Number of Nodes |
| --- | --- | --- |
| A | 127 | 16,777,214 |
| B | 16,383 | 65,534 |
| C | 2,097,151 | 254 |

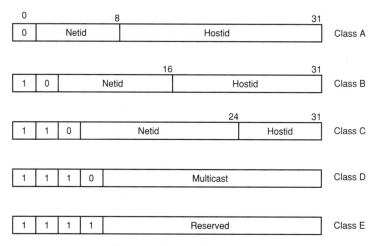

**Figure 2.18**   IP address classes.

ARPANET is an example of a class A network. Class B networks are medium-sized networks and are suited for medium to large organizations. Class C networks are suited for small organizations, in which each network can have no more than 254 nodes.

The 32-bit number is represented for convenience as four decimal numbers corresponding to the decimal value of the four bytes that make up the 32-bit IP address. The decimal numbers are separated by periods (.). This shorthand notation for IP addresses is called *dotted decimal notation*. Figure 2.19 shows the format of an IP packet.

The following shows an IP address in its binary form and also in dotted decimal notation:

IP Address = 10010000 00010011 01001010 11001010

IP Address = 144.19.74.202

In Figure 2.19, the version number field is four bits long and indicates the format of the IP header. This allows future IP packet structures to be defined. The current version number is four. Table 2.8 shows the other possible values of the version number field. IP version 6 is the new IP version format and is referred to as IPv6.

Table 2.8  **IP Version Number Values**

| IP Version | Meaning |
| --- | --- |
| 0 | Reserved |
| 1–3 | Unassigned |
| 4 | IP |
| 5 | Stream IP (Experimental IP) |
| 6 | IPv6 |
| 7–14 | Unassigned |
| 15 | Reserved |

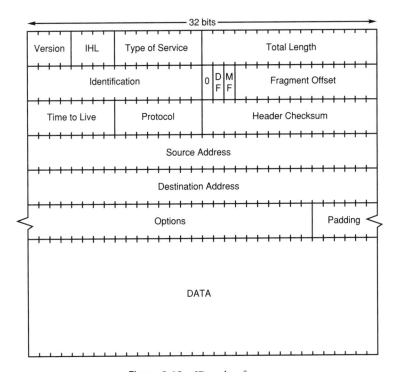

**Figure 2.19**  IP packet format.

The Internet Header Length (IHL) is the length of the header in 32-bit words. This field is required because the IP header contains a variable-length option field.

The Type of Service (TOS) field informs the networks of the Quality of Service (QOS) desired, such as precedence, delay, throughput, and reliability. Figure 2.20 shows the meaning of this eight-bit field.

The Precedence field reflects the military origin of IP networks. The following are the meanings of some of the precedence values:

■ Flash. ASAP (As Soon As Possible); maximum priority on all circuits

■ Immediate. Within four hours

■ Priority. Same day

■ Routine. Within one day

Most IP implementations and routing protocols (RIP, HELLO, and so on) ignore the Type of Service field.

The Precedence field is intended for Department of Defense applications of the Internet protocols. The use of nonzero values in this field is outside the scope of the IP standard specification. Vendors should consult the Defense Information Systems

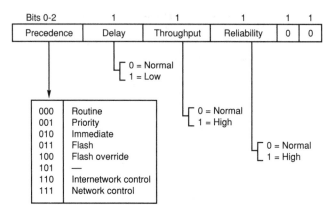

**Figure 2.20** Type of Service (TOS) field for IP packets.

Agency (DISA) for guidance on the IP Precedence field and its implications for other protocol layers.

Vendors should note that the use of precedence most likely requires that its value be passed between protocol layers in much the same way as the TOS field is passed. The IP layer must provide a means for the Transport layer to set the TOS field of every datagram sent; the default is all zero bits. The IP layer should pass received TOS values up to the Transport layer.

Although little used in the past, the TOS field is expected to play an increasing role in the near future with routing protocols such as OSPF that could use the TOS field. The TOS field is expected to be used to control two aspects of router operations: routing and queuing algorithms. The TOS field also can be mapped into the Data Link layer for effective sharing of serial lines by different classes of TCP traffic.

The Total Length field contains the length of the IP header and data in bytes. The maximum size of the datagram is 65,535 bytes. All IP nodes must be prepared to receive a minimum size of 576 bytes (512 bytes of data plus 64 bytes of protocol overhead).

The Identification field is set uniquely for each datagram, and is the datagram number. It is used with the fragment flags DF (Don't Fragment), MF (More Fragments), and Fragment Offset fields to reassemble the datagram. If the DF flag is set to 1, the datagram should not be fragmented. An MF flag set to 1 indicates to the receiver that more fragments are to come. An MF set to 0 indicates the last fragment.

The Fragment Offset field indicates the position of the fragment's data relative to the start of the original datagram. This is a 13-bit field and is measured in 8-byte groups. This means that the Fragment Offset value must be multiplied by 8 to get the byte offset.

The Time to Live (TTL) is measured in seconds and represents the maximum time an IP datagram can live on the network. It should be decremented at each router by the amount of time taken to process the packet. The intent is that TTL expiration causes a datagram to be discarded by a router, but not by the destination host. Hosts that act as routers by forwarding datagrams (such as Windows NT) must follow the router rules for TTL. The TTL field has two functions: limiting the lifetime of TCP segments and terminating Internet routing loops. Although TTL is time in seconds, it also has some attributes of a hop count because each gateway is required to reduce the TTL field by the number of seconds that a router holds the packet, or at least by 1 second. This is why some implementors mistakenly set it to 16, because 16 is infinity for RIP. But TTL is independent of RIP metrics.

Other considerations for TTL fields follow:

■ A host must not send a datagram with a TTL value of zero, and a host must not discard a datagram just because it is received with TTL less than two.

■ An upper-layer protocol may want to set the TTL to implement an expanding scope search for some Internet resource. This is used by some diagnostic tools and is expected to be useful for locating the "nearest" server of a given class using IP multicasting, for example. A particular transport protocol also may want to specify its own TTL boundary on maximum datagram lifetime.

■ A fixed value must be at least big enough for the Internet diameter—the longest possible path. A reasonable value is about twice the diameter, which allows for continued Internet growth.

■ The IP layer must provide a means for the Transport layer to set the TTL field of every datagram sent. When a fixed TTL value is used, that value must be configurable. Unfortunately, most implementations do not allow the initial TTL value to be set. A default value of 32 or 64 is very common.

The Protocol field indicates the upper-layer protocol that is to receive the IP data. It is similar in function to the Packet Type field for IPX packets. The "assigned numbers" RFC 1060 contains the defined values for this field; for example, TCP has a protocol field value of 6, UDP has a value of 17, and ICMP has a value of 1.

The header checksum is used for the IP header only. The 1s complement of each 16-bit value making up the header is added (excluding the Header Checksum field). Then the 1s complement of the sum is taken. This field is recomputed at each router because the TTL field is decremented, and the header is modified.

The source address and destination address are the 32-bit IP addresses of the source and destination nodes.

The IP options are security, loose source routing, strict source routing, record route, and Internet timestamp.

## The TCP Protocol

TCP is the primary transport protocol used to provide reliable, full-duplex, virtual-circuit connections. The connections are made between port numbers of the sender and the receiver nodes. TCP has an octet-stream orientation. An octet is a group of eight bits.

Therefore, an octet stream is an 8-bit stream. There is no inherent notion of a block of data. TCP can be used to provide multiple virtual-circuit connections between two TCP hosts.

Figure 2.21 shows the TCP packet structure. The source port and destination port numbers identify the end-point processes in the TCP virtual circuit. Some port numbers are well known, whereas others are assigned dynamically. RFC 1066 contains a description of some of the well-known port numbers. A few of these are shown in Table 2.9.

The 32-bit sequence number is the number of the first byte of data in the current message. If the SYN flag is set to 1, this field defines the initial sequence number to be used for that session. A 32-bit value is used to avoid using old sequence numbers that already may be assigned to data in transit on the network.

The acknowledgment number indicates the sequence number of the next byte expected by the receiver. TCP acknowledgments are cumulative—that is, a single acknowledgment can be used to acknowledge a number of prior TCP message segments.

The Data Offset field is the number of 32-bit words in the TCP header. This field is needed because the TCP options field can be variable in length.

Table 2.9  **Some Well-Known TCP Port Numbers**

| Port Number | Description |
| --- | --- |
| 0 | Reserved |
| 5 | Remote Job Entry |
| 7 | Echo |
| 9 | Discard |
| 11 | Systat |
| 13 | Daytime |
| 15 | Netstat |
| 17 | Quotd (quote of the day) |
| 20 | ftp_data |
| 21 | ftp (Control) |
| 23 | telnet |
| 25 | smtp |
| 37 | time |
| 53 | name server |
| 102 | ISO-TSAP |
| 103 | X.400 |
| 104 | X.400 sending service |
| 111 | Sun RPC |
| 139 | NetBIOS session source |
| 160–223 | Reserved |

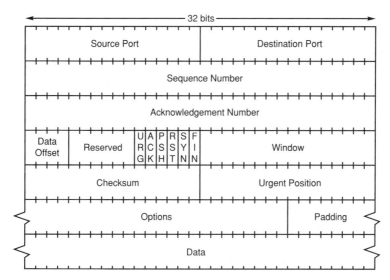

**Figure 2.21**   TCP packet format.

The flags that follow have the following meanings:

- URG. This flag is used to send out-of-band data without waiting for the receiver to process octets already in the stream. When the URG flag is set, the Urgent Pointer field is valid. RFC 1122 states that the Urgent pointer points to the sequence number of the LAST octet (not LAST + 1) in a sequence of urgent data, and that RFC 793 describes it incorrectly as LAST + 1. A TCP implementation must support a sequence of urgent data of any length. A TCP layer must inform the Application layer asynchronously whenever the TCP layer receives an Urgent pointer with no previous pending urgent data, or whenever the Urgent pointer advances in the data stream.

    There must be a way for the application to learn how much urgent data remains to be read from the connection, or at least to determine whether more urgent data remains to be read. Although the Urgent mechanism can be used for any application, it normally is used to send interrupt-type commands to a Telnet program. The asynchronous, or out-of-band, notification allows the application to go into urgent mode, reading data from the TCP connection. This allows control commands to be sent to an application whose normal input buffers are full of unprocessed data.

- ACK. The ACK flag indicates that the Acknowledgment Number field is valid.

- PSH. This flag tells TCP to immediately deliver data for this message to the upper-layer process. When an application issues a series of send calls without setting the PSH flag, the TCP may aggregate the data internally without sending it.

Similarly, when a series of segments is received without the PSH bit, a TCP may queue the data internally without passing it to the receiving application.

The PSH bit is not a record marker and is independent of segment boundaries. Some implementations incorrectly regard the PSH as a record marker, however. The transmitter should collapse successive PSH bits when it packetizes data to send the largest possible segment.

A TCP can implement PSH flags on send calls. If PSH flags are not implemented, then the sending TCP must not buffer data indefinitely and must set the PSH bit in the last buffered segment (for example, when no more queued data is to be sent).

RFC-793 erroneously implies that a received PSH flag must be passed to the Application layer. Passing a received PSH flag to the Application layer now is optional.

An application program is logically required to set the PSH flag in a send call whenever it needs to force delivery of the data to avoid a communication deadlock. A TCP should send a maximum-size segment whenever possible to improve performance, however. This means that on the sender side, a PSH may not result in the segment being immediately transmitted.

When the PSH flag is not implemented on send TCP calls (or when the application/TCP interface uses a pure streaming model), responsibility for aggregating any tiny data fragments to form reasonable-size segments is partially borne by the Application layer. Generally, an interactive application protocol must set the PSH flag at least in the last send call in each command or response sequence. A bulk transfer protocol like FTP should set the PSH flag on the last segment of a file, or when necessary to prevent buffer deadlock.

At the receiver, the PSH bit forces buffered data to be delivered to the application (even if less than a full buffer is received). Conversely, the lack of a PSH can be used to avoid unnecessary wake-up calls to the application process; this can be an important performance optimization for large time-sharing hosts.

- RST. The RST bit resets the virtual circuit due to unrecoverable errors. The reason could be a host crash or delayed duplicate SYN packets.

- SYN. This flag indicates the opening of a virtual-circuit connection. TCP connections are opened using the three-way-handshake procedure. The SYN and the ACK flags are used to indicate the following packets:

  SYN = 1 and ACK = 0   Open connection packet

  SYN = 1 and ACK = 1   Open connection acknowledgment

  SYN = 0 and ACK = 1   Data packet or ACK packet

- FIN. The FIN flag terminates the connection. Connection termination in TCP is accomplished by using a graceful close mechanism: Both sides must agree to terminate by sending a FIN = 1 flag before connection termination can occur. The graceful close ensures that data is not unexpectedly lost by either side by an abrupt connection termination.

The Window field implements flow control and is used by the receiver to advertise the number of additional bytes of data it is willing to accept.

The Checksum field is 1's complement of the sum of all the 16-bit words in the TCP packet. A 96-bit pseudoheader (see Figure 2.22) is prepended to the TCP header for checksum computation. The pseudoheader identifies whether the packet has arrived at the right destination. The pseudoheader has the protocol ID (6 for TCP), source, and destination IP address. Because the TCP header contains the source and destination port number, this describes the connection between the endpoints.

The Options field currently defines only the Maximum Segment Size (MSS) option, which is negotiated during connection establishment.

### The UDP Protocol

There are a number of applications in which the robustness of TCP is not required. Instead, what is needed is a transport protocol that can identify the applications on the computers and provides a rudimentary error check. The User Datagram Protocol (UDP) provides these capabilities.

Unlike TCP, which is connection oriented, UDP (as its name suggests) operates in the datagram mode. UDP makes no attempt to create a connection. Data is sent by encapsulating it in a UDP header and passing it to the IP layer. The IP layer sends the UDP packet in a single IP datagram unless fragmentation is required. UDP does not attempt to provide sequencing of data. It is therefore possible for data to arrive in a different order in which it was sent. Applications that need sequencing services must

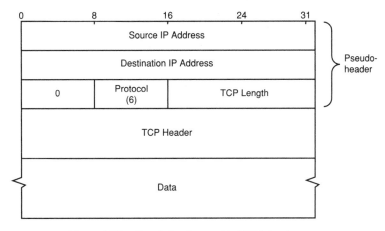

**Figure 2.22**    Pseudoheader used in TCP checksum.

either build their own sequencing mechanism as part of the application or use TCP instead of UDP. In many LAN environments the chances of data being received out of sequence is small because of small predictable delays and simple network topology.

UDP is useful in applications that are command/response oriented and where the commands and responses can be sent in a single datagram. There is no overhead of having to open a connection, and then close the connection just to send a small amount of data. Another advantage of UDP is for applications that require broadcast/multicast. In TCP, if a broadcast must be sent to 1000 stations, the sender must open 1000 connections, send data on each connection, and then close the 1000 connections. The overhead of opening these connections, maintaining them (resource utilization), and then closing them is high. If UDP is used, the sender can send the data to the IP module requesting a broadcast/multicast distribution. The underlying networks broadcast/multicast capability may be used in sending the data.

UDP provides a rudimentary form of optional error checking over the integrity of the data. If the underlying network is known to be reliable, the UDP checksums can be disabled, which speeds up UDP processing.

The features of UDP are summarized as follows:

- Provision for identifying application processes by using UDP port numbers.

- Datagram oriented. No overhead of opening, maintaining, and closing a connection.

- Efficient for broadcast/multicast applications.

- No sequencing of data. Data cannot be guaranteed for delivery correctly.

- Optional error checksum of data only.

- Faster, simpler, and more efficient than TCP. Also less robust than TCP.

UDP is said to provide unreliable connectionless delivery services over TCP. UDP is regarded as a Transport layer protocol. As a Transport layer protocol, UDP is somewhat of a paradox, because the function of a Transport layer is to provide end-to-end data integrity, which is something UDP does not do. Despite this fact, a large number of practical applications are built around UDP. These include the following:

- Trivial File Transfer Protocol (TFTP)
- DNS (Domain Name System)
- NFS (Network File System) version 2
- SNMP (Simple Network Management Protocol)
- RIP (Routing Information Protocol)
- NetBIOS datagrams
- Many services that broadcast data, such as WHOD (the Who daemon on UNIX servers)

## UDP Header Format

The UDP header has a fixed length of eight octets. The format of the UDP header is shown in Figure 2.23.

The Source Port is a 16-bit, optional field. When meaningful, it indicates the following:

- The port number of the sending process.

- The source port number is the port to which a reply should be addressed in the absence of any other information.

- When set to 0, it indicates that the source port number is not used.

The Destination Port field identifies the process at the destination IP address that is to receive the UDP data being sent. Like TCP, UDP performs demultiplexing of data to the destination process using port number values. If UDP receives a datagram with a port number that is not in use (no UDP application associated with the port), it generates an ICMP port unreachable error message and rejects the datagram.

The Length field is the length of this UDP packet in octets. This length includes the UDP header and its data. The minimum value of the Length field is 8 and indicates a 0 size data field.

The Checksum field is the 16-bit 1's complement of the 1's complement sum of a pseudoheader of information from the IP header, the UDP header, and the data, padded with 0 octets at the end (if necessary) to make a multiple of two octets. The checksum procedure is the same as is used in TCP.

The pseudoheader is conceptually prefixed to the UDP header and contains the source address, the destination address, the protocol (UDP protocol number is 17), and the UDP length (see Figure 2.24). This information provides protection against misrouted datagrams. The pseudoheader has a fixed size of 12 octets. The information in the UDP pseudoheader completely specifies the half association of the destination, even though no connection is being set up.

If the computed checksum is 0, it is transmitted as all 1s (the equivalent in 1's complement arithmetic). Therefore, an all 0 checksum is never generated by the previous calculation, and is used to indicate a special condition: An all 0 transmitted checksum value means that checksums are not being used. Another way of looking at this is that

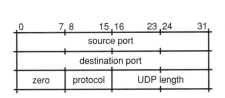

**Figure 2.23**   UDP header format.

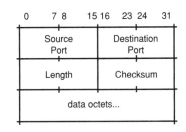

**Figure 2.24**   UDP pseudoheader used in checksum calculations.

0 has two representations using 1's complement arithmetic: all 0s, and all 1s. All 1s is used for calculated checksum and all 0s indicates that checksumming is disabled. If running an application on a reliable IP network, such as a LAN, you may want to disable the extra overhead of generating checksums on transmission and verifying them on receiving the UDP datagram.

The UDP protocol runs on top of IP. The IP checksum is done only over the header, whereas the UDP checksum is done over the UDP header and data. The UDP checksum is needed to guarantee the integrity of the data field.

# Installing the TCP/IP Protocol and Services

## 3

T HE PREVIOUS CHAPTERS HAVE DISCUSSED IN detail the network components and TCP/IP protocol components of Windows networks. This chapter addresses how the network components and TCP/IP protocols are installed on Windows workstations. The installation procedure and issues associated with Windows NT and Windows 98 workstations are also covered. Normally, TCP/IP should be installed during the installation of network services when installing the operating system. However, there may be situations when a standalone computer must connect with a network after the addition of suitable networking hardware. In this case you must explicitly install TCP/IP software.

You also learn to configure the TCP/IP stack to make use of name services such as WINS and DNS. Detailed configuration of TCP/IP application services such as Dynamic Host Configuration Protocol (DHCP), WINS, and DNS are discussed in later chapters in the book.

## Installing TCP/IP

A Windows NT installation automatically includes the TCP/IP protocol stack if you choose to install any network services. This section discusses the procedures for installing and configuring the Windows NT TCP/IP protocol stack. You must install the TCP/IP protocol stack manually only if you have previously removed it but now need to add support for TCP/IP services.

1. Log on to the Windows NT computer as an Administrator user.

2. Double-click the Network icon in the Control Panel. The Network dialog box appears (see Figure 3.1). Select the Protocols tab. Alternatively, you can right-click on Network Neighborhood and choose Properties to get to the Network properties.

3. If you are reinstalling the TCP/IP protocol stack, click the Add button (see Figure 3.2). You should see a list of protocols you can add.

4. Select TCP/IP Protocol and then choose OK.

5. A Windows NT TCP/IP Installation Options dialog box appears and asks whether you want to obtain an IP address from a DHCP server on your network or you want to manually configure the IP address. If you choose Obtain an IP Address from a DHCP Server, the Windows NT TCP/IP stack requests its IP address from a DHCP server when it initializes. Make sure that all the other TCP/IP configuration entries are empty; otherwise, they will override the parameters assigned by the DHCP server.

   If you have a DHCP server on your network, choose Yes; otherwise, select No. See the later section "Configuring the DHCP Relay" for additional information on configuring DHCP.

6. You see a dialog box prompting you for the path of the distribution files. If you have a CD-ROM on the Windows NT Server, the Path field contains the path to the CD-ROM distribution files. If the Windows NT Server distribution files are not in the path displayed, enter their drive and directory or the UNC name if the source files are on a network server.

   Choose Continue.

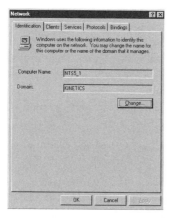

**Figure 3.1**  Network dialog box.

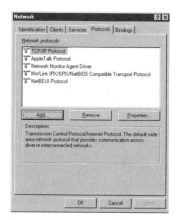

**Figure 3.2**  Network Protocols tab.

You see a status of the copy operation as files are copied. The Configuring Network status screen appears as the setup program performs binding analysis and configuration.

The TCP/IP protocol is now installed. Your next step is to configure at least the basic TCP/IP settings.

## Configuring the IP Address

If you're not using DHCP to assign a TCP/IP address to the Windows NT Server dynamically, the Microsoft TCP/IP Protocol Properties dialog box appears (see Figure 3.3). You can also get to this dialog box by highlighting the TCP/IP protocol in the Protocols tab of the Network panel and selecting the Properties button. In this dialog box, you specify the IP Address, Subnet Mask, and Default Gateway address of the network interface.

1. If a DHCP server already is on the network and you want to use it to configure the Windows NT computer, you should choose the Obtain an IP Address from a DHCP Server option. A DHCP server contains TCP/IP configuration information for other TCP/IP hosts. When a TCP/IP host starts, it requests its configuration information from the DHCP server.

   If you choose Obtain an IP Address from a DHCP Server, the Windows NT computer obtains the IP address and subnet mask values from the DHCP server. If you enter values for the IP address and subnet mask, you effectively disable the DHCP client and you will not download any information from the DHCP server.

   If no DHCP server is yet on the network, or if you are installing the Windows NT Server for use as a DHCP server, you must set the IP address and subnet mask manually. Enter the IP address and subnet mask for the Windows NT Server's network interface as shown in Figure 3.3.

2. If your network is connected to other TCP/IP networks or subnetworks, you must specify a value for the Default Gateway field so that you can reach the other networks. TCP/IP recognizes whether the destination address is on another network and forwards the packet to the default gateway (or default *router*, correctly speaking). (The term *default gateway* is still used because historically the devices known as routers today were called gateways.)

3. If you have multiple network adapters, each must be configured individually. Specify the IP address configuration (IP address, subnet mask, default gateway, use of DHCP server) for each adapter bound to the TCP/IP protocol by selecting the network cards in the Adapter field one at a time.

**IP Addresses for Multiple Adapters**

Each network adapter must have a unique IP address, even if the adapter is in the same Windows NT computer.

4. Click the Advanced button if you want to configure multiple IP addresses for a single network adapter, multiple default gateways for a network adapter, or security options. Select the network adapter to configure from the Adapter field in the Advanced IP Addressing dialog box (see Figure 3.4). Note that the IP configuration settings in this dialog box apply only to the selected network adapter.

5. You can enter multiple IP addresses and subnet masks for the selected adapter by entering the IP address and subnet mask values in the IP Address and Subnet Mask boxes of the Advanced IP Addressing dialog box (see Figure 3.4) and clicking the Add button.

   Multiple IP addresses and subnet masks are particularly useful when you want a single physical system to look like several systems. The mail server might be 199.245.180.1, for example, the DNS server 200.1.180.2, the FTP server 203.24.10.3, and so on. Also, multiple IP addresses and subnet masks can help during transition to a different IP network number assignment for the network. You also can use multiple IP addresses if your network consists of multiple logical IP networks. During the transition phase, it is useful to have both IP network numbers be applicable. You can specify up to five additional IP addresses and subnet masks for a selected network adapter through this dialog box. If you need more than six IP addresses for a single interface, you can add more addresses by editing the Registry directly.

   (To remove an IP address and subnet mask combination, highlight it and click the Remove button.)

6. If you must specify alternative default gateways, you can enter the IP addresses of the default gateways in the Gateways field of the Advanced IP Addressing dialog box (see Figure 3.4) and choose the corresponding Add button.

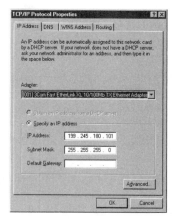

**Figure 3.3**   TCP/IP Protocol Properties dialog box.

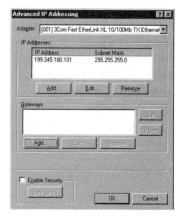

**Figure 3.4**   Advanced IP Addressing dialog box.

The default gateway field is the IP address of a router on the local network. When a packet is sent to an IP address that is not on the local network and not specified in the local routing table at the Windows NT computer, the default gateway is used. If you have specified multiple default gateways, they are tried in the order in which they are listed if an attempt to use a particular gateway is unsuccessful. You can change the order in which the default gateways are tried by selecting a gateway's address and moving it by using the Up and Down buttons.

To remove a gateway, highlight it and choose the Remove button.

7. You can enable and configure security on each adapter. Check the Enable Security box and click the Configure button. The TCP/IP Security dialog box appears (see Figure 3.5). The security options act as a type of filter. This may be appropriate if you want to accept traffic only for some well-defined services with specific port numbers. You can find the official port and protocol numbers in the Assigned Numbers RFC (RFC 1700).

By default, all TCP ports, UDP ports, and the IP protocol are enabled. This means that the NT computer accepts packets destined to any TCP or UDP port in an IP packet. To change the default values, select the option Permit Only and use the Add and Remove buttons to edit the criteria for filtering of IP packets.

## Configuring the DNS Settings

If you want to use DNS for host name resolution on Windows networks, select the DNS tab from the Microsoft TCP/IP Properties dialog box. DNS is the most commonly used name-resolution method on the Internet and other UNIX-based networks. If you enable DNS name resolution, you must have a DNS server that the Windows NT computer can contact, or have the Windows NT computer configured as a DNS server. The Windows NT computer needs to know the IP address of the DNS server. The IP address of the DNS server is specified in the TCP/IP DNS tab. This section discusses the DNS client software.

When accessing other TCP/IP hosts on the network, you can use their IP addresses. Users typically find it easier to remember and use symbolic names for computers rather than IP addresses. This is why the computer names usually are used for Windows NT computers rather than just IP addresses. The Domain Name System (DNS) is used for naming TCP/IP nodes, such as Windows NT computers and UNIX hosts. The naming scheme is hierarchical and consists of names such as wks1.kinetics.com or wks2.cello.org. DNS is the most widely used name service for UNIX hosts and on the Internet. If you plan to use your Windows NT computer on a UNIX network or the

### Host Names for DNS Compatibility

In host names, you cannot use some characters that you can use in Windows NT computer names, particularly the underscore (_). If you are connected to the Internet, you probably should use DNS-compatible names so that both naming systems can use the same names for the same computers.

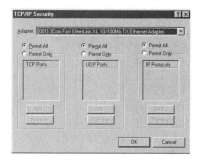

**Figure 3.5**   TCP/IP Security dialog box.

Internet, you should configure your Windows NT computer to use DNS. TCP/IP applications written to use the Windows Sockets API, such as Internet Explorer, FTP, and Telnet, use DNS or the local HOSTS file to resolve symbolic names.

When the TCP/IP connectivity components are installed on a Windows NT computer, the DNS client software for resolving DNS names is also installed. The DNS client software is, in addition to dynamic name resolution, used for resolving NetBIOS computer names through WINS servers and NetBIOS over TCP/IP. When you configure DNS on a Windows NT computer, it applies to all network adapters installed on the computer.

The following steps outline the procedure to follow to configure your Windows NT computer to use DNS client software:

1. The Host Name field in the DNS tab in the Microsoft TCP/IP Protocol Properties dialog box is where you enter the TCP/IP host name of the computer (see Figure 3.6). You usually just use the same name as the computer name. If you want to use another TCP/IP host name, you can enter the name in the Host Name field without affecting the computer name. The host name can be any combination of letters A to Z, digits 0 to 9, and the hyphen (-) character used as a separator.

   Host names to IP address mappings are stored on DNS servers. The Berkeley r★ utilities, such as rcp, rsh, rexec, and so on, use the host names for authentication.

2. Enter an optional domain name in the Domain field (see Figure 3.6). If, for example, the host name is NTWS1 in the domain name KINETICS.COM, you should enter the name KINETICS.COM in the Domain field. A DNS domain differs from a Windows NT or LAN Manager domain. Windows NT domains and LAN Manager domains are proprietary in nature, whereas DNS domains are universal and also apply to non-Microsoft products.

3. Use the DNS Service Search Order box (see Figure 3.6), to enter the IP address of the DNS servers that are used for domain name resolution. After you enter the IP address of the DNS server in the field, choose the Add button to move the IP address to the list of IP addresses for the DNS servers.

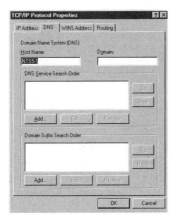

**Figure 3.6**  DNS configuration.

You can specify up to three IP addresses for DNS servers. The DNS servers that you specify are queried in the order in which they are listed. You can change the order in which the DNS servers are searched by highlighting the IP address of a DNS server and using the Up and Down buttons to move it within the list.

To remove a DNS server from the list, highlight its IP address and choose the Remove button.

### Defining FQDNs

The domain name is optional, because a small organization not connected to the Internet doesn't need to use hierarchical domain names. The domain name is combined with the host name to create a *fully qualified domain name (FQDN)* for the computer.

        FQDN = host name + domain name

In the preceding example, the FQDN for host NTWS1 is the following:

        FQDN = NTWS1 + KINETICS.COM = NTWS1.KINETICS.COM

When the Windows NT computer uses a DNS query to resolve a name that is a simple host name without the domain extension, the domain name specified in the Domain Name field is appended to the host name.

The domain name can be any combination of letters A to Z, digits 0 to 9, and the hyphen (-), using the period (.) character as a separator. Domain names are not case sensitive; so KINETICS.COM is the same as kinetics.com. A domain name usually reflects the name of an organization or its function. Domain names used on the Internet are registered with the InterNIC. Certain domain names may already be taken. You can check the availability of domain names with your Internet Service Provider or use the whois domain-name command on a UNIX system connected to the Internet to find out if the domain name is taken.

4.  In the Domain Suffix Search Order box (refer to Figure 3.6), enter the domain suffixes that are appended to host names during domain name resolution.

    You can add up to six domain suffixes. If you need to change the search order of the domain suffixes, highlight the domain name and use the Up and Down buttons to move the domain name.

    To remove a domain name, highlight it in the Domain Suffix Search Order list and choose the Remove button.

    Figure 3.7 shows a sample DNS configuration for the host NTS5-1. The local domain name is KINETICS.COM. The DNS servers are 199.245.180.10 and 199.245.180.16. First, the DNS server with IP address 199.245.180.10 is used to resolve a name. If this server can't resolve the name to its IP address, then the DNS server at 199.245.180.16 is used. The domain suffix search order is SCS.COM and LTREE.COM.

5.  Choose OK after you set the DNS configuration options.

## Configuring the WINS Address

If you have WINS (Windows Name Services) servers installed on the network, you can use WINS servers in combination with name query broadcasts to resolve computer names. The WINS server is an example of a NetBIOS Name Server (NBNS) type of server used for resolving NetBIOS names, as per the rules specified in RFC 1001 and RFC 1002.

If you are not using the WINS server, the Windows NT computer uses name query broadcasts and the local LMHOSTS file to resolve computer names to IP addresses. Broadcast resolution is confined to the local network.

The name query broadcasts use the b-mode for NetBIOS over TCP/IP and are discussed in greater detail in Chapter 9, "TCP/IP Name Resolution Using WINS."

1.  To specify that you are using WINS servers, enter the IP addresses of the primary and secondary WINS servers (see Figure 3.8). The secondary WINS server is used as a backup in case the primary WINS server cannot respond.

    If a computer is configured to use DHCP, name resolution using WINS is automatically enabled and configured for that computer as long as the DHCP server is configured to send the IP addresses of the WINS servers to the client. If you manually enter IP addresses for the WINS servers here, those settings will override any settings sent by DHCP.

    If the computer being configured is a WINS server, then the computer automatically uses WINS to resolve computer names, regardless of how you configure name resolution for the local computer.

2.  Enable the Enable DNS for Windows Resolution by checking the check box next to it.

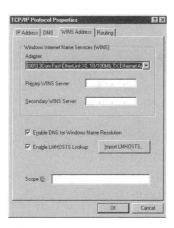

**Figure 3.7**  Sample DNS configuration.    **Figure 3.8**  WINS Address tab.

You can use the local file LMHOSTS for resolving NetBIOS computer names on Windows networks. If you want to use the LMHOSTS file, enable the Enable LMHOSTS Lookup check box. You can import computer names and IP addresses from an existing LMHOSTS file by clicking the Import LMHOSTS button and specifying the directory path for the LMHOSTS file. You can use the Import LMHOSTS option when you have already created an LMHOSTS file for the computer names on your network and want to use the information in this file for all computers on the network.

3. Use the Scope ID field to specify the computer's scope identifier on a network that uses NetBIOS over TCP/IP. You use scope IDs only for NetBIOS over TCP/IP. Computers using NetBIOS over TCP/IP to talk to each other must have the same scope ID. By default, this field is left blank. If this field is left blank, the computers have the same Scope ID by default. If you want to set up groups of Windows NT computers that can only communicate among themselves using NetBIOS over TCP/IP, you can have different Scope IDs for different groups.

### When to Use the LMHOSTS File

By default, the LMHOSTS file is found in the \%SystemRoot%\SYSTEM32\DRIVERS\ETC directory. If you are using a WINS server, the LMHOSTS file is consulted last after trying the WINS server. Using LMHOSTS files works well for Windows networks that have a small number of computers and for networks that do not experience many changes, but using LMHOSTS files is problematic for larger, more dynamic networks. Keeping all the different computers' LMHOSTS files in sync becomes difficult on a larger network, and creating situations in which two computers (even ones sitting next to each other) may have different views of the network becomes all too easy. The LMHOSTS file is discussed in Chapter 9.

## Configuring the DHCP Relay

If you want to set up your Windows NT computer to relay BOOTP and DHCP messages to a server on a different network or subnet, you can enable this option from the DHCP Relay tab (see Figure 3.9). This tab is enabled only on NT Servers and not on NT Workstations. This option is good for branch offices where you don't want to set up a separate DHCP server.

1. The *seconds threshold* is based on the number of seconds since the client was initialized. If the secs field in the DHCP request is larger than this setting, the DHCP relay agent cannot forward the packet. Set the Seconds threshold. The default is 4 seconds, which works in most environments.

2. Set the Maximum hops. This is the total number of DHCP relay hops a DHCP request can cross. If the NT server receives a DHCP request packet that has reached the maximum number of hops, it cannot forward the request. You can use this setting to expire packets caught in a loop between two DHCP relays.

3. You must configure a DHCP relay agent if you are using DHCP and not all the DHCP clients are on the same subnet as a DHCP server. Type the IP addresses of the DHCP servers and choose the Add button.

## Configuring the Routing

You can use a Windows NT Workstation or Windows NT Server as a simple IP router (see Figure 3.10). Such a router routes only between two IP subnetworks. The Windows NT IP router understands only static routes, unless you install the RIP for Internet protocol service.

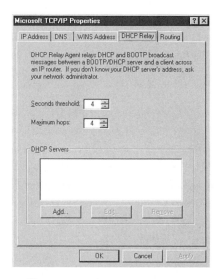

**Figure 3.9** The DHCP Relay tab.

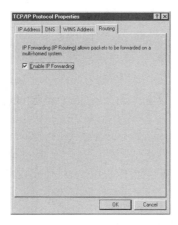

**Figure 3.10**   Routing tab.

The Enable IP Routing option in the Routing tab enables the Windows NT computer to participate in routing on a network. This option does not turn the Windows NT Server into a general-purpose dynamic router. It enables the Windows NT Server to perform static IP routing, but does not enable any form of dynamic routing. In *dynamic routing*, routers exchange information about the networks and routes they know about, but in *static routing* the routers are silent and know only about the networks they have been connected to or otherwise configured to know about.

If your Windows NT Server has more than one network interface and you want the system to perform static routing, be sure to enable the Enable IP Routing option. If you have the Windows NT Server connected to multiple different networks but have chosen not to have the Windows NT Server route between them, be sure to disable this option.

The Enable IP Routing option is not available if your Windows NT Server has only one network adapter and one IP address. To configure the Windows NT computer as a simple IP router, you must have at least two network adapters, such as Ethernet, Token Ring, or FDDI adapters, installed in the Windows NT computer.

The SLIP/PPP connection does not count as a network interface for the purpose of enabling IP routing. If you need to enable IP routing with a SLIP/PPP connection, specify a second IP address for your network interface, which then allows you to access the Enable IP Routing option. This specification is accomplished in the following manner:

1. To enable simple IP routing, check the Enable IP Routing check box in the Routing tab.

2. Choose OK after you set the TCP/IP properties.

3. When the Network Protocols dialog box reappears, choose Close.

4. When the Network Settings Change dialog box reappears, choose Yes to complete the TCP/IP configuration, and to restart the computer so the changes can take effect.

You can also enable routing by editing a Registry setting if you don't want to add a secondary address. In the following key, set EnableRouter to 1:

```
HKEY_LOCAL_MACHINE\SYSTEM\CurrentControlSet\Services\Tcpip\Parameters\IP
```

# Removing TCP/IP Components in Windows NT

After you have installed TCP/IP on a Windows NT computer, its removal should probably never be necessary. If you have a major reorganization of your network, however, and are no longer using TCP/IP applications and services, you can remove TCP/IP from the Windows NT computer. For example, if you are downsizing to a small isolated network you may want to use a simpler protocol such as NetBEUI or IPX. TCP/IP configuration and maintenance require more knowledge than for the NetBEUI and IPX protocols.

Use the following as a guideline for removing TCP/IP:

1. Log on to the Windows NT Server as an administrator user.
2. Double-click the Network icon in the Control Panel.
3. Select the Protocols tab and highlight the TCP/IP Protocol from the list box, then choose the Remove button.

   Windows NT warns you that the action permanently removes that component. Also, you cannot reinstall a component that has been removed until after you restart the computer. If other services are currently using the TCP/IP protocol, you must remove these services *before* removing TCP/IP.

4. After removing the component or service, choose Close. The Network Settings Change dialog box prompts you to restart the computer so the changes can take effect. Select Yes.

# Installing TCP/IP in Windows 98

A Windows 98 installation automatically includes the TCP/IP protocol stack if you choose to install any network services. The following list of steps discusses the procedures for installing and configuring the Windows 98 TCP/IP protocol stack. You only have to install the TCP/IP protocol stack manually if you have previously removed it but now need to add support for TCP/IP services or if that machine previously was not part of the network.

1. Log on to the Windows 98 computer. This may involve specifying a user account and password for the Microsoft Network.
2. Select Start, Settings, Control Panel. Double-click the Network icon in the Control Panel. The Network dialog box appears (see Figure 3.11).
3. If you are reinstalling the TCP/IP protocol stack, click the Add button. You should see a list of network component types that you can install (see Figure 3.12).

**Figure 3.11**   Network dialog box.

4. Highlight Protocol and click the Add button. You should see a list of vendors that are providers of network protocols (see Figure 3.13).

5. Highlight the vendor name (such as Microsoft Corp.). Select TCP/IP and select OK.

6. Follow instructions onscreen to complete the installation.

## Basic Configuration of Windows 98 TCP/IP

After installing the TCP/IP protocol stack, you must perform at least some basic configuration of TCP/IP, such as IP address assignments for the network interfaces, and so on. The following is an outline of the basic configuration steps:

1. Start the Network applet in the Control Panel.

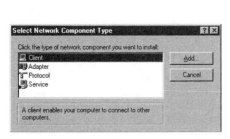

**Figure 3.12**   Select Network Component Type dialog box.

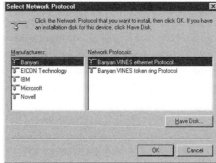

**Figure 3.13**   Select Network Protocol dialog box.

**When to Disable Routing**

You might want to disable routing when connected to multiple networks if the Windows NT Server is performing an important function (such as a web server) and you do not want it to use CPU cycles to deal with other tasks that you already have other systems dedicated to performing.

You should also disable routing on firewalls and proxy servers. You do not want the packets to bypass the firewall/proxy software that subjects the packet to the network security policy. If routing is enabled, the packets could be forwarded by the router regardless of any restrictions on the packet placed by the firewall/proxy software.

2.  In the Configuration tab of the Network panel, select the TCP/IP network interface (see Figure 3.14) whose properties are to be entered.

3.  Select the Properties button. You should see the TCP/IP Properties dialog box (see Figure 3.15).

4.  If the IP Address tab is not initially shown, select it (see Figure 3.15).

5.  If you select the option to Obtain an IP Address Automatically, the DHCP client on the Windows 98 computer will be enabled. This DHCP client contacts DHCP servers on the network to obtain its IP address and subnet mask. If you specify an IP address, you must enter the network interface's IP address and subnet mask. Each network interface must be assigned a separate and unique IP

**Host Names and Domain Names**

The Host field is where you enter the TCP/IP host name of the computer. You usually just use the same name as the computer name. If you want to use another TCP/IP host name, you can enter the name in the Host Name field without affecting the computer name. The host name can be any combination of the letters A to Z, digits 0 to 9, and the hyphen (-), plus the period (.) character used as a separator. Host name to IP address mappings are stored on DNS servers. The Berkeley r* utilities, such as rcp, rsh, rexec, and so on, use the host names for authentication.

You can enter an optional domain name in the Domain field. If, for example, the host name is W98-1 in the domain name KINETICS.COM, you should enter the name KINETICS.COM in the Domain field. A DNS domain differs from a Windows NT or LAN Manager domain. Windows NT domains and LAN Manager domains are proprietary in nature, whereas DNS domains are universal and also apply to non-Microsoft products. The domain name is optional, because a small organization not connected to the Internet doesn't need to use hierarchical domain names.

When the Windows 98 computer uses a DNS query to resolve a name that is a simple host name without the domain extension, the domain name specified in the Domain Name field is appended to the host name.

The domain name can be any combination of letters A to Z, digits 0 to 9, and the hyphen (-), using the period (.) character as a separator. Domain names are not case sensitive; so KINETICS.COM is the same as kinetics.com.

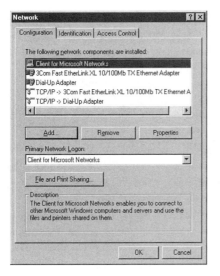

**Figure 3.14**   Network panel for Windows 98.

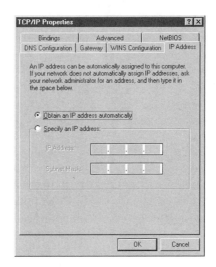

**Figure 3.15**   TCP/IP properties for Windows 98.

address and subnet mask. Repeat the steps outlined in this section for each network interface.

6. If you select the WINS Configuration tab, you see the screen in Figure 3.16. You have a choice of using DHCP for WINS resolution. This means that the DHCP server returns the IP address of the WINS server to use in addition to the IP address and subnet mask. Alternatively, you can explicitly specify the IP address of the WINS server to use by enabling the option Enable WINS Resolution. If you do not want to use WINS for name resolution, you can select the Disable WINS Resolution option. If WINS is not used, the HOSTS file on the local Windows 98 computer can be used to perform name resolution.

7. If you select the Gateway tab, you see the screen in Figure 3.17. This screen is used to enter the default gateway (correctly speaking, the default *router*) address for each network interface. The default gateway is necessary for the Windows 98 computer to perform host routing to remote networks. To specify a gateway IP address, enter the value in the New Gateway field, and click on Add. The gateways are tried in the order in which they are listed. To remove a gateway, highlight it in the list Installed Gateways, and click the Remove button.

8. If you select the DNS Configuration tab, you see the screen in Figure 3.18. This screen is used to enter the parameters for resolving DNS names. If DNS is not to be used, you must select the option Disable DNS; otherwise, select Enable DNS, which enables you to specify the DNS settings.

9. Use the DNS Server Search Order box (see Figure 3.18), to enter the IP address of the DNS servers that are used for domain name resolution. After you enter

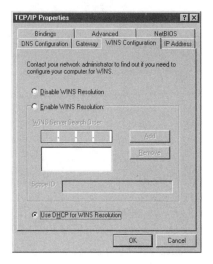

**Figure 3.16**   WINS Configuration tab for Windows 98.

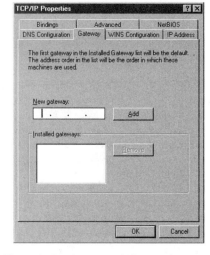

**Figure 3.17**   Gateway tab for Windows 98.

the IP address of the DNS server in the field, choose the Add button to move the IP address to the list of IP addresses for the DNS servers.

10.  Specify up to three IP addresses for DNS servers. The DNS servers that you specify are queried in the order they are listed. You can change the order in which the DNS servers are searched by highlighting the IP address of a DNS server and using the Up and Down buttons to move it within the list. To remove a DNS server from the list, highlight its IP address and choose the Remove button.

11.  In the Domain Suffix Search Order box (see Figure 3.18), enter the domain suffixes that are appended to host names during domain name resolution. If you need to change the search order of the domain suffixes, highlight the domain name and use the up and down buttons to move the domain name.

12.  To remove a domain name, highlight it in the Domain Suffix Search Order list and choose the Remove button.

13.  If you select the NetBIOS tab, you can specify whether you want to enable NetBIOS over TCP/IP (see Figure 3.19). With TCP/IP installed this option is automatically enabled and therefore appears checked and grayed out.

14.  If you select the Advanced tab (see Figure 3.20), you can specify any advanced parameters for the protocol by selecting the value that you want to change on the left and then selecting its new value on the right. You can also use this screen to make the selected protocol the default protocol by enabling the option Set This Protocol to Be the Default Protocol.

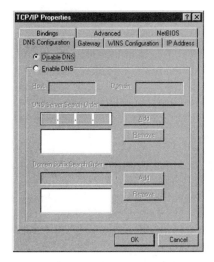

**Figure 3.18**   DNS Configuration tab for Windows 98.

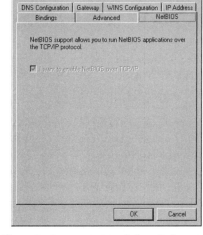

**Figure 3.19**   NetBIOS tab for Windows 98.

15. If you select the Bindings tab (see Figure 3.21), you can see the list of network components that use the TCP/IP protocol. You can use this screen to enable or disable network components. To improve your computer's speed, select only the network components that you need.

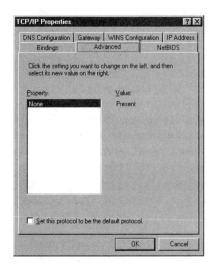

**Figure 3.20**   Advanced tab for Windows 98.

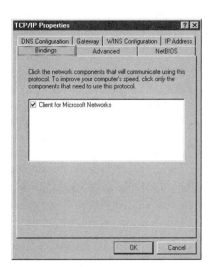

**Figure 3.21**   Bindings tab for Windows 98.

## Installation Considerations for WinSock 2 on Windows 98

Both Windows NT 5 and Windows 98 support WinSock 2. A primary goal of Windows Sockets 2 is to provide a protocol-independent interface that supports other protocol stacks besides TCP/IP. WinSock 2 is designed to support emerging networking requirements such as the requirement for real-time multimedia communications.

Prior to WinSock 2, Windows Sockets programming centered on TCP/IP. Some of the programming practices that worked with TCP/IP do not work with every protocol. As a result, the Windows Sockets 2 API added new functions where necessary. When previous versions of Windows sockets supported only TCP/IP, a developer could create an application that supported only two socket types: connectionless and connection-oriented. Connectionless protocols used SOCK_DGRAM sockets and connection-oriented protocols used SOCK_STREAM sockets. To support additional protocols such as IPX and NetBEUI, new socket types have been defined. In addition, developers can no longer rely on socket type to describe all the essential attributes of a transport protocol.

The new Windows Sockets 2 extends functionality in the following areas:

- **Access to protocols other than TCP/IP.** Windows Sockets 2 enables an application to use the familiar socket interface to achieve simultaneous access to a number of installed transport protocols.

- **Overlapped I/O with scatter/gather.** Windows Sockets 2 incorporates the overlapped model for socket I/O that increases the efficiency of the model. The addition of scatter/gather capabilities enables data from several sources to be combined when sending or distributing to different data areas while receiving. This is consistent with the data I/O model established in Win32 environments.

- **Protocol-independent name resolution facilities.** Windows Sockets 2 applications discover what types of name-resolution facilities are provided.

- **Protocol-independent multicast and multipoint.** Windows Sockets 2 applications discover what types of multipoint or multicast capabilities a transport provides and use these facilities in a general manner.

- **Quality of service.** Window Sockets 2 establishes the conventions that applications use to negotiate required service levels for parameters such as bandwidth and latency. Other QOS-related enhancements include socket grouping and prioritization, and mechanisms for network-specific QOS extensions.

- **Socket extensions.** Windows Sockets 2 incorporates shared sockets and conditional acceptance, exchange of user data at connection setup/teardown time, and protocol-specific extension mechanisms.

The installation of WinSock 2 also installs the Resource Reservation Protocol (RSVP). *RSVP* is a protocol for reserving network resources that can be implemented on existing networks. It has been proposed as an Internet standard and is designed to work with any network protocol, especially TCP/IP. RSVP is also explicitly designed to handle multicast traffic effectively.

RSVP has the following attributes:

■ RSVP handles reservations for unicast and for one-to-many and many-to-many multicast applications. It can respond dynamically to changing group membership and routes.

■ RSVP is simple. Quality of Service (QOS) for each direction of data flow is established separately and need not be the same.

■ RSVP is receiver-oriented. The receiver, not the sender, of the data stream is responsible for requesting and maintaining the reservation.

■ RSVP reservations are maintained in a "soft state" on participating routers. If the reservation is not periodically updated, it is canceled.

■ RSVP is not a routing protocol. It uses present and future routing protocols to determine the paths by which data is transmitted.

■ RSVP provides opaque transport for policy and traffic control messages. These protocols are independent of RSVP.

■ RSVP provides several reservation styles to accommodate a variety of applications.

■ RSVP functions transparently through routers that do not support it (although the specified QOS is no longer guaranteed).

The RSVP functionality is available to programmers through APIs. It is available to WinSock application programmers through the Generic Quality of Service (GQOS) APIs in WinSock 2. To use GQOS through RSVP, the sockets programmer must enumerate the available protocols by using the WSAEnumProtocols API to look for one that supports QOS (using a service flag) and passes the protocol information structure in on the call to WSASocket().

Because there are several alternative TCP/IP protocol stacks for the Windows 9x environment, you may encounter some difficulties using WinSock 2 with other vendors stacks, especially if you are not using upgraded versions of other vendor's protocol stacks and interfaces.

Microsoft's documentation on Windows 98 specifies that during the Windows 98 installation, all WinSock 1.1 components are backed up. If you experience interoperability problems with WinSock 2 and are unable to work around the problem, you may want to remove WinSock 2 and reinstall the older Winsock components. To remove WinSock 2, perform the following steps:

1. Double-click Add/Remove Programs in Control Panel.

2. Click Restore WinSock 1.x Configuration.

3. Click Yes.

When WinSock 2 is removed, only the WinSock 2–related files are removed. The Windows 98 versions of the Microsoft TCP/IP and IPX/SPX stacks stay installed, and will run with WinSock 1.1.

The Winsock 1.1 environment is backed up only the first time you upgrade your computer from Windows 95 to Windows 98. Subsequent reinstallation of Windows 98 onto Windows 98 does not back up the Winsock environment. After you remove WinSock 2, the only way to put it back on the computer is to reinstall Windows 98.

# 4

# Configuring TCP/IP

**A**FTER INSTALLING TCP/IP, YOU MAY HAVE to perform additional configuration. An important consideration in performing additional configuration is the manner in which name resolution is expected to be performed on the network. This chapter explains the basic considerations for computer name resolution, including the purpose and structure of the LMHOSTS and HOSTS files.

You may also need to configure additional TCP/IP services such as FTP, an Internet printer, SNMP, and Web Services. The configuration of FTP and Internet printer services is described in this chapter. Configuring SNMP is described in Chapter 11, "Network Management for Microsoft Networks Using SNMP."

## Configuring Name Resolution Services in Windows NT

In Chapter 3, "Installing the TCP/IP Protocol and Services," you learned how to specify the WINS server and DNS server in the IP configuration parameters for Windows NT computers. WINS and DNS servers are used for resolving names on a Windows network. There are two additional files that are useful in configuring name resolution. These are the LMHOSTS file and the HOSTS file.

## NetBIOS Services

NetBIOS provides name services, datagram services, and session services (see Table 4.1). The name and datagram services use ports 137 and 138 of the UDP Transport layer protocol. The session services use port 139 of the TCP Transport layer protocol. Name and datagram services use UDP because the nature of the traffic generated by these services tends to be request-reply oriented. Also, name services make frequent use of broadcasts to resolve names, and UDP is better suited than TCP for handling broadcasts. On large networks, broadcasts can be a problem because they can lead to broadcast storms. For this reason, many routers are by default configured to block broadcasts.

The session services in NetBIOS use TCP; TCP guarantees data delivery, whereas UDP does not. Also, the model of a TCP session more accurately reflects the behavior of a NetBIOS session. Both TCP and NetBIOS issue open primitives to open a connection and the close primitive to close a connection.

Initially NetBIOS referred to computer names only. There was only a single user for a computer. A message sent to the computer was received by the sole user on the computer.

As the networks became large with many users on the network, NetBIOS names were added for the user and the workgroup or domain. The NetBIOS username allowed a user to receive a message. If more than one instance of the username existed (user logged in several times), only the first username that was registered receives the message.

The workgroup/domain name was added to group different systems under a common name for ease of browsing, manageability, and domain security in the Windows NT domain model. These group names are registered as NetBIOS names on the network.

On a given computer, there could be several processes. Processes that provide services are called *application services*. Some of these application services are registered as NetBIOS names. Windows NT allows up to 250 NetBIOS names to be registered on a computer. Examples of application services on a Windows computer include the following:

- **Server Service.** This identifies the application service that is running. This typically refers to the service that allows the sharing of files and printers on the computer.

Table 4.1  **NetBIOS Services**

| Service Name | Port | Protocol | Short Name |
| --- | --- | --- | --- |
| NetBIOS Name Service | 137 | UDP | nbname |
| NetBIOS Datagram Service | 138 | UDP | Nbdatagram |
| NetBIOS Session Service | 139 | TCP | Nbsession |

■ **Workstation Service.** This enables a workstation to act as a client and use services provided by the Server service on another computer.

■ **Messenger Service.** This receives and displays messages for names that are registered on the computer.

The maximum length of NetBIOS names is 16 characters. Of these characters, the first 15 characters specify the NetBIOS name, and the last character is a byte that specifies the type of the NetBIOS name. This one-byte identifier can have a value from 0 to 255. The following shows a list of the names of some of the services that may be registered. The numbers in brackets are the hexadecimal values of the one-byte identifiers.

■ **Computername[0x00].** This is the Workstation service registered for the computer.

■ **Computername[0x03].** This is the Messenger service registered for the computer.

■ **Username[0x03].** This is the username registered by the Messenger for the logged-on username.

■ **Computername[0x20].** This is the Server service registered for the computer.

■ **Domainname[0x00].** This registers the computer as a member of the domain name/workgroup.

■ **Domainname[0x1E].** This is used to facilitate browser elections.

■ **Domainname[0x1B].** This registers the computer as the domain master browser.

■ **Domainname[0x1C].** This registers the computer as a domain controller.

■ **Domainname[0x1D].** This registers the computer as the local subnetwork's master browser.

For example, if user Phylos on Windows NT workstation WS1 in domain KINETD wants to retrieve files from a Windows NT server called NTS, the username Phylos[0x03] uses the workstation service with NetBIOS name WS1[0x00] to be first authenticated by the domain controller with NetBIOS name KINETD[0x1C]. After the authentication, the workstation service WS1[0x00] communicates with the server service NTS[0x20] to retrieve files.

## Types of Name Resolution Methods

Windows NT name resolution methods can be grouped into the following categories:

■ Standard resolution

■ Specific resolution

These methods are discussed in the following sections.

### Standard Resolution

The *standard resolution* method is used by UNIX systems and software ported from UNIX to the Windows environment. The standard resolution method is performed in the following order:

1. Local hostname
2. Using the HOSTS file
3. Using DNS
4. NetBIOS name resolution, if DNS fails

The *local host* is the name of the locally configured machine. The name to be resolved is first checked to determine whether it is the name of the local machine.

If the name to be resolved is not that of the local machine, the HOSTS file is consulted. The HOSTS *file* is a table of mappings of IP addresses and hostnames. The format of the HOSTS file is taken from the 4.3 BSD UNIX hosts file. The HOSTS file is consulted by applications such as Telnet, FTP, and PING. The HOSTS file is not kept at a central location. Instead, each computer is required to maintain its own HOSTS file. If the HOSTS file is to be changed for the network, it must be changed on all the computers on the network.

If the name to be resolved is not found in the HOSTS file, a name query is sent to the DNS server. The DNS servers hold, among other things, the name-to-IP address mappings in a distributed database on the network. Most DNS servers on the Internet are UNIX based, although DNS implementations are available on platforms such as Windows NT.

### Specific Resolution

The *specific resolution* method is unique to Windows networks. It consists of a combination of the following methods:

■ Local broadcast
■ Windows Internet Name Service (WINS)
■ Using the LMHOSTS file

The *local broadcast* is a broadcast request sent on the local network requesting the IP address of the name that is to be resolved. The computer that recognizes its name in the broadcast request responds with its IP address. If no such computer exists, no response to the broadcast is received and the local broadcast is unable to resolve the name to its IP address. The local broadcast is also called the *b-node* name resolution method.

The *Windows Internet Name Service (WINS)* is an example of a NetBIOS Name Server (NBNS). The most common example of NBNS is the WINS implementation on Windows NT Server. NBNS name resolution is specified by RFCs 1001 and 1002.

The LMHOSTS *file* is a table of mappings between IP addresses and NetBIOS names. The structure of the LMHOSTS file is similar to the HOSTS file, with the added distinction that it contains a number of additional directives to make name resolution configuration easier. Windows NT checks the LMHOSTS file only when other name resolution methods fail.

The exact order in which the specific name resolution method is implemented depends on the name resolution configuration for the Windows NT computer. These name resolution methods include the following: b-node, p-node, m-node, and h-node. The following list describes each method:

- In the *b-node (broadcast node)* name resolution, only broadcast packets are used for name registration and resolution. Because roadcasts can quickly flood the network, this name resolution mode should be used only for small local networks that do not have a WINS server. To configure your network to use this mode, ensure that there are no WINS servers on the network, and that the Windows computers are configured to not use WINS. That is, for the Windows client computers, ensure that you do not specify the IP address of a WINS server.

- The *p-node (peer node)* name resolution uses WINS servers exclusively to resolve names. If the name cannot be resolved using WINS, other name resolution methods are not attempted.

- The *m-node (mixed node)* name resolution is a combination of b-node and p-node methods. First, the b-node name resolution method is attempted. If the b-node fails, the client resorts to using p-node name resolution. This method tends to generate broadcast traffic first, and then attempt WINS resolution. It is suitable for small networks that have a WINS server, and where it is known that the WINS server's database has not been updated for some time with new host-name entries.

- The *h-node (hybrid node)* name resolution is also a combination of b-node and p-node methods. However, this method first tries the p-node name resolution. If the p-node fails, the client resorts to using b-node name resolution. This method tends to generate broadcast traffic as a last resort, because the first attempt is to contact a WINS server. This is the most efficient of all the methods, and is suitable for larger networks that have a reliable WINS server, and in which it is known that the WINS server's database has been updated with new hostname entries.

## Configuring the NetBIOS Name Cache

A Windows NT computer requesting name resolution first consults a special area in memory called the NetBIOS name cache. This data area contains a list of computer names and their IP addresses. Because this information is cached in memory, retrieval of the information, if found, is quick. The name cache entries come from two sources:

- Answers of resolved name queries
- Preloading of the name cache from the LMHOSTS file using the #PRE directive

With the exception of the preloaded name cache entries, all other entries are timed out and flushed from the cache. The default timeout period is 10 minutes. Readers who are familiar with the Address Resolution Protocol (ARP) will recognize that the NetBIOS name cache acts in a similar manner.

In order to purge and reload the name cache, you can use the following command:
`nbtstat -R`

The `-R` option is case sensitive. There is another option, `-r`, that is used for displaying name resolution statistics.

There are two Registry entries that can be used to configure the name cache parameters. These Registry entries can be found under the following Registry key:

`HKEY_LOCAL_MACHINE\SYSTEM\CurrentControlSet\Services\NetBT\Parameters`

The name cache entries are as follows:

- **Size/Small/Medium/Large.** This is used to specify the number of names kept in the name cache. The settings are for small, medium, and large. Small corresponds to a value of 1 and sets the name size cache to 16 names. Medium corresponds to a value of 2 and sets the name size cache to 64 names. Large corresponds to a value of 3 and sets the name size cache to 128 names. The default value is 1, which is adequate for many networks. The parameter type is `REG_DWORD`.

- **CacheTimeout.** This is used to specify the number of seconds an entry is to remain in the name cache. The default value is 0x927c0 (600,000 seconds or 10 minutes), which is adequate for many networks. The parameter type is `REG_DWORD`.

These parameter entries and others for NetBT are shown in Figure 4.1.

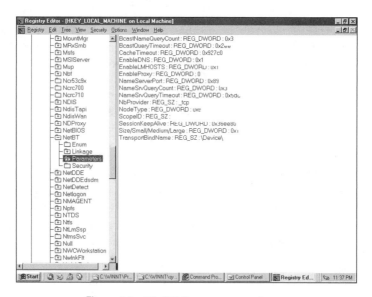

**Figure 4.1**   NetBT Parameter entry keys.

## Configuring the Name Broadcasts

If the name resolution process does not find the name to be resolved in the name cache, it may send a broadcast if it is configured as b-node, m-node, or h-node. NetBIOS broadcasts a Name Query packet to the local network on UDP port 137 (refer to Table 4.1). Every computer processes the broadcast packet. If a computer on the network is configured for the NetBT protocol, the NetBIOS module in the computer receives the broadcast. The NetBIOS module compares the name request with the name of the registered computer name. If there is a match, the NetBIOS module sends a Positive Name Query Response packet.

If there is more than one response, this indicates a duplicate NetBIOS name, which is reported on the computer console of the computer that receives the response. It is interesting to note that the Name Query broadcast is processed by every computer up to the Session layer, whether or not the computer has the answer. Therefore, the broadcast not only generates network traffic but results in wasted CPU cycles on many computers.

There are two Registry entries that can be used to configure the name query broadcast parameters. These Registry entries can be found under the following Registry key:

```
HKEY_LOCAL_MACHINE\SYSTEM\CurrentControlSet\Services\NetBT\Parameters
```

The broadcast entries are as follows:

- **BcastNameQueryCount.** This is used to specify the number of times the system tries to send a Name Query broadcast. The default value is 3, which is adequate for many networks. The parameter type is `REG_DWORD`.

- **BcastQueryTimeout.** This is used to specify the number of seconds to wait before retrying the Name Query broadcast. The default value is 7.5 seconds. The parameter type is `REG_DWORD`. The default is in 1/100 seconds.

## Configuring the *LMHOSTS* File

On small Windows NT networks that use NetBIOS over TCP/IP, the name resolution for computer names typically is provided by the `LMHOSTS` file. If you have WINS servers on the networks, it is not necessary to use the `LMHOSTS` file, except as a backup. Use of `LMHOSTS` is adequate for small networks in which broadcast network traffic usually is not a major concern. On larger networks, however, broadcast network traffic can consume a substantial amount of available network bandwidth and generally is avoided by the network designer.

### Understanding the Syntax of the *LMHOSTS* File

The `LMHOSTS` file contains mappings between Windows NT NetBIOS computer names and their IP addresses. The file is located in the `\%SystemRoot%\SYSTEM32\DRIVERS\ETC` directory and is compatible with the `LMHOSTS` file syntax used in Microsoft LAN Manager 2.x.

The following is a sample Windows NT LMHOSTS file that is installed on Windows NT computers:

```
# Copyright (c)  1993-1995 Microsoft Corp.
#
# This is a sample LMHOSTS file used by the Microsoft TCP/IP for Windows
# NT.
#
# This file contains the mappings of IP addresses to NT computernames
# (NetBIOS) names.  Each entry should be kept on an individual line.
# The IP address should be placed in the first column followed by the
# corresponding computername. The address and the computername
# should be separated by at least one space or tab. The "#" character
# is generally used to denote the start of a comment (see the exceptions
# below).
#
# This file is compatible with Microsoft LAN Manager 2.x TCP/IP lmhosts
# files and offers the following extensions:
#
#      #PRE
#      #DOM:<domain>
#      #INCLUDE <filename>
#      #BEGIN_ALTERNATE
#      #END_ALTERNATE
#      \0xnn (non-printing character support)
#
# Following any entry in the file with the characters "#PRE" will cause
# the entry to be preloaded into the name cache. By default, entries are
# not preloaded, but are parsed only after dynamic name resolution fails.
#
# Following an entry with the "#DOM:<domain>" tag will associate the
# entry with the domain specified by <domain>. This affects how the
# browser and logon services behave in TCP/IP environments. To preload
# the hostname associated with #DOM entry, it is necessary to also add a
# #PRE to the line. The <domain> is always preloaded although it will not
# be shown when the name cache is viewed.
#
# Specifying "#INCLUDE <filename>" will force the RFC NetBIOS (NBT)
# software to seek the specified <filename> and parse it as if it were
# local. <filename> is generally a UNC-based name, allowing a
# centralized lmhosts file to be maintained on a server.
# It is ALWAYS necessary to provide a mapping for the IP address of the
# server prior to the #INCLUDE. This mapping must use the #PRE directive.
# In addition the share "public" in the example below must be in the
# LanManServer list of "NullSessionShares" in order for client machines
# to be able to read the lmhosts file successfully. This key is under
# \machine\
# system\currentcontrolset\services\lanmanserver\parameters\
  ↪nullsessionshares
```

```
# in the Registry. Simply add "public" to the list found there.
#
# The #BEGIN_ and #END_ALTERNATE keywords allow multiple #INCLUDE
# statements to be grouped together. Any single successful include
# will cause the group to succeed.
#
# Finally, non-printing characters can be embedded in mappings by
# first surrounding the NetBIOS name in quotations, then using the
# \0xnn notation to specify a hex value for a non-printing character.
#
# The following example illustrates all of these extensions:
#
102.54.94.97     rhino            #PRE #DOM:networking  #net group's DC
102.54.94.102    "appname   \0x14"                      #special app server
102.54.94.123    popular          #PRE                  #source server
102.54.94.117    localsrv         #PRE                  #needed for the
➥include
#
# #BEGIN_ALTERNATE
# #INCLUDE \\localsrv\public\lmhosts
# #INCLUDE \\rhino\public\lmhosts
# #END_ALTERNATE
#
# In the above example, the "appname" server contains a special
# character in its name, the "popular" and "localsrv" server names are
# preloaded, and the "rhino" server name is specified so it can be used
# to later #INCLUDE a centrally maintained lmhosts file if the "localsrv"
# system is unavailable.
#
# Note that the whole file is parsed including comments on each lookup,
# so keeping the number of comments to a minimum will improve
performance.
# Therefore it is not advisable to simply add lmhosts file entries onto
# the end of this file.
```

Comments are preceded with the # character. If the first several characters following # match any of the keywords explained in Table 4.2, they are treated as commands to perform special processing. Because the keywords are preceded with the comment character, the contents of the files are compatible with the syntax used by the HOSTS file. The HOSTS file is used by Windows Socket applications and UNIX applications.

Notice that the previous sample LMHOSTS file has the following entry:

```
102.54.94.102    "appname   \0x14"  #special app server
```

There are eight spaces of "padding" between the name and the special character; the total length of the name is 16 characters.

The code 0x14 is the 1-byte identifier identifying the application service.

Table 4.2  **LMHOSTS Keywords**

| Keyword | Description |
| --- | --- |
| #PRE | This keyword is added after an entry in LMHOSTS to preload the entry into the name cache. Entries that do not have a #PRE keyword are not preloaded into the name cache and are parsed only after WINS and Name Query broadcasts fail to resolve a name. You must preload entries that are added using the #INCLUDE statement. #PRE, therefore, must be appended for entries in the files referenced in #INCLUDE statements; otherwise, the entry is ignored. |
| #DOM: *domain_name* | This keyword is used to identify that the computer name is that of a domain controller (PDC or BDC). *domain_name* is the name of the Windows NT domain that the computer is a domain controller of. #DOM affects the behavior of the Browser and Logon services on a network consisting of network segments joined by routers. |
| #INCLUDE *filename* | The specified filename is processed for computer name mappings. The filename can use UNC names, which enable the mappings file to be on remote computers. If the computer referenced in the UNC name is outside the local broadcast region, you must include a mapping for the computer name in the LMHOSTS file so that it can be found. You can add #PRE for the UNC computer name mapping to ensure that it is preloaded. Entries that appear in the INCLUDE file must be preloaded using the #PRE keyword, or the entries are ignored. |
| #BEGIN_ALTERNATE | Used to mark the beginning of a group of #INCLUDE statements. The name resolver attempts to use the #INCLUDE statements in the order in which they are listed. Any single successful attempt to use one of the #INCLUDE statements causes the group to succeed, in which case none of the other #INCLUDE statements in the group are processed. If none of the files in the #INCLUDE statement can be accessed, an event is added to the Event log indicating that the block inclusion failed. You can examine this Event log by using the Event Viewer program. |
| #END_ALTERNATE | This marks the end of the #INCLUDE block. Every #BEGIN_ALTERNATE must have a corresponding #END_ALTERNATE. |
| \0xnn | Escape code for including non-printable characters in NetBIOS names. The NetBIOS names that use this code must have double quotes around the names. Use this code only for special device names and custom applications. When using this notation, take into account the fact that the NetBIOS name in quotes is padded with spaces if it is fewer than 16 characters. |

### Understanding How the *LMHOSTS* File Is Processed

The LMHOSTS file is particularly useful if the network segment on which the Windows NT client resides does not have a WINS server. In this case, broadcast name resolution is used. Broadcast name resolution makes use of IP-level broadcast packets that are usually blocked by IP routers. The broadcast name resolution, therefore, never is transmitted beyond a router boundary. To solve this problem, Windows NT name resolution operates in the following manner when a WINS server is not specified:

1. Windows NT maintains a local cache of names that is initialized during system startup. The name cache is consulted first to see whether the name can be resolved.

2. If no matching entry is in the name cache, Windows NT uses broadcast to resolve names. The broadcast name resolution is called the b-node broadcast protocol and is documented in RFCs 1001 and 1002.

3. If the broadcast name resolution fails, the LMHOSTS file is parsed and any matching entry is used.

4. If no matching entry is in the LMHOSTS file, name resolution fails, and an error message is generated.

Figure 4.2 illustrates the name resolution for the LMHOSTS file. The name cache is initialized with entries that are marked with the #PRE keyword in the LMHOSTS file. For example, the LMHOSTS could contain the following entries, with only some of the entries marked with the #PRE keyword:

```
144.19.74.1   uziel
144.19.74.2   zadkiel #PRE
144.19.74.3   gabriel
144.19.74.4   uriel
144.19.74.5   michael #PRE
144.19.74.6   chamuel
```

You may want to preload entries for hosts such as servers that are always expected to be up.

In this LMHOSTS file, the mappings for host zadkiel and michael are preloaded into the name cache on system startup. If the Windows NT computer needs to resolve the names zadkiel and michael, no broadcast packets are generated, because the name cache provides the name resolution. If the Windows NT computer needs to resolve the names uziel, gabriel, uriel, and chamuel, broadcast name resolution is used. If the broadcast name resolution is unsuccessful, the LMHOSTS file is parsed for these names. When a non-preloaded name is resolved by parsing the LMHOSTS file, it is cached for a period of time so that it can be reused. Names resolved through broadcasts are also saved in cache until the timeout period expires.

The preloaded cache has a limit of 100 entries. If more than 100 entries in the LMHOSTS file are marked with #PRE, only the first 100 entries are preloaded. Additional entries are not loaded in the name cache, but are resolved if the LMHOSTS file is parsed.

If you have made changes to the LMHOSTS file in terms of the entries that are marked with the #PRE keyword, you can purge and reload the name cache by using the following command:

```
nbtstat -R
```

The advantage of using nbtstat is that you can preload the cache without restarting the Windows NT computer.

### Strategy for Using Common *LMHOSTS* Files

The LMHOSTS file is kept on the local Windows NT computer in the \%SystemRoot%\ SYSTEM32\DRIVERS\ETC directory. The maintenance of this local LMHOSTS file on every computer can become a problem when frequent changes are made.

The use of the #INCLUDE statement can simplify the maintenance of the LMHOSTS file. You could keep the LMHOSTS file on a Windows NT server named NTKS and include the following reference to this file on other Windows NT computers:

```
#INCLUDE \\NTKS\ETC\LMHOSTS
```

In this example, the ETC is the shared name of the \%SystemRoot%\SYSTEM32\ DRIVERS\ETC directory on the NTKS computer. The advantage of this approach is that all the common names that need to be preloaded are kept in a common file. If the NTKS computer is not in the broadcast region, you must include a specific mapping for it. If the NTKS has an IP address of 134.21.22.13, for example, you could use the

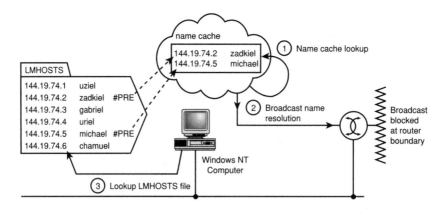

**Figure 4.2**   LMHOSTS name resolution.

following entries in the LMHOSTS file:

```
134.21.22.13    NTK           #PRE
#INCLUDE        \\NTKS\ETC\LMHOSTS
```

To ensure that the common LMHOSTS file is always available, you can replicate this file to other Windows NT computers using the Windows NT replicator service. The common LMHOSTS file must be on Windows NT Server because only the Windows NT Server can act as an export server for replication.

If you have redundant servers, you need to specify that the LMHOSTS file can be found on any of the redundant servers. In this situation, using the #BEGIN_ALTERNATIVE and #END_ALTERNATIVE commands comes in handy. Recall from Table 4.1 that these statements mark a block of #INCLUDE statements so that any one of the #INCLUDE statements can be used.

Consider the following example, in which an alternate list of LMHOSTS files are specified on Windows NT computers on network segment:

```
#BEGIN_ALTERNATIVE
#INCLUDE \\NTKS\ETC\LMHOSTS  # Main source of LMHOSTS file
#INCLUDE \\NTBC1\ETC\LMHOSTS # Backup 1
#INCLUDE \\NTBC2\ETC\LMHOSTS # Backup 2
#END_ALTERNATIVE
```

In this example, the LMHOSTS file on NTKS is assumed to be replicated to backup Windows NT computers NTBC1 and NTBC2. The shared name for the \%SystemRoot%\SYSTEM32\DRIVERS\ETC directory is ETC on all the Windows NT computers. The block inclusion is successful if any of the files on the three Windows NT computers is available. If the file is not available because the Windows NT computers are down or an incorrect path is specified, an event is added to the Windows NT computer's Event log.

### Specifying Domain Controllers in the *LMHOSTS* File

The domain controllers contain the user account security database, and are frequently accessed by clients in a domain. Besides logon authentication, domain controllers are involved with activities such as user account database synchronization (also called *domain pulses*), password changes, master browser list synchronization, and other changes. On a large network, controllers for the domain may be on different network segments separated by routers from the Windows NT computer requesting access to the domain controller.

You can use the #DOM keyword for Windows NT domain controller computer names in the LMHOSTS file. Entries that are marked with the #DOM keyword are loaded in a special Internet group name cache that is used to limit the distribution of requests for a local domain controller.

If the domain controller is on a local network segment, it can be reached by broadcast name resolution requests. If, however, the domain controller is beyond a router boundary, perhaps on a different subnet, the domain controller is not reachable by broadcast requests. By marking an entry in the LMHOSTS file with the #DOM keyword,

Microsoft TCP/IP uses IP datagrams with a destination address of the domain controller. Because these IP datagrams are not broadcast datagrams, the local routers are
able to route the request to the proper destination beyond the router boundary. Figure
4.3 shows that the entry for the domain controller NTS1 in the file `LMHOSTS` does not
have the `#DOM` keyword, whereas the following entry for NTS2 specifies that it is a
domain controller for the domain `KINETD`:

```
192.12.60.2    NTS2         #DOM:KINETD
```

In the example in Figure 4.3, the broadcast name resolution request for NTS1 is
blocked by the IP router, whereas the name resolution request for NTS2 is forwarded
by the IP router because it is marked with the `#DOM` keyword.

If a name resolution request involves a domain controller name that is in the
Internet group name cache, the name is resolved first through a WINS server (if one
exists) or a name broadcast. If this name resolution fails, the datagram request is sent to
the domain controllers for the domain listed in the Internet group name cache, and a
local broadcast occurs.

Because domains can span multiple IP subnetworks, you can use the following as a
guideline to ensure proper name resolution:

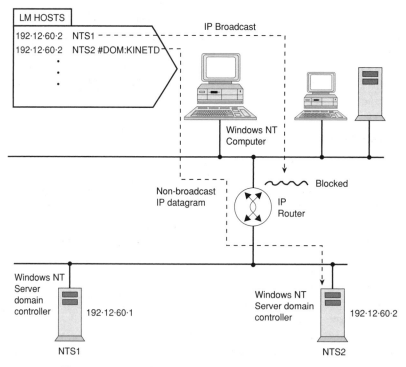

**Figure 4.3**   Use of the `#DOM` keyword in the `LMHOSTS` file.

- All domain controller names referenced in Windows NT computers' local LMHOSTS files must have a #DOM keyword to ensure that domain controllers can be reached across IP routers.

- All domain controllers for a domain must have mappings in their LMHOSTS files for all other domain controllers so that if a BDC is promoted to a PDC, the names are properly resolved. These mappings also ensure that the domain controllers are able to communicate properly with one another.

- If you want to browse another domain, you must make sure that the local LMHOSTS file has the IP address mapping for the PDC of that domain and also for the BDCs in case one of the BDCs is promoted to a PDC.

- If a trust relationship exists between domains, ensure that the domain controllers in the trusting domains are listed in the LMHOSTS file.

## Configuring the *HOSTS* File

The HOSTS file is used by UNIX TCP/IP–derived tools such as PING, NETSTAT, and so on, to resolve hostnames to their IP addresses.

The HOSTS file syntax is similar to the syntax of the LMHOSTS file. The HOSTS file is also found in the same directory (\%SystemRoot%\SYSTEM32\DRIVERS\ETC) as the LMHOSTS file. The HOSTS file syntax differs from the LMHOSTS file in the following ways:

- There are no special tags such as #PRE, #DOM, and so on, in the HOSTS file.

- You can define several alias names for an IP address by listing the names on the same line separated by spaces.

The general syntax of each line in the HOSTS file can be either of the following:

```
IPAddress    Name1 [Name2 ... NameN] # Comment
# Comment
```

*Name2* and *NameN* are optional aliases for the name *Name1*. As with the LMHOSTS configuration file, anything after the symbol # is treated as a comment.

The following is an example of a HOSTS file:

```
# Copyright (c) 1993-1995 Microsoft Corp.
#
# This is a sample HOSTS file used by Microsoft TCP/IP for Windows NT.
#
# This file contains the mappings of IP addresses to hostnames. Each
# entry should be kept on an individual line. The IP address should
# be placed in the first column followed by the corresponding hostname.
# The IP address and the hostname should be separated by at least one
# space.
#
# Additionally, comments (such as these) may be inserted on individual
# lines or following the machine name denoted by a '#' symbol.
#
# For example:
```

```
#
#        102.54.94.97     rhino.acme.com         # source server
#        38.25.63.10      x.acme.com             # x client host

127.0.0.1    localhost
199.245.180.1   ntws1
199.245.180.2   ntws2
199.245.180.3   ntws3
199.245.180.4   ntws4
199.245.180.5   ntws5
199.245.180.6   ntws6 phylos anzimee
ntsmain ntc ntcontroller
```

# Other Support Files for TCP/IP Services

As mentioned earlier, the HOSTS file must be configured for many UNIX-based services ported to Windows NT. In addition to the HOSTS file, there are three other files that may be used by the Windows NT port of UNIX-based services. These files are the NETWORKS, PROTOCOL, and SERVICES files that are found in the \%SystemRoot%\ SYSTEM32\DRIVERS\ETC directory. For the most part you need not configure these files unless you want to add symbolic names for networks or you are a software developer porting new services and protocols to the Windows environment.

## The *NETWORKS* File

The NETWORKS file is used to identify the networks that exist on the internetwork. The NETWORKS file is similar in concept to the HOSTS file. Whereas the HOSTS file contains the association between host addresses and hostnames, the NETWORKS file contains the association between network addresses and network names.

Each line in the NETWORK text file contains information in the following format:

*network_name*        *network_number*[*/subnet_mask*]        *alias* #comment

*network_name* is an identifier representing the name of the network and *network_number* is the *netid* part of the IP address for the network. The network name cannot contain a tab, space, or number (#) character, and must be unique in the NETWORKS file.

*subnet_mask* is the subnet mask for the network. It can be expressed in dotted decimal or dotted hexadecimal notation. The square brackets ([ ]) in the previously stated syntax for the NETWORKS file entry indicate that the subnet mask is optional. If the subnet mask is left out, a default mask indicates that no subnet mask is being used.

The optional *alias* identifies other names by which this network is known. Usually the *network_name* is in lowercased characters and an alias is included that lists the service in uppercased characters.

*#comment* is used to place comments. All characters between the # and the end of the line are ignored and treated as comments. The #comment can occur on a line by itself.

The network names specified in the NETWORKS file can be used in configuration utilities and commands that deal with the network address. For example, the network name can be used as an alternative to using the network addresses. This file can be modified by network administrators to enable the use of network names in configuration commands and utilities rather than using the more difficult to remember network addresses.

The following is a sample of a NETWORKS file:

```
# Copyright (c) 1993-1995 Microsoft Corp.
#
# This file contains network name/network number mappings for
# local networks. Network numbers are recognized in dotted decimal form.
#
# Format:
#
# <network name>  <network number>    [aliases...]  [#<comment>]
#
# For example:
#
#    loopback    127
#    campus      284.122.107
#    london      284.122.108

loopback                127
Kinet                                199.245.180
SCSnet                               200.24.4.0
MyNet                      144.19
```

## The *PROTOCOL* File

The PROTOCOL file is used to identify the names of protocols and the corresponding protocol number. The protocol number for the Internet suite of protocols is the value protocol identifier (protocol id) field of the IP header. The *protocol id* field is used to identify the upper-layer protocol that uses the Internet Protocol.

The PROTOCOL file accompanies the TCP/IP protocol module and contains common protocols; you should not have to modify the file.

Each line in the PROTOCOL text file contains information in the following format:

```
protocol_name      protocol_number     [alias]    #comment
```

*protocol_name* is an identifier representing the name of the protocol and *protocol_number* is the number used in the IP header to identify the protocol. The protocol name cannot contain a tab, space, or number (#) character and must be unique in the PROTOCOL file.

The optional *alias* identifies other names by which this protocol is known. Usually the *protocol_name* is in lowercased characters and an alias is included that lists the service in uppercased characters.

*#comment* is used to place comments. All characters between the # and the end of the line are ignored and treated as comments. #comment can occur on a line by itself. An example PROTOCOL file for Windows NT is listed next:

```
# Copyright (c) 1993-1995 Microsoft Corp.
#
# This file contains the Internet protocols as defined by RFC 1060
# (Assigned Numbers).
#
# Format:
#
# <protocol name>  <assigned number>  [aliases...]   [#<comment>]

ip        0    IP        # Internet protocol
icmp      1    ICMP      # Internet control message protocol
ggp       3    GGP       # Gateway-gateway protocol
tcp       6    TCP       # Transmission control protocol
egp       8    EGP       # Exterior gateway protocol
pup       12   PUP       # PARC universal packet protocol
udp       17   UDP       # User datagram protocol
hmp       20   HMP       # Host monitoring protocol
xns-idp   22   XNS-IDP   # Xerox NS IDP
rdp       27   RDP       # "reliable datagram" protocol
rvd       66   RVD       #
```

## The *SERVICES* File

The SERVICES file is used to identify the following:

- Names of services
- Transport protocol
- Port number used by the service

The names of services are programs that run in the Process/Application layer of the DoD model. Examples of these services are Telnet, FTP, SMTP, SNMP, and so on. These services could use a Transport protocol such as TCP or UDP. The SERVICES configuration file identifies the Transport protocol that is used. Some services are available through both the TCP and UDP transport protocols. In this case, the service is listed twice: once for the TCP protocol and once for the UDP protocol. The port number identifies the application service that uses the Transport protocol.

This SERVICES file accompanies the TCP/IP protocol module and contains common TCP/IP services; you should not have to modify the file.

Each line in the SERVICES text file contains information in the following format:

*service*          *port/transport*          [*alias*]      #*comment*

*service* is an identifier representing the name of the service. Example values of services are Telnet, FTP, FTP-DATA, SMTP, and SNMP. The service name cannot contain a tab, space, or number (#) character and must be unique in the SERVICES file.

The optional *alias* identifies other names by which this service is known.

*#comment* is used to place comments. All characters between the # and the end of the line are ignored and treated as comments. #comment can occur on a line by itself.

A sample SERVICES file for a Windows NT computer is shown next:

```
# Copyright (c) 1993-1995 Microsoft Corp.
#
# This file contains port numbers for well-known services as defined by
# RFC 1060 (Assigned Numbers).
#
# Format:
#
# <service name>   <port number>/<protocol>   [aliases...]   [#<comment>]
#

echo              7/tcp
echo              7/udp
discard           9/tcp     sink null
discard           9/udp     sink null
systat           11/tcp
systat           11/tcp     users
daytime          13/tcp
daytime          13/udp
netstat          15/tcp
qotd             17/tcp     quote
qotd             17/udp     quote
chargen          19/tcp     ttytst source
chargen          19/udp     ttytst source
ftp-data         20/tcp
ftp              21/tcp
telnet           23/tcp
smtp             25/tcp     mail
time             37/tcp     timeserver
time             37/udp     timeserver
rlp              39/udp     resource      # resource location
name             42/tcp     nameserver
name             42/udp     nameserver
whois            43/tcp     nicname       # usually to sri-nic
domain           53/tcp     nameserver    # name-domain server
domain           53/udp     nameserver
nameserver       53/tcp     domain        # name-domain server
nameserver       53/udp     domain
mtp              57/tcp                   # deprecated
bootp            67/udp                   # boot program server
tftp             69/udp
rje              77/tcp     netrjs
finger           79/tcp
link             87/tcp     ttylink
```

```
supdup          95/tcp
hostnames       101/tcp   hostname      # usually from sri-nic
iso-tsap        102/tcp
dictionary      103/tcp   webster
x400            103/tcp                 # ISO Mail
x400-snd        104/tcp
csnet-ns        105/tcp
pop             109/tcp   postoffice
pop2            109/tcp                 # Post Office
pop3            110/tcp   postoffice
portmap         111/tcp
portmap         111/udp
sunrpc          111/tcp
sunrpc          111/udp
auth            113/tcp   authentication
sftp            115/tcp
path            117/tcp
uucp-path       117/tcp
nntp            119/tcp   usenet        # Network News Transfer
ntp             123/udp   ntpd ntp      # network time protocol (exp)
nbname          137/udp
nbdatagram      138/udp
nbsession       139/tcp
NeWS            144/tcp   news
sgmp            153/udp   sgmp
tcprepo         158/tcp   repository    # PCMAIL
snmp            161/udp   snmp
snmp-trap       162/udp   snmp
print-srv       170/tcp                 # network PostScript
vmnet           175/tcp
load            315/udp
vmnet0          400/tcp
sytek           500/udp
biff            512/udp   comsat
exec            512/tcp
login           513/tcp
who             513/udp   whod
shell           514/tcp   cmd           # no passwords used
syslog          514/udp
printer         515/tcp   spooler       # line printer spooler
talk            517/udp
ntalk           518/udp
efs             520/tcp                 # for LucasFilm
route           520/udp   router routed
timed           525/udp   timeserver
tempo           526/tcp   newdate
courier         530/tcp   rpc
conference      531/tcp   chat
```

```
rvd-control        531/udp    MIT disk
netnews            532/tcp    readnews
netwall            533/udp               # for emergency broadcasts
uucp               540/tcp    uucpd      # uucp daemon
klogin             543/tcp               # Kerberos authenticated
➥rlogin
kshell             544/tcp    cmd        # and remote shell
new-rwho           550/udp    new-who    # experimental
remotefs           556/tcp    rfs_server rfs# Brunhoff remote filesystem
rmonitor           560/udp    rmonitord  # experimental
monitor            561/udp               # experimental
garcon             600/tcp
maitrd             601/tcp
busboy             602/tcp
acctmaster         700/udp
acctslave          701/udp
acct               702/udp
acctlogin          703/udp
acctprinter        704/udp
elcsd              704/udp               # errlog
acctinfo           705/udp
acctslave2         706/udp
acctdisk           707/udp
kerberos           750/tcp    kdc        # Kerberos authentication—tcp
kerberos           750/udp    kdc        # Kerberos authentication—udp
kerberos_master    751/tcp               # Kerberos authentication
kerberos_master    751/udp               # Kerberos authentication
passwd_server      752/udp               # Kerberos passwd server
userreg_server     753/udp               # Kerberos userreg server
krb_prop           754/tcp               # Kerberos slave propagation
erlogin            888/tcp               # Login and environment
➥passing
kpop               1109/tcp              # Pop with Kerberos
phone              1167/udp
ingreslock         1524/tcp
maze               1666/udp
nfs                2049/udp              # sun nfs
knetd              2053/tcp              # Kerberos de-multiplexor
eklogin            2105/tcp              # Kerberos encrypted rlogin
rmt                5555/tcp   rmtd
mtb                5556/tcp   mtbd       # mtb backup
man                9535/tcp              # remote man server
w                  9536/tcp
mantst             9537/tcp              # remote man server, testing
bnews              10000/tcp
rscs0              10000/udp
queue              10001/tcp
rscs1              10001/udp
```

```
poker          10002/tcp
rscs2          10002/udp
gateway        10003/tcp
rscs3          10003/udp
remp           10004/tcp
rscs4          10004/udp
rscs5          10005/udp
rscs6          10006/udp
rscs7          10007/udp
rscs8          10008/udp
rscs9          10009/udp
rscsa          10010/udp
rscsb          10011/udp
qmaster        10012/tcp
qmaster        10012/udp
```

# Installing and Configuring the FTP Server Service

Windows NT Servers and Workstations can be set up as FTP servers to enable files in the Windows NT computer to be accessed by FTP clients. The FTP clients can be other Windows NT computers, UNIX computers, DOS/Windows computers, Macintosh computers, VMS computers, and so on.

The Windows NT FTP Server supports all the FTP client commands, is implemented as a multithreaded Win32 application, and complies with RFCs 959 and 1123, which describe the FTP protocols and services.

FTP servers use the user accounts of the host operating system. In the case of Windows NT, the FTP user accounts are the ones created on the FTP computer and the FTP anonymous user account.

The FTP Server is a part of the Microsoft Internet Information Server (IIS). The following section includes some general installation and utilization information.

### Installing and Configuring the FTP Server Service on Windows NT Server

You can choose to install the FTP Service and other Internet services when you do your original NT installation. Select the Microsoft Internet Information Server box during installation. The FTP Server is automatically installed as a part of IIS on the Windows NT Server.

If you have already installed the NT Server without the Internet Information Server, you can add IIS now. The FTP Server service relies on the TCP/IP protocol, so you must install and configure the TCP/IP protocol before you can install FTP Server services.

You can install the FTP Server service on a Windows NT Workstation. However, the number of licensed connections to the Windows NT Workstation cannot exceed

10 simultaneous connections. For this reason it is more common to install FTP Server services on a Windows NT Server which does not have the license restrictions of 10 simultaneous connections.

Follow these steps to install the FTP Server on a Windows NT Server:

1. Log on as an administrator user on the Windows NT computer (Windows NT Server or Workstation).

2. Double-click the Network icon in the Control Panel to display the Network dialog box.

3. Select the Services tab and choose the Add button.

4. Select Microsoft Internet Information Server from the list in the Add Network Services dialog box. Choose OK. Enter the path for the installation files when prompted.

   The Microsoft Internet Server Setup Welcome screen appears. Click OK.

5. Check the FTP Service option and choose OK.

6. The Publishing directories screen appears next. Choose OK to accept the default directory or specify another directory.

7. You see the status of files being copied to the Windows NT computer.

   At the end of the file copy, you see the Services tab again. Select Close to exit the Network dialog box.

8. To configure the FTP Service, click the Microsoft Internet Server (Common) icon in the Programs folder and select Internet Service Manager. Double-click the server running the FTP service to bring up the FTP Service Properties dialog box (see Figure 4.4).

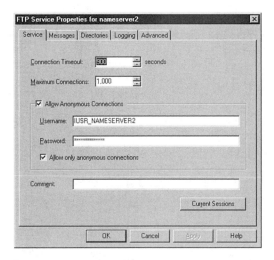

**Figure 4.4**  The FTP Service Properties dialog box.

9. Use the Maximum Connections field to specify the number of simultaneous FTP sessions to the FTP server. The default value is 20, and the maximum is 32,767. If a value of 0 is entered, it indicates that no maximum limits exist and it enables an unlimited number of user connections. Use this field to perform appropriate load balancing. Restricting the number of FTP connections to between 50 and 250 connections to avoid overwhelming a server is common practice.

10. Use the Connection Timeout field to specify how long an FTP user can remain connected without generating any activity before being disconnected. The default value is 10 minutes and the maximum is 60 minutes. A value of 0 disables the idle timeout feature. The value is primarily used for security reasons to reduce the threat of unattended FTP sessions.

11. Enable the option Allow Anonymous Connections to allow users with the user account named anonymous or FTP to log on to the FTP server. A user is not required to enter a password when logging on as an anonymous user, although the user is prompted for an email address as a password. The username anonymous is reserved on the Windows NT computer for anonymous logon. You cannot, therefore, use a Windows NT user account named anonymous.

    By default, anonymous connections are not allowed and, therefore, this option is not set.

12. Use the Username field to specify the name of the Windows NT user account to be used for the user who logs on as anonymous. The access permissions for the anonymous FTP user are the same as that for the specified user. By default, the Guest system account is used for the anonymous user.

13. Use the Password field to specify the password for the user account specified in the Username field.

14. Enable the Allow Only Anonymous Connections check box option if you want only anonymous user logons to ensure that Windows NT users do not log on with their Windows NT usernames and passwords. Remember that FTP passwords are not encrypted; if they are used on the network, passwords could be compromised. By default, this option is disabled.

    You can see the FTP User Sessions screen (see Figure 4.5) by clicking on the Current Sessions button.

    Other configuration options are available on the other FTP Service Properties tabs.

15. Choose OK to save your FTP service settings.

**Figure 4.5**   The initial FTP User Sessions screen.

## Managing FTP Services

After the FTP Server service is installed and configured, it is automatically started each time the server computer is started. To administer the FTP server, you must log on to the Windows NT computer as an administrator user.

You can use the NET STOP and NET START commands to stop and start the FTP Service. If you want to stop the FTP Services on the Windows NT computer, for example, use the following command:

```
NET STOP FTPSVC
```

This command abruptly disconnects all FTP users from the FTP server. If you want to determine if any FTP users are connected, use the FTP Server icon in the Control Panel.

Instead of abruptly disconnecting users with the NET STOP command, you can temporarily pause FTP Services by using the following command:

```
NET PAUSE FTPSVC
```

Pausing the FTP Services prevents new users from connecting to the FTP server, but does not disconnect currently logged-on users. New users connecting to the FTP server receive the following message:

```
421-Service not available, closing control connection.
```

After users who are logged on are disconnected, you can stop the FTP Service without causing users to lose their sessions.

In addition to the Internet Service Manager, you can use the Services icon in the Control Panel for starting, stopping, and pausing FTP Services.

You can use the Microsoft Internet Server Manager to manage existing user sessions. The FTP User Sessions dialog box displays the following information:

- Name of connected user
- IP address of connected computer
- Duration of connection
- For anonymous users, their passwords (usually email accounts) are displayed

- Anonymous users have a question mark (?) next to their icons, whereas users authenticated by Windows NT do not

You can disconnect any single user or all users from the FTP User Sessions dialog box.

## Advanced FTP Server Configuration

The configuration of the FTP server described so far is adequate for most FTP server installations. This section describes additional configuration that can be done on the FTP server. These configuration options are built into the Microsoft Internet Service Manager for FTP Services. You can also do many of the advanced FTP server configurations by making direct changes to the Registry.

All of the FTP Service parameters discussed in this section are found under the following Registry key:

HKEY_LOCAL_MACHINE\SYSTEM\CurrentControlSet\Services\MSFTPSRV\Parameters

Figure 4.6 shows the default entries under this Registry key. If a value entry does not exist, its default value is used. To change to a non-default value, you must create the value entry. The value entries and their data types and values are discussed in this section.

You can perform all FTP server configuration by editing the Registry, or the following value entries can be set when configuring the FTP server in the Network Settings dialog box:

- AllowAnonymous

- AllowNonAnonymous

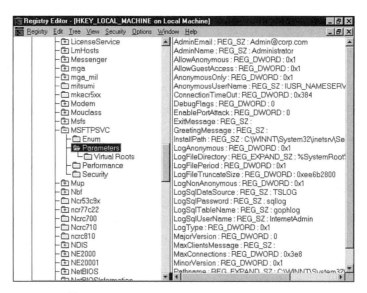

**Figure 4.6**  FTP Service parameters in Registry.

- `AnonymousUsername`
- `ConnectionTimeout`
- `HomeDirectory`
- `MaxConnections`

The following value entries can be set by using the FTP Server icon in the Control Panel, and then selecting the Security button:

- `ReadAccessMask`
- `WriteAccessMask`

### Specifying Annotated Directory Descriptions

When a user changes to a directory on the FTP server, you can display for the user a text filenamed `~FTPSVC~.CKM`, which contains a description of the directory. It also is a good idea to flag this file as hidden so that it does not show up in directory listings. You can use the File Manager for this purpose or use the following command:

```
ATTRIB +H ~FTPSVC~.CKM
```

On many FTP clients the directory descriptions can be toggled by using the FTP site–specific `CKM` command:

```
QUOTE SITE CKM
```

The `AnnotatedDirectories` value entry defines the behavior of directory annotation for newly connected FTP users. The value entry is of data type `REG_DWORD`. It has a value of `0` or `1`. A value of `1` means that the directory-annotated file `~FTPSVC~.CKM` is used to display directory description to the user. The default value is `0`, which means that directory annotation is off.

### Customizing Greeting and Exit Messages

When a user logs on to an FTP server, you can display a customized greeting message that informs the user of the usage policy on the server or some other site-specific information. The greeting message is not sent if the user logs on as anonymous and uses the minus character (–) before the username.

The greeting message is stored in the `GreetingMessage` value entry. This value entry is of data type `REG_SZ`. You can use any string characters. The default is no greeting messages.

When a user logs off, you can display a signoff message. The signoff message is specified in the value entry `ExitMessage`. This value entry is of data type `REG_SZ`, and has a default value of `Goodbye`.

### Logging FTP Connections

As FTP users connect to the FTP server, you can log the connections in the system event log by setting the value entries `LogAnonymous` and `LogNonAnonymous`.

The `LogAnonymous` value entry is of data type `REG_DWORD` and has a value of `0` or `1`. If set to `1`, anonymous user connections are logged in the system event log; otherwise, logging is disabled. The default value is `0`, which means that logging is disabled.

The `LogNonAnonymous` value entry is similar to the `LogAnonymous` value entry, except that it applies to non-anonymous users such as Windows NT user accounts. The `LogNonAnonymous` value entry is of data type `REG_DWORD` and has a value of `0` or `1`. If set to `1`, non-anonymous user connections are logged in the system event log; otherwise, logging is disabled. The default value is `0`, which means that logging is disabled.

The `LogFileAccess` value entry controls the logging of file access to the `FTPSVC.LOG`, which is kept in the `\SystemRoot\SYSTEM32` directory. The `LogFileAccess` is of data type `REG_DWORD` and has a value of `0` or `1`. If set to `1`, file accesses are logged in the `FTPSVC.LOG` file; otherwise, logging is disabled. The default value is `0`, which means that logging is disabled. The following is an example of the contents of the `FTPSVC.LOG` file:

```
************** FTP SERVER SERVICE STARTING Fri July 10 11:05:00 am 1998
132.12.23.13 kss opened d:\FTP\sample.txt Fri July 10 11:10:03 am 1998
132.12.23.12 kss appended d:\FTP\sample.txt Fri July 10 11:22:12 am 1998
132.12.23.12 kss created d:\FTP\readme.txt Fri July 10 11:55:32 am 1998
************** FTP SERVER SERVICE STOPPING Fri July 10 11:59:56 am 1998
```

From the previous sample log, you can see that the log file contains entries for the IP address of the connecting computer, the username, the operation on the file (created, deleted, opened, appended), pathname of file, and date/timestamp information.

### Configuring the Display Format for Directory Listings

You can use the following FTP command to toggle the directory listing format between MS-DOS– and UNIX-style formats:

```
QUOTE SITE DIRSTYLE
```

The directory listing format is important in those applications that depend on a particular directory listing format. Most of these are UNIX-based applications.

The initial format of directory listings is controlled by the `MsdosDirOutput` value entry. The `MsdosDirOutput` value entry is of data type `REG_DWORD` and has a value of `0` or `1`. If set to `1`, directory listings look like that for MS-DOS when the `DIR` command is used; otherwise, directory listings look like that for UNIX when the `ls` command is used. The default value is `1`, which means that directory listings look like that for MS-DOS. If the value is set to `1`, backward slashes (\) are used in the `pwd` command, and if set to `0`, forward slashes (/) are used in the `pwd` command.

Another parameter that affects directory listings is `LowercaseFiles`. The `LowercaseFiles` value entry is of data type `REG_DWORD` and has a value of `0` or `1`. If set to `1`, filenames returned by the `list` and `nlst` commands are mapped to lowercase for non-case-preserving file systems, such as FAT. If set to `0`, the mapping to lowercase names is not performed. This flag has no effect on HPFS and NTFS filenames because these file systems are case-preserving.

### Changing the Maximum Clients Message

If you have set limits to the number of maximum FTP user sessions, and this limit is exceeded, the new FTP users receive the following message:

```
Maximum clients reached, service unavailable.
```

If you want to change this default message you can change the `MaxClientsMessage` value entry. The `MaxClientsMessage` value entry is of data type `REG_SZ` and can be set to any string value.

# Configuring TCP/IP to Print from Windows NT to UNIX Printers

Another aspect of TCP/IP configuration is configuring Windows NT to print to UNIX printers on the network. The print jobs are sent using the TCP/IP protocol. Windows NT printing support for UNIX printers conforms to RFC 1179.

To print to a UNIX computer, only one Windows NT computer (workstation or server) must have the TCP/IP protocol installed and configured as well as the Microsoft TCP/IP Printing Service. This Windows NT computer then acts as print gateway for other Microsoft clients (see Figure 4.7). The other Microsoft clients do not need TCP/IP installed on them to use the print gateway. Figure 4.7 shows that the computer named NTKS has TCP/IP print support and has defined the shared printers \\NTKS\Unix_PR1 and \\NTKS\Unix_PR2. These printers correspond to a directly connected UNIX printer, and a printer attached to a UNIX computer. Other Microsoft clients connect to the shared printers as if they were Microsoft print devices. A print job sent to the shared printer names \\NTKS\Unix_PR1 and \\NTKS\Unix_PR2 is redirected by NTKS to the corresponding UNIX printer.

## Installing and Configuring TCP/IP Printing

The following is an outline for installing and configuring TCP/IP printing:

1. Log on as administrator user on the Windows NT computer (Windows NT Server or Workstation).

2. Double-click the Network icon in the Control Panel to display the Network dialog box.

3. Choose the Services tab in the Network dialog box.

4. Choose the Add button. Select Microsoft TCP/IP Printing by highlighting it in the Select Network Service list box and then choosing OK.

5. When prompted, enter the path for the distribution files and choose Continue.

   You see the status of files being copied to the Windows NT computer.

6. When the Network Services dialog box reappears, choose Close.

7. The Network Settings Change dialog box prompts you to restart the computer to ensure that the changes take effect. Choose Yes.

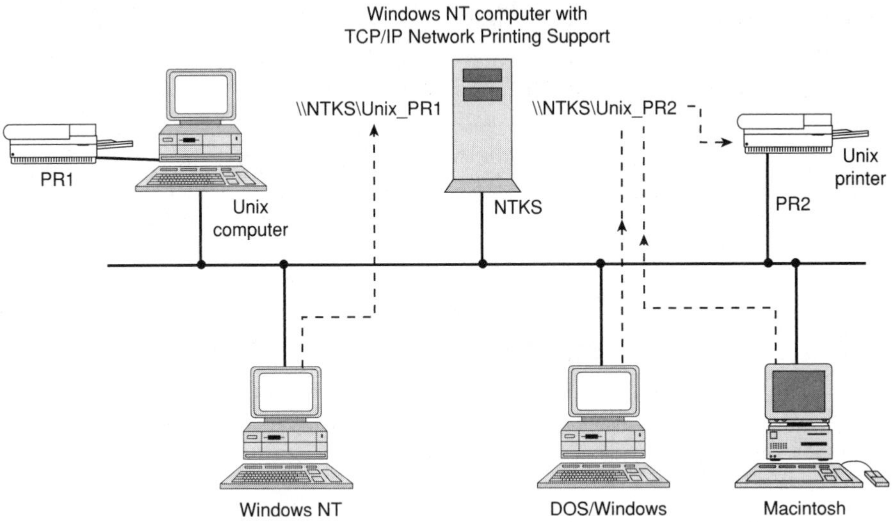

**Figure 4.7** TCP/IP printing using Windows NT.

After the Windows NT computer restarts, you must create a TCP/IP printer so that Microsoft clients can use it as a print gateway to UNIX computers. After the Windows NT computer restarts, proceed with the remaining steps to create the TCP/IP printer.

8. Double-click the Printers icon in the Control Panel, and click the Add Printer icon. The Add Printer Wizard appears (see Figure 4.8). To install a TCP/IP printer, you need to choose Local Printer, then add an LPR port specifying the UNIX host and print queue.

9. Select a printer choice under Windows NT Internet Printing (see Figure 4.9). These servers are typically print servers running the line printer daemon (lpd) process.

10. Follow the prompts on the screen to define the new printer. This may involve selecting the printer manufacturer and printer properties.

11. At the completion of print configuration, an icon for the new printer in the Printers window appears.

## Printing to a Windows NT Computer from a UNIX Computer

The previous section outlined the configuration procedure for printing to a UNIX printer from Microsoft clients. On a network consisting of a mix of UNIX computers and Microsoft clients, you might need to print from a UNIX client to a Windows NT printer.

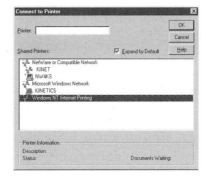

**Figure 4.8**   The Add Printer Wizard.          **Figure 4.9**   Connect to Printer screen.

To print from a UNIX client to a Windows NT computer, you must have TCP/IP Print Services running on the Windows NT computer. UNIX print clients expect to communicate with a UNIX line printer daemon (lpd). You can start the Windows NT Lpdsvc service, which emulates a UNIX line printer daemon. Figure 4.10 shows how UNIX clients can print to a Windows NT computer.

You can start, pause, continue, or stop the Windows NT lpdsvc by using the following NET commands:

- NET START LPDSVC
- NET PAUSE LPDSVC

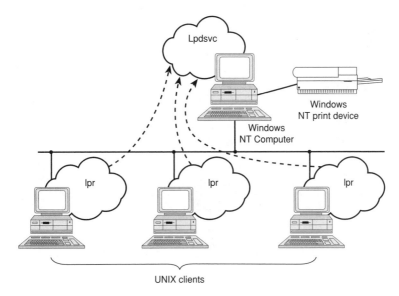

**Figure 4.10**   TCP/IP printing from UNIX to Windows NT print servers.

- NET CONTINUE LPDSVC

- NET STOP LPDSVC

Alternatively, you can use the Microsoft Management Console (MMC) to start, pause, continue, or stop the lpdsvc. To start MMC, select Start, Programs, Adminstrator Tools, System Service Management. The lpdsvc is called TCP/IP Print Server in the MMC console (see Figure 4.11). By default, this service is started manually. You can right-click on the service name and select the Startup option to start this service. You can similarly select the Properties option to set the starting option of this service to automatic, which ensures that the service will be started when the Windows NT computer is started.

On the UNIX printer, you must use the appropriate UNIX command, usually lpr, to submit print jobs to the Windows NT computer. Consult your UNIX documentation for the details of this command. The general syntax of the lpr command is as follows:

```
lpr -s NTHost -P NTPrinter filename
```

The NTHost is the DNS name of the Windows NT computer running the lpdsvc. The NTPrinter is the name of the Windows NT printer created on the NTHost, and filename is the name of the UNIX file to be printed.

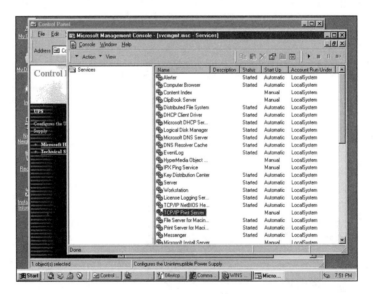

**Figure 4.11**   The TCP/IP Print Server in the System Services dialog box.

# Advanced TCP/IP Configuration
# Using the Registry and Perl

**M**OST OF THE TRADITIONAL ADMINISTRATIVE TASKS on Windows NT can be done using the system tools in the Administrative Tools group and using the Network applet in the Control Panel. Changes made by these tools are entered in to the Registry. The Registry is the internal database for storing configuration information on the system.

There are times, however, in which you may want to make a configuration change or bug fix by editing the Registry directly. You can do this by using the Registry Editor or through writing a program in a language like C/C++, Perl, or Basic. It is best to use the Registry Editor for making custom changes to a few systems. If you need to make the same changes to a large number of systems, it may be convenient to do so by writing a custom program. The Perl language has become very popular on many operating systems. While the language is a little bit more difficult to master than languages like Basic, Perl is considerably more flexible and powerful. This chapter exposes you to how you can access the Registry from Perl.

## The Architecture and Layout of the Registry

The *Registry* is the internal databases used in Windows NT and Windows 9x to store configuration information for the system. The configuration information includes settings for TCP/IP and other protocols. The Registry is used in the following ways:

- Provide startup information during system boot

- Store general system configuration data

- Manage device driver configuration parameters

- Store new configuration data for added applications and system tools

- Assist system administrators to modify Windows NT system configuration

The Registry database is organized in a tree structure similar to the directory and files in a file system. The nodes in this tree are called *keys* and the leaves of the tree are called *value entries*. A key can contain other subkeys just as a directory can contain other subdirectories. Keys and subkeys are primarily used to organize categories of information. Figure 5.1 shows the structure of the Registry as seen using the Registry Editor. This is the Regedt32.exe program for Windows NT and the Regedit.exe program for Windows 9x. You can also use REGEDIT.EXE in Windows NT, which gives a more "explorer"-like style to editing the Registry.

The Registry consists of several hierarchical subtrees that are local to each Windows NT computer. The subtrees contain information on the computer and user accounts defined on the Windows NT computer. The subtrees (see Figure 5.2) in the Windows NT Registry are as follows:

- HKEY_LOCAL_MACHINE. This shows how the machine is configured at boot time.

- HKEY_CLASSES_ROOT. This is primarily used to provide backward compatibility with earlier versions of Windows. It handles file associations and data. This is actually a symbolic link (pointer) to the HKEY_LOCAL_MACHINE\Software\Classes.

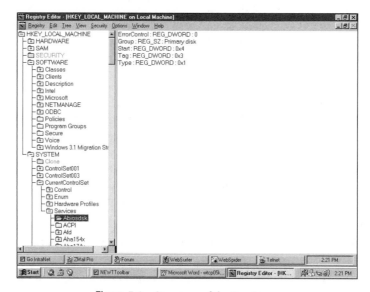

**Figure 5.1**  Structure of the Registry.

- **HKEY_CURRENT_USER.** This contains the profile of the currently logged-on user.

- **HKEY_USERS.** This is meant to contain details of users logged on to the system. In reality, only two users are shown: the default user and the user logged on locally.

- **HKEY_CURRENT_CONFIG.** This is used to store hardware configuration profiles. The profiles can be selected at boot time.

The root keys of the Registry subtrees begin with an **HKEY_** prefix to indicate that this is a handle key that can be used within programs to identify that subtree. The previously listed subtrees all have this prefix.

Value entries consist of a *value name*, *value type*, and the actual *value*. Each value entry in the Registry has a type that is described in Table 5.1. Value types begin with an **AREG_@** prefix. The suffix **A_SZ@** indicates a string terminated with a zero. A value entry is limited to a storage size of 1 MB, which is sufficient for most applications. If an application needs larger sizes, it can split the data into several value entries. The values from **0** to **7FFFFFFF** (hexadecimal) are reserved for system use. Values from **80000000** (hexadecimal) to **FFFFFFFF** (hexadecimal) are reserved for use by applications.

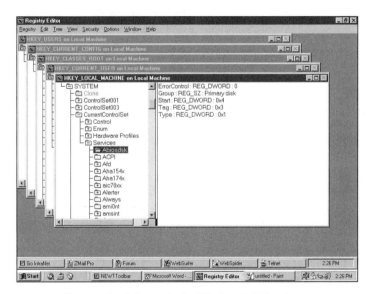

**Figure 5.2** Subtrees in the Windows NT Registry.

Table 5.1   **Data Types for Value Entries in the Registry**

| Data Type | Description |
| --- | --- |
| REG_SZ | This is a sequence of characters forming a string value. An example of this data type is the computer name ComputerName : REG_SZ : NTUS. Many Registry values that are more easily changeable by the system administrator are of this type. |
| REG_DWORD | This a numeric value that is 4 bytes long (double word). Device parameters, service values, and numeric configuration values such as interrupt levels, and so on, are expressed as this data type. The Registry Editor can display this value in decimal, hexadecimal, or binary format. An example of this data type is memory address for a network adapter: MemoryAddress : REG_DWORD : 0xd0000. The A0x@ prefix indicates that the value is expressed as a hexadecimal number. This is a common way of displaying the values of the REG_DWORD data type. |
| REG_MULTI_SZ | This contains multiple string values in a human-readable text. The string values are separated by null (ASCII 0), a common convention used in the AC@ programming language. An example of this is the value that describes the dependencies for the CD-ROM file system: DependOnGroup : REG_MULTI_SZ : SCSI CDROM Class |
| REG_EXPAND_SZ | This is an expandable data string that contains a variable to be replaced when the value is accessed by an application. For example, a value that references the system variable %SystemRoot% would be of REG_EXPAND_SZ data type. The %SystemRoot% refers to the directory in which the Windows NT system is installed. When an application accesses a value that contains the system variable %SystemRoot%, it replaces this variable with the actual directory location where Windows NT was installed. An example of |

| Data Type | Description |
|---|---|
| | this is the image path of the network adapter driver, which contains a reference to the %SystemRoot%: ImagePath : REG_EXPAND_SZ: %SystemRoot%\System32\drivers\ CENDIS3.sys |
| REG_BINARY | This is the raw binary data format. Hardware configuration information is stored in this format. The Registry Editor can also display this data in hexadecimal format. Unless you have documentation on the meaning of the individual bits, it is risky to modify this information. You can use the Windows NT Diagnostic program (WINMSD.EXE) to view hardware-specific information stored in the REG_BINARY format. An example of this is the component information for a peripheral device: Component Information : REG_BINARY : 64 00 00 00 … |
| REG_FULL_RESOURCE_DESCRIPTOR | This is used to hold configuration data for hardware devices. It represents a record of information that has field names describing the individual components of this record. An example of this is the configuration data for a hard disk controller: Configuration Data : REG_FULL_RESOURCE_DESCRIPTOR : … |
| REG_NONE | This is used to indicate an undefined value type. |
| REG_LINK | This is a Unicode symbolic link. |
| REG_RESOURCE_LIST | This is used to hold information on Windows NT device drivers. |
| REG_DWORD_LITTLE_ENDIAN | Same as REG_DWORD but with the most significant byte in the higher memory address. |
| REG_DWORD_BIG_ENDIAN | Same as REG_DWORD but with the most significant byte in the lower memory address. |

The TCP/IP protocol parameters are placed in the HKEY_LOCAL_MACHINE tree. Changing TCP/IP parameters therefore results in changing the value entries in the HKEY_LOCAL_MACHINE. Because the HKEY_LOCAL_MACHINE is the most important key for the configuration of TCP/IP parameters, its structure and organization are discussed next.

## The HKEY_LOCAL_MACHINE Subtree

The HKEY_LOCAL_MACHINE contains information about the local computer hardware, software, security accounts database, and system configuration information. Examples of hardware information are bus type, adapter cards, system memory, device drivers, startup order of device drivers, services to load, application specific data, and so on. The information in the HKEY_LOCAL_MACHINE remains the same regardless of the user that is logged on.

Most system information is stored in HKEY_LOCAL_MACHINE. The HKEY_LOCAL_MACHINE tree has five subkeys. These are the HARDWARE, SAM (Security Accounts Manager), SECURITY, SOFTWARE, and SYSTEM subkeys, and are described in Table 5.2.

Table 5.2 **Hives under** *HKEY_LOCAL_MACHINE*

| Subtree Key Name | Description |
| --- | --- |
| HARDWARE | This describes the physical configuration of the computer, how the hardware uses device drivers, kernel-mode mode drivers, device maps, and resource maps. The data in this subtree is volatile, which means it is re-created on system startup. The Windows NT Diagnostic program (WINMSD.EXE) uses the information in this subtree and displays it in an easier-to-understand format. Most of the data in this subtree is in binary format, which makes it difficult to decode. The subtree contains the following major subkeys: DESCRIPTION, DEVICEMAP, and RESOURCEMAP. The DESCRIPTION key contains the information on the hardware that was recognized by NTDETECT.COM and the Windows NT Executive. The DEVICEMAP key contains information used by device driver classes in a special format. The RESOURCEMAP key maps device drivers to the hardware resources they use. |
| SAM | This contains the user and group accounts information for the domain (for Windows NT Server) or local computer (for Windows NT Workstations). This information is managed by the User Manager administration tool, and the list of users and groups is displayed in File Manager. This subtree is mapped to the key HKEY_LOCAL_MACHINE\SECURITY\SAM, which means that changes made in any of these subkeys automatically appear in the other subkey. |
| SECURITY | This contains information on the security policy and user rights. This information is used by the Windows NT security subsystem. |
| SOFTWARE | This contains information on the software installed on the computer, and miscellaneous configuration data. This includes the parameter settings for protocols such as TCP/IP. |
| SYSTEM | This controls the system boot, loading of device drivers, startup of Windows NT services, and various other operating system behavior. |

SECURITY, SAM, SOFTWARE, and SYSTEM are called *hives* and have corresponding files located for them in the %SystemRoot%\System32\Config directory. Table 5.3 shows the standard hive files on a Windows NT computer.

# Tools to Access and Configure the Registry

The recommended method for accessing and configuring the Registry is to use the network configuration and administration tools. In Windows NT the primary tool used for network configuration is the Network applet in the Control Panel.

However, for certain types of configuration tasks it may be more convenient to edit the Registry directly. Editing the Registry directly is done by using the Registry Editor (REGEDIT.EXE or REGEDT32.EXE). This must be done with care and extreme caution because inadvertent changes to the Registry can crash your system. You should also back up the Registry prior to making major changes in the Registry. You can do this by using the REGBACK program.

You can also use the Registry Editor to connect to and edit the Registry of a remote machine. This is particularly useful when you may not be able to access the remote machines conveniently.

The Registry Editor runs in an interactive mode and is good for making specific changes on a computer system. If you want to make the same changes in the Registry on every computer on your network by running a program that does not involve user input, you can write a custom program or script. For example, you can write a custom program in C/C++ that uses the Registry APIs to modify the Registry. You can also use the Perl scripting language for Win32 systems (Windows NT and Windows 9x) to write scripts to read or modify the Registry.

Another useful method of modifying the Registry is by merging text files with the parameters that you need to change. Then you can use regedit *sample.reg*, in which *sample.reg* contains the values to be edited.

The remaining sections give you a walk-through of using the Registry Editor and the Perl scripting language.

Table 5.3   **Standard Hives**

| Hive Name | Associated Files |
| --- | --- |
| HKEY_LOCAL_MACHINE\SAM | SAM, SAM.LOG |
| HKEY_LOCAL_MACHINE\SECURITY | SECURITY, SECURITY.LOG |
| HKEY_LOCAL_MACHINE\SOFTWARE | SOFTWARE, SOFTWARE.LOG |
| HKEY_LOCAL_MACHINE\SYSTEM | SYSTEM, SYSTEM.ALT |
| HKEY_CURRENT_USER | USER###, USER###.LOG, ADMIN###, ADMIN###.LOG |
| HKEY_USERS\DEFAULT | DEFAULT, DEFAULT.LOG |

## Using REGEDIT to View TCP/IP–Related Parameters

The TCP/IP–related parameters in the Registry are kept under the following key:
```
HKEY_LOCAL_MACHINE\SYSTEM\CurrentControlSet\Services\Tcpip
```

This key contains TCP/IP parameter information for the entire computer system, such as host name, domain name, name servers, router discovery options, and so on.
```
HKEY_LOCAL_MACHINE\SYSTEM\CurrentControlSet\Control\ComputerName
```

This key defines the computer name that is used for the system. The IP address mapping in this file should be consistent with the IP address of the computer name.
```
HKEY_LOCAL_MACHINE\SYSTEM\CurrentControlSet\Enum\Root
```

This key contains the status of the network adapters that exist on the current system. A Windows NT hardware profile can contain many network adapter definitions, but not all of these network adapters may actually be installed or functioning on the computer system. This key can be used to determine which network adapters are active.
```
HKEY_LOCAL_MACHINE\SYSTEM\CurrentControlSet\Services
```

This key contains the parameters and linkage information for the network adapters. Only the parameter information for the active network adapters are in use on the computer system.

You can start the Registry Editor on Windows NT by running the `REGEDT32.EXE` program. All of the TCP/IP parameters are in the `HKEY_LOCAL_MACHINE\SYSTEM\CurrentControlSet`. The `CurrentControlSet` is a symbolic link (pointer) to a control set key such as `HKEY_LOCAL_MACHINE\SYSTEM\CurrentControlSet001` or `HKEY_LOCAL_MACHINE\SYSTEM\CurrentControlSet002`. The *control set* defines the set of parameters needed to boot the computer system successfully. Several copies of the control set are kept. This enables you to back out of a faulty control set and go back to a last known good control set. The control set pointed to by the `HKEY_LOCAL_MACHINE\SYSTEM\CurrentControlSet` pointer is defined in the key `HKEY_LOCAL_MACHINE\SYSTEM\Select`. The value entries under this key are of type `REG_DWORD` and include the following:

- `Current`: This contains the control set number pointed to by `HKEY_LOCAL_MACHINE\SYSTEM\CurrentControlSet`.

- `Default`: This contains the number of the default control set.

- `Failed`: This contains the number of the control set that is known to have failed.

- `LastKnownGood`: This contains the number of the control set that was last known to be good. A control set is known to be good if the boot process is successful and a user is able to log on successfully to the computer system.

Figure 5.3 shows the value entries under the `HKEY_LOCAL_MACHINE\SYSTEM\Select` key. From this figure you can see that the current control set number is 1 and corresponds to the key `HKEY_LOCAL_MACHINE\SYSTEM\CurrentControlSet001`. The default control set (value 1) is the same as the current control set. The failed control set is 0,

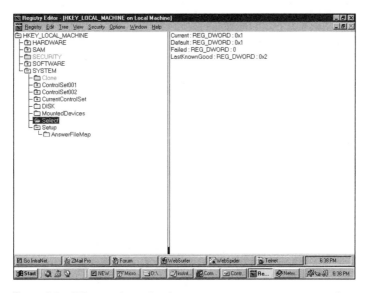

**Figure 5.3** Value entries under the HKEY_LOCAL_MACHINE\SYSTEM\Select key.

which implies that there is no failed control set. The last control set that was known to be good is 2, and corresponds to the key HKEY_LOCAL_MACHINE\SYSTEM\CurrentControlSet002.

Figure 5.4 shows the value entries and subkeys under the key HKEY_LOCAL_MACHINE\SYSTEM\CurrentControlSet\Services\Tcpip. This key contains the value entries for the TCP/IP protocol driver. The image path of the TCP/IP driver is System32\DRIVERS\tcpip.sys; its display name is TCP/IP Protocol Driver.

Figure 5.5 shows the entries and subkeys under the key HKEY_LOCAL_MACHINE\ SYSTEM\CurrentControlSet\Control\ComputerName. This key contains the definitions of the computer names. If you are modifying the hostname of the computer, you must ensure that the modified hostname matches the value entries under this subkey. This is because the hostname is resolved to its IP address by using one of the name resolution techniques. See Chapter 9, "TCP/IP Name Resolution Using WINS," for additional information on name resolution techniques.

Figure 5.6 shows the entries and subkeys under the key HKEY_LOCAL_MACHINE\ SYSTEM\CurrentControlSet\Enum\Root. This key enumerates all the network adapters whose drivers are registered on the system.

Figure 5.7 shows the entries and subkeys under the key HKEY_LOCAL_MACHINE\ SYSTEM\CurrentControlSet\Services. This key shows information for the services running on the computer system. The information includes parameters and linkage information for the network adapters.

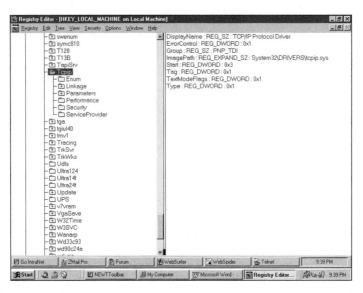

**Figure 5.4** The HKEY_LOCAL_MACHINE\SYSTEM\CurrentControlSet\Services\Tcpip key.

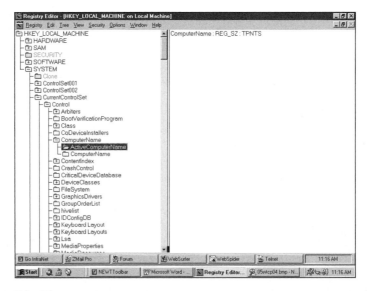

**Figure 5.5** The HKEY_LOCAL_MACHINE\SYSTEM\CurrentControlSet\Control\ComputerName key.

**Figure 5.6** The HKEY_LOCAL_MACHINE\SYSTEM\CurrentControlSet\Enum\Root key.

**Figure 5.7** The HKEY_LOCAL_MACHINE\SYSTEM\CurrentControlSet\Services key.

## Using the Perl Tool to Access the Windows NT Registry

*Perl* is a script programming language that has its origins in the UNIX community. Perl was originally designed for processing system-oriented tasks for the UNIX operating system but can be used on any operating system. Perl has been ported to run on many operating systems including Microsoft's Win32 systems, Windows 9x, and Windows NT.

Perl for Win32 systems can be obtained through CD-ROM publishers such as Walnut Creek (800-261-6630, 408-261-6630) and InfoMagic, Inc. (800-800-6613, 602-526-9565). The standard Perl distribution can be found at `http://www.perl.com/CPAN/`.

Perl scripts that operate properly on the Registry can be used to automate the configuration of network administration tasks. This is particularly valuable in situations in which the same administration task must be repeated on many computers.

The sections that follow discusses how Perl can be used to automate access to the Registry and perform various Registry-related tasks.

# Using Perl to Configure TCP/IP

This section describes several examples of using Perl scripts to access the TCP/IP parameters in the Windows NT Registry. The examples are written using Perl version 5, also called Perl5.

To test these examples, you must have Perl5 installed on your system, along with the appropriate Win32 extensions that are included as part of the standard Perl5 distribution for Win32 systems.

## Reading the Active Computer Name

Consider a situation in which you want to read the active computer name setting on a computer. You probably will not write a script to do this simple task that you can accomplish by using the standard GUI interface on the Windows system. However, the active computer name can be valuable when you are using it as a part of a script to change or configure the computer name.

Here is a Perl script to read the active computer name:

```
$status = NTRegOpenKeyEx ( &HKEY_LOCAL_MACHINE,
'SYSTEM\CurrentControlSet\Control\ComputerName\ActiveComputerName',
&NULL, &KEY_ALL_ACCESS, $hkey );
if ($status)
{
   print "Opening ComputerName key 1:\n" ;
}
else
{
   print "Couldn't retrieve current ComputerName!!\n";
   exit;
}

NTRegQueryValueEx( $hkey, 'ComputerName', &NULL, $type,
➥$oldcomputername);
```

```
print "Active ComputerName is: $oldcomputername\n";
NTRegCloseKey( $hkey );
```

The `NTRegOpenKey()` used in the first statement in the script is used to open the key specified in the second parameter:

```
$status = NTRegOpenKeyEx ( &HKEY_LOCAL_MACHINE,
 'SYSTEM\CurrentControlSet\Control\ComputerName\ActiveComputerName',
 &NULL, &KEY_ALL_ACCESS, $hkey );
```

The opened key exists under the root key, `HKEY_LOCAL_MACHINE`, specified in the first parameter. The handle to the opened key, `$hkey`, is returned in the last parameter. This handle is used in subsequent Registry operations and remains valid until the Registry key is closed. The third parameter is reserved and a `NULL` value is passed in its place. The fourth parameter contains the operations that are permitted on the key. In this case `KEY_ALL_ACCESS` indicates all possible operations. The `KEY_ALL_ACCESS` is meant to be treated as a symbolic constant with a predefined value defined in Windows NT. Since Perl does not support symbolic constants, `KEY_ALL_ACCESS` is written as a subroutine that returns a constant value. In Perl, a subroutine is invoked by preceding it by an & symbol—hence the use of `&KEY_ALL_ACCESS` to indicate a call to subroutine `KEY_ALL_ACCESS()` that returns the constant value. Other possible values for key operations along with their subroutine definitions are as follows:

```
sub DELETE {(0x00010000);}

sub READ_CONTROL {(0x00020000);}

sub WRITE_DAC {(0x00040000);}

sub WRITE_OWNER {(0x00080000);}

sub SYNCHRONIZE {(0x00100000);}

sub STANDARD_RIGHTS_REQUIRED {(0x000F0000);}

sub STANDARD_RIGHTS_READ {( &READ_CONTROL);}

sub STANDARD_RIGHTS_WRITE {( &READ_CONTROL);}

sub STANDARD_RIGHTS_EXECUTE {( &READ_CONTROL);}

sub STANDARD_RIGHTS_ALL {(0x001F0000);}

sub SPECIFIC_RIGHTS_ALL {(0x0000FFFF);}

sub ACCESS_SYSTEM_SECURITY {(0x01000000);}

sub MAXIMUM_ALLOWED {(0x02000000);}

sub GENERIC_READ {(0x80000000);}

sub GENERIC_WRITE {(0x40000000);}

sub GENERIC_EXECUTE {(0x20000000);}

sub GENERIC_ALL {(0x10000000);}

sub KEY_QUERY_VALUE {(0x0001);}

sub KEY_SET_VALUE {(0x0002);}

sub KEY_CREATE_SUB_KEY {(0x0004);}

sub KEY_ENUMERATE_SUB_KEYS {(0x0008);}
```

```
sub KEY_NOTIFY {(0x0010);}

sub KEY_CREATE_LINK {(0x0020);}

sub KEY_READ {(( &STANDARD_RIGHTS_READ | &KEY_QUERY_VALUE |
➥&KEY_ENUMERATE_SUB_KEYS | &KEY_NOTIFY) & (~ &SYNCHRONIZE));}

sub KEY_WRITE {(( &STANDARD_RIGHTS_WRITE | &KEY_SET_VALUE |
➥&KEY_CREATE_SUB_KEY) & (~ &SYNCHRONIZE));}

sub KEY_EXECUTE {(( &KEY_READ) & (~ &SYNCHRONIZE));}

sub KEY_ALL_ACCESS {(( &STANDARD_RIGHTS_ALL | &KEY_QUERY_VALUE |
➥&KEY_SET_VALUE | &KEY_CREATE_SUB_KEY | &KEY_ENUMERATE_SUB_KEYS |
➥&KEY_NOTIFY | &KEY_CREATE_LINK) & (~ &SYNCHRONIZE));}
```

The keyword `sub` preceding the subroutine name defines the beginning of the subroutine. After the `sub` comes the name of the subroutine, which is followed by braces ({}) that enclose the body of the subroutine. Because no parameters are passed to the previously listed subroutines, they can be written as `&KEY_ALL_ACCESS` instead of `&KEY_ALL_ACCESS()`.

Other subroutines used as parameters in the `NTRegOpenEx()` call that return a constant value are the `HKEY_LOCAL_MACHINE` and `NULL` that return the values `0x80000002` and `0`, respectively. These are defined as follows:

```
sub HKEY_LOCAL_MACHINE {( 0x80000002 );}

sub NULL { (0);}
```

The `HKEY_LOCAL_MACHINE` subroutine returns a predefined Registry handle: `0x80000002`. The predefined Registry handles are defined as follows:

```
sub HKEY_CLASSES_ROOT {( 0x80000000 );}

sub HKEY_CURRENT_USER {( 0x80000001 );}

sub HKEY_LOCAL_MACHINE {( 0x80000002 );}

sub HKEY_USERS {( 0x80000003 );}

sub HKEY_PERFORMANCE_DATA {( 0x80000004 );}

sub HKEY_PERFORMANCE_TEXT {( 0x80000050 );}

sub HKEY_PERFORMANCE_NLSTEXT {( 0x80000060 );}
```

The value returned by the call to `NTRegOpenEx()` is a scalar value and is stored in the scalar variable `$status`. In Perl, values can be single valued, or multi-valued. *Single value* objects are stored in variables called *scalar* variables, which always begin with the $ symbol. *Multi-valued* objects are called lists or vectors and are stored in array variables. *Array* variables begin with an @ symbol. Another type of multi-valued object is the hash variable. *Hash* variables are indexed arrays and begin with the % symbol.

A non-zero scalar value returned by a subroutine usually indicates success of the requested subroutine operation. A `0` value indicates a failure in performing the requested subroutine operation. In the previous Perl script, the status value returned by `NTRegOpenEx()` is tested, and appropriate status or error messages are generated:

```
if ($status)
{
   print "Opening ComputerName key 1:\n" ;
}
```

```
else
{
   print "Couldn't retrieve current ComputerName!!\n";
   exit;
}
```

If the `NTRegOpenEx()` fails, the `else` part of the `if` statement is executed. The statement `exit;` causes immediate halting of the Perl script with an exit status code of `0`.

After the successful completion of the `NTRegOpenEx()`, the `NTRegQueryValueEx()` is invoked to query the `ComputerName` value entry:

```
NTRegQueryValueEx( $hkey, 'ComputerName', &NULL, $type,
➥$oldcomputername);
```

The `NTRegQueryValueEx()`takes the handle to the Registry key, `$hkey`, as its first parameter. The second parameter, `ComputerName`, is the name of the value entry to be read. The third parameter is reserved and a `NULL` value is passed in its place. The fourth parameter, `$type`, is the type of the value entry returned. The fifth and last parameter is the value of the value entry that was queried. You can use the `$type` value that is returned to determine the type of the value entry. Alternatively, if you know the name of the value entry, you can view the Registry with the Registry Editor to determine the type of the value entry. Perl defines the following Registry data types for Windows NT:

```
sub REG_NONE {( 0 );}

sub REG_SZ {( 1 );}

sub REG_EXPAND_SZ {( 2 );}

sub REG_BINARY {( 3 );}

sub REG_DWORD {( 4 );}

sub REG_DWORD_LITTLE_ENDIAN {( 4 );}

sub REG_DWORD_BIG_ENDIAN {( 5 );}

sub REG_LINK {( 6 );}

sub REG_MULTI_SZ {( 7 );}

sub REG_RESOURCE_LIST {( 8 );}

sub REG_FULL_RESOURCE_DESCRIPTOR {( 9 );}

sub REG_RESOURCE_REQUIREMENTS_LIST {( 10 );}
```

Finally, the Registry key is closed by a call to `NTRegClosekey()`, which relinquishes any internal data structures associated with the opened key:

```
NTRegCloseKey( $hkey );
```

In order to run the Perl script, the appropriate library routines and subroutine definitions for running the script must be specified. This can be done by adding the following at the beginning of the previous Perl script:

```
BEGIN{
@INC = qw( Lib
   Ext );

};
```

```
require "NT.ph";
```

The `BEGIN` `{}` ensures that the statements listed in the braces are run at the beginning of execution of the script. The `BEGIN` block is used to define the `@INC` list that lists the `include` directories. The `qw()` is called the "quote-word" syntax and forces the words `Lib` and `Ext` to be treated as a list of quoted words:

```
("Lib", "Ext")
```

This statement is equivalent to the following:

```
@INC = ("Lib", "Ext");
```

The `require` statement that follows ensures that the contents of `NT.ph` are processed at compile time and the definitions in this file are known before processing the statements that follow.

The complete Perl script including these definitions therefore becomes the following:

```
BEGIN{
@INC = qw( Lib
   Ext );

};

require "NT.ph";

$status = NTRegOpenKeyEx ( &HKEY_LOCAL_MACHINE,
'SYSTEM\CurrentControlSet\Control\ComputerName\ActiveComputerName',
&NULL, &KEY_ALL_ACCESS, $hkey );
if ($status)
{
   print "Opening ComputerName key 1:\n" ;
}
else
{
   print "Couldn't retrieve current ComputerName!!\n";
   exit;
}

NTRegQueryValueEx( $hkey, 'ComputerName', &NULL, $type,
➥$oldcomputername);
print "Active ComputerName is: $oldcomputername\n";
NTRegCloseKey( $hkey );
```

If you want to ensure that the code is to be executed only on Windows NT systems, you can use the `Win32::IsWinNT()` subroutine that returns a non-zero value if it is executed on Windows NT, and a zero value for other systems. The `Win32::` prefix to `IsWinNT()` is the name of the Windows 32 module in which the subroutine `IsWinNT()` is defined. You could use the following `if` statement to perform the test for a Windows NT system:

```
if( Win32::IsWinNT() )
{

    # Add code specific to Windows NT

}
```

In the previous Perl script there is code that is specific to Windows NT. To ensure that this code will be executed only for a Windows NT system, you can write the Perl script as follows:

```
BEGIN{
@INC = qw( Lib
   Ext );

};

require "NT.ph";

if Win32::IsWinNT())
{
    $status = NTRegOpenKeyEx ( &HKEY_LOCAL_MACHINE,
    'SYSTEM\CurrentControlSet\Control\ComputerName\ActiveComputerName',
    &NULL, &KEY_ALL_ACCESS, $hkey );
    if ($status)
    {
      print "Opening ComputerName key 1:\n" ;
    }
    else
    {
      print "Couldn't retrieve current ComputerName!!\n";
      exit;
    }

    NTRegQueryValueEx( $hkey, 'ComputerName', &NULL, $type,
    ➡$oldcomputername);
    print "Active ComputerName is: $oldcomputername\n";
    NTRegCloseKey( $hkey );
}
```

## Modifying IP Addresses

The IP address of a network adapter is stored in the key HKEY_LOCAL_MACHINE\ SYSTEM\CurrentControlSet\Services\*adapter*\Parameters\Tcpip under the value entry IPAddress. To read this value entry, you can use the NTRegOpenKeyEx(), NTRegQueryValueEx(), and NTRegCloseKey() that were used in the Perl script of the previous section. However, to change its value you must use NTRegSetValueEx(). The following Perl script reads, displays, and sets the IP address:

```
BEGIN{
@INC = qw( Lib
   Ext );

};

require "NT.ph";

$ip = "144.19.75.2"; # New IP address to change to

NTRegOpenKeyEx ( &HKEY_LOCAL_MACHINE,
   'SYSTEM\CurrentControlSet\Services\El90x2\Parameters\Tcpip',
   &NULL, &KEY_ALL_ACCESS, $hkey ) ?
   &log( "Opening 3COM 3C905 IPAddress key.\n" ):
   &gripe( "Couldn't retrieve current 3COM 3C905 IPaddress!!\n" );

NTRegQueryValueEx( $hkey, 'IPAddress', &NULL, $type, $oldipaddress );
print "Old 3COM 3C905 IPAddress was: $oldipaddress\n";

NTRegSetValueEx( $hkey, 'IPAddress', &NULL, $type, $ip ) ?
   &log( "Updated 3COM 3C905 ipaddress to $ip\n" ):
   &gripe( "Couldn't update 3COM 3C905 ipaddress!!\n" );

NTRegQueryValueEx( $hkey, 'IPAddress', &NULL, $type, $oldipaddress );
if ( $oldipaddress eq $ip )
{
   print "New 3COM 3C905 IPAddress verified as: $ip\n";
}

NTRegCloseKey( $hkey );

#
# Support subroutines to log and complain.
#
sub log
{
   ( $message ) = @_;
   print $message;
}

sub gripe
{
   ( $message ) = @_;
   warn $message;
}
```

The call to NTRegOpenKeyEx() is used to obtain the handle $hkey to the key
SYSTEM\CurrentControlSet\Services\El90x2\Parameters\Tcpip in

HKEY_LOCAL_MACHINE. If the value returned by NTRegOpenKeyEx() is non zero (success), the call to the log() subroutine is executed. If this value is zero (failure), the call to gripe() is executed. Log() and gripe() are defined as subroutines at the end of the script:

```
NTRegOpenKeyEx ( &HKEY_LOCAL_MACHINE,
    'SYSTEM\CurrentControlSet\Services\El90x2\Parameters\Tcpip',
    &NULL, &KEY_ALL_ACCESS, $hkey ) ?
    &log( "Opening 3COM 3C905 IPAddress key.\n" ):
    &gripe( "Couldn't retrieve current 3COM 3C905 IPaddress!!\n" );
```

After obtaining a handle to the key, the IPaddress value entry is read and displayed using the NTRegQueryValueEx():

```
NTRegQueryValueEx( $hkey, 'IPAddress', &NULL, $type, $oldipaddress );
print "Old 3COM 3C905 IPAddress was: $oldipaddress\n";
```

Next, the NTRegSetValueEx() is executed to set the new IP address. The number and format of the parameters is the same as that in NTRegQueryValueEx(). The new IP address is stored in the variable $ip and is passed as the last parameter to NTRegSetValueEx():

```
NTRegSetValueEx( $hkey, 'IPAddress', &NULL, $type, $ip ) ?
    &log( "Updated 3COM 3C905 ipaddress to $ip\n" ):
    &gripe( "Couldn't update 3COM 3C905 ipaddress!!\n" );
```

After updating the value entry, the next few statements verify that the IP address was changed as expected. The NTRegQueryValueEx() is used to re-read the value that was written:

```
NTRegQueryValueEx( $hkey, 'IPAddress', &NULL, $type, $oldipaddress );
if ( $oldipaddress eq $ip )
{
    print "New 3COM 3C905 IPAddress verified as: $ip\n";
}

NTRegCloseKey( $hkey );
```

In the previous example, the new IP address was hard coded into the script. If there is a need to query the network administrator to change the IP address, you can do so by using the following modified Perl script. This Perl script also checks to see if the code is run on a Windows NT system by calling Win32::IsWinNT():

```
BEGIN{
@INC = qw( Lib
    Ext );

};

require "NT.ph";

print <<'--end--';
This script will modify the network configuration.
Do you wish to proceed? [Y/n]
```

```
--end--
$in = <STDIN>;
until ( $in eq "\n" || $in =~ /^y/i )
{
    exit if ( $in =~ /^no?\n$/i );
    print "Do you wish to proceed? [Y/n]";
    $in = <STDIN>;
}


print "Enter your IP address:";
$ip = <STDIN>;

if (Win32::IsWinNT())
{
    NTRegOpenKeyEx ( &HKEY_LOCAL_MACHINE,
        'SYSTEM\CurrentControlSet\Services\El90x2\Parameters\Tcpip',
        &NULL, &KEY_ALL_ACCESS, $hkey ) ?
        &log( "Opening 3COM 3C905 IPAddress key.\n" ):
        &gripe( "Couldn't retrieve current 3COM 3C905 IPaddress!!\n" );

    NTRegQueryValueEx( $hkey, 'IPAddress', &NULL, $type, $oldipaddress );
    print "Old 3COM 3C905 IPAddress was: $oldipaddress\n";

    NTRegSetValueEx( $hkey, 'IPAddress', &NULL, $type, $ip ) ?
        &log( "Updated 3COM 3C905 ipaddress to $ip\n" ):
        &gripe( "Couldn't update 3COM 3C905 ipaddress!!\n" );

    NTRegQueryValueEx( $hkey, 'IPAddress', &NULL, $type, $oldipaddress );
    if ( $oldipaddress eq $ip )
    {
        print "New 3COM 3C905 IPAddress verified as: $ip\n";
    }

    NTRegCloseKey( $hkey );

}

#
# Support subroutines to log and complain.
#
sub log
{
    ( $message ) = @_;
    print $message;
}

sub gripe
{
```

```
    ( $message ) = @_;
    warn $message;
}
```

## Deleting Registry Keys

In all the examples given so far there is no need to delete a Registry key. If you are configuring TCP/IP parameters, you do not need to delete Registry keys. You may, however, wish to delete keys to clean up the Registry of unneeded configuration information such as old network adapters. To delete a Registry key, you can use the NTRegDeleteKey(). You must first, however, delete all subkeys under the key to be deleted. The syntax for using the NTRegDeleteKey() is as follows:

```
    NTRegDeleteKey(handle, keystringname);
```

The first parameter, *handle,* is the handle that was opened for the Registry. The second parameter, *keystringname,* is a string value that is the name of the key to be deleted.

## Enumerating TCP/IP Information Using Perl5 Objects

The examples of TCP/IP configuration script given so far have not used Registry objects that can be defined in Perl5. All the operations to the Registry were specified in relationship to the handle to the Registry. In Perl5, you can create a reference to an object so that all references are then performed by executing methods for that object. Object methods are similar to standard Perl subroutines except that they are performed with respect to an object.

Consider the following Perl script, which, if run on a Windows NT system, lists all of the TCP/IP parameters stored under the key
HKEY_LOCAL_MACHINE\SYSTEM\CurrentControlSet\Services\Tcpip\Parameters:

```
    BEGIN{
    @INC = qw( Lib
        Ext );

    };

    use Win32::Registry;

    $keyname = "SYSTEM\\CurrentControlSet\\Services\\Tcpip\\Parameters";
    $main::HKEY_LOCAL_MACHINE->Open($keyname, $param) ||
        die "Open: $!";
    $param->GetValues(\%value_entries);

    foreach $k (keys %value_entries)
    {
        $key = $value_entries{$k};
        print "$$key[0] = $$key[2]\n";

    }
```

The first statement of interest is the use statement:

```
use Win32::Registry;
```

This is used to include the Win32:Registry package for subsequent use. The variable $keyname contains the key
SYSTEM\CurrentControlSet\Services\Tcpip\Parameters relative to the root key HKEY_LOCAL_MACHINE.

The next statement uses the predefined object $main::HKEY_LOCAL_MACHINE for the root key HKEY_LOCAL_MACHINE in the Registry module, and invokes the method Open():

```
$main::HKEY_LOCAL_MACHINE->Open($keyname, $param) ||
    die "Open: $!";
```

If the value returned by the call to the Open() method is 0, the die statement is executed. The $! refers to the last error status code.

The param$ variable contains the object corresponding to the opened key. This is used in the next statement to obtain a hash array of all the value entries.

```
$param->GetValues(\%value_entries);
```

The use of the backslash (\) before %value_entries indicates that this is a reference to a hash array. The *hash array* is populated with value entries on the return from the call to the GetValues() method. Each hash element contains the name of the Registry value and a value that is a reference to a three-element list. The three elements are the value name, the data type, and the actual value. The foreach statement causes the variable $k to iterate over each of the key values:

```
foreach $k (keys %value_entries)
{
    $key = $value_entries{$k};
    print "$$key[0] = $$key[2]\n";

}
```

The keys operator returns an array of keys for the hash array %value_entries. The following statement returns the three-element list:

```
$key = $value_entries{$k};
```

The $key[0] is the first element of the list and is the value entry name; the $key[2] is the third element of the list and this is the actual value. The second element of the list, the Registry data type, is $key[1], which is not displayed. The following print statement, therefore, displays the value name and its value:

```
print "$$key[0] = $$key[2]\n";
```

## Running Perl Scripts

You can run Perl scripts from the command line by typing the following command:

```
Perl perfilename
```

Replace *perfilename* with the name of the file containing the Perl script.

It is also possible to place the perl command in a batch file. One clever method of placing the perl command in a batch file is as follows:

```
#!c:\winnt\system32\perl5\perl.exe
@rem = '--*-Perl-*--';
@rem = '
echo off
if exist perl.exe goto perlhere
print Could not find Perl interpreter!!
print *gasp* *wheeze* *choke*
pause
goto endofperl
:perlhere
if exist perl100.dll goto perldllhere
print Could not find Perl100.dll
print *gasp* *wheeze* *choke*
pause
goto endofperl
:perldllhere
perl.exe nameofbatchfile %1 %2 %3 %4 %5 %6 %7 %8 %9
goto endofperl

@rem ';

BEGIN{
@INC = qw( Lib
      Ext );

};

require "NT.ph";

Rest of the Perl script goes here

:endofperl
```

The statement #!c:\winnt\system32\perl5\perl.exe at the beginning of the file is treated as a comment by UNIX command processors such as the Korn Shell or C shell that has been ported to Windows NT. Should you be using these command processors, the first line specifies that the remaining lines should be processed using the program found in file c:\winnt\system32\perl5\perl.exe.

When this batch file is run, the following statement is treated as a comment by the Win32 command interpreter, CMD.EXE, which is compatible to the MS-DOS command processor:

```
@rem = '--*-Perl-*--';
```

The next statement is treated as a comment also by the Win32 command interpreter:

```
@rem = '
```

The statements that follow are treated as commands for the Win32 command interpreter:

```
echo off
if exist perl.exe goto perlhere
print Could not find Perl interpreter!!
print *gasp* *wheeze* *choke*
pause
goto endofperl
:perlhere
if exist perl100.dll goto perldllhere
print Could not find Perl100.dll
print *gasp* *wheeze* *choke*
pause
goto endofperl
:perldllhere
perl.exe nameofbatchfile %1 %2 %3 %4 %5 %6 %7 %8 %9
goto endofperl

@rem ';
```

The previous commands check the existence of the `perl.exe` and `perl100.dll` files. If they do not exist, appropriate error messages are displayed and the execution of the batch file branches to a point at the end of the file labeled `:endofperl`. The last statement is treated as a comment:

```
@rem ';
```

If the files `perl.exe` and `perl100.dll` exist, the following command is invoked:

```
perl.exe nameofbatchfile %1 %2 %3 %4 %5 %6 %7 %8 %9
```

The *nameofbatchfile* should be the same name as the batch file that contains these commands. The arguments are passed as %1 to %9.

When `perl.exe` is invoked, it starts executing the batch file as a Perl script. When the first statement is encountered, it is treated as an array variable:

```
@rem = '--*-Perl-*--';
```

Next, the following second statement is encountered:

```
@rem = '
```

The Perl interpreter scans the rest of the lines looking for a matching quote ('), which is found several lines down:

```
@rem ';
```

In the process of scanning for a matching quote, the DOS-like commands are skipped. The remaining statements are processed by the Perl interpreter as valid Perl statements.

# 6

# TCP/IP Protocol Traces

WINDOWS NETWORKS PROVIDE MANY APPLICATION SERVICES. When these application services run on the network, their application data is sent using a transport protocol such as TCP/IP. There are a number of application services that are sent using special Application layer protocols such as SMB and Session layer protocols such as NetBIOS. It is very useful for a network administrator to understand the nature of network traffic that is generated when certain actions are performed or applications run. For example, an understanding of the amount of network traffic generated with a specific application can give you an understanding of how the application affects the overall network performance.

You can monitor network traffic using protocol analyzers. Windows NT Server comes with a Network Monitor tool that can be used to capture network traffic going in and out of that Windows NT server. A more full-featured Network Monitor tool that can capture any network traffic is bundled with Microsoft's Systems Management Server (SMS) product. You can also use third-party protocol analyzer tools such as Network General's Sniffer, Novell's LANalyzer, Precision Guesswork's Lanwatch32, and so on.

This chapter discusses how you can use the Network Monitor Tool and performs a detailed analysis of several sample protocol traces generated on a Windows network.

# Analyzing Network Traffic with Network Monitor

In this section only the basics on how to effectively use the Network Monitor tool are discussed. This includes running the Network Monitor tool and setting capture filters. For additional details on the Network Monitor tool, refer to the product documentation.

The Network Monitor tool is installed when you install network services on Windows NT Server version 5. You can run the Network Monitor tool when logged on as an Administrator user by selecting Programs, Network Administration, Microsoft Network Monitor Tools.

You should see the main Network Monitor screen (see Figure 6.1). In order to start capturing packets you can press F10, select Capture, Start from the menu bar, or click the Play button on the toolbar.

If the Windows NT server is connected to the network, you begin to see statistics on network traffic information being captured and other information such as network utilization, frames per second, bytes per second, and so on (see Figure 6.2).

To view the network traffic that you have captured, you must stop the capture and view the packet trace. You can do this using the Shift+F11 key, or choosing Capture, Stop and View.

Figure 6.3 shows the captured traffic. If you double-click on any packet you will see the detailed decode of the packet (see Figure 6.4). You can expand any of the protocol layers in the detailed decode by clicking on the plus sign next to that protocol layer.

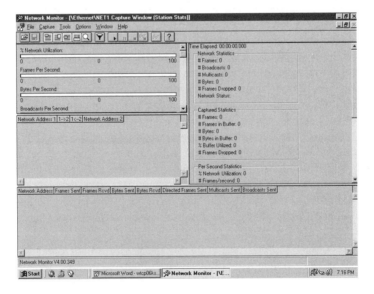

**Figure 6.1**   Network Monitor main screen.

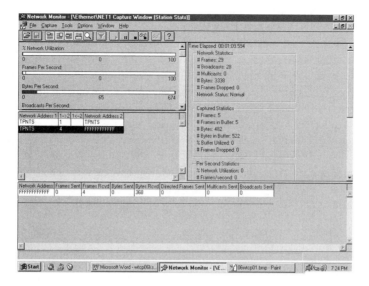

**Figure 6.2**    Network Monitor screen showing packets being captured.

**Figure 6.3**    Network Monitor screen showing packet trace.

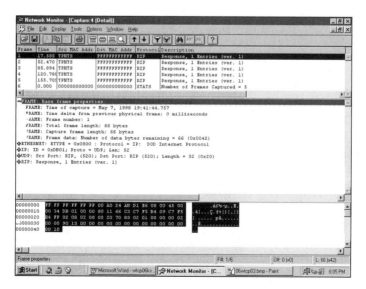

**Figure 6.4**    Network Monitor screen showing detailed view of a packet in the packet trace.

## Setting Capture Filter Options

On a large network you will be capturing traffic from potentially many stations. Also in a multiprotocol environment you will be capturing protocols in addition to the one you are interested in examining. It is useful to be able to set a filter to capture only the type of traffic of interest to you. The Network Monitor tool comes with two types of filters: the capture filter, and the display filter. The *capture* filter restricts the packets captured in the packet buffers based on the criteria on that filter. For example, you may be interested in only capturing IP related traffic and not other traffic such as IPX (used in NetWare networks), DDP (used in AppleTalk), and so on. You can set a capture filter, and even save it so that it can be reloaded for later use. The *display* filter, on the other hand, is used to selectively display packets that have already been captured in the packet buffers according to the criteria specified in the display filter. The procedures for setting capture and display filters are similar.

The following is an outline of a procedure to set a capture filter for capturing IP related traffic:

1. Start the Network Monitor.

2. Select Capture, Filter. Alternatively, you can press F8.

3. In the capture filter that is displayed (see Figure 6.5), double-click on the line SAP/ETYPE = Any SAP or Any ETYPE. This means that by default any SAP value in a 802.2 frame or ETYPE (Ethertype) value in a Ethernet II frame will be captured.

4. By default all the protocols are enabled (see Figure 6.6).

5. You can remove the protocols that are enabled by highlighting them and clicking the Disable button. Alternatively, you can disable all the protocols by clicking the Disable All button and then selecting only the IP–related protocols. (This alternative approach is faster.)

6. Enable the following protocols:

   - ARP
   - IP with SAP value of 6
   - IP with ETYPE value of 800 (hex)

   ARP stands for Address Resolution Protocol and is a support protocol used in TCP/IP networks. The IP with SAP value of 6 is not really used in Windows NT and most TCP/IP implementations. Nevertheless, it is a good idea to include it in case you run into an uncommon TCP/IP implementation. There is no need to select protocols such as TCP or UDP because these are always encapsulated in an IP packet. Figure 6.7 shows the capture filter for the IP–related parameters.

### Pseudo STATS entry in Network Monitor
The last entry in the capture buffer is a *pseudo* entry that contains statistics on the packets captured so far. In other words, the last entry (STATS) is not a real packet that was captured on the network.

 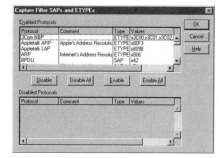

**Figure 6.5**  Default capture filter.      **Figure 6.6**  Capturing SAPs and ETYPEs.

7. Select OK.

8. Select Save.

9. Specify the name of the capture filter file (such as `IPONLY.CAP`).

10. You can load the capture filter file any time before starting the capture of packets.

# Examples of IP Traffic on a Windows Network

In this section, several examples of TCP/IP traces on a Windows network are presented and analyzed. The examples are meant as a guideline on how you can capture and decode network traffic on your own to further your understanding of TCP/IP on a Windows–based network.

It is instructive to examine the protocol layering and details of some of the packets in the protocol traces. It is not practical to do this for every packet in the trace files because there are hundreds of such packets, and to do a detailed analysis of packets in every trace file would exceed the scope and page count restriction of this book.

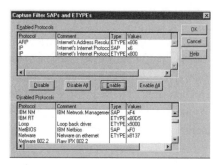

**Figure 6.7**  Capture filter for IP related protocols.

## How Windows Computers Detect Duplicate IP Addresses

The TCP/IP implementation on Windows computers has the useful capability of detecting duplicate IP addresses. If you are using a DHCP server to assign IP addresses, assignment of duplicate IP addresses is unlikely to happen: IP addresses are assigned from a central DHCP server that does not give out duplicate IP addresses. However, if you are assigning IP addresses manually on each computer, there is always the possibility of assigning duplicate IP addresses by mistake. This could still happen in a mixed DHCP/non-DHCP environment because IP addresses are allocated manually for the non-DHCP computers.

Windows computers detect duplicate IP addresses by sending an ARP request that includes a request to resolve the computer's IP address.

*ARP (Address Resolution Protocol)* is used in broadcast networks such as Ethernet, Token Ring, and FDDI to discover the *MAC address* (hardware address) of stations given their IP address. In other words, ARP is used to discover the bindings between IP addresses and MAC addresses. For example, if a Windows station wants to connect to a Windows NT server whose IP address is 199.245.180.102, it will broadcast an ARP request that contains the address 199.245.180.102 to be resolved. Because this ARP request is sent using a MAC address broadcast, all stations on the network process the ARP broadcast request. However, only the computer that has the address of 199.245.180.102 will respond. The response contains the hardware address of the computer. The computer that initiates the ARP request caches the IP address and its hardware address that it resolved in an ARP cache table, which can be examined using the ARP command. You can use the ARP ? command to see the options for this command.

The following sections discuss two scenarios. The first scenario is meant to illustrate the normal behavior of ARP resolution, with no duplicate address detected. Its purpose is to provide you with information to understand the second scenario. The second scenario discusses what happens when there is a duplicate IP address conflict on a Windows network, and how this conflict is detected.

### Normal ARP Resolution

When a Windows NT computer attempts to discover the MAC address of a target computer, it broadcasts an ARP request with the target IP address. Figure 6.8 shows the decode of such an ARP request. There are several instructive points to note about this ARP request:

■ The ETYPE (Ethernet Type) value for the ARP frame is 806 (hex), which is a standard value that uniquely identifies ARP frames.

■ The Ethernet destination address is FFFFFFFFFFFF, which indicates a broadcast address.

■ The ARP opcode field has a value of 1, which indicates an ARP request.

■ The `Hardware Address Space` field indicates the type of physical network that ARP is used on. In this case a value of `1` indicates that the physical network is Ethernet.

■ The `Protocol Address Space` has a value of `800` (hex), which indicates that the protocol address being resolved is for the Internet Protocol (IP). The value of `800` (hex) is the same as that used in the `Ethernet Type` field to identify that the Ethernet header encapsulates an IP datagram.

■ The Hardware Address Length has a value of `6`, which means that the MAC address—Ethernet MAC address, in this case—is `6` octets long.

■ The Protocol Address Length has a value of `4`, which means that the IP address is 4 octets long.

The following fields are significant in the ARP request:

```
Sender's Hardware Address = 0060083671DE
Sender's Protocol Address = 199.245.180.101
Target's Hardware Address = 000000000000
Target's Protocol Address = 199.245.180.20
```

The station making the request has an IP address of 199.245.180.201 and the target station whose hardware address is to be found has an IP address of 199.245.180.20. In the Windows NT TCP/IP implementation, the target's hardware address is set to `0` in the ARP request. However, any value is valid in the target's hardware address because the address is not known.

```
Frame    Time    Src MAC Addr   Dst MAC Addr   Protocol   Description
                                Src Other Addr  Dst Other Addr  Type Other Addr
1        15.950  NTS5_1         FFFFFFFFFFFF   ARP_RARP   ARP: Request, Target IP: 199.245.180.20


    FRAME: Base frame properties
        FRAME: Time of capture = May 9, 1998 11:7:18.803
        FRAME: Time delta from previous physical frame: 8 milliseconds
        FRAME: Frame number: 5
        FRAME: Total frame length: 42 bytes
        FRAME: Capture frame length: 42 bytes
        FRAME: Frame data: Number of data bytes remaining = 42 (0x002A)
    ETHERNET: ETYPE = 0x0806 : Protocol = ARP:  Address Resolution Protocol
        ETHERNET: Destination address : FFFFFFFFFFFF
            ETHERNET: .......1 = Group address
            ETHERNET: ......1. = Locally administered address
        ETHERNET: Source address : 0060083671DE
            ETHERNET: .......0 = No routing information present
            ETHERNET: ......0. = Universally administered address
        ETHERNET: Frame Length : 42 (0x002A)
        ETHERNET: Ethernet Type : 0x0806 (ARP:  Address Resolution Protocol)
        ETHERNET: Ethernet Data: Number of data bytes remaining = 28 (0x001C)
    ARP_RARP: ARP: Request, Target IP: 199.245.180.20
        ARP_RARP: Hardware Address Space = 1 (0x1)
        ARP_RARP: Protocol Address Space = 2048 (0x800)
        ARP_RARP: Hardware Address Length = 6 (0x6)
        ARP_RARP: Protocol Address Length = 4 (0x4)
        ARP_RARP: Opcode = 1 (0x1)
        ARP_RARP: Sender's Hardware Address = 0060083671DE
        ARP_RARP: Sender's Protocol Address = 199.245.180.101
        ARP_RARP: Target's Hardware Address = 000000000000
        ARP_RARP: Target's Protocol Address = 199.245.180.20

00000:  FF FF FF FF FF FF 00 60 08 36 71 DE 08 06 00 01   .......`.6q.....
00010:  08 00 06 04 00 01 00 60 08 36 71 DE C7 F5 B4 65   .......`.6q....e
00020:  00 00 00 00 00 00 C7 F5 B4 14                     ..........
```

**Figure 6.8** ARP Request packet.

The ARP reply shown in Figure 6.9 is sent directly to the ARP requester because the identity of the ARP requester is known by examining the `Sender's Hardware Address` and `Sender's Protocol Address` fields.

The answer to the ARP request is contained in the `Sender's Hardware Address` field in the ARP reply; this is sent by the computer that responds with the answer.

```
Sender's Hardware Address = 00A024ABD1E6   (Answer)
Sender's Protocol Address = 199.245.180.20
Target's Hardware Address = 0060083671DE
Target's Protocol Address = 199.245.180.101
```

### Detecting Duplicate Addresses Using ARP

Now that you understand the normal ARP resolution mechanism, you can better understand how ARP is used by Windows computers to detect duplicate IP addresses.

When a Windows computer boots up, it sends an ARP request to resolve its own IP address. That is, the ARP request's target protocol address is the same as the IP address of the Windows computer making the ARP request. Figure 6.10 shows such a

```
Frame    Time    Src MAC Addr   Dst MAC Addr   Protocol   Description
                 Src Other Addr  Dst Other Addr  Type Other Addr
1        15.950  NTS5_1          FFFFFFFFFFFF   ARP_RARP   ARP: Request, Target IP: 199.245.180.20


   FRAME: Base frame properties
       FRAME: Time of capture = May 9, 1998 11:7:18.803
       FRAME: Time delta from previous physical frame: 8 milliseconds
       FRAME: Frame number: 5
       FRAME: Total frame length: 42 bytes
       FRAME: Capture frame length: 42 bytes
       FRAME: Frame data: Number of data bytes remaining = 42 (0x002A)
   ETHERNET: ETYPE = 0x0806 : Protocol = ARP:  Address Resolution Protocol
       ETHERNET: Destination address : FFFFFFFFFFFF
           ETHERNET: .......1 = Group address
           ETHERNET: ......1. = Locally administered address
       ETHERNET: Source address : 0060083671DE
           ETHERNET: .......0 = No routing information present
           ETHERNET: ......0. = Universally administered address
       ETHERNET: Frame Length : 42 (0x002A)
       ETHERNET: Ethernet Type : 0x0806 (ARP:  Address Resolution Protocol)
       ETHERNET: Ethernet Data: Number of data bytes remaining = 28 (0x001C)
   ARP_RARP: ARP: Request, Target IP: 199.245.180.20
       ARP_RARP: Hardware Address Space = 1 (0x1)
       ARP_RARP: Protocol Address Space = 2048 (0x800)
       ARP_RARP: Hardware Address Length = 6 (0x6)
       ARP_RARP: Protocol Address Length = 4 (0x4)
       ARP_RARP: Opcode = 1 (0x1)
       ARP_RARP: Sender's Hardware Address = 0060083671DE
       ARP_RARP: Sender's Protocol Address = 199.245.180.101
       ARP_RARP: Target's Hardware Address = 000000000000
       ARP_RARP: Target's Protocol Address = 199.245.180.20

00000:  FF FF FF FF FF FF 00 60 08 36 71 DE 08 06 00 01    .......`.6q....
00010:  08 00 06 04 00 01 00 60 08 36 71 DE C7 F5 B4 65    .......`.6q....e
00020:  00 00 00 00 00 00 C7 F5 B4 14                      ..........
```

**Figure 6.9**  ARP Request packet.

packet with the following important fields in the ARP request packet:

```
Sender's Hardware Address = 0060083671DE
Sender's Protocol Address = 199.245.180.101
Target's Hardware Address = 000000000000
Target's Protocol Address = 199.245.180.101
```

Note that the Sender's Protocol Address and the Target's Protocol Address fields have the same value of 199.245.180.101. If there is no other station with an IP address of 199.245.180.101, then there will be no ARP reply. However, if there exists a station with a duplicate IP address of 199.245.180.101, that station will respond with an ARP reply and its hardware address. Figure 6.11 shows an ARP reply from a station with the duplicate IP address of 199.245.180.101.

When a station sees an ARP reply from a station with a duplicate IP address, it reports this problem on the computer screen. If you monitor the protocol traffic when this message occurs, you can detect the computer with the duplicate IP address.

## TCP/IP Trace for Joining a Domain

When a Windows NT computer joins a domain, a special computer account for that Windows NT computer is created in the domain database. This computer account

```
Frame   Time    Src MAC Addr   Dst MAC Addr    Protocol   Description
                         Src Other Addr  Dst Other Addr   Type Other Addr
1       25.950  NTS5_1           FFFFFFFFFFFF   ARP_RARP   ARP: Request, Target IP: 199.245.180.20

   FRAME: Base frame properties
       FRAME: Time of capture = May 9, 1998 12:8:20.231
       FRAME: Time delta from previous physical frame: 8 milliseconds
       FRAME: Frame number: 1
       FRAME: Total frame length: 42 bytes
       FRAME: Capture frame length: 42 bytes
       FRAME: Frame data: Number of data bytes remaining = 42 (0x002A)
   ETHERNET: ETYPE = 0x0806 : Protocol = ARP: Address Resolution Protocol
       ETHERNET: Destination address : FFFFFFFFFFFF
           ETHERNET: .......1 = Group address
           ETHERNET: ......1. = Locally administered address
       ETHERNET: Source address : 0060083671DE
           ETHERNET: .......0 = No routing information present
           ETHERNET: ......0. = Universally administered address
       ETHERNET: Frame Length : 42 (0x002A)
       ETHERNET: Ethernet Type : 0x0806 (ARP: Address Resolution Protocol)
       ETHERNET: Ethernet Data: Number of data bytes remaining = 28 (0x001C)
   ARP_RARP: ARP: Request, Target IP: 199.245.180.101
       ARP_RARP: Hardware Address Space = 1 (0x1)
       ARP_RARP: Protocol Address Space = 2048 (0x800)
       ARP_RARP: Hardware Address Length = 6 (0x6)
       ARP_RARP: Protocol Address Length = 4 (0x4)
       ARP_RARP: Opcode = 1 (0x1)
       ARP_RARP: Sender's Hardware Address = 0060083671DE
       ARP_RARP: Sender's Protocol Address = 199.245.180.101
       ARP_RARP: Target's Hardware Address = 000000000000
       ARP_RARP: Target's Protocol Address = 199.245.180.101

00000:   FF FF FF FF FF FF 00 60 08 36 71 DE 08 06 00 01    .......`.6q.....
00010:   08 00 06 04 00 01 00 60 08 36 71 DE C7 F5 B4 65    .......`.6q....e
00020:   00 00 00 00 00 00 C7 F5 B4 65                      ..........
```

Figure 6.10  ARP request packet with target address same as sender.

```
Frame   Time    Src MAC Addr   Dst MAC Addr   Protocol  Description
                          Src Other Addr  Dst Other Addr  Type Other Addr
2       25.960  00A024ABD1E6   NTS5_1         ARP_RARP  ARP: Reply, Target IP: 199.245.180.101
Target Hdwr Addr: 00600836

    FRAME: Base frame properties
        FRAME: Time of capture = May 9, 1998 12:8:20.233
        FRAME: Time delta from previous physical frame: 0 milliseconds
        FRAME: Frame number: 2
        FRAME: Total frame length: 60 bytes
        FRAME: Capture frame length: 60 bytes
        FRAME: Frame data: Number of data bytes remaining = 60 (0x003C)
    ETHERNET: ETYPE = 0x0806 : Protocol = ARP:  Address Resolution Protocol
        ETHERNET: Destination address : 0060083671DE
            ETHERNET: .......0 = Individual address
            ETHERNET: ......0. = Universally administered address
        ETHERNET: Source address : 00A024ABD1E6
            ETHERNET: .......0 = No routing information present
            ETHERNET: ......0. = Universally administered address
        ETHERNET: Frame Length : 60 (0x003C)
        ETHERNET: Ethernet Type : 0x0806 (ARP:  Address Resolution Protocol)
        ETHERNET: Ethernet Data: Number of data bytes remaining = 46 (0x002E)
    ARP_RARP: ARP: Reply, Target IP: 199.245.180.101 Target Hdwr Addr: 0060083671DE
        ARP_RARP: Hardware Address Space = 1 (0x1)
        ARP_RARP: Protocol Address Space = 2048 (0x800)
        ARP_RARP: Hardware Address Length = 6 (0x6)
        ARP_RARP: Protocol Address Length = 4 (0x4)
        ARP_RARP: Opcode = 2 (0x2)
        ARP_RARP: Sender's Hardware Address = 00A024ABD1E6
        ARP_RARP: Sender's Protocol Address = 199.245.180.101
        ARP_RARP: Target's Hardware Address = 0060083671DE
        ARP_RARP: Target's Protocol Address = 199.245.180.101
        ARP_RARP: Frame Padding

00000:  00 60 08 36 71 DE 00 A0 24 AB D1 E6 08 06 00 01   .`.6q...$.......
00010:  08 00 06 04 00 02 00 A0 24 AB D1 E6 C7 F5 B4 65   ........$.......
00020:  00 60 08 36 71 DE C7 F5 B4 65 65 65 65 65 65 65   .`.6q....eeeeeee
00030:  65 65 65 65 65 65 65 65 65 65 65 65               eeeeeeeeeeee
```

Figure 6.11   ARP reply packet from a station with duplicate IP address.

is used to authenticate the computer as a legitimate member of the domain. Figure 6.12 shows a summary of the packets that were produced by a station named LTREE1 joining an NT domain called NTDOMAIN.

The first two packets are ARP request/reply packets for resolving IP addresses to hardware addresses. ARP resolution was discussed in the previous section and is therefore not discussed here.

Packet 3 is a NETLOGON request for logging into the Primary Domain Controller of the domain.

Packets 4 to 8 deal with identifying which SMB protocol variant the client and server understand. The client in this case is the NT workstation, LTREE1, and the server is the primary domain controller, NTSRVR. The client identifies the protocol

```
1   12.886  NTSRVR         FFFFFFFFFFFF  ARP_RARP  ARP: Request, Target IP: 199.245.180.1
2   12.887  LTREE1         NTSRVR        ARP_RARP  ARP: Reply, Target IP: 199.245.180.101
                                                   Target Hdwr Addr: 00600836
3   12.889  LTREE1         NTSRVR        NETLOGON  Query for Primary DC
                                                     LTREE1          NTSRVR          IP
4   13.325  LTREE1         NTSRVR        TCP       ....S., len:    4,
            seq: 1735525-1735528, ack:        0, win: 8 LTREE1        NTSRVR          IP
5   13.325  LTREE1         NTSRVR        TCP       .A...., len:    0,
            seq: 1735526-1735526, ack:   439492, win: 8 LTREE1        NTSRVR          IP
```

```
6    13.326  LTREE1        NTSRVR        NBT       SS: Session Request,
              Dest: NTSRVR       , Source: LTREE1        LTREE1          NTSRVR       IP
7    13.329  LTREE1        NTSRVR        SMB       C negotiate, Dialect = NT LM 0.12
                                                                  LTREE1          NTSRVR       IP
8    13.454  LTREE1        NTSRVR        TCP       .A....., len:    0,
              seq:  1735772-1735772, ack:    439595, win: 8 LTREE1          NTSRVR       IP
9    13.599  LTREE1        NTSRVR        SMB       C session setup & X,
              Username = Administrator, and C tree connect LTREE1          NTSRVR       IP
10   13.755  LTREE1        NTSRVR        TCP       .A....., len:    0,
              seq:  1736044-1736044, ack:    439743, win: 8 LTREE1          NTSRVR       IP
11   13.760  LTREE1        NTSRVR        SMB       C NT create & X, File = \srvsvc
                                                                  LTREE1          NTSRVR       IP
12   13.798  LTREE1        NTSRVR        MSRPC     c/o RPC Bind:
              UUID 4B324FC8-1670-01D3-1278-5A47BF6EE188  LTREE1          NTSRVR       IP
13   13.802  LTREE1        NTSRVR        MSRPC     c/o RPC Request:     call 0x1
              opnum 0x15  context 0x0  hint 0x2 LTREE1          NTSRVR       IP
14   13.807  LTREE1        NTSRVR        SMB       C close file, FID = 0x800
                                                                  LTREE1          NTSRVR       IP
15   13.844  LTREE1        NTSRVR        NETLOGON  Query for Primary DC
                                                                  LTREE1          NTSRVR       IP
16   13.955  LTREE1        NTSRVR        TCP       .A....., len:    0,
              seq:  1736506-1736506, ack:    440181, win: 8 LTREE1          NTSRVR       IP
17   14.012  LTREE1        NTSRVR        SMB       C NT create & X, File = \samr
                                                                  LTREE1          NTSRVR       IP
18   14.017  LTREE1        NTSRVR        MSRPC     c/o RPC Bind:
              UUID 12345778-1234-ABCD-EF00-0123456789AC  LTREE1          NTSRVR       IP
19   14.021  LTREE1        NTSRVR        MSRPC     c/o RPC Request:
              call 0x1  opnum 0x39  context 0x0  hint 0x2 LTREE1          NTSRVR       IP
20   14.032  LTREE1        NTSRVR        SMB       C NT create & X, File = \lsarpc
                                                                  LTREE1          NTSRVR       IP
21   14.037  LTREE1        NTSRVR        MSRPC     c/o RPC Bind:
              UUID 12345778-1234-ABCD-EF00-0123456789AB  LTREE1          NTSRVR       IP
22   14.040  LTREE1        NTSRVR        MSRPC     c/o RPC Request:
              call 0x1  opnum 0x2C  context 0x0  hint 0x4 LTREE1          NTSRVR       IP
23   14.046  LTREE1        NTSRVR        MSRPC     c/o RPC Request:
              call 0x2  opnum 0x7  context 0x0  hint 0x16 LTREE1          NTSRVR       IP
24   14.050  LTREE1        NTSRVR        MSRPC     c/o RPC Request:
              call 0x3  opnum 0x0  context 0x0  hint 0x14 LTREE1          NTSRVR       IP
25   14.053  LTREE1        NTSRVR        SMB       C close file, FID = 0x802
                                                                  LTREE1          NTSRVR       IP
26   14.088  LTREE1        NTSRVR        MSRPC     c/o RPC Request:
              call 0x2  opnum 0x7  context 0x0  hint 0x34 LTREE1          NTSRVR       IP
27   14.092  LTREE1        NTSRVR        MSRPC     c/o RPC Request:
              call 0x3  opnum 0x32  context 0x0  hint 0x4 LTREE1          NTSRVR       IP
28   14.171  LTREE1        NTSRVR        MSRPC     c/o RPC Request:
              call 0x4  opnum 0x24  context 0x0  hint 0x1 LTREE1          NTSRVR       IP
29   14.177  LTREE1        NTSRVR        MSRPC     c/o RPC Request:
              call 0x5  opnum 0x2C  context 0x0  hint 0x1 LTREE1          NTSRVR       IP
30   14.247  LTREE1        NTSRVR        MSRPC     c/o RPC Request:
              call 0x6  opnum 0x3A  context 0x0  hint 0x3 LTREE1          NTSRVR       IP
31   14.316  LTREE1        NTSRVR        MSRPC     c/o RPC Request:
              call 0x7  opnum 0x1  context 0x0  hint 0x14 LTREE1          NTSRVR       IP
32   14.320  LTREE1        NTSRVR        MSRPC     c/o RPC Request:
              call 0x8  opnum 0x1  context 0x0  hint 0x14 LTREE1          NTSRVR       IP
33   14.330  LTREE1        NTSRVR        SMB       C NT create & X, File = \lsarpc
                                                                  LTREE1          NTSRVR       IP
34   14.336  LTREE1        NTSRVR        MSRPC     c/o RPC Bind:
              UUID 12345778-1234-ABCD-EF00-0123456789AB  LTREE1          NTSRVR       IP
35   14.339  LTREE1        NTSRVR        MSRPC     c/o RPC Request:
              call 0x1  opnum 0x2C  context 0x0  hint 0x4 LTREE1          NTSRVR       IP
36   14.344  LTREE1        NTSRVR        MSRPC     c/o RPC Request:
              call 0x2  opnum 0x7  context 0x0  hint 0x16 LTREE1          NTSRVR       IP
37   14.348  LTREE1        NTSRVR        MSRPC     c/o RPC Request:
              call 0x3  opnum 0x0  context 0x0  hint 0x14 LTREE1          NTSRVR       IP
38   14.351  LTREE1        NTSRVR        SMB       C close file, FID = 0x803
                                                                  LTREE1          NTSRVR       IP
39   14.456  LTREE1        NTSRVR        TCP       .A....., len:    0,
              seq:  1740289-1740289, ack:    442556, win: 8 LTREE1          NTSRVR       IP
40   16.811  LTREE1        NTSRVR        SMB       C NT create & X, File = \lsarpc
                                                                  LTREE1          NTSRVR       IP
41   16.816  LTREE1        NTSRVR        MSRPC     c/o RPC Bind:
              UUID 12345778-1234-ABCD-EF00-0123456789AB  LTREE1          NTSRVR       IP
42   16.820  LTREE1        NTSRVR        MSRPC     c/o RPC Request:
              call 0x1  opnum 0x2C  context 0x0  hint 0x4 LTREE1          NTSRVR       IP
43   16.825  LTREE1        NTSRVR        MSRPC     c/o RPC Request:
              call 0x2  opnum 0xD  context 0x0  hint 0x1C LTREE1          NTSRVR       IP
```

```
43   16.825  LTREE1          NTSRVR         MSRPC     c/o RPC Request:
              call 0x2 opnum 0xD context 0x0 hint 0x1C LTREE1          NTSRVR       IP
44   16.834  LTREE1          NTSRVR         MSRPC     c/o RPC Request:
              call 0x3 opnum 0x0 context 0x0 hint 0x14 LTREE1          NTSRVR       IP
45   16.838  LTREE1          NTSRVR         SMB       C close file, FID = 0x804
                                                                LTREE1          NTSRVR       IP
46   16.960  LTREE1          NTSRVR         TCP       .A...., len:    0,
              seq:  1741055-1741055, ack:    443146, win: 8 LTREE1          NTSRVR       IP
47   18.602  LTREE1          NTSRVR         MSRPC     c/o RPC Request:
              call 0x9 opnum 0x1 context 0x0 hint 0x14 LTREE1          NTSRVR       IP
48   18.907  LTREE1          NTSRVR         SMB       C close file, FID = 0x801
                                                                LTREE1          NTSRVR       IP
49   18.926  LTREE1          NTSRVR         SMB       C tree disconnect
                                                                LTREE1          NTSRVR       IP
50   18.928  LTREE1          NTSRVR         SMB       C logoff & X
                                                                LTREE1          NTSRVR       IP
51   18.930  LTREE1          NTSRVR         TCP       .A...F, len:    0,
              seq:  1741315-1741315, ack:    443375, win: 7 LTREE1          NTSRVR       IP
52   18.931  LTREE1          NTSRVR         TCP       .A...., len:    0,
              seq:  1741316-1741316, ack:    443376, win: 7 LTREE1          NTSRVR       IP
```

**Figure 6.12**   Summary of packets for joining a domain.

by sending the SMB `negprot` command to the server in packet 7, listing the protocol dialects that it understands. In this case, the dialect that the client understands is NT LM 0.12. Figure 6.13 shows the details of packet 7.

At the IP datagram level, you can see the source and destination addresses of this packet:

```
IP: Source Address = 199.245.180.1
IP: Destination Address = 199.245.180.101
```

This is a packet sent from 199.245.180.1 (LTREE1) to the server 199.245.180.101 (NTSRVR).

```
FRAME: Base frame properties
    FRAME: Time of capture = May 9, 1998 17:2:14.491
    FRAME: Time delta from previous physical frame: 3 milliseconds
    FRAME: Frame number: 7
    FRAME: Total frame length: 228 bytes
    FRAME: Capture frame length: 228 bytes
    FRAME: Frame data: Number of data bytes remaining = 228 (0x00E4)
ETHERNET: ETYPE = 0x0800 : Protocol = IP:  DOD Internet Protocol
    ETHERNET: Destination address : 0060083671DE
        ETHERNET: .......0 = Individual address
        ETHERNET: ......0. = Universally administered address
    ETHERNET: Source address : 0000C07A2D5C
        ETHERNET: .......0 = No routing information present
        ETHERNET: ......0. = Universally administered address
    ETHERNET: Frame Length : 228 (0x00E4)
    ETHERNET: Ethernet Type : 0x0800 (IP:  DOD Internet Protocol)
    ETHERNET: Ethernet Data: Number of data bytes remaining = 214 (0x00D6)
IP: ID = 0xA900; Proto = TCP; Len: 214
    IP: Version = 4 (0x4)
    IP: Header Length = 20 (0x14)
    IP: Service Type = 0 (0x0)
        IP: Precedence = Routine
        IP: ...0.... = Normal Delay
        IP: ....0... = Normal Throughput
        IP: .....0.. = Normal Reliability
    IP: Total Length = 214 (0xD6)
```

```
      IP: Identification = 43264 (0xA900)
      IP: Flags Summary = 2 (0x2)
          IP: .......0 = Last fragment in datagram
          IP: ......1. = Cannot fragment datagram
      IP: Fragment Offset = 0 (0x0) bytes
      IP: Time to Live = 128 (0x80)
      IP: Protocol = TCP - Transmission Control
      IP: Checksum = 0x58CF
      IP: Source Address = 199.245.180.1
      IP: Destination Address = 199.245.180.101
      IP: Data: Number of data bytes remaining = 194 (0x00C2)
TCP: .AP..., len:  174, seq:   1735598-1735771, ack:     439496, win: 8756, src: 1029
          dst:  139 (NBT Session)
      TCP: Source Port = 0x0405
      TCP: Destination Port = NETBIOS Session Service
      TCP: Sequence Number = 1735598 (0x1A7BAE)
      TCP: Acknowledgement Number = 439496 (0x6B4C8)
      TCP: Data Offset = 20 (0x14)
      TCP: Reserved = 0 (0x0000)
      TCP: Flags = 0x18 : .AP...
          TCP: ..0..... = No urgent data
          TCP: ...1.... = Acknowledgement field significant
          TCP: ....1... = Push function
          TCP: .....0.. = No Reset
          TCP: ......0. = No Synchronize
          TCP: .......0 = No Fin
      TCP: Window = 8756 (0x2234)
      TCP: Checksum = 0x6757
      TCP: Urgent Pointer = 0 (0x0)
      TCP: Data: Number of data bytes remaining = 174 (0x00AE)
NBT: SS: Session Message, Len: 170
      NBT: Packet Type = Session Message
      NBT: Packet Flags = 0 (0x0)
          NBT: .......0 = Add 0 to Length
      NBT: Packet Length = 170 (0xAA)
      NBT: SS Data: Number of data bytes remaining = 170 (0x00AA)
SMB: C negotiate, Dialect = NT LM 0.12
      SMB: SMB Status = Error Success
          SMB: Error class = No Error
          SMB: Error code = No Error
      SMB: Header: PID = 0xCAFE TID = 0x0000 MID = 0x0000 UID = 0x0000
          SMB: Tree ID     (TID) = 0 (0x0)
          SMB: Process ID  (PID) = 51966 (0xCAFE)
          SMB: User ID     (UID) = 0 (0x0)
          SMB: Multiplex ID (MID) = 0 (0x0)
          SMB: Flags Summary = 24 (0x18)
              SMB: .......0 = Lock & Read and Write & Unlock not supported
              SMB: ......0. = Send No Ack not supported
              SMB: ....1... = Using caseless pathnames
              SMB: ...1.... = Canonicalized pathnames
              SMB: ..0..... = No Opportunistic lock
              SMB: .0...... = No Change Notify
              SMB: 0....... = Client command
          SMB: flags2 Summary = 3 (0x3)
              SMB: ...............1 = Understands long filenames
              SMB: ..............1. = Understands extended attributes
              SMB: ...0............ = No DFS capabilities
              SMB: ..0............. = No paging of IO
              SMB: .0.............. = Using SMB status codes
              SMB: 0............... = Using ASCII strings
      SMB: Command = C negotiate
          SMB: Word count = 0
          SMB: Byte count = 135
          SMB: Byte parameters
          SMB: Dialect Strings Understood
              SMB: Dialect String = PC NETWORK PROGRAM 1.0
              SMB: Dialect String = XENIX CORE
              SMB: Dialect String = MICROSOFT NETWORKS 1.03
              SMB: Dialect String = LANMAN1.0
              SMB: Dialect String = Windows for Workgroups 3.1a
              SMB: Dialect String = LM1.2X002
              SMB: Dialect String = LANMAN2.1
              SMB: Dialect String = NT LM 0.12
```

```
00000:  00 60 08 36 71 DE 00 00 C0 7A 2D 5C 08 00 45 00    .`.6q....z-\..E.
00010:  00 D6 A9 00 40 00 80 06 58 CF C7 F5 B4 01 C7 F5    ....@...X.......
00020:  B4 65 04 05 00 8B 00 1A 7B AE 00 06 B4 C8 50 18    .e......{.....P.
00030:  22 34 67 57 00 00 00 00 00 AA FF 53 4D 42 72 00    "4gW.......SMBr.
00040:  00 00 00 18 03 00 00 00 00 00 00 00 00 00 00 00    ................
```

**Figure 6.13**   The SMB `negprot` command for negotiating SMB dialect.

At the TCP level for packet 7, you can see the source and destination port numbers as the following:

```
TCP: Source Port = 0x0405
TCP: Destination Port = NETBIOS Session Service
```

This identifies the port number endpoints of the TCP session. This packet is being sent from the port number 405 (hex) on LTREE1 to the NetBIOS session service at TCP port number 139 on NTSRVR.

The TCP header in packet 7 encapsulates the NBT packet. This describes the NetBIOS session over TCP/IP. The fields in this packet are the following:

```
NBT: Packet Type = Session Message
NBT: Packet Flags = 0 (0x0)
    NBT: .......0 = Add 0 to Length
NBT: Packet Length = 170 (0xAA)
```

This is part of a NetBIOS session message indicated by the `Packet Type` field value of `0`. The packet flags are `0`, and the packet length is `170` (AA hex).

NBT can be viewed as a Session layer protocol that encapsulates SMB, the Application layer protocol. You may want to refer to the packet structure of SMB packets discussed in Chapter 2, "TCP/IP Protocols Infrastructure for Windows Networks," for additional details on SMB. The SMB packet contains the following information:

```
SMB: SMB Status = Error Success
    SMB: Error class = No Error
    SMB: Error code = No Error
SMB: Header: PID = 0xCAFE TID = 0x0000 MID = 0x0000 UID = 0x0000
    SMB: Tree ID     (TID) = 0 (0x0)
    SMB: Process ID  (PID) = 51966 (0xCAFE)
    SMB: User ID     (UID) = 0 (0x0)
    SMB: Multiplex ID (MID) = 0 (0x0)
    SMB: Flags Summary = 24 (0x18)
        SMB: .......0 = Lock & Read and Write & Unlock not supported
        SMB: ......0. = Send No Ack not supported
        SMB: ....1... = Using caseless pathnames
        SMB: ...1.... = Canonicalized pathnames
        SMB: ..0..... = No Opportunistic lock
        SMB: .0...... = No Change Notify
        SMB: 0....... = Client command
    SMB: flags2 Summary = 3 (0x3)
```

```
           SMB: ..............1 = Understands long filenames
           SMB: .............1. = Understands extended attributes
           SMB: ...0........... = No DFS capabilities
           SMB: ..0............ = No paging of IO
           SMB: .0............. = Using SMB status codes
           SMB: 0.............. = Using ASCII strings
      SMB: Command = C negotiate
         SMB: Word count = 0
         SMB: Byte count = 135
         SMB: Byte parameters
         SMB: Dialect Strings Understood
            SMB: Dialect String = PC NETWORK PROGRAM 1.0
            SMB: Dialect String = XENIX CORE
            SMB: Dialect String = MICROSOFT NETWORKS 1.03
            SMB: Dialect String = LANMAN1.0
            SMB: Dialect String = Windows for Workgroups 3.1a
            SMB: Dialect String = LM1.2X002
            SMB: Dialect String = LANMAN2.1
            SMB: Dialect String = NT LM 0.12
```

The SMB Status, Error class, and Error code fields have a value of 0 indicating a success and no errors.

The Tree ID (TID) field identifies the shared resource that is being connected to. This field is valid when a resource is being used in the SMB command. In the case of the SMB negprot command this field does not specify a shared resource and its value is set to 0.

The Process ID (PID) field is the caller's process identifier. It is generated by the consumer (redirector or the client) to uniquely identify a process within the consumer's system. The term *consumer* here is a computer science term used commonly to describe the software that processes or "consumes" the message. A response message will always contain the same value in the PID as in the corresponding request message. In this example, the PID has a value of 51966 (0xCAFE).

The User ID (UID) identifies the authenticated process. It is used when the server is executing in the User level security mode to validate access on protocols which reference symbolically named resources. Thus different users accessing the same TID may be granted different access to the resources defined by the TID based on the UID.

The Multiplex ID (MID) is used for multiplexing multiple messages on a single Virtual Circuit (VC) normally when multiple requests are from the same process. The PID and the MID fields uniquely identify a request and are used by the consumer to correlate incoming responses to previously sent requests.

There are two flag fields in the SMB packet: flags and flags2. The flags field has a value of 24 (0x18) and indicates that caseless, *canonicalized* (standard form) pathnames are used:

```
   SMB: .......0 = Lock & Read and Write & Unlock not supported
   SMB: ......0. = Send No Ack not supported
```

```
SMB: ....1... = Using caseless pathnames
SMB: ...1.... = Canonicalized pathnames
SMB: ..0..... = No Opportunistic lock
SMB: .0...... = No Change Notify
SMB: 0....... = Client command
```

The flags2 field has a value of 3 and indicates that long names and extended attributes are understood:

```
SMB: ...............1 = Understands long filenames
SMB: ..............1. = Understands extended attributes
SMB: ...0........... = No DFS capabilities
SMB: ..0............ = No paging of IO
SMB: .0............. = Using SMB status codes
SMB: 0.............. = Using ASCII strings
```

The SMB Command field indicates that this is the C negotiate command. The Byte count field value of 135 indicates the size of the byte parameters sent. This portion of the SMB packet is the variable length part of the packet. The byte parameters contain the strings of the dialects understood by the client. These dialects are listed as "dialect strings" in the decode of the packet and include the following SMB dialects:

```
PC NETWORK PROGRAM 1.0
XENIX CORE
MICROSOFT NETWORKS 1.03
LANMAN1.0
Windows for Workgroups 3.1a
LM1.2X002
LANMAN2.1
NT LM 0.12
```

After the SMB protocol variant has been established as seen in packet 7, the client can proceed to log on to the server. This is done using the SMB SesssetupX command shown in packets 9 to 10 (refer to Figure 6.12). Figure 6.14 shows the detailed decode of packet 9.

The Command field indicates that this a C session setup & X command (0x73). The reference to & X is due to the capability in this SMB packet structure of specifying several SMB commands in one SMB packet. Note that after the first Command field with a value of C session setup & X(0x75) there is another Command field set to C

```
FRAME: Base frame properties
    FRAME: Time of capture = May 9, 1998 17:2:14.761
    FRAME: Time delta from previous physical frame: 145 milliseconds
    FRAME: Frame number: 9
    FRAME: Total frame length: 326 bytes
    FRAME: Capture frame length: 326 bytes
    FRAME: Frame data: Number of data bytes remaining = 326 (0x0146)
ETHERNET: ETYPE = 0x0800 : Protocol = IP:  DOD Internet Protocol
    ETHERNET: Destination address : 0060083671DE
        ETHERNET: .......0 = Individual address
        ETHERNET: ......0. = Universally administered address
```

```
        ETHERNET: Source address : 0000C07A2D5C
            ETHERNET: .......0 = No routing information present
            ETHERNET: ......0. = Universally administered address
        ETHERNET: Frame Length : 326 (0x0146)
        ETHERNET: Ethernet Type : 0x0800 (IP:  DOD Internet Protocol)
        ETHERNET: Ethernet Data: Number of data bytes remaining = 312 (0x0138)
IP: ID = 0xAB00; Proto = TCP; Len: 312
    IP: Version = 4 (0x4)
    IP: Header Length = 20 (0x14)
    IP: Service Type = 0 (0x0)
        IP: Precedence = Routine
        IP: ...0.... = Normal Delay
        IP: ....0... = Normal Throughput
        IP: .....0.. = Normal Reliability
    IP: Total Length = 312 (0x138)
    IP: Identification = 43776 (0xAB00)
    IP: Flags Summary = 2 (0x2)
        IP: .......0 = Last fragment in datagram
        IP: ......1. = Cannot fragment datagram
    IP: Fragment Offset = 0 (0x0) bytes
    IP: Time to Live = 128 (0x80)
    IP: Protocol = TCP - Transmission Control
    IP: Checksum = 0x566D
    IP: Source Address = 199.245.180.1
    IP: Destination Address = 199.245.180.101
    IP: Data: Number of data bytes remaining = 292 (0x0124)
TCP: .AP..., len:  272, seq:  1735772-1736043, ack:     439595, win: 8657, src: 1029
            dst:  139 (NBT Session)
    TCP: Source Port = 0x0405
    TCP: Destination Port = NETBIOS Session Service
    TCP: Sequence Number = 1735772 (0x1A7C5C)
    TCP: Acknowledgement Number = 439595 (0x6B52B)
    TCP: Data Offset = 20 (0x14)
    TCP: Reserved = 0 (0x0000)
    TCP: Flags = 0x18 : .AP...
        TCP: ..0..... = No urgent data
        TCP: ...1.... = Acknowledgement field significant
        TCP: ....1... = Push function
        TCP: .....0.. = No Reset
        TCP: ......0. = No Synchronize
        TCP: .......0 = No Fin
    TCP: Window = 8657 (0x21D1)
    TCP: Checksum = 0xBB39
    TCP: Urgent Pointer = 0 (0x0)
    TCP: Data: Number of data bytes remaining = 272 (0x0110)
NBT: SS: Session Message, Len: 268
    NBT: Packet Type = Session Message
    NBT: Packet Flags = 0 (0x0)
        NBT: .......0 = Add 0 to Length
    NBT: Packet Length = 268 (0x10C)
    NBT: SS Data: Number of data bytes remaining = 268 (0x010C)
SMB: C session setup & X, Username = Administrator, and C tree connect & X,
        Share = \\NTSRVR\IPC$
    SMB: SMB Status = Error Success
        SMB: Error class = No Error
        SMB: Error code = No Error
    SMB: Header: PID = 0xCAFE TID = 0x0000 MID = 0x0000 UID = 0x0000
        SMB: Tree ID    (TID) = 0 (0x0)
        SMB: Process ID  (PID) = 51966 (0xCAFE)
        SMB: User ID    (UID) = 0 (0x0)
        SMB: Multiplex ID (MID) = 0 (0x0)
        SMB: Flags Summary = 24 (0x18)
            SMB: .......0 = Lock & Read and Write & Unlock not supported
            SMB: ......0. = Send No Ack not supported
            SMB: ....1... = Using caseless pathnames
            SMB: ...1.... = Canonicalized pathnames
            SMB: ..0..... = No Opportunistic lock
            SMB: .0...... = No Change Notify
            SMB: 0....... = Client command
        SMB: flags2 Summary = 32771 (0x8003)
```

```
              SMB: .......0 = Lock & Read and Write & Unlock not supported
              SMB: ......0. = Send No Ack not supported
              SMB: ....1... = Using caseless pathnames
              SMB: ...1.... = Canonicalized pathnames
              SMB: ..0..... = No Opportunistic lock
              SMB: .0...... = No Change Notify
              SMB: 0....... = Client command
         SMB: flags2 Summary = 32771 (0x8003)
              SMB: ...............1 = Understands long filenames
              SMB: ..............1. = Understands extended attributes
              SMB: ...0............ = No DFS capabilities
              SMB: ..0............. = No paging of IO
              SMB: .0.............. = Using SMB status codes
              SMB: 1............... = Using UNICODE strings
    SMB: Command = C session setup & X
       SMB: Word count = 13
       SMB: Word parameters
       SMB: Next offset = 0x00DE
       SMB: Max Buffer Size = 4356 (0x1104)
       SMB: Max MPX requests = 50
       SMB: VC number = 0
       SMB: Session Key = 0
       SMB: Password length = 24 (0x18)
       SMB: Unicode Password length = 24 (0x18)
       SMB: Capabilities = 212 (0xD4)
          SMB: ............................0 = No Raw Reads and Writes.
          SMB: ...........................0. = No support for multiplexed commands.
          SMB: ...........................1.. = Supports UNICODE strings.
          SMB: ..........................0... = Does not support large files.
          SMB: .........................1.... = Supports the NT SMB extensions.
          SMB: ........................0..... = RPC remote API's not supported.
          SMB: .......................1...... = Recognizes NT Status codes.
          SMB: ......................1....... = Supports level II oplocks.
          SMB: .....................0........ = Does not support Lock and Read.
          SMB: ....................0......... = Does not support NT Find.
          SMB: ...................0.......... = Does not support bulk transfers.
          SMB: ..................0........... = Does not support compressed bulk transfers.
          SMB: .................0............ = This server is NOT DFS aware.
          SMB: ................0............. = ReadX responses must be within negotiated
                                                buffer sizes.
       SMB: Byte count = 161
       SMB: Byte parameters
       SMB: Account name = Administrator
       SMB: Domain name = NTDOMAIN
       SMB: Native OS = Windows NT 1381
       SMB: Native Lanman = Windows NT 4.0
    SMB: Command = C tree connect & X
       SMB: Word count = 4
       SMB: Word parameters
       SMB: Next offset = 0x0000
       SMB: Disconnect flag = 0x0000
       SMB: Password length = 1 (0x1)
       SMB: Byte count = 35
       SMB: Byte parameters
       SMB: Password =
       SMB: File name = \\NTSRVR\IPC$
       SMB: Service Name = ?????
    SMB: Command = No secondary command

00000:  00 60 08 36 71 DE 00 00 C0 7A 2D 5C 08 00 45 00    .`.6q....z-\..E.
00010:  01 38 AB 00 40 00 80 06 56 6D C7 F5 B4 01 C7 F5    .8..@...Vm......
00020:  B4 65 04 05 00 8B 00 1A 7C 5C 00 06 B5 2B 50 18    .e......|\...+P.
00030:  21 D1 BB 39 00 00 00 00 01 0C FF 53 4D 42 73 00    !..9.......SMBs.
00040:  00 00 00 18 03 80 00 00 00 00 00 00 00 00 00 00    ................
```

**Figure 6.14** SMB decode of SesssetupX command.

`tree connect & X`. This indicates that after the session is set up, a shared resource is connected. The file name of this shared resource is \\NTSRVR\IPC$.

The last SMB `Command` field indicates that there is no secondary command (0xFF).

There are a few other interesting points to note about the SMB command in packet 9. The `PID` value of `51966` (0xCAFE) is the same as that in packet 7 indicating that this is the same consumer process. The `flags` field in packet 9 is the same as for packet 7, but the `flags2` field indicates that UNICODE strings are used.

Under the `C session setup & X`, the word `parameters` shows that there is a list of interesting capabilities in the `Capabilities` field, which is set to `212` (0xD4). The bits in this field are decoded as follows:

```
SMB: ..............0 = No Raw Reads and Writes.
SMB: .............0. = No support for multiplexed commands.
SMB: ............1.. = Supports UNICODE strings.
SMB: ...........0... = Does not support large files.
SMB: ..........1.... = Supports the NT SMB extensions.
SMB: .........0..... = RPC remote API's not supported.
SMB: ........1...... = Recognizes NT Status codes.
SMB: .......1....... = Supports level II oplocks.
SMB: ......0........ = Does not support Lock and Read.
SMB: .....0......... = Does not support NT Find.
SMB: ....0.......... = Does not support bulk transfers.
SMB: ...0........... = Does not support compressed bulk transfers.
SMB: ..0............ = This server is NOT DFS aware.
SMB: .0............. = ReadX responses must be within negotiated buffer
sizes.
```

The byte parameters under the `C session setup & X` command show the following values:

```
SMB: Account name = Administrator
SMB: Domain name = NTDOMAIN
SMB: Native OS = Windows NT 1381
SMB: Native Lanman = Windows NT 4.0
```

These parameters indicate the account name (Administrator) and domain name (NTDOMAIN). The native operating system is Windows NT Build 1381, and the Native Lanman class of the operating system is Windows NT 4.0.

In packet 11 a connection is made to the server service \srvsvc (see Figure 6.15).

```
FRAME: Base frame properties
    FRAME: Time of capture = May 9, 1998 17:2:14.960
    FRAME: Time delta from previous physical frame: 38 milliseconds
    FRAME: Frame number: 12
    FRAME: Total frame length: 214 bytes
    FRAME: Capture frame length: 214 bytes
    FRAME: Frame data: Number of data bytes remaining = 214 (0x00D6)
ETHERNET: ETYPE = 0x0800 : Protocol = IP:  DOD Internet Protocol
    ETHERNET: Destination address : 0060083671DE
        ETHERNET: .......0 = Individual address
        ETHERNET: ......0. = Universally administered address
    ETHERNET: Source address : 0000C07A2D5C
        ETHERNET: .......0 = No routing information present
        ETHERNET: ......0. = Universally administered address
    ETHERNET: Frame Length : 214 (0x00D6)
    ETHERNET: Ethernet Type : 0x0800 (IP:  DOD Internet Protocol)
    ETHERNET: Ethernet Data: Number of data bytes remaining = 200 (0x00C8)
IP: ID = 0xAE00; Proto = TCP; Len: 200
    IP: Version = 4 (0x4)
    IP: Header Length = 20 (0x14)
    IP: Service Type = 0 (0x0)
        IP: Precedence = Routine
        IP: ...0.... = Normal Delay
        IP: ....0... = Normal Throughput
        IP: .....0.. = Normal Reliability
    IP: Total Length = 200 (0xC8)
    IP: Identification = 44544 (0xAE00)
    IP: Flags Summary = 2 (0x2)
        IP: .......0 = Last fragment in datagram
        IP: ......1. = Cannot fragment datagram
    IP: Fragment Offset = 0 (0x0) bytes
    IP: Time to Live = 128 (0x80)
    IP: Protocol = TCP - Transmission Control
    IP: Checksum = 0x53DD
    IP: Source Address = 199.245.180.1
    IP: Destination Address = 199.245.180.101
    IP: Data: Number of data bytes remaining = 180 (0x00B4)
TCP: .AP..., len:  160, seq:  1736148-1736307, ack:     439850, win: 8402, src: 1029
     dst:  139 (NBT Session)
    TCP: Source Port = 0x0405
    TCP: Destination Port = NETBIOS Session Service
    TCP: Sequence Number = 1736148 (0x1A7DD4)
    TCP: Acknowledgement Number = 439850 (0x6B62A)
    TCP: Data Offset = 20 (0x14)
    TCP: Reserved = 0 (0x0000)
    TCP: Flags = 0x18 : .AP...
        TCP: ..0..... = No urgent data
        TCP: ...1.... = Acknowledgement field significant
        TCP: ....1... = Push function
        TCP: .....0.. = No Reset
        TCP: ......0. = No Synchronize
        TCP: .......0 = No Fin
    TCP: Window = 8402 (0x20D2)
    TCP: Checksum = 0x77B5
    TCP: Urgent Pointer = 0 (0x0)
    TCP: Data: Number of data bytes remaining = 160 (0x00A0)
NBT: SS: Session Message, Len: 156
    NBT: Packet Type = Session Message
    NBT: Packet Flags = 0 (0x0)
        NBT: .......0 = Add 0 to Length
    NBT: Packet Length = 156 (0x9C)
    NBT: SS Data: Number of data bytes remaining = 156 (0x009C)
SMB: C transact TransactNmPipe, FID = 0x800
    SMB: SMB Status = Error Success
        SMB: Error class = No Error
        SMB: Error code = No Error
    SMB: Header: PID = 0xB6C0 TID = 0x0800 MID = 0x0080 UID = 0x0800
        SMB: Tree ID     (TID) = 2048 (0x800)
        SMB: Process ID  (PID) = 46784 (0xB6C0)
        SMB: User ID     (UID) = 2048 (0x800)
        SMB: Multiplex ID (MID) = 128 (0x80)
        SMB: Flags Summary = 24 (0x18)
            SMB: .......0 = Lock & Read and Write & Unlock not supported
            SMB: ......0. = Send No Ack not supported
            SMB: ....1... = Using caseless pathnames
            SMB: ...1.... = Canonicalized pathnames
            SMB: ..0..... = No Opportunistic lock
            SMB: .0...... = No Change Notify
            SMB: 0....... = Client command
```

```
            SMB: flags2 Summary = 32771 (0x8003)
                SMB: ...............1 = Understands long filenames
                SMB: ..............1. = Understands extended attributes
                SMB: ...0............ = No DFS capabilities
                SMB: ..0............. = No paging of IO
                SMB: .0.............. = Using SMB status codes
                SMB: 1............... = Using UNICODE strings
        SMB: Command = R transact
            SMB: Word count = 16
            SMB: Word parameters
            SMB: Total parm bytes = 0
            SMB: Total data bytes = 72
            SMB: Max parm bytes = 0
            SMB: Max data bytes = 1024
            SMB: Max setup words = 0 (0x0)
            SMB: Transact Flags Summary = 0 (0x0)
                SMB: ...............0 = Leave session intact
                SMB: ..............0. = Response required
            SMB: Transact timeout = 0 (0x0)
            SMB: Parameter bytes = 0 (0x0)
            SMB: Parameter offset = 84 (0x54)
            SMB: Data bytes = 72 (0x48)
            SMB: Data offset = 84 (0x54)
            SMB: Max setup words = 2
            SMB: Setup words
            SMB: Pipe function = Transact named pipe (TransactNmPipe)
            SMB: File ID (FID) = 2048 (0x800)
            SMB: Byte count = 89
            SMB: Byte parameters
            SMB: File name = \PIPE\
            SMB: Transaction data
        SMB: Data: Number of data bytes remaining = 72 (0x0048)
    MSRPC: c/o RPC Bind:        UUID 4B324FC8-1670-01D3-1278-5A47BF6EE188   call 0x7A53D0
              assoc grp 0x0   xmit 0x1630   recv 0x1630
        MSRPC: Version = 5 (0x5)
        MSRPC: Version (Minor) = 0 (0x0)
        MSRPC: Packet Type = Bind
        MSRPC: Flags 1 = 0 (0x0)
            MSRPC: .......0 = Reserved -or- Not the first fragment (AES/DC)
            MSRPC: ......0. = Not a last fragment -or- No cancel pending
            MSRPC: .....0.. = Not a fragment -or- No cancel pending (AES/DC)
            MSRPC: ....0... = Receiver to repond with a fack PDU -or- Reserved (AES/DC)
            MSRPC: ...0.... = Not used -or- Does not support concurrent multiplexing (AES/DC)
            MSRPC: ..0..... = Not for an idempotent request -or- Did not execute guaranteed
                               call (Fault PDU only) (AES/DC)
            MSRPC: .0...... = Not for a broadcast request -or- 'Maybe' call semantics
                               not requested (AES/DC)
            MSRPC: 0....... = Reserved -or- No object UUID specified in the optional
                               object field (AES/DC)
        MSRPC: Packed Data Representation
        MSRPC: Fragment Length = 72 (0x48)
        MSRPC: Authentication Length = 0 (0x0)
        MSRPC: Call Identifier = 8016848 (0x7A53D0)
        MSRPC: Max Trans Frag Size = 5680 (0x1630)
        MSRPC: Max Recv Frag Size = 5680 (0x1630)
        MSRPC: Assoc Group Identifier = 0 (0x0)
        MSRPC: Presentation Context List
            MSRPC: Number of Context Elements = 1 (0x1)
            MSRPC: Presentation Context Identifier = 0 (0x0)
            MSRPC: Number of Transfer Syntaxs = 1 (0x1)
            MSRPC: Abstract Interface UUID = 4B324FC8-1670-01D3-1278-5A47BF6EE188
            MSRPC: Abstract Interface Version = 3 (0x3)
            MSRPC: Transfer Interface UUID = 8A885D04-1CEB-11C9-9FE8-08002B104860
            MSRPC: Transfer Interface Version = 2 (0x2)

00000:  00 60 08 36 71 DE 00 00 C0 7A 2D 5C 08 00 45 00   .`.6q....z-\..E.
00010:  00 C8 AE 00 40 00 80 06 53 DD C7 F5 B4 01 C7 F5   ....@...S.......
00020:  B4 65 04 05 00 8B 00 1A 7D D4 00 06 B6 2A 50 18   .e......}....*P.
00030:  20 D2 77 B5 00 00 00 00 00 9C FF 53 4D 42 25 00    .w........SMB%.
00040:  00 00 00 18 03 80 68 FF 00 00 00 00 00 00 00 00   ......h.........
```

**Figure 6.15**   SMB command C NT Create & X for connecting to server service \srvsvc.

Packet 12 is used to record a transaction using the SMB command `R transact`(see Figure 6.16). In this command a named pipe (`\PIPE`) is set up. The transaction data is actually a Microsoft RPC (MSRPC) call. Thus the SMB packet encapsulates the MSRPC packet. The MSRPC packet is used for binding the abstract interface from client to server. An RPC is a remote invocation of a programming API that is executed at the server and the results sent back to the client.

```
FRAME: Base frame properties
    FRAME: Time of capture = May 9, 1998 17:2:14.960
    FRAME: Time delta from previous physical frame: 38 milliseconds
    FRAME: Frame number: 12
    FRAME: Total frame length: 214 bytes
    FRAME: Capture frame length: 214 bytes
    FRAME: Frame data: Number of data bytes remaining = 214 (0x00D6)
ETHERNET: ETYPE = 0x0800 : Protocol = IP: DOD Internet Protocol
    ETHERNET: Destination address : 0060083671DE
        ETHERNET: .......0 = Individual address
        ETHERNET: ......0. = Universally administered address
    ETHERNET: Source address : 0000C07A2D5C
        ETHERNET: .......0 = No routing information present
        ETHERNET: ......0. = Universally administered address
    ETHERNET: Frame Length : 214 (0x00D6)
    ETHERNET: Ethernet Type : 0x0800 (IP: DOD Internet Protocol)
    ETHERNET: Ethernet Data: Number of data bytes remaining = 200 (0x00C8)
IP: ID = 0xAE00; Proto = TCP; Len: 200
    IP: Version = 4 (0x4)
    IP: Header Length = 20 (0x14)
    IP: Service Type = 0 (0x0)
        IP: Precedence = Routine
        IP: ...0.... = Normal Delay
        IP: ....0... = Normal Throughput
        IP: .....0.. = Normal Reliability
    IP: Total Length = 200 (0xC8)
    IP: Identification = 44544 (0xAE00)
    IP: Flags Summary = 2 (0x2)
        IP: .......0 = Last fragment in datagram
        IP: ......1. = Cannot fragment datagram
    IP: Fragment Offset = 0 (0x0) bytes
    IP: Time to Live = 128 (0x80)
    IP: Protocol = TCP - Transmission Control
    IP: Checksum = 0x53DD
    IP: Source Address = 199.245.180.1
    IP: Destination Address = 199.245.180.101
    IP: Data: Number of data bytes remaining = 180 (0x00B4)
TCP: .AP..., len:  160, seq:   1736148-1736307, ack:    439850, win: 8402, src: 1029  dst:  139 (NBT Session)
    TCP: Source Port = 0x0405
    TCP: Destination Port = NETBIOS Session Service
    TCP: Sequence Number = 1736148 (0x1A7DD4)
    TCP: Acknowledgement Number = 439850 (0x6B62A)
    TCP: Data Offset = 20 (0x14)
    TCP: Reserved = 0 (0x0000)
    TCP: Flags = 0x18 : .AP...
        TCP: ..0..... = No urgent data
        TCP: ...1.... = Acknowledgement field significant
        TCP: ....1... = Push function
        TCP: .....0.. = No Reset
        TCP: ......0. = No Synchronize
        TCP: .......0 = No Fin
    TCP: Window = 8402 (0x20D2)
    TCP: Checksum = 0x77B5
    TCP: Urgent Pointer = 0 (0x0)
    TCP: Data: Number of data bytes remaining = 160 (0x00A0)
NBT: SS: Session Message, Len: 156
    NBT: Packet Type = Session Message
    NBT: Packet Flags = 0 (0x0)
        NBT: .......0 = Add 0 to Length
    NBT: Packet Length = 156 (0x9C)
    NBT: SS Data: Number of data bytes remaining = 156 (0x009C)
SMB: C transact TransactNmPipe, FID = 0x800
    SMB: SMB Status = Error Success
        SMB: Error class = No Error
        SMB: Error code = No Error
```

```
     SMB: Header: PID = 0xB6C0 TID = 0x0800 MID = 0x0080 UID = 0x0800
        SMB: Tree ID      (TID) = 2048 (0x800)
        SMB: Process ID   (PID) = 46784 (0xB6C0)
        SMB: User ID      (UID) = 2048 (0x800)
        SMB: Multiplex ID (MID) = 128 (0x80)
        SMB: Flags Summary = 24 (0x18)
              SMB: .......0 = Lock & Read and Write & Unlock not supported
              SMB: ......0. = Send No Ack not supported
              SMB: ....1... = Using caseless pathnames
              SMB: ...1.... = Canonicalized pathnames
              SMB: ..0..... = No Opportunistic lock
              SMB: .0...... = No Change Notify
              SMB: 0....... = Client command
        SMB: flags2 Summary = 32771 (0x8003)
              SMB: ...............1 = Understands long filenames
              SMB: ..............1. = Understands extended attributes
              SMB: ...0............ = No DFS capabilities
              SMB: ..0............. = No paging of IO
              SMB: .0.............. = Using SMB status codes
              SMB: 1............... = Using UNICODE strings
     SMB: Command = R transact
        SMB: Word count = 16
        SMB: Word parameters
        SMB: Total parm bytes = 0
        SMB: Total data bytes = 72
        SMB: Max parm bytes = 0
        SMB: Max data bytes = 1024
        SMB: Max setup words = 0 (0x0)
        SMB: Transact Flags Summary = 0 (0x0)
              SMB: ..............0 = Leave session intact
              SMB: ..............0. = Response required
        SMB: Transact timeout = 0 (0x0)
        SMB: Parameter bytes = 0 (0x0)
        SMB: Parameter offset = 84 (0x54)
        SMB: Data bytes = 72 (0x48)
        SMB: Data offset = 84 (0x54)
        SMB: Max setup words = 2
        SMB: Setup words
        SMB: Pipe function = Transact named pipe (TransactNmPipe)
        SMB: File ID (FID) = 2048 (0x800)
        SMB: Byte count = 89
        SMB: Byte parameters
        SMB: File name = \PIPE\
        SMB: Transaction data
     SMB: Data: Number of data bytes remaining = 72 (0x0048)
  MSRPC: c/o RPC Bind:       UUID 4B324FC8-1670-01D3-1278-5A47BF6EE188  call 0x7A53D0  assoc grp 0x0  xmit 0x1630  recv 0x1630
     MSRPC: Version = 5 (0x5)
     MSRPC: Version (Minor) = 0 (0x0)
     MSRPC: Packet Type = Bind
     MSRPC: Flags 1 = 0 (0x0)
           MSRPC: .......0 = Reserved -or- Not the first fragment (AES/DC)
           MSRPC: ......0. = Not a last fragment -or- No cancel pending
           MSRPC: .....0.. = Not a fragment -or- No cancel pending (AES/DC)
           MSRPC: ....0... = Receiver to repond with a fack PDU -or- Reserved (AES/DC)
           MSRPC: ...0.... = Not used -or- Does not support concurrent multiplexing (AES/DC)
           MSRPC: ..0..... = Not for an idempotent request -or- Did not execute guaranteed call (Fault PDU only) (AES/DC)
           MSRPC: .0...... = Not for a broadcast request -or- 'Maybe' call semantics not requested (AES/DC)
           MSRPC: 0....... = Reserved -or- No object UUID specified in the optional object field (AES/DC)
     MSRPC: Packed Data Representation
     MSRPC: Fragment Length = 72 (0x48)
     MSRPC: Authentication Length = 0 (0x0)
     MSRPC: Call Identifier = 8016848 (0x7A53D0)
     MSRPC: Max Trans Frag Size = 5680 (0x1630)
     MSRPC: Max Recv Frag Size = 5680 (0x1630)
     MSRPC: Assoc Group Identifier = 0 (0x0)
     MSRPC: Presentation Context List
        MSRPC: Number of Context Elements = 1 (0x1)
        MSRPC: Presentation Context Identifier = 0 (0x0)
        MSRPC: Number of Transfer Syntaxes = 1 (0x1)
        MSRPC: Abstract Interface UUID = 4B324FC8-1670-01D3-1278-5A47BF6EE188
        MSRPC: Abstract Interface Version = 3 (0x3)
        MSRPC: Transfer Interface UUID = 8A885D04-1CEB-11C9-9FE8-08002B104860
        MSRPC: Transfer Interface Version = 2 (0x2)

00000:  00 60 08 36 71 DE 00 00 C0 7A 2D 5C 08 00 45 00   .`.6q....z-\..E.
00010:  00 C8 AE 00 40 00 80 06 53 DD C7 F5 B4 01 C7 F5   ....@...S.......
00020:  B4 65 04 05 00 8B 00 1A 7D D4 00 06 B6 2A 50 18   .e......}....*P.
00030:  20 D2 77 B5 00 00 00 00 00 9C FF 53 4D 42 25 00    .w........SMB%.
00040:  00 00 00 18 03 80 68 FF 00 00 00 00 00 00 00 00   ......h.........
```

Figure 6.16  Embedding of MSRPC Bind command in SMB.

Packet 13 contains the RPC request whose `Operation Number` field is `c/o Request prop. dg header prop` (0x15). This operation number identifies the remote procedure that is executed.

After the RPC request is executed, packet 14 indicates that the share file (`\srvsvc`) that was opened in packet 11 is closed.

Packets 15 and 16 form a query for a primary domain controller. Packet 15 contains NETLOGON data that is sent encapsulated in an SMB packet (see Figure 6.17). The SMB packet is used to create a transaction, and sent using mailslots. Mailslot messages are sent as datagrams and not as part of a virtual circuit such as that created by TCP. As you examine Figure 6.17, you can see that the message is sent using the UDP datagram rather than a TCP packet.

```
FRAME: Base frame properties
     FRAME: Time of capture = May 9, 1998 17:2:15.6
     FRAME: Time delta from previous physical frame: 37 milliseconds
     FRAME: Frame number: 15
     FRAME: Total frame length: 270 bytes
     FRAME: Capture frame length: 270 bytes
     FRAME: Frame data: Number of data bytes remaining = 270 (0x010E)
ETHERNET: ETYPE = 0x0800 : Protocol = IP:  DOD Internet Protocol
     ETHERNET: Destination address : 0060083671DE
          ETHERNET: .......0 = Individual address
          ETHERNET: ......0. = Universally administered address
     ETHERNET: Source address : 0000C07A2D5C
          ETHERNET: .......0 = No routing information present
          ETHERNET: ......0. = Universally administered address
     ETHERNET: Frame Length : 270 (0x010E)
     ETHERNET: Ethernet Type : 0x0800 (IP:  DOD Internet Protocol)
     ETHERNET: Ethernet Data: Number of data bytes remaining = 256 (0x0100)
IP: ID = 0xB100; Proto = UDP; Len: 256
     IP: Version = 4 (0x4)
     IP: Header Length = 20 (0x14)
     IP: Service Type = 0 (0x0)
          IP: Precedence = Routine
          IP: ...0.... = Normal Delay
          IP: ....0... = Normal Throughput
          IP: .....0.. = Normal Reliability
     IP: Total Length = 256 (0x100)
     IP: Identification = 45312 (0xB100)
     IP: Flags Summary = 0 (0x0)
          IP: .......0 = Last fragment in datagram
          IP: ......0. = May fragment datagram if necessary
     IP: Fragment Offset = 0 (0x0) bytes
     IP: Time to Live = 128 (0x80)
     IP: Protocol = UDP - User Datagram
     IP: Checksum = 0x909A
     IP: Source Address = 199.245.180.1
     IP: Destination Address = 199.245.180.101
     IP: Data: Number of data bytes remaining = 236 (0x00EC)
UDP: Src Port: NETBIOS Datagram Service, (138); Dst Port: NETBIOS Datagram Service (138);
     Length = 236 (0xEC)
     UDP: Source Port = NETBIOS Datagram Service
     UDP: Destination Port = NETBIOS Datagram Service
     UDP: Total length = 236 (0xEC) bytes
     UDP: UDP Checksum = 0x6FB3
     UDP: Data: Number of data bytes remaining = 228 (0x00E4)
NBT: DS: Type = 16 (DIRECT UNIQUE)
     NBT: Datagram Packet Type = DIRECT UNIQUE
     NBT: Datagram Flags = 2 (0x2)
          NBT: 0000.... = Reserved
          NBT: ....00.. = B Node
          NBT: ......1. = First Packet
          NBT: .......0 = More Fragments Follow
     NBT: Datagram ID = 32938 (0x80AA)
```

```
      NBT: Source IP Address = 199.245.180.1
      NBT: Source Port = 138 (0x8A)
      NBT: Datagram Length = 214 (0xD6)
      NBT: Packet Offset = 0 (0x0)
      NBT: Source Name = LTREE1          <00>
      NBT: Destination Name = NTDOMAIN       <1B>
      NBT: DS Data: Number of data bytes remaining = 146 (0x0092)
   SMB: C transact, File = \MAILSLOT\NET\NETLOGON
      SMB: SMB Status = Error Success
         SMB: Error class = No Error
         SMB: Error code = No Error
      SMB: Header: PID = 0xCAFE TID = 0x0000 MID = 0x0000 UID = 0x0000
         SMB: Tree ID     (TID) = 0 (0x0)
         SMB: Process ID   (PID) = 51966 (0xCAFE)
         SMB: User ID     (UID) = 0 (0x0)
         SMB: Multiplex ID (MID) = 0 (0x0)
         SMB: Flags Summary = 24 (0x18)
            SMB: .......0 = Lock & Read and Write & Unlock not supported
            SMB: ......0. = Send No Ack not supported
            SMB: ....1... = Using caseless pathnames
            SMB: ...1.... = Canonicalized pathnames
            SMB: ..0..... = No Opportunistic lock
            SMB: .0...... = No Change Notify
            SMB: 0....... = Client command
         SMB: flags2 Summary = 3 (0x3)
            SMB: ...............1 = Understands long filenames
            SMB: ..............1. = Understands extended attributes
            SMB: ...0............ = No DFS capabilities
            SMB: ..0............. = No paging of IO
            SMB: .0.............. = Using SMB status codes
            SMB: 0............... = Using ASCII strings
      SMB: Command = C transact
         SMB: Word count = 17
         SMB: Word parameters
         SMB: Total parm bytes = 0
         SMB: Total data bytes = 54
         SMB: Max parm bytes = 2
         SMB: Max data bytes = 0
         SMB: Max setup words = 0 (0x0)
         SMB: Transact Flags Summary = 2 (0x2)
            SMB: ..............0 = Leave session intact
            SMB: ..............1. = No response required
         SMB: Transact timeout = 4294967295 (0xFFFFFFFF)
         SMB: Parameter bytes = 0 (0x0)
         SMB: Parameter offset = 92 (0x5C)
         SMB: Data bytes = 54 (0x36)
         SMB: Data offset = 92 (0x5C)
         SMB: Max setup words = 3
         SMB: Setup words
         SMB: Mailslot opcode = Write mailslot
         SMB: Transaction priority = 0
         SMB: Mailslot class = Unreliable (broadcast)
         SMB: Byte count = 77
         SMB: Byte parameters
         SMB: File name = \MAILSLOT\NET\NETLOGON
         SMB: Transaction data
      SMB: Data: Number of data bytes remaining = 54 (0x0036)
   NETLOGON: Query for Primary DC
      NETLOGON: Opcode = Query for Primary DC
      NETLOGON: Computer Name = LTREE1
      NETLOGON: Mailslot Name = \MAILSLOT\NET\GETDC995
      NETLOGON: Unicode Computer Name = LTREE1
      NETLOGON: NT Version = 1 (0x1)
      NETLOGON: LMNT Token = WindowsNT Networking
      NETLOGON: LM20 Token = OS/2 LAN Manager 2.0 (or later) Networking

00000:  00 60 08 36 71 DE 00 00 C0 7A 2D 5C 08 00 45 00   .`.6q....z-\..E.
00010:  01 00 B1 00 00 00 80 11 90 9A C7 F5 B4 01 C7 F5   ................
00020:  B4 65 00 8A 00 8A 00 EC 6F B3 10 02 80 AA C7 F5   .e......o.......
00030:  B4 01 00 8A 00 D6 00 00 20 45 4D 46 45 46 43 45   ........ EMFEFCE
00040:  46 45 46 44 42 43 41 43 41 43 41 43 41 43 41 43   FEFDBCACACACACAC
```

Figure 6.17   NETLOGON data sent in an SMB packet.

Packets 17 to 19 are used to create a connection to the SAM database (\samr), and send an RPC operation, 0x39. Note that the repeated pattern for the RPC call consists of an MSRPC bind request followed by the RPC containing the operation number.

Packets 20 to 48 are used to create a connection to the local security agent RPC (\lsarpc) under different modes, and sent a series of RPC operations.

The purpose of the RPC operations sent from packets 17 to 48 is to authenticate the NT workstation, LTREE1, to the domain NTDOMAIN. Also, a computer account is created on the domain controller NTSRVR for the member computer LTREE1.

Packet 49 is used to disconnect from the tree resource (see Figure 6.18) and packet 50 is used to log off the network connection (see Figure 6.19).

```
FRAME: Base frame properties
    FRAME: Time of capture = May 9, 1998 17:2:20.88
    FRAME: Time delta from previous physical frame: 19 milliseconds
    FRAME: Frame number: 49
    FRAME: Total frame length: 93 bytes
    FRAME: Capture frame length: 93 bytes
    FRAME: Frame data: Number of data bytes remaining = 93 (0x005D)
ETHERNET: ETYPE = 0x0800 : Protocol = IP:  DOD Internet Protocol
    ETHERNET: Destination address : 0060083671DE
        ETHERNET: .......0 = Individual address
        ETHERNET: ......0. = Universally administered address
    ETHERNET: Source address : 0000C07A2D5C
        ETHERNET: .......0 = No routing information present
        ETHERNET: ......0. = Universally administered address
    ETHERNET: Frame Length : 93 (0x005D)
    ETHERNET: Ethernet Type : 0x0800 (IP:  DOD Internet Protocol)
    ETHERNET: Ethernet Data: Number of data bytes remaining = 79 (0x004F)
IP: ID = 0xD300; Proto = TCP; Len: 79
    IP: Version = 4 (0x4)
    IP: Header Length = 20 (0x14)
    IP: Service Type = 0 (0x0)
        IP: Precedence = Routine
        IP: ...0.... = Normal Delay
        IP: ....0... = Normal Throughput
        IP: .....0.. = Normal Reliability
    IP: Total Length = 79 (0x4F)
    IP: Identification = 54016 (0xD300)
    IP: Flags Summary = 2 (0x2)
        IP: .......0 = Last fragment in datagram
        IP: ......1. = Cannot fragment datagram
    IP: Fragment Offset = 0 (0x0) bytes
    IP: Time to Live = 128 (0x80)
    IP: Protocol = TCP - Transmission Control
    IP: Checksum = 0x2F56
    IP: Source Address = 199.245.180.1
    IP: Destination Address = 199.245.180.101
    IP: Data: Number of data bytes remaining = 59 (0x003B)
TCP: .AP..., len:   39, seq:   1741233-1741271, ack:    443293, win: 7984, src: 1029
    dst:  139 (NBT Session)
    TCP: Source Port = 0x0405
    TCP: Destination Port = NETBIOS Session Service
    TCP: Sequence Number = 1741233 (0x1A91B1)
    TCP: Acknowledgement Number = 443293 (0x6C39D)
    TCP: Data Offset = 20 (0x14)
    TCP: Reserved = 0 (0x0000)
    TCP: Flags = 0x18 : .AP...
        TCP: ..0..... = No urgent data
        TCP: ...1.... = Acknowledgement field significant
        TCP: ....1... = Push function
        TCP: .....0.. = No Reset
        TCP: ......0. = No Synchronize
        TCP: .......0 = No Fin
```

```
        TCP: Window = 7984 (0x1F30)
        TCP: Checksum = 0xBDEE
        TCP: Urgent Pointer = 0 (0x0)
        TCP: Data: Number of data bytes remaining = 39 (0x0027)
  NBT: SS: Session Message, Len: 35
        NBT: Packet Type = Session Message
        NBT: Packet Flags = 0 (0x0)
            NBT: .......0 = Add 0 to Length
        NBT: Packet Length = 35 (0x23)
        NBT: SS Data: Number of data bytes remaining = 35 (0x0023)
  SMB: C tree disconnect
        SMB: SMB Status = Error Success
            SMB: Error class = No Error
            SMB: Error code = No Error
        SMB: Header: PID = 0xCAFE TID = 0x0800 MID = 0x08C0 UID = 0x0800
            SMB: Tree ID     (TID) = 2048 (0x800)
            SMB: Process ID  (PID) = 51966 (0xCAFE)
            SMB: User ID     (UID) = 2048 (0x800)
            SMB: Multiplex ID (MID) = 2240 (0x8C0)
            SMB: Flags Summary = 24 (0x18)
                SMB: .......0 = Lock & Read and Write & Unlock not supported
                SMB: ......0. = Send No Ack not supported
                SMB: ....1... = Using caseless pathnames
                SMB: ...1.... = Canonicalized pathnames
                SMB: ..0..... = No Opportunistic lock
                SMB: .0...... = No Change Notify
                SMB: 0....... = Client command
            SMB: flags2 Summary = 32771 (0x8003)
                SMB: ...............1 = Understands long filenames
                SMB: ..............1. = Understands extended attributes
                SMB: ...0............ = No DFS capabilities
                SMB: ..0............. = No paging of IO
                SMB: .0.............. = Using SMB status codes
                SMB: 1............... = Using UNICODE strings
        SMB: Command = C tree disconnect
            SMB: Word count = 0
            SMB: Byte count = 0

00000:  00 60 08 36 71 DE 00 00 C0 7A 2D 5C 08 00 45 00   .`.6q....z-\..E.
00010:  00 4F D3 00 40 00 80 06 2F 56 C7 F5 B4 01 C7 F5   .O..@.../V......
00020:  B4 65 04 05 00 8B 00 1A 91 B1 00 06 C3 9D 50 18   .e............P.
00030:  1F 30 BD EE 00 00 00 00 00 00 23 FF 53 4D 42 71 00   .0.......#.SMBq.
00040:  00 00 00 18 03 80 00 00 00 00 00 00 00 00 00 00   ................
```

Figure 6.18   SMB c tree disconnect packet.

```
  FRAME: Base frame properties
        FRAME: Time of capture = May 9, 1998 17:2:20.90
        FRAME: Time delta from previous physical frame: 2 milliseconds
        FRAME: Frame number: 50
        FRAME: Total frame length: 97 bytes
        FRAME: Capture frame length: 97 bytes
        FRAME: Frame data: Number of data bytes remaining = 97 (0x0061)
  ETHERNET: ETYPE = 0x0800 : Protocol = IP:  DOD Internet Protocol
        ETHERNET: Destination address : 0060083671DE
            ETHERNET: .......0 = Individual address
            ETHERNET: ......0. = Universally administered address
        ETHERNET: Source address : 0000C07A2D5C
            ETHERNET: .......0 = No routing information present
            ETHERNET: ......0. = Universally administered address
        ETHERNET: Frame Length : 97 (0x0061)
        ETHERNET: Ethernet Type : 0x0800 (IP:  DOD Internet Protocol)
        ETHERNET: Ethernet Data: Number of data bytes remaining = 83 (0x0053)
  IP: ID = 0xD400; Proto = TCP; Len: 83
        IP: Version = 4 (0x4)
        IP: Header Length = 20 (0x14)
        IP: Service Type = 0 (0x0)
            IP: Precedence = Routine
```

```
        IP: ...0.... = Normal Delay
        IP: ....0... = Normal Throughput
        IP: .....0.. = Normal Reliability
    IP: Total Length = 83 (0x53)
    IP: Identification = 54272 (0xD400)
    IP: Flags Summary = 2 (0x2)
        IP: .......0 = Last fragment in datagram
        IP: ......1. = Cannot fragment datagram
    IP: Fragment Offset = 0 (0x0) bytes
    IP: Time to Live = 128 (0x80)
    IP: Protocol = TCP - Transmission Control
    IP: Checksum = 0x2E52
    IP: Source Address = 199.245.180.1
    IP: Destination Address = 199.245.180.101
    IP: Data: Number of data bytes remaining = 63 (0x003F)
TCP: .AP..., len:   43, seq:    1741272-1741314, ack:     443332, win: 7945, src: 1029
        dst:   139 (NBT Session)
    TCP: Source Port = 0x0405
    TCP: Destination Port = NETBIOS Session Service
    TCP: Sequence Number = 1741272 (0x1A91D8)
    TCP: Acknowledgement Number = 443332 (0x6C3C4)
    TCP: Data Offset = 20 (0x14)
    TCP: Reserved = 0 (0x0000)
    TCP: Flags = 0x18 : .AP...
        TCP: ..0..... = No urgent data
        TCP: ...1.... = Acknowledgement field significant
        TCP: ....1... = Push function
        TCP: .....0.. = No Reset
        TCP: ......0. = No Synchronize
        TCP: .......0 = No Fin
    TCP: Window = 7945 (0x1F09)
    TCP: Checksum = 0x77C0
    TCP: Urgent Pointer = 0 (0x0)
    TCP: Data: Number of data bytes remaining = 43 (0x002B)
NBT: SS: Session Message, Len: 39
    NBT: Packet Type = Session Message
    NBT: Packet Flags = 0 (0x0)
        NBT: .......0 = Add 0 to Length
    NBT: Packet Length = 39 (0x27)
    NBT: SS Data: Number of data bytes remaining = 39 (0x0027)
SMB: C logoff & X
    SMB: SMB Status = Error Success
        SMB: Error class = No Error
        SMB: Error code = No Error
    SMB: Header: PID = 0xCAFE TID = 0x0800 MID = 0x0900 UID = 0x0800
        SMB: Tree ID      (TID) = 2048 (0x800)
        SMB: Process ID   (PID) = 51966 (0xCAFE)
        SMB: User ID      (UID) = 2048 (0x800)
        SMB: Multiplex ID (MID) = 2304 (0x900)
        SMB: Flags Summary = 24 (0x18)
            SMB: .......0 = Lock & Read and Write & Unlock not supported
            SMB: ......0. = Send No Ack not supported
            SMB: ....1... = Using caseless pathnames
            SMB: ...1.... = Canonicalized pathnames
            SMB: ..0..... = No Opportunistic lock
            SMB: .0...... = No Change Notify
            SMB: 0....... = Client command
        SMB: flags2 Summary = 32771 (0x8003)
            SMB: ...............1 = Understands long filenames
            SMB: ..............1. = Understands extended attributes
            SMB: ...0............ = No DFS capabilities
            SMB: ..0............. = No paging of IO
            SMB: .0.............. = Using SMB status codes
            SMB: 1............... = Using UNICODE strings
    SMB: Command = C logoff & X
        SMB: Word count = 2
        SMB: Word parameters
        SMB: Next offset = 0xFFFF
    SMB: Command = No secondary command
```

```
00000:   00 60 08 36 71 DE 00 00 C0 7A 2D 5C 08 00 45 00    .`.6q....z-\..E.
00010:   00 53 D4 00 40 00 80 06 2E 52 C7 F5 B4 01 C7 F5    .S..@....R......
00020:   B4 65 04 05 00 8B 00 1A 91 D8 00 06 C3 C4 50 18    .e............P.
00030:   1F 09 77 C0 00 00 00 00 00 00 27 FF 53 4D 42 74 00    ..w......'.SMBt.
00040:   00 00 00 18 03 80 00 00 00 00 00 00 00 00 00 00    ................
```

**Figure 6.19**   SMB C Logoff & X packet.

## TCP/IP Trace for Browser Activation

This section discusses the network traffic produced when a user performs a browse operation. The browse operation is typically performed when you try to list the share names on the network to make a connection to. For example, you can do this by using the Network Neighborhood, through the Windows Explorer, or by right-clicking on the My Computer icon on the desktop and selecting Map Network Drive.

Figure 6.20 shows a summary of the trace file produced by a browse operation.

Packets 1 and 2 indicate the creation of a TCP session over which the browser data is sent. You can see this by observing that the S (SYN) flag is set in packet 1 indicating the creation of a TCP session (see Figure 6.21).

```
Network Monitor trace   Mon 05/11/98 22:37:32   D:\WINNT\system32\NETMON\CAPTURES\browses.txt

Frame    Time    Src MAC Addr    Dst MAC Addr    Protocol   Description
                                                 Src Other Addr  Dst Other Addr  Type Other Addr

1        12.117  LTREE1          NTSRVR          TCP        ....S., len:    4,
    seq:  3757693-3757696, ack:        0, win: 8 LTREE1            NTSRVR          IP
2        12.118  LTREE1          NTSRVR          TCP        .A...., len:    0,
    seq:  3757694-3757694, ack:  4572065, win: 8 LTREE1            NTSRVR          IP
3        12.118  LTREE1          NTSRVR          NBT        SS: Session Request,
    Dest: NTSRVR          , Source: LTREE1        LTREE1            NTSRVR          IP
4        12.121  LTREE1          NTSRVR          SMB        C negotiate, Dialect = NT LM 0.12
                                                 LTREE1            NTSRVR          IP
5        12.147  LTREE1          NTSRVR          SMB        C session setup & X,
    Username = Administrator, and C tree connect LTREE1            NTSRVR          IP
6        12.156  LTREE1          NTSRVR          SMB        C NT create & X, File = \srvsvc
                                                 LTREE1            NTSRVR          IP
7        12.161  LTREE1          NTSRVR          MSRPC      c/o RPC Bind:
    UUID 4B324FC8-1670-01D3-1278-5A47BF6EE188    LTREE1            NTSRVR          IP
8        12.165  LTREE1          NTSRVR          MSRPC      c/o RPC Request:
    call 0x1  opnum 0xF  context 0x0  hint 0x40 LTREE1            NTSRVR          IP
9        12.170  LTREE1          NTSRVR          SMB        C close file, FID = 0x800
                                                 LTREE1            NTSRVR          IP
10       12.301  LTREE1          NTSRVR          TCP        .A...., len:    0,
    seq:  3758696-3758696, ack:  4573082, win: 7 LTREE1            NTSRVR          IP
```

**Figure 6.20**   Trace file for a browse operation.

```
FRAME: Base frame properties
    FRAME: Time of capture = May 9, 1998 18:11:7.53
    FRAME: Time delta from previous physical frame: 0 milliseconds
    FRAME: Frame number: 1
    FRAME: Total frame length: 60 bytes
    FRAME: Capture frame length: 60 bytes
    FRAME: Frame data: Number of data bytes remaining = 60 (0x003C)
ETHERNET: ETYPE = 0x0800 : Protocol = IP:  DOD Internet Protocol
    ETHERNET: Destination address : 0060083671DE
        ETHERNET: .......0 = Individual address
        ETHERNET: ......0. = Universally administered address
```

```
        ETHERNET: Source address : 0000C07A2D5C
          ETHERNET: .......0 = No routing information present
          ETHERNET: ......0. = Universally administered address
        ETHERNET: Frame Length : 60 (0x003C)
        ETHERNET: Ethernet Type : 0x0800 (IP: DOD Internet Protocol)
        ETHERNET: Ethernet Data: Number of data bytes remaining = 46 (0x002E)
IP: ID = 0x8E00; Proto = TCP; Len: 44
    IP: Version = 4 (0x4)
    IP: Header Length = 20 (0x14)
    IP: Service Type = 0 (0x0)
        IP: Precedence = Routine
        IP: ...0.... = Normal Delay
        IP: ....0... = Normal Throughput
        IP: .....0.. = Normal Reliability
    IP: Total Length = 44 (0x2C)
    IP: Identification = 36352 (0x8E00)
    IP: Flags Summary = 2 (0x2)
        IP: .......0 = Last fragment in datagram
        IP: ......1. = Cannot fragment datagram
    IP: Fragment Offset = 0 (0x0) bytes
    IP: Time to Live = 128 (0x80)
    IP: Protocol = TCP - Transmission Control
    IP: Checksum = 0x7479
    IP: Source Address = 199.245.180.1
    IP: Destination Address = 199.245.180.101
    IP: Data: Number of data bytes remaining = 24 (0x0018)
TCP: ....S., len:    4, seq:    3757693-3757696, ack:        0, win: 8192, src: 1033
      dst:  139 (NBT Session)
    TCP: Source Port = 0x0409
    TCP: Destination Port = NETBIOS Session Service
    TCP: Sequence Number = 3757693 (0x39567D)
    TCP: Acknowledgement Number = 0 (0x0)
    TCP: Data Offset = 24 (0x18)
    TCP: Reserved = 0 (0x0000)
    TCP: Flags = 0x02 : ....S.
        TCP: ..0..... = No urgent data
        TCP: ...0.... = Acknowledgement field not significant
        TCP: ....0... = No Push function
        TCP: .....0.. = No Reset
        TCP: ......1. = Synchronize sequence numbers
        TCP: .......0 = No Fin
    TCP: Window = 8192 (0x2000)
    TCP: Checksum = 0x248A
    TCP: Urgent Pointer = 0 (0x0)
    TCP: Options
            TCP: Option Kind (Maximum Segment Size) = 2 (0x2)
            TCP: Option Length = 4 (0x4)
            TCP: Option Value = 1460 (0x5B4)
    TCP: Frame Padding

00000:  00 60 08 36 71 DE 00 00 C0 7A 2D 5C 08 00 45 00    .`.6q....z-\..E.
00010:  00 2C 8E 00 40 00 80 06 74 79 C7 F5 B4 01 C7 F5    .,..@...ty......
00020:  B4 65 04 09 00 8B 00 39 56 7D 00 00 00 00 60 02    .e.....9V}....`.
00030:  20 00 24 8A 00 00 02 04 05 B4 4D 46                 .$.......MF
```

**Figure 6.21**  TCP open connection packet.

Packet 3 is used to create a NetBIOS session using NBT (see Figure 6.22). Note that the NBT frame contains the following information:

```
NBT: Packet Type = Session Request
NBT: Packet Flags = 0 (0x0)
    NBT: .......0 = Add 0 to Length
NBT: Packet Length = 68 (0x44)
NBT: Called Name = NTSRVR
NBT: Calling Name = LTREE1          <00>
```

```
FRAME: Base frame properties
    FRAME: Time of capture = May 9, 1998 18:11:7.54
    FRAME: Time delta from previous physical frame: 0 milliseconds
    FRAME: Frame number: 3
    FRAME: Total frame length: 126 bytes
    FRAME: Capture frame length: 126 bytes
    FRAME: Frame data: Number of data bytes remaining = 126 (0x007E)
ETHERNET: ETYPE = 0x0800 : Protocol = IP:  DOD Internet Protocol
    ETHERNET: Destination address : 0060083671DE
        ETHERNET: .......0 = Individual address
        ETHERNET: ......0. = Universally administered address
    ETHERNET: Source address : 0000C07A2D5C
        ETHERNET: .......0 = No routing information present
        ETHERNET: ......0. = Universally administered address
    ETHERNET: Frame Length : 126 (0x007E)
    ETHERNET: Ethernet Type : 0x0800 (IP:  DOD Internet Protocol)
    ETHERNET: Ethernet Data: Number of data bytes remaining = 112 (0x0070)
IP: ID = 0x9000; Proto = TCP; Len: 112
    IP: Version = 4 (0x4)
    IP: Header Length = 20 (0x14)
    IP: Service Type = 0 (0x0)
        IP: Precedence = Routine
        IP: ...0.... = Normal Delay
        IP: ....0... = Normal Throughput
        IP: .....0.. = Normal Reliability
    IP: Total Length = 112 (0x70)
    IP: Identification = 36864 (0x9000)
    IP: Flags Summary = 2 (0x2)
        IP: .......0 = Last fragment in datagram
        IP: ......1. = Cannot fragment datagram
    IP: Fragment Offset = 0 (0x0) bytes
    IP: Time to Live = 128 (0x80)
    IP: Protocol = TCP - Transmission Control
    IP: Checksum = 0x7235
    IP: Source Address = 199.245.180.1
    IP: Destination Address = 199.245.180.101
    IP: Data: Number of data bytes remaining = 92 (0x005C)
TCP: .AP..., len:   72, seq:   3757694-3757765, ack:   4572065, win: 8760, src: 1033
        dst:   139 (NBT Session)
    TCP: Source Port = 0x0409
    TCP: Destination Port = NETBIOS Session Service
    TCP: Sequence Number = 3757694 (0x39567E)
    TCP: Acknowledgement Number = 4572065 (0x45C3A1)
    TCP: Data Offset = 20 (0x14)
    TCP: Reserved = 0 (0x0000)
    TCP: Flags = 0x18 : .AP...
        TCP: ..0..... = No urgent data
        TCP: ...1.... = Acknowledgement field significant
        TCP: ....1... = Push function
        TCP: .....0.. = No Reset
        TCP: ......0. = No Synchronize
        TCP: .......0 = No Fin
    TCP: Window = 8760 (0x2238)
    TCP: Checksum = 0x4FFF
    TCP: Urgent Pointer = 0 (0x0)
    TCP: Data: Number of data bytes remaining = 72 (0x0048)
NBT: SS: Session Request, Dest: NTSRVR        , Source: LTREE1        <00>, Len: 68
    NBT: Packet Type = Session Request
    NBT: Packet Flags = 0 (0x0)
        NBT: .......0 = Add 0 to Length
    NBT: Packet Length = 68 (0x44)
    NBT: Called Name = NTSRVR
    NBT: Calling Name = LTREE1        <00>

00000:  00 60 08 36 71 DE 00 00 C0 7A 2D 5C 08 00 45 00   .`.6q....z-\..E.
00010:  00 70 90 00 40 00 80 06 72 35 C7 F5 B4 01 C7 F5   .p..@...r5......
00020:  B4 65 04 09 00 8B 00 39 56 7E 00 45 C3 A1 50 18   .e.....9V~.E..P.
00030:  22 38 4F FF 00 00 81 00 00 44 20 45 4F 46 45 46   "80......D EOFEF
00040:  44 46 43 46 47 46 43 43 41 43 41 43 41 43 41 43   DFCFGFCCACACACAC
```

Figure 6.22  NBT Session Create packet.

```
FRAME: Base frame properties
    FRAME: Time of capture = May 9, 1998 18:11:7.57
    FRAME: Time delta from previous physical frame: 3 milliseconds
    FRAME: Frame number: 4
    FRAME: Total frame length: 228 bytes
    FRAME: Capture frame length: 228 bytes
    FRAME: Frame data: Number of data bytes remaining = 228 (0x00E4)
ETHERNET: ETYPE = 0x0800 : Protocol = IP:  DOD Internet Protocol
    ETHERNET: Destination address : 0060083671DE
        ETHERNET: .......0 = Individual address
        ETHERNET: ......0. = Universally administered address
    ETHERNET: Source address : 0000C07A2D5C
        ETHERNET: .......0 = No routing information present
        ETHERNET: ......0. = Universally administered address
    ETHERNET: Frame Length : 228 (0x00E4)
    ETHERNET: Ethernet Type : 0x0800 (IP:  DOD Internet Protocol)
    ETHERNET: Ethernet Data: Number of data bytes remaining = 214 (0x00D6)
IP: ID = 0x9100; Proto = TCP; Len: 214
    IP: Version = 4 (0x4)
    IP: Header Length = 20 (0x14)
    IP: Service Type = 0 (0x0)
        IP: Precedence = Routine
        IP: ...0.... = Normal Delay
        IP: ....0... = Normal Throughput
        IP: .....0.. = Normal Reliability
    IP: Total Length = 214 (0xD6)
    IP: Identification = 37120 (0x9100)
    IP: Flags Summary = 2 (0x2)
        IP: .......0 = Last fragment in datagram
        IP: ......1. = Cannot fragment datagram
    IP: Fragment Offset = 0 (0x0) bytes
    IP: Time to Live = 128 (0x80)
    IP: Protocol = TCP - Transmission Control
    IP: Checksum = 0x70CF
    IP: Source Address = 199.245.180.1
    IP: Destination Address = 199.245.180.101
    IP: Data: Number of data bytes remaining = 194 (0x00C2)
TCP: .AP..., len:  174, seq:   3757766-3757939, ack:   4572069, win: 8756, src: 1033
    dst:  139 (NBT Session)
    TCP: Source Port = 0x0409
    TCP: Destination Port = NETBIOS Session Service
    TCP: Sequence Number = 3757766 (0x3956C6)
    TCP: Acknowledgement Number = 4572069 (0x45C3A5)
    TCP: Data Offset = 20 (0x14)
    TCP: Reserved = 0 (0x0000)
    TCP: Flags = 0x18 : .AP...
        TCP: ..0..... = No urgent data
        TCP: ...1.... = Acknowledgement field significant
        TCP: ....1... = Push function
        TCP: .....0.. = No Reset
        TCP: ......0. = No Synchronize
        TCP: .......0 = No Fin
    TCP: Window = 8756 (0x2234)
    TCP: Checksum = 0x7D00
    TCP: Urgent Pointer = 0 (0x0)
    TCP: Data: Number of data bytes remaining = 174 (0x00AE)
NBT: SS: Session Message, Len: 170
    NBT: Packet Type = Session Message
    NBT: Packet Flags = 0 (0x0)
        NBT: .......0 = Add 0 to Length
    NBT: Packet Length = 170 (0xAA)
    NBT: SS Data: Number of data bytes remaining = 170 (0x00AA)
SMB: C negotiate, Dialect = NT LM 0.12
    SMB: SMB Status = Error Success
        SMB: Error class = No Error
        SMB: Error code = No Error
    SMB: Header: PID = 0xCAFE TID = 0x0000 MID = 0x0000 UID = 0x0000
        SMB: Tree ID       (TID) = 0 (0x0)
        SMB: Process ID    (PID) = 51966 (0xCAFE)
        SMB: User ID       (UID) = 0 (0x0)
        SMB: Multiplex ID (MID) = 0 (0x0)
        SMB: Flags Summary = 24 (0x18)
```

```
        SMB: flags2 Summary = 3 (0x3)
            SMB: .............1 = Understands long filenames
            SMB: ............1. = Understands extended attributes
            SMB: ...0............ = No DFS capabilities
            SMB: ..0............. = No paging of IO
            SMB: .0.............. = Using SMB status codes
            SMB: 0............... = Using ASCII strings
    SMB: Command = C negotiate
        SMB: Word count = 0
        SMB: Byte count = 135
        SMB: Byte parameters
        SMB: Dialect Strings Understood
            SMB: Dialect String = PC NETWORK PROGRAM 1.0
            SMB: Dialect String = XENIX CORE
            SMB: Dialect String = MICROSOFT NETWORKS 1.03
            SMB: Dialect String = LANMAN1.0
            SMB: Dialect String = Windows for Workgroups 3.1a
            SMB: Dialect String = LM1.2X002
            SMB: Dialect String = LANMAN2.1
            SMB: Dialect String = NT LM 0.12
00000:  00 60 08 36 71 DE 00 00 C0 7A 2D 5C 08 00 45 00   .`.6q....z-\..E.
00010:  00 D6 91 00 40 00 80 06 70 CF C7 F5 B4 01 C7 F5   ....@...p.......
00020:  B4 65 04 09 00 8B 00 39 56 C6 00 45 C3 A5 50 18   .e.....9V..E..P.
00030:  22 34 7D 00 00 00 00 00 00 AA FF 53 4D 42 72 00   "4}........SMBr.
00040:  00 00 00 18 03 00 00 00 00 00 00 00 00 00 00 00   ................
```

**Figure 6.22**   NBT Session Create packet.

The `Called Name` is the name of the NetBIOS node at the remote end (NTSRVR), and the `Calling Name` is the name of the originator of the session (LTREE1).

Packet 4 is used to negotiate the SMB dialect to be used (see Figure 6.23). The byte parameters under the `C negotiate` section list the SMB dialects that the client understands.

```
    FRAME: Base frame properties
        FRAME: Time of capture = May 9, 1998 18:11:7.57
        FRAME: Time delta from previous physical frame: 3 milliseconds
        FRAME: Frame number: 4
        FRAME: Total frame length: 228 bytes
        FRAME: Capture frame length: 228 bytes
        FRAME: Frame data: Number of data bytes remaining = 228 (0x00E4)
    ETHERNET: ETYPE = 0x0800 : Protocol = IP:  DOD Internet Protocol
        ETHERNET: Destination address : 0060083671DE
            ETHERNET: .......0 = Individual address
            ETHERNET: ......0. = Universally administered address
        ETHERNET: Source address : 0000C07A2D5C
            ETHERNET: .......0 = No routing information present
            ETHERNET: ......0. = Universally administered address
        ETHERNET: Frame Length : 228 (0x00E4)
        ETHERNET: Ethernet Type : 0x0800 (IP:  DOD Internet Protocol)
        ETHERNET: Ethernet Data: Number of data bytes remaining = 214 (0x00D6)
    IP: ID = 0x9100; Proto = TCP; Len: 214
        IP: Version = 4 (0x4)
        IP: Header Length = 20 (0x14)
        IP: Service Type = 0 (0x0)
            IP: Precedence = Routine
            IP: ...0.... = Normal Delay
            IP: ....0... = Normal Throughput
            IP: .....0.. = Normal Reliability
        IP: Total Length = 214 (0xD6)
        IP: Identification = 37120 (0x9100)
        IP: Flags Summary = 2 (0x2)
            IP: .......0 = Last fragment in datagram
            IP: ......1. = Cannot fragment datagram
        IP: Fragment Offset = 0 (0x0) bytes
        IP: Time to Live = 128 (0x80)
        IP: Protocol = TCP - Transmission Control
        IP: Checksum = 0x70CF
```

```
    IP: Source Address = 199.245.180.1
    IP: Destination Address = 199.245.180.101
    IP: Data: Number of data bytes remaining = 194 (0x00C2)
TCP: .AP..., len:  174, seq:   3757766-3757939, ack:   4572069, win: 8756, src: 1033
        dst: 139 (NBT Session)
    TCP: Source Port = 0x0409
    TCP: Destination Port = NETBIOS Session Service
    TCP: Sequence Number = 3757766 (0x3956C6)
    TCP: Acknowledgement Number = 4572069 (0x45C3A5)
    TCP: Data Offset = 20 (0x14)
    TCP: Reserved = 0 (0x0000)
    TCP: Flags = 0x18 : .AP...
        TCP: ..0..... = No urgent data
        TCP: ...1.... = Acknowledgement field significant
        TCP: ....1... = Push function
        TCP: .....0.. = No Reset
        TCP: ......0. = No Synchronize
        TCP: .......0 = No Fin
    TCP: Window = 8756 (0x2234)
    TCP: Checksum = 0x7D00
    TCP: Urgent Pointer = 0 (0x0)
    TCP: Data: Number of data bytes remaining = 174 (0x00AE)
NBT: SS: Session Message, Len: 170
    NBT: Packet Type = Session Message
    NBT: Packet Flags = 0 (0x0)
        NBT: .......0 = Add 0 to Length
    NBT: Packet Length = 170 (0xAA)
    NBT: SS Data: Number of data bytes remaining = 170 (0x00AA)
SMB: C negotiate, Dialect = NT LM 0.12
    SMB: SMB Status = Error Success
        SMB: Error class = No Error
        SMB: Error code = No Error
    SMB: Header: PID = 0xCAFE TID = 0x0000 MID = 0x0000 UID = 0x0000
        SMB: Tree ID      (TID) = 0 (0x0)
        SMB: Process ID   (PID) = 51966 (0xCAFE)
        SMB: User ID      (UID) = 0 (0x0)
        SMB: Multiplex ID (MID) = 0 (0x0)
        SMB: Flags Summary = 24 (0x18)
            SMB: .......0 = Lock & Read and Write & Unlock not supported
            SMB: ......0. = Send No Ack not supported
            SMB: ....1... = Using caseless pathnames
            SMB: ...1.... = Canonicalized pathnames
            SMB: ..0..... = No Opportunistic lock
            SMB: .0...... = No Change Notify
            SMB: 0....... = Client command
        SMB: flags2 Summary = 3 (0x3)
            SMB: ..............1 = Understands long filenames
            SMB: .............1. = Understands extended attributes
            SMB: ...0.......... = No DFS capabilities
            SMB: ..0........... = No paging of IO
            SMB: .0............ = Using SMB status codes
            SMB: 0............. = Using ASCII strings
    SMB: Command = C negotiate
        SMB: Word count = 0
        SMB: Byte count = 135
        SMB: Byte parameters
        SMB: Dialect Strings Understood
            SMB: Dialect String = PC NETWORK PROGRAM 1.0
            SMB: Dialect String = XENIX CORE
            SMB: Dialect String = MICROSOFT NETWORKS 1.03
            SMB: Dialect String = LANMAN1.0
            SMB: Dialect String = Windows for Workgroups 3.1a
            SMB: Dialect String = LM1.2X002
            SMB: Dialect String = LANMAN2.1
            SMB: Dialect String = NT LM 0.12

00000:  00 60 08 36 71 DE 00 00 C0 7A 2D 5C 08 00 45 00    .`.6q....z-\..E.
00010:  00 D6 91 00 40 00 80 06 70 CF C7 F5 B4 01 C7 F5    ....@...p.......
00020:  B4 65 04 09 00 8B 00 39 56 C6 00 45 C3 A5 50 18    .e.....9V..E..P.
00030:  22 34 7D 00 00 00 00 00 00 00 AA FF 53 4D 42 72 00   "4}........SMBr.
00040:  00 00 00 18 03 00 00 00 00 00 00 00 00 00 00 00    ................
```

Figure 6.23   SMB C Negotiate packet.

Packet 5 (see Figure 6.24) is used to create the session, pass the user name account (in this case the Administrator account) and NT domain, and connect to the share name \\NTSRVR\IPC$.

```
06-24  FRAME: Base frame properties
      FRAME: Time of capture = May 9, 1998 18:11:7.83
      FRAME: Time delta from previous physical frame: 26 milliseconds
      FRAME: Frame number: 5
      FRAME: Total frame length: 324 bytes
      FRAME: Capture frame length: 324 bytes
      FRAME: Frame data: Number of data bytes remaining = 324 (0x0144)
    ETHERNET: ETYPE = 0x0800 : Protocol = IP:  DOD Internet Protocol
      ETHERNET: Destination address : 0060083671DE
          ETHERNET: .......0 = Individual address
          ETHERNET: ......0. = Universally administered address
      ETHERNET: Source address : 0000C07A2D5C
          ETHERNET: .......0 = No routing information present
          ETHERNET: ......0. = Universally administered address
      ETHERNET: Frame Length : 324 (0x0144)
      ETHERNET: Ethernet Type : 0x0800 (IP:  DOD Internet Protocol)
      ETHERNET: Ethernet Data: Number of data bytes remaining = 310 (0x0136)
    IP: ID = 0x9200; Proto = TCP; Len: 310
      IP: Version = 4 (0x4)
      IP: Header Length = 20 (0x14)
      IP: Service Type = 0 (0x0)
          IP: Precedence = Routine
          IP: ...0.... = Normal Delay
          IP: ....0... = Normal Throughput
          IP: .....0.. = Normal Reliability
      IP: Total Length = 310 (0x136)
      IP: Identification = 37376 (0x9200)
      IP: Flags Summary = 2 (0x2)
          IP: .......0 = Last fragment in datagram
          IP: ......1. = Cannot fragment datagram
      IP: Fragment Offset = 0 (0x0) bytes
      IP: Time to Live = 128 (0x80)
      IP: Protocol = TCP - Transmission Control
      IP: Checksum = 0x6F6F
      IP: Source Address = 199.245.180.1
      IP: Destination Address = 199.245.180.101
      IP: Data: Number of data bytes remaining = 290 (0x0122)
    TCP: .AP..., len:  270, seq:  3757940-3758209, ack:   4572168, win: 8657, src: 1033
          dst:  139 (NBT Session)
      TCP: Source Port = 0x0409
      TCP: Destination Port = NETBIOS Session Service
      TCP: Sequence Number = 3757940 (0x395774)
      TCP: Acknowledgement Number = 4572168 (0x45C408)
      TCP: Data Offset = 20 (0x14)
      TCP: Reserved = 0 (0x0000)
      TCP: Flags = 0x18 : .AP...
          TCP: ..0..... = No urgent data
          TCP: ...1.... = Acknowledgement field significant
          TCP: ....1... = Push function
          TCP: .....0.. = No Reset
          TCP: ......0. = No Synchronize
          TCP: .......0 = No Fin
      TCP: Window = 8657 (0x21D1)
      TCP: Checksum = 0x7593
      TCP: Urgent Pointer = 0 (0x0)
      TCP: Data: Number of data bytes remaining = 270 (0x010E)
    NBT: SS: Session Message, Len: 266
      NBT: Packet Type = Session Message
      NBT: Packet Flags = 0 (0x0)
          NBT: .......0 = Add 0 to Length
      NBT: Packet Length = 266 (0x10A)
      NBT: SS Data: Number of data bytes remaining = 266 (0x010A)
    SMB: C session setup & X, Username = Administrator, and C tree connect & X,
       Share = \\NTSRVR\IPC$
      SMB: SMB Status = Error Success
          SMB: Error class = No Error
          SMB: Error code = No Error
```

```
SMB: Header: PID = 0xCAFE TID = 0x0000 MID = 0x0000 UID = 0x0000
       SMB: Tree ID      (TID) = 0 (0x0)
       SMB: Process ID   (PID) = 51966 (0xCAFE)
       SMB: User ID      (UID) = 0 (0x0)
       SMB: Multiplex ID (MID) = 0 (0x0)
       SMB: Flags Summary = 24 (0x18)
             SMB: .......0 = Lock & Read and Write & Unlock not supported
             SMB: ......0. = Send No Ack not supported
             SMB: ....1... = Using caseless pathnames
             SMB: ...1.... = Canonicalized pathnames
             SMB: ..0..... = No Opportunistic lock
             SMB: .0...... = No Change Notify
             SMB: 0....... = Client command
       SMB: flags2 Summary = 32771 (0x8003)
             SMB: ...............1 = Understands long filenames
             SMB: ..............1. = Understands extended attributes
             SMB: ...0............ = No DFS capabilities
             SMB: ..0............. = No paging of IO
             SMB: .0.............. = Using SMB status codes
             SMB: 1............... = Using UNICODE strings
SMB: Command = C session setup & X
       SMB: Word count = 13
       SMB: Word parameters
       SMB: Next offset = 0x00DE
       SMB: Max Buffer Size = 4356 (0x1104)
       SMB: Max MPX requests = 50
       SMB: VC number = 0
       SMB: Session Key = 0
       SMB: Password length = 24 (0x18)
       SMB: Unicode Password length = 24 (0x18)
       SMB: Capabilities = 212 (0xD4)
             SMB: ............................0 = No Raw Reads and Writes.
             SMB: ............................0. = No support for multiplexed commands.
             SMB: ...........................1.. = Supports UNICODE strings.
             SMB: ..........................0... = Does not support large files.
             SMB: .........................1.... = Supports the NT SMB extensions.
             SMB: ........................0..... = RPC remote API's not supported.
             SMB: .......................1...... = Recognizes NT Status codes.
             SMB: ......................1....... = Supports level II oplocks.
             SMB: .....................0........ = Does not support Lock and Read.
             SMB: ....................0......... = Does not support NT Find.
             SMB: ...................0.......... = Does not support bulk transfers.
             SMB: ..................0........... = Does not support compressed bulk transfers.
             SMB: .................0............ = This server is NOT DFS aware.
             SMB: ................0............. = ReadX responses must be within
                                                   negotiated buffer sizes.
       SMB: Byte count = 161
       SMB: Byte parameters
       SMB: Account name = Administrator
       SMB: Domain name = NTDOMAIN
       SMB: Native OS = Windows NT 1381
       SMB: Native Lanman = Windows NT 4.0
SMB: Command = C tree connect & X
       SMB: Word count = 4
       SMB: Word parameters
       SMB: Next offset = 0x0000
       SMB: Disconnect flag = 0x0000
       SMB: Password length = 1 (0x1)
       SMB: Byte count = 33
       SMB: Byte parameters
       SMB: Password =
       SMB: File name = \\NTSRVR\IPC$
       SMB: Service Name = IPC
SMB: Command = No secondary command

00000:  00 60 08 36 71 DE 00 00 C0 7A 2D 5C 08 00 45 00    .`.6q....z-\..E.
00010:  01 36 92 00 40 00 80 06 6F 6F C7 F5 B4 01 C7 F5    .6..@...oo......
00020:  B4 65 04 09 00 8B 00 39 57 74 00 45 C4 08 50 18    .e.....9Wt.E..P.
00030:  21 D1 75 93 00 00 00 01 0A FF 53 4D 42 73 00       !.u.......SMBs.
00040:  00 00 00 18 03 80 00 00 00 00 00 00 00 00 00 00    ................
```

**Figure 6.24**  SMB C session setup & X, Username = Administrator, and C tree connect.

Packet 6 (see Figure 6.25) is used to create a connection to the shared resource (\srvsvc).

```
FRAME: Base frame properties
      FRAME: Time of capture = May 9, 1998 18:11:7.92
      FRAME: Time delta from previous physical frame: 9 milliseconds
      FRAME: Frame number: 6
      FRAME: Total frame length: 158 bytes
      FRAME: Capture frame length: 158 bytes
      FRAME: Frame data: Number of data bytes remaining = 158 (0x009E)
ETHERNET: ETYPE = 0x0800 : Protocol = IP: DOD Internet Protocol
      ETHERNET: Destination address : 0060083671DE
          ETHERNET: .......0 = Individual address
          ETHERNET: ......0. = Universally administered address
      ETHERNET: Source address : 0000C07A2D5C
          ETHERNET: .......0 = No routing information present
          ETHERNET: ......0. = Universally administered address
      ETHERNET: Frame Length : 158 (0x009E)
      ETHERNET: Ethernet Type : 0x0800 (IP: DOD Internet Protocol)
      ETHERNET: Ethernet Data: Number of data bytes remaining = 144 (0x0090)
IP: ID = 0x9300; Proto = TCP; Len: 144
      IP: Version = 4 (0x4)
      IP: Header Length = 20 (0x14)
      IP: Service Type = 0 (0x0)
          IP: Precedence = Routine
          IP: ...0.... = Normal Delay
          IP: ....0... = Normal Throughput
          IP: .....0.. = Normal Reliability
      IP: Total Length = 144 (0x90)
      IP: Identification = 37632 (0x9300)
      IP: Flags Summary = 2 (0x2)
          IP: .......0 = Last fragment in datagram
          IP: ......1. = Cannot fragment datagram
      IP: Fragment Offset = 0 (0x0) bytes
      IP: Time to Live = 128 (0x80)
      IP: Protocol = TCP - Transmission Control
      IP: Checksum = 0x6F15
      IP: Source Address = 199.245.180.1
      IP: Destination Address = 199.245.180.101
      IP: Data: Number of data bytes remaining = 124 (0x007C)
TCP: .AP..., len:  104, seq:    3758210-3758313, ack:    4572316, win: 8509, src: 1033
      dst:  139 (NBT Session)
      TCP: Source Port = 0x0409
      TCP: Destination Port = NETBIOS Session Service
      TCP: Sequence Number = 3758210 (0x395882)
      TCP: Acknowledgement Number = 4572316 (0x45C49C)
      TCP: Data Offset = 20 (0x14)
      TCP: Reserved = 0 (0x0000)
      TCP: Flags = 0x18 : .AP...
          TCP: ..0..... = No urgent data
          TCP: ...1.... = Acknowledgement field significant
          TCP: ....1... = Push function
          TCP: .....0.. = No Reset
          TCP: ......0. = No Synchronize
          TCP: .......0 = No Fin
      TCP: Window = 8509 (0x213D)
      TCP: Checksum = 0xB47D
      TCP: Urgent Pointer = 0 (0x0)
      TCP: Data: Number of data bytes remaining = 104 (0x0068)
NBT: SS: Session Message, Len: 100
      NBT: Packet Type = Session Message
      NBT: Packet Flags = 0 (0x0)
          NBT: .......0 = Add 0 to Length
      NBT: Packet Length = 100 (0x64)
      NBT: SS Data: Number of data bytes remaining = 100 (0x0064)
SMB: C NT create & X, File = \srvsvc
      SMB: SMB Status = Error Success
          SMB: Error class = No Error
          SMB: Error code = No Error
      SMB: Header: PID = 0x0940 TID = 0x0801 MID = 0x0040 UID = 0x0801
          SMB: Tree ID    (TID) = 2049 (0x801)
          SMB: Process ID  (PID) = 2368 (0x940)
          SMB: User ID    (UID) = 2049 (0x801)
          SMB: Multiplex ID (MID) = 64 (0x40)
          SMB: Flags Summary = 24 (0x18)
              SMB: .......0 = Lock & Read and Write & Unlock not supported
              SMB: ......0. = Send No Ack not supported
              SMB: ....1... = Using caseless pathnames
              SMB: ...1.... = Canonicalized pathnames
              SMB: ..0..... = No Opportunistic lock
              SMB: .0...... = No Change Notify
              SMB: 0....... = Client command
          SMB: flags2 Summary = 32771 (0x8003)
              SMB: ..............1 = Understands long filenames
```

```
            SMB: .............1. = Understands extended attributes
            SMB: ...0............ = No DFS capabilities
            SMB: ..0............. = No paging of IO
            SMB: .0.............. = Using SMB status codes
            SMB: 1............... = Using UNICODE strings
       SMB: Command = R NT create & X
         SMB: Word count = 24
         SMB: Word parameters
         SMB: Next offset = 0x0000
         SMB: Word count = 24
         SMB: Word parameters
         SMB: Name Length (NT) = 14 (0xE)
         SMB: Create Flags DWord = 0x00000006
            SMB: ............................1. = Request Oplock
            SMB: ...........................1.. = Request OpBatch
            SMB: ..........................0... = No Open Target Dir
         SMB: Root Dir FID = 0x00000000
         SMB: Desired Access = 0x0002019F
            SMB: ............................1 = Read Data Allowed
            SMB: ...........................1. = Write Data Allowed
            SMB: ..........................1.. = Append Data Allowed
            SMB: .........................1... = Read EA Allowed
            SMB: ........................1.... = Write EA Allowed
            SMB: .......................0..... = File Execute Denied
            SMB: ......................0...... = File Delete Denied
            SMB: .....................1....... = File Read Attributes Allowed
            SMB: ....................1........ = File Write Attributes Allowed
         SMB: File Allocation Size = 0x0000000000000000
         SMB: NT File Attributes = 0x00000000
            SMB: ............................0 = Not Read Only
            SMB: ...........................0. = Not Hidden
            SMB: ..........................0.. = Not System
            SMB: .........................0... = Not Directory
            SMB: ........................0.... = Not Archive
            SMB: .......................0..... = Not Normal
            SMB: ......................0...... = Not Temporary
            SMB: .....................0....... = Not Atomic Write
            SMB: ....................0........ = Not XAction Write
         SMB: File Share Access = 0x00000003
            SMB: ............................1 = Read allowed
            SMB: ...........................1. = Write allowed
            SMB: ..........................0.. = Delete not allowed
         SMB: Create Disposition = Open:  If exist, Open, else fail
         SMB: Create Options = 0 (0x0)
            SMB: ............................0 = non-directory
            SMB: ...........................0. = non-write through
            SMB: ..........................0.. = non-sequential writing allowed
            SMB: .........................0... = intermediate buffering allowed
            SMB: ........................0.... = IO alerts bits not set
            SMB: .......................0..... = IO non-alerts bit not set
            SMB: ......................0...... = non-directory file bit is not set
            SMB: .....................0....... = tree connect bit not set
            SMB: ....................0........ = complete if oplocked bit is not set
            SMB: ...................0......... = no EA knowledge bit is not set
            SMB: ..................0.......... = 8.3 filenames bit is not set
            SMB: .................0........... = random access bit is not set
            SMB: ................0............ = delete on close bit is not set
            SMB: ...............0............. = open by filename
            SMB: ..............0.............. = open for backup bit not set
         SMB: Impersonation Level = 0x00000002
         SMB: Security Flags = 0x01
            SMB: .......1 = dynamic tracking
            SMB: ......0. = effective only bit not set
         SMB: Byte count = 17
         SMB: File name = \srvsvc

00000:  00 60 08 36 71 DE 00 00 C0 7A 2D 5C 08 00 45 00   .`.6q....z-\..E.
00010:  00 90 93 00 40 00 80 06 6F 15 C7 F5 B4 01 C7 F5   ....@...o.......
00020:  B4 65 04 09 00 8B 00 39 58 82 00 45 C4 9C 50 18   .e.....9X..E..P.
00030:  21 3D B4 7D 00 00 00 00 00 64 FF 53 4D 42 A2 00   !=.}.....d.SMB..
00040:  00 00 00 18 03 80 71 FF 00 00 00 00 00 00 00 00   ......q.........
```

**Figure 6.25**  SMB C NT create & X, File = \srvsvc.

Packets 7 to 10 are used to create an RPC binding and process the browse information.

## TCP/IP Broadcasts for Windows NT Configured as a Router

This section discusses the network traffic produced by an NT server configured as a RIP router. Configuring a router with the RIP protocol results in periodic broadcasts on the network. Every RIP router on the network sends these broadcasts. As the number of routers and networks increases, so do the number of RIP broadcast messages. On a large network, RIP broadcasts can use up a significant portion of the network bandwidth. Figure 6.26 shows a summary of the RIP broadcast messages and Figure 6.27 shows a detailed decode of one of these messages.

```
1      17.585  TPNTS          FFFFFFFFFFFF    RIP       Response, 1 Entries (ver. 1)
                                              TPNTS          199.245.180.255 IP
2      52.470  TPNTS          FFFFFFFFFFFF    RIP       Response, 1 Entries (ver. 1)
                                              TPNTS          199.245.180.255 IP
3      85.894  TPNTS          FFFFFFFFFFFF    RIP       Response, 1 Entries (ver. 1)
                                              TPNTS          199.245.180.255 IP
4     120.788  TPNTS          FFFFFFFFFFFF    RIP       Response, 1 Entries (ver. 1)
                                              TPNTS          199.245.180.255 IP
5     155.709  TPNTS          FFFFFFFFFFFF    RIP       Response, 1 Entries (ver. 1)
                                              TPNTS          199.245.180.255 IP
```

**Figure 6.26**   RIP broadcast messages.

```
FRAME: Base frame properties
    FRAME: Time of capture = May 7, 1998 19:41:44.757
    FRAME: Time delta from previous physical frame: 0 milliseconds
    FRAME: Frame number: 1
    FRAME: Total frame length: 66 bytes
    FRAME: Capture frame length: 66 bytes
    FRAME: Frame data: Number of data bytes remaining = 66 (0x0042)
ETHERNET: ETYPE = 0x0800 : Protocol = IP:  DOD Internet Protocol
    ETHERNET: Destination address : FFFFFFFFFFFF
        ETHERNET: .......1 = Group address
        ETHERNET: ......1. = Locally administered address
    ETHERNET: Source address : 00A024ABD1E6
        ETHERNET: .......0 = No routing information present
        ETHERNET: ......0. = Universally administered address
    ETHERNET: Frame Length : 66 (0x0042)
    ETHERNET: Ethernet Type : 0x0800 (IP:  DOD Internet Protocol)
    ETHERNET: Ethernet Data: Number of data bytes remaining = 52 (0x0034)
IP: ID = 0xDB01; Proto = UDP; Len: 52
    IP: Version = 4 (0x4)
    IP: Header Length = 20 (0x14)
    IP: Service Type = 0 (0x0)
        IP: Precedence = Routine
        IP: ...0.... = Normal Delay
        IP: ....0... = Normal Throughput
        IP: .....0.. = Normal Reliability
    IP: Total Length = 52 (0x34)
    IP: Identification = 56065 (0xDB01)
    IP: Flags Summary = 0 (0x0)
        IP: .......0 = Last fragment in datagram
        IP: ......0. = May fragment datagram if necessary
    IP: Fragment Offset = 0 (0x0) bytes
    IP: Time to Live = 128 (0x80)
    IP: Protocol = UDP - User Datagram
    IP: Checksum = 0x66C3
    IP: Source Address = 199.245.180.9
```

```
      IP: Destination Address = 199.245.180.255
      IP: Data: Number of data bytes remaining = 32 (0x0020)
 UDP: Src Port: RIP, (520); Dst Port: RIP (520); Length = 32 (0x20)
      UDP: Source Port = RIP
      UDP: Destination Port = RIP
      UDP: Total length = 32 (0x20) bytes
      UDP: UDP Checksum = 0x7083
      UDP: Data: Number of data bytes remaining = 24 (0x0018)
 RIP: Response, 1 Entries (ver. 1)
      RIP: Command = Response
      RIP: Version = 1 (0x1)
      RIP: Unused = 0 (0x0)
      RIP: Data Frame: IP Address = 144.19.0.0, Metric = 16
          RIP: Address Family Identifier = 2 (0x2)
          RIP: Unused = 0 (0x0)
          RIP: IP Address = 144.19.0.0
          RIP: Unused = 0 (0x0)
          RIP: Unused = 0 (0x0)
          RIP: Metric = 16 (0x10)

00000:  FF FF FF FF FF FF 00 A0 24 AB D1 E6 08 00 45 00   ........$.....E.
00010:  00 34 DB 01 00 00 80 11 66 C3 C7 F5 B4 09 C7 F5   .4......f.......
00020:  B4 FF 02 08 02 08 00 20 70 83 02 01 00 00 00 02   ....... p.......
00030:  00 00 90 13 00 00 00 00 00 00 00 00 00 00 00 00   ...............
00040:  00 10                                             ..
```

**Figure 6.27** Detailed decode of RIP broadcast message.

In the Ethernet frame in Figure 6.27, the address FFFFFFFFFFFF indicates that the information is broadcast to all nodes on the router's Ethernet interface. The Ethernet source address, 00A024ABD1E6, is the MAC address of the router port.

```
ETHERNET: Destination address : FFFFFFFFFFFF
    ETHERNET: .......1 = Group address
    ETHERNET: ......1. = Locally administered address
ETHERNET: Source address : 00A024ABD1E6
    ETHERNET: .......0 = No routing information present
    ETHERNET: ......0. = Universally administered address
```

The IP datagram encapsulates the UDP transport protocol. RIP, because it is broadcast based, uses UDP instead of TCP. It is more efficient to send broadcast messages using UDP rather than using TCP. The UDP header contains the following information:

```
UDP: Source Port = RIP
UDP: Destination Port = RIP
UDP: Total length = 32 (0x20) bytes
UDP: UDP Checksum = 0x7083
```

The UDP port numbers identify the sending and receiving processes. In this case the UDP port number value of **520** indicates the RIP process.

The RIP packet is encapsulated by the UDP header and contains the following information:

```
RIP: Command = Response
RIP: Version = 1 (0x1)
RIP: Unused = 0 (0x0)
RIP: Address Family Identifier = 2 (0x2)
RIP: Unused = 0 (0x0)
```

```
RIP: IP Address = 144.19.0.0
RIP: Unused = 0 (0x0)
RIP: Unused = 0 (0x0)
RIP: Metric = 16 (0x10)
```

The RIP `Command` field value indicates that this is a response message with a value of 2, which is decoded by Network Monitor as a response type message. In this case it is an unsolicited response message sent at periodic intervals. A RIP response message can also be sent on receipt of a RIP request message. The `Version` field has a value of 1, which indicates that the RIP message format is version 1 for RIP version 1 of the protocol. There is a more enhanced version of RIP called RIP version 2. The `Address_Family Identifier` field with a value of 2 indicates that an Internet address format is used. The IP address uses only 4 octets. The `IP Address` field value of 144.19.0.0 indicates that the network 144.19.0.0 is being advertised. A RIP metric value can be 1 to 16. The RIP metric value of 16 indicates that the destination network is unreachable.

## TCP/IP Trace for Broadcast Name Resolution

Name resolution can occur using any of the following techniques:

- WINS
- Broadcast Name Resolution
- LMHOSTS file
- DNS

An overview of these different name resolution techniques is discussed in Chapters 9, "TCP/IP Name Resolution Using WINS," and 10, "TCP/IP Name Resolution Using DNS."

Figure 6.28 shows broadcast name resolution when an attempt is made to ping a node with the name of TPNTS using the command `ping tpnts`.

In this case, because neither the WINS, LMHOSTS/HOSTS file, or DNS was set to resolve the name, the broadcast name resolution method was used.

```
1    2.716   TPNTS      LTREE1       NBT     NS: Query (Node Status) resp. for TPNTS
                                             <00>, Success   TPNTS       LTREE1       IP
2    2.959   LTREE1     TPNTS        ICMP    Echo,     From 199.245.180.01
                        To   199.245.180.09                 LTREE1       TPNTS        IP
3    2.959   TPNTS      LTREE1       ICMP    Echo Reply, To 199.245.180.01
                        From 199.245.180.09                 TPNTS        LTREE1       IP
4    3.967   LTREE1     TPNTS        ICMP    Echo,     From 199.245.180.01
                        To   199.245.180.09                 LTREE1       TPNTS        IP
5    3.968   TPNTS      LTREE1       ICMP    Echo Reply, To 199.245.180.01
                        From 199.245.180.09                 TPNTS        LTREE1       IP
6    4.979   LTREE1     TPNTS        ICMP    Echo,     From 199.245.180.01
                        To   199.245.180.09                 LTREE1       TPNTS        IP
7    4.979   TPNTS      LTREE1       ICMP    Echo Reply, To 199.245.180.01
                        From 199.245.180.09                 TPNTS        LTREE1       IP
8    5.990   LTREE1     TPNTS        ICMP    Echo,     From 199.245.180.01
                        To   199.245.180.09                 LTREE1       TPNTS        IP
9    5.991   TPNTS      LTREE1       ICMP    Echo Reply, To 199.245.180.01
                        From 199.245.180.09                 TPNTS        LTREE1       IP
```

**Figure 6.28** Broadcast name resolution for `ping` command.

Packet 1 in Figure 6.29 shows the name resolution response from the TPNTS node. The UDP header shows the following information:

```
UDP: Source Port = NETBIOS Name Service
UDP: Destination Port = NETBIOS Name Service
UDP: Total length = 70 (0x46) bytes
UDP: UDP Checksum = 0x43EA
```

The NETBIOS Name Service uses a UDP port number of 137. The NBT query response contains the following information:

```
NBT: Transaction ID = 32802 (0x8022)
NBT: Flags Summary = 0x8500 - Resp.; Query; Success
    NBT: 1............... = Response
    NBT: .0000.......... = Query
    NBT: .....1......... = Authoritative Answer
    NBT: ......0........ = Datagram not truncated
    NBT: .......1....... = Recursion desired
    NBT: ........0...... = Recursion not available
    NBT: .........0..... = Reserved
    NBT: ..........0.... = Reserved
    NBT: ...........0... = Not a broadcast packet
    NBT: ............0000 = Success
NBT: Question Count = 0 (0x0)
NBT: Answer Count = 1 (0x1)
NBT: Name Service Count = 0 (0x0)
NBT: Additional Record Count = 0 (0x0)
NBT: Resource Record Name = TPNTS          <00>
NBT: Resource Record Type = NetBIOS General Name Service
NBT: Resource Record Class = Internet Class
NBT: Time To Live = 300000 (0x493E0)
NBT: RDATA Length = 6 (0x6)
NBT: Resource Record Flags = 24576 (0x6000)
    NBT: 0.............. = Unique NetBIOS Name
    NBT: .00............ = B Node
    NBT: ...0000000000000 = Reserved
NBT: Owner IP Address = 199.245.180.9
```

```
FRAME: Base frame properties
    FRAME: Time of capture - May 9, 1998 18:58:9.237
    FRAME: Time delta from previous physical frame: 0 milliseconds
    FRAME: Frame number: 1
    FRAME: Total frame length: 104 bytes
    FRAME: Capture frame length: 104 bytes
    FRAME: Frame data: Number of data bytes remaining = 104 (0x0068)
ETHERNET: ETYPE = 0x0800 : Protocol = IP: DOD Internet Protocol
    ETHERNET: Destination address : 0000C07A2D5C
        ETHERNET: .......0 = Individual address
        ETHERNET: ......0. = Universally administered address
    ETHERNET: Source address : 00A024ABD1E6
        ETHERNET: .......0 = No routing information present
        ETHERNET: ......0. = Universally administered address
    ETHERNET: Frame Length : 104 (0x0068)
    ETHERNET: Ethernet Type : 0x0800 (IP: DOD Internet Protocol)
    ETHERNET: Ethernet Data: Number of data bytes remaining = 90 (0x005A)
```

```
       IP: ID = 0x4303; Proto = UDP; Len: 90
          IP: Version = 4 (0x4)
          IP: Header Length = 20 (0x14)
          IP: Service Type = 0 (0x0)
             IP: Precedence = Routine
             IP: ...0.... = Normal Delay
             IP: ....0... = Normal Throughput
             IP: .....0.. = Normal Reliability
          IP: Total Length = 90 (0x5A)
          IP: Identification = 17155 (0x4303)
          IP: Flags Summary = 0 (0x0)
             IP: .......0 = Last fragment in datagram
             IP: ......0. = May fragment datagram if necessary
          IP: Fragment Offset = 0 (0x0) bytes
          IP: Time to Live = 128 (0x80)
          IP: Protocol = UDP - User Datagram
          IP: Checksum = 0xFF99
          IP: Source Address = 199.245.180.9
          IP: Destination Address = 199.245.180.1
          IP: Data: Number of data bytes remaining = 70 (0x0046)
       UDP: Src Port: NETBIOS Name Service, (137); Dst Port: NETBIOS Name Service (137);
            Length = 70 (0x46)
          UDP: Source Port = NETBIOS Name Service
          UDP: Destination Port = NETBIOS Name Service
          UDP: Total length = 70 (0x46) bytes
          UDP: UDP Checksum = 0x43EA
          UDP: Data: Number of data bytes remaining = 62 (0x003E)
       NBT: NS: Query (Node Status) resp. for TPNTS        <00>, Success
          NBT: Transaction ID = 32802 (0x8022)
          NBT: Flags Summary = 0x8500 - Resp.; Query; Success
             NBT: 1............... = Response
             NBT: .0000.......... = Query
             NBT: .....1......... = Authoritative Answer
             NBT: ......0........ = Datagram not truncated
             NBT: .......1....... = Recursion desired
             NBT: ........0...... = Recursion not available
             NBT: .........0..... = Reserved
             NBT: ..........0.... = Reserved
             NBT: ...........0... = Not a broadcast packet
             NBT: ............0000 = Success
          NBT: Question Count = 0 (0x0)
          NBT: Answer Count = 1 (0x1)
          NBT: Name Service Count = 0 (0x0)
          NBT: Additional Record Count = 0 (0x0)
          NBT: Resource Record Name = TPNTS        <00>
          NBT: Resource Record Type = NetBIOS General Name Service
          NBT: Resource Record Class = Internet Class
          NBT: Time To Live = 300000 (0x493E0)
          NBT: RDATA Length = 6 (0x6)
          NBT: Resource Record Flags = 24576 (0x6000)
             NBT: 0............... = Unique NetBIOS Name
             NBT: .00............. = B Node
             NBT: ...0000000000000 = Reserved
          NBT: Owner IP Address = 199.245.180.9

00000:  00 00 C0 7A 2D 5C 00 A0 24 AB D1 E6 08 00 45 00    ...z-\..$.....E.
00010:  00 5A 43 03 00 00 80 11 FF 99 C7 F5 B4 09 C7 F5    .ZC.............
00020:  B4 01 00 89 00 89 00 46 43 EA 80 22 85 00 00 00    .......FC..".....
00030:  00 01 00 00 00 00 20 46 45 46 41 45 4F 46 45 46    ...... FEFAEOFEF
00040:  44 43 41 43 41 43 41 43 41 43 41 43 41 43 41 43    DCACACACACACACAC
00050:  41 43 41 43 41 41 41 00 00 20 00 01 00 04 93 E0    ACACAAA.. ......
00060:  00 06 60 00 C7 F5 B4 09                            ..`.....
```

**Figure 6.29**  NBT Name Query response.

The `Flags Summary` field value of `0x8500` indicates that a response that is authoritative is desired, and if necessary recursion can be used.

The NetBIOS name service response packet contains an answer, and therefore the `Answer Count` field is set to 1. The `Resource Record Name` that was used is TPNTS. The `Resource Record Type` field is NetBIOS General Service (0x0020). The `Resource`

Record Class is the Internet Class (0x0001), which indicates that IP addresses are being resolved. The Time To Live (0x6000) indicates the number of seconds that the information should be cached by the requester. After this time, the requester should assume that the information is old and issue another name resolution request.

The RDATA Length indicates the size of the resource record answer that follows. In this case the RDATA is 6 octets long and includes 2 octets of the Resource Record Flags and 4 octets of Owner IP Address, which is the resolved name's IP address.

The Resource Record Flags value of 0x6000 indicates that the result is a unique NetBIOS name that was resolved using the b-node (broadcast) method (see Chapters 9 and 10 for additional details on the different modes of name resolution). The result of the name resolution is specified in the Owner IP Address field that is set to 199.245.180.9.

Once the name is resolved, you can see in packets 2 to 10 a repeated ICMP (Internet Control Message Protocol) echo request (the PING request packet) and the corresponding ICMP echo response (the PING reply packet). The node that is being pinged is 199.245.180.9.

Figures 6.30 and 6.31 show the detailed views of the ICMP echo request and ICMP echo reply, respectively.

Note that the ICMP packet is encapsulated by an IP packet. The IP header field Protocol is set to a value of 1 and indicates that the IP header encapsulates an ICMP message.

```
FRAME: Base frame properties
    FRAME: Time of capture = May 9, 1998 18:58:9.480
    FRAME: Time delta from previous physical frame: 243 milliseconds
    FRAME: Frame number: 2
    FRAME: Total frame length: 74 bytes
    FRAME: Capture frame length: 74 bytes
    FRAME: Frame data: Number of data bytes remaining = 74 (0x004A)
ETHERNET: ETYPE = 0x0800 : Protocol = IP: DOD Internet Protocol
    ETHERNET: Destination address : 00A024ABD1E6
        ETHERNET: .......0 = Individual address
        ETHERNET: ......0. = Universally administered address
    ETHERNET: Source address : 0000C07A2D5C
        ETHERNET: .......0 = No routing information present
        ETHERNET: ......0. = Universally administered address
    ETHERNET: Frame Length : 74 (0x004A)
    ETHERNET: Ethernet Type : 0x0800 (IP: DOD Internet Protocol)
    ETHERNET: Ethernet Data: Number of data bytes remaining = 60 (0x003C)
IP: ID = 0x4600; Proto = ICMP; Len: 60
    IP: Version = 4 (0x4)
    IP: Header Length = 20 (0x14)
    IP: Service Type = 0 (0x0)
        IP: Precedence = Routine
        IP: ...0.... = Normal Delay
        IP: ....0... = Normal Throughput
        IP: .....0.. = Normal Reliability
    IP: Total Length = 60 (0x3C)
    IP: Identification = 17920 (0x4600)
    IP: Flags Summary = 0 (0x0)
        IP: .......0 = Last fragment in datagram
        IP: ......0. = May fragment datagram if necessary
    IP: Fragment Offset = 0 (0x0) bytes
    IP: Time to Live = 32 (0x20)
    IP: Protocol = ICMP - Internet Control Message
    IP: Checksum = 0x5CCB
    IP: Source Address = 199.245.180.1
    IP: Destination Address = 199.245.180.9
    IP: Data: Number of data bytes remaining = 40 (0x0028)
```

```
ICMP: Echo,      From 199.245.180.01 To   199.245.180.09
    ICMP: Packet Type = Echo
    ICMP: Checksum = 0x4B5C
    ICMP: Identifier = 256 (0x100)
    ICMP: Sequence Number = 256 (0x100)
    ICMP: Data: Number of data bytes remaining = 32 (0x0020)

00000:  00 A0 24 AB D1 E6 00 00 C0 7A 2D 5C 08 00 45 00    ..$......z-\..E.
00010:  00 3C 46 00 00 00 20 01 5C CB C7 F5 B4 01 C7 F5    .<F... .\.......
00020:  B4 09 08 00 4B 5C 01 00 01 00 61 62 63 64 65 66    ....K\....abcdef
00030:  67 68 69 6A 6B 6C 6D 6E 6F 70 71 72 73 74 75 76    ghijklmnopqrstuv
00040:  77 61 62 63 64 65 66 67 68 69                      wabcdefghi
```

**Figure 6.30**   ICMP Echo Request.

```
FRAME: Base frame properties
    FRAME: Time of capture = May 9, 1998 18:58:9.480
    FRAME: Time delta from previous physical frame: 0 milliseconds
    FRAME: Frame number: 3
    FRAME: Total frame length: 74 bytes
    FRAME: Capture frame length: 74 bytes
    FRAME: Frame data: Number of data bytes remaining = 74 (0x004A)
ETHERNET: ETYPE = 0x0800 : Protocol = IP:  DOD Internet Protocol
    ETHERNET: Destination address : 0000C07A2D5C
        ETHERNET: .......0 = Individual address
        ETHERNET: ......0. = Universally administered address
    ETHERNET: Source address : 00A024ABD1E6
        ETHERNET: .......0 = No routing information present
        ETHERNET: ......0. = Universally administered address
    ETHERNET: Frame Length : 74 (0x004A)
    ETHERNET: Ethernet Type : 0x0800 (IP:  DOD Internet Protocol)
    ETHERNET: Ethernet Data: Number of data bytes remaining = 60 (0x003C)
IP: ID = 0x4403; Proto = ICMP; Len: 60
    IP: Version = 4 (0x4)
    IP: Header Length = 20 (0x14)
    IP: Service Type = 0 (0x0)
        IP: Precedence = Routine
        IP: ...0.... = Normal Delay
        IP: ....0... = Normal Throughput
        IP: .....0.. = Normal Reliability
    IP: Total Length = 60 (0x3C)
    IP: Identification = 17411 (0x4403)
    IP: Flags Summary = 0 (0x0)
        IP: .......0 = Last fragment in datagram
        IP: ......0. = May fragment datagram if necessary
    IP: Fragment Offset = 0 (0x0) bytes
    IP: Time to Live = 128 (0x80)
    IP: Protocol = ICMP - Internet Control Message
    IP: Checksum = 0xFEC7
    IP: Source Address = 199.245.180.9
    IP: Destination Address = 199.245.180.1
    IP: Data: Number of data bytes remaining = 40 (0x0028)
ICMP: Echo Reply, To 199.245.180.01 From 199.245.180.09
    ICMP: Packet Type = Echo Reply
    ICMP: Checksum = 0x535C
    ICMP: Identifier = 256 (0x100)
    ICMP: Sequence Number = 256 (0x100)
    ICMP: Data: Number of data bytes remaining = 32 (0x0020)

00000:  00 00 C0 7A 2D 5C 00 A0 24 AB D1 E6 08 00 45 00    ...z-\..$.....E.
00010:  00 3C 44 03 00 00 80 01 FE C7 C7 F5 B4 09 C7 F5    .<D.............
00020:  B4 01 00 00 53 5C 01 00 01 00 61 62 63 64 65 66    ....S\....abcdef
00030:  67 68 69 6A 6B 6C 6D 6E 6F 70 71 72 73 74 75 76    ghijklmnopqrstuv
00040:  77 61 62 63 64 65 66 67 68 69                      wabcdefghi
```

**Figure 6.31**   ICMP Echo Reply.

# Routing with Microsoft TCP/IP

THE INTERNET PROTOCOL CAN BE USED to build arbitrarily complex networks. If the IP network is primarily Windows NT based, you may want to use Windows NT computers as routers to save on the cost of buying dedicated router hardware. This chapter explains some of the advantages and disadvantages of Windows NT–based router solutions.

You can use Windows NT to build complex networks that extend the range of networks to span large distances. Complex IP networks are joined together with IP routers. IP routers understand the format of the IP header and can forward IP datagrams based on the information in the IP header. The forwarding of IP datagrams to their destinations is called routing. The routers act as packet-switching devices that select one path over another based on specified criteria.

This chapter explains IP routing concepts that you need to understand to design large IP networks. The configuration of routing services on Windows NT is examined. Finally, some advanced topics dealing with efficient subnet design, variable-length subnet masks, and supernetting are discussed.

## IP Routing Concepts

As explained in Chapter 1, "TCP/IP Architecture for Windows," routers are OSI layer 3 devices. Layer 3 in the OSI model is concerned with routing functions. Figure 7.1 shows a simplified model for a router.

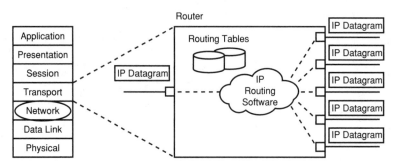

**Figure 7.1** A simplified router model.

A router has multiple ports; it must have a minimum of two ports. IP datagrams arrive at the router's port. The IP routing software examines the header of the IP datagram to determine how the datagram should be forwarded. The most important piece of information the routing software examines is the destination address of the IP datagram. The routing software consults the routing table in the router and forwards the datagram through one of the router's ports.

## Static Versus Dynamic Routing

The routing table contains a list of destination networks and hosts and information about the best way to reach these destinations. How is the information in the routing table set up? There are two ways to initialize a router's routing table:

- Static method
- Dynamic method

The *static* method requires that the information in the routing table be entered manually. In the *dynamic* method, the router can dynamically learn information about how to route to other networks and hosts. The router learns this information via routing protocols.

---

**Exceptions**

A system that has only one port but two or more addresses on different subnets would be an example of a router that has only one physical port, but this is an exception. This is a simplified model for the purpose of explaining these concepts.

## Routing Protocols

*Routing protocols* define how routers exchange information among themselves to learn the best route to destinations on the Internet. Because routing protocols must exchange messages in an IP network, the routing protocols are carried in IP datagrams. Routing protocols may run directly on top of IP, as in the case of OSPF (Open Shortest Path First); they may run on top of the UDP Transport layer protocol, as in the case of RIP (Routing Information Protocol); or they may run on top of the TCP Transport layer protocol, as in the case of BGP (Border Gateway Protocol).

Because routing protocols are clients of IP, TCP, or UDP, they can be treated as a class of special Application layer protocols.

## Router Configuration Issues

Regardless of the routing protocol that is used by a router, a certain amount of manual configuration needs to be done for a router before it can operate in a network. The reason for this is that a router is an OSI layer 3 device whose network interfaces are identified by IP addresses. The IP addresses and related parameters for each network interface of the router must be configured, and this is a manual process. In some commercial routers, the configuration parameters can be set up in a file, which can then be downloaded from a local or network device. By using configuration files you can automate the setup of routers, but you still need to manually set up the configuration file properly.

Traditionally, many routers were application hosts, such as UNIX computers that also performed routing functions. In fact, many UNIX systems automatically act as routers by default, if they have more than one network interface (multi-homed hosts).

Today, routers can be built using Windows NT Server. It is possible to build routers using Windows NT Workstation or Windows 9x computers, but you may have to resort to using third-party software. If you are using Windows NT Server, you can use the standard distribution software to set up the server as an IP router.

If a server or application host is configured to act as a router, it has to perform the dual job of providing routing and application services. Because each IP datagram needs to be routed separately, the routing algorithm can consume a substantial amount of the server or application host's processor time on a busy network. This can seriously affect the performance of the computer as an application server. For this reason, dedicated hardware devices are sold by router vendors such as Cisco, Bay Networks, 3Com, and others, which perform only routing functions. By using dedicated hardware devices that contain specialized hardware designed to speed routing functions, the communications and applications functions can be more easily separated. This leads to easier management of communications and applications and avoids conflict of interest.

Nevertheless, if the network is small, and performance and throughput not a critical issue because network traffic is light, it may be desirable to use a Windows NT computer as a router. You do not have to buy additional router hardware, and the router configuration can be done by the Windows NT Administrator rather than a specialist knowledgeable about the hardware-based routers.

## Datagram Delivery by Hosts and Routers

In traditional IP router discussion, the terms hosts and routers are used. *Hosts* are computers such as Windows NT Workstation and Windows 9x computers. *Routers* are special devices that actively perform routing tasks. As discussed in the previous section, a Windows NT server can be configured as a router.

Both hosts and routers participate in the process of routing an IP datagram. IP datagrams are generated by a sending host that wants to contact services at another host. Figure 7.2 shows a network that has hosts and routers. The routers provide connections to outside networks.

When the sending host sends an IP datagram, it must make a decision about whether to send the datagram directly to a host on the network, or forward the datagram to one of the routers on that network. This decision is the routing that is performed at each host.

Although a router's ports are connected to the network, the router only forwards IP datagrams that are sent to the router port. It is the responsibility of the sending host to forward the IP datagram specifically to a router port. In the example in Figure 7.2, the sender host does this by discovering the hardware address of the router port that is connected to the network, and using the hardware address of the router port in the destination address field of the Data Link layer frame. In a broadcast network, a protocol such as ARP is used to discover the hardware address of the router port.

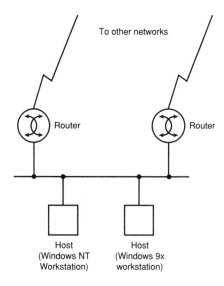

**Figure 7.2** Hosts and routers.

### Host and Router Routing Tables

Both hosts and routers have IP routing tables. The routing table consists of information on destinations and how to reach the destination. Hosts and routers consult their routing tables to determine how to route a datagram.

In the case of hosts, the IP module consults the host routing table for outgoing datagrams that are not on the local network. Routers consult their routing tables for incoming datagrams, and route based on information in their routing tables.

What kind of information on destinations is kept in the routing table? If the routing table listed every possible destination host, the routing table would become too large to be manageable. This is because the routing table would have to contain an entry for every possible IP address destination. There are about four billion IPv4 addresses. In a completely connected Internet, the routing tables would have to have about four billion entries! The computers would quickly run out of memory space to store the routing table, and the network managers would run out of patience in managing such large tables! Clearly, a more manageable solution is needed.

The IP routing table is designed so that routing can be performed with a minimum of information in the routing table. Rather than storing the IP addresses of every reachable host, the network number of the destination network is stored. Recall that an IP address consists of a netid and a hostid. The *netid* is the network number and is the same for all hosts that are on that network. In other words, hosts on the same physical network share a common IP address prefix called the *netid*. Rather than storing routing information on all the hosts on a network, it is more efficient to store only the information on their network number. This vastly reduces the number of entries in a routing table and keeps the routing table small. If there are $H$ host bits in the IP address for a network, using a network number instead of the host addresses for the destination network, reduces the number of routing table entries by a factor of $2^H$.

A routing table entry contains the destination and the next hop router to forward the datagram to reach the destination. The next hop router is a router that is connected to any directly connected segment of the source router. The traversal of a datagram through a router is called a *hop*. Figure 7.3 shows that routers R1, R2, and R3 are next hop routers for the router R0, because they are connected to the same network segment. Routers R0 and R1 are connected by a point-to-point link. Similarly routers R0, R2 and R0, R3 are also connected by a point-to-point link.

It is important to realize that the routing table points only to the next router on the same physical network; the table does not contain the complete path to the destination. In other words, the routing entry does not contain a list of all routers that a datagram must travel through. In the example of Figure 7.3, the routing table for router R0 contains entries for R1, R2, and R3 only. The routing table for R0 does not list routers R4, R5, R6, R7, R8, and R9 because they are not next hop routers with respect to router R0.

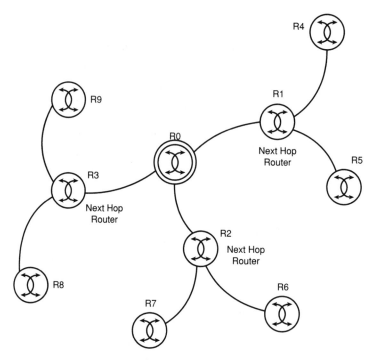

**Figure 7.3**    Next hop router.

The next hop router is so selected to represent a minimum cost to reach the destination. The minimum cost can be measured in terms of time delays, monetary cost, or hop count. The routing protocol that is used by the routers to communicate routing information specifies how the minimum cost should be determined. The cost associated with sending a datagram through a particular next hop router represents a global awareness of the topology of the network. However, the next hop router only represents an awareness of the local network topology.

Because the routing table contains information only on the neighboring routers, the routing table is kept simple. The routing table must keep track of the neighbor routers. The routing protocol is responsible for computing the cost of selecting a particular neighbor router.

Using the network suffix in the routing table instead of the IP address of hosts reduces the size of the routing table but leads to other consequences. All hosts for a particular network have only one entry in the routing table, and therefore only one path. Even if there are multiple paths to a particular host, they cannot be used concurrently. In this simple model of the routing table, there is no provision for taking into account delay, priority, or throughput of network traffic. Some routing protocols attempt to take into account these factors by associating a cost for each route in the routing table. The destination host is reached by a series of direct deliveries from the sender to final router. Until the final router attempts to deliver the datagram to the destination host, there is no way of knowing that the destination host exists. If the final router in the chain of direct deliveries attempts is not able to deliver the datagram, the final router sends an error report in the form of an ICMP message to the sender. If the destination host is on a broadcast network such as an Ethernet LAN, the final router attempts to deliver the datagram by using ARP to bind the destination IP address to its hardware address. If the ARP binding fails, it assumes that the destination host is not reachable.

### Example of a Host Routing Table on a Windows NT Computer

The routing table for a host such as a Windows NT computer is similar to that for a router. The difference is that hosts only route IP datagrams that originate from that host; they do not forward datagrams received from other IP nodes. Routers, on the other hand, forward IP datagrams received from other IP nodes.

Figure 7.4 shows the routing table for a Windows NT computer. The network contains three routers. Host A has a choice of selecting any of the routers, but it does not make this selection in an arbitrary manner. The host consults its routing table to determine how to send an IP datagram. The routing table for the host A contains the following entries:

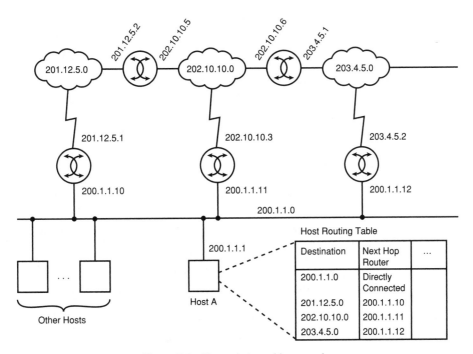

**Figure 7.4**   Host routing table example.

| Destination | Next Hop Router |
|---|---|
| 200.1.1.0 | Directly connected |
| 201.12.5.0 | 200.1.1.10 |
| 202.10.10.0 | 200.1.1.11 |
| 203.4.5.0 | 200.1.1.12 |

The first entry in the routing table is for the local network 200.1.1.0. The next hop router column indicates that this is a directly connected network. This means that the host can use direct delivery to reach the destination and there is no need to forward to a router any datagrams destined for the local network 200.1.1.0. The host uses the physical transport mechanism to forward the datagram to any host on network 200.1.1.0. For a broadcast network such as Ethernet, this may involve using ARP to discover the hardware address of the local destination host before sending the IP datagram.

The second entry in the routing table indicates that all datagrams for network 201.12.5.0 should be forwarded to the router port 200.1.1.10. Note that the network 201.12.5.0 can be reached through other local routers, but the path would involve traversing other networks such as 202.10.10.0 and 203.4.5.0. The routing protocol is smart enough to figure out that the optimal path to reach network 201.12.5.0 is through the router at 201.1.1.10. If the router at 201.1.1.10 was down, the routing entry for destination 201.12.5.0 would indicate other routers to reach the destination.

The third entry in the routing table specifies that all datagrams for network 202.10.10.0 should be forwarded to the router port 200.1.1.11. Again, note that the network 202.10.10.0 can be reached through other local routers, but the path would involve traversing other networks such as 201.12.5.0 and 203.4.5.0. The routing protocol is smart enough to figure out that the optimal path to reach network 202.10.10.0 is through the router at 201.1.1.11. If the router at 201.1.1.11 was down, the routing entry for destination 202.10.10.0 would indicate other routers to reach the destination.

The last entry in the routing table indicates that all datagrams for network 203.4.5.0 should be forwarded to the router port 200.1.1.12. Again, note that the network 203.4.5.0 can be reached through other local routers, but the path would involve traversing other networks such as 201.12.5.0 and 202.10.10.0. The routing protocol is smart enough to figure out that the optimal path to reach network 203.4.5.0 is through the router at 201.1.1.12. If the router at 201.1.1.12 was down, the routing entry for destination 203.4.5.0 would indicate other routers to reach the destination.

If you examine the next hop router IP addresses, you notice that the port connected to the local network has the same IP address prefix of 200.1.1. Moreover, this network prefix is the same as that of the local network and all hosts connected to the local network 200.1.1.0. This is an important point to note about next hop routers: They share a common network prefix with the network their ports are connected to. Because the routers must have more than one port, the other ports also must have the same network prefix as the port they connect to (refer to Figure 7.4).

Usually the last entry in the routing table is the default route and is represented as a destination of 0.0.0.0. The default route is selected only if there is no match in the routing table.

## Host-Specific Routes

Most routing entries specify the network number as their destination. However, many implementations include a provision for specifying a host IP address as the destination. When the host IP address is used as the destination in a routing table, you have more control over how a host should be reached because you can specify the next hop router on a host IP address basis rather than on a network number basis. The ability to specify a particular next hop router that should be used is very useful in testing and debugging. Consider the network in Figure 7.5, which shows the routing table for a host as follows:

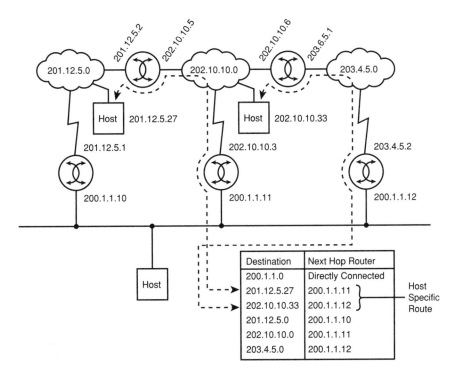

**Figure 7.5**  Host-specific route.

| Destination | Next Hop Router |
|---|---|
| 200.1.1.0 | Directly connected |
| 201.12.5.27 | 200.1.1.11 (*Host-specific route*) |
| 202.10.10.33 | 200.1.1.12 (*Host-specific route*) |
| 201.12.5.0 | 200.1.1.10 |
| 202.10.10.0 | 200.1.1.11 |
| 203.4.5.0 | 200.1.1.12 |

The example in Figure 7.5 is similar to that in Figure 7.4, with the difference that destination hosts 201.12.5.27 and 202.10.10.33 are specified as having host-specific routes in the routing table for host A.

Without the host-specific route for the destination, 201.12.5.27 would be reached via the router 200.1.1.10 that is specified for the destination network 201.12.5.0.

Similarly, without the host-specific route, the destination 202.10.10.33 would be reached via the router 200.1.1.11 that is specified for the destination network 202.10.10.0. For debugging and testing purposes you may want to send the data for a destination host through a specific next hop router. You can do this using host-specific routes as illustrated in Figure 7.5.

## Default Routes

If a network has only one next hop router, all remote destinations must be reached through this next hop router (see Figure 7.6). In this case it does not make sense to specify each destination explicitly. It is better to specify a default route to act as a "catch all" for all destinations. The router specified by this default route is called the default router. The terms *default router* and *default gateway* are synonymous. Routers were historically called *gateways*. The Windows 9x and NT implementations use the term default gateway.

In Figure 7.6, the router table for the hosts consists of only two entries: one for the local network, and the other for the default route. The routing software must make only two tests to determine how to route the IP datagram.

In general, the default route can be useful in keeping the routing table small where many destinations must be reached through the same next hop router (see Figure 7.7). The routing software looks at the routing table to determine whether there is an exact match for the destination. If a match cannot be found, the default route is used. The default route is represented in the routing table with a special destination value of 0.0.0.0.

In Figure 7.7, the routing table for a host can be written as follows without using default routes:

| Destination | Next Hop Router |
|---|---|
| 200.1.1.0 | Directly connected |
| 201.1.1.0 | 200.1.1.33 |

202.1.1.0        200.1.1.34

203.1.1.0        200.1.1.34

204.1.1.0        200.1.1.34

This routing table has five route entries. Using a default route, you can consolidate the last three route entries into a single route as shown in the following routing table, which is equivalent to the previous routing table:

| **Destination** | **Next Hop Router** |
| --- | --- |
| 200.1.1.0 | Directly connected |
| 201.1.1.0 | 200.1.1.33 |
| 0.0.0.0 | 200.1.1.34 (default route) |

On a Windows NT computer you can set the default route by performing the following steps:

1. Start the Network applet from the Control Panel.

2. Select the Protocols tab.

3. Highlight the TCP/IP Protocol.

4. Select Properties.

5. Select the IP Address tab.

6. Enter the default router address in the Default Gateway field.

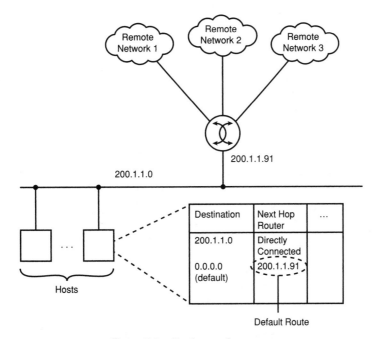

**Figure 7.6**  Single next hop router.

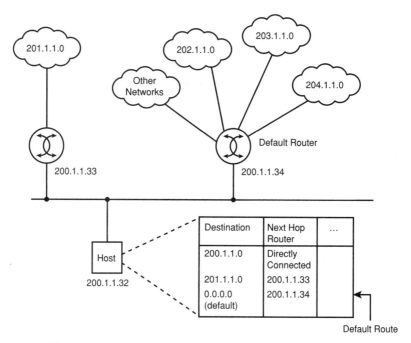

**Figure 7.7** Use of default route to minimize size of routing table.

## Subnetting and Its Advantages

*Subnetting* is a scheme that allows you to divide a network into smaller networks by using the same network number assignment. The advantages of subnetting are as follows:

- Simplified administration
- Restructuring of the internal network without affecting external networks
- Improved security
- Isolation of network traffic

The simplified administration results from the fact that one can use routers to partition networks by using logical boundaries. This often allows the smaller networks to be administered independently and more efficiently. The smaller networks may even be managed by their own independent network administration staff. This can even avoid or eliminate certain types of political problems between department staffs that may desire to have greater control over their networks.

Using subnets allows the network to be structured internally without the rest of the connected network being aware of changes in the internal network. In Figure 7.8, the internal network has been divided into two subnets, but external traffic coming from the internal network is still sent to the network address 149.108.0.0. It is up to the router that belongs to the organization to make a further distinction between IP addresses belonging to its subnets. A very important aspect of the internal network being "invisible" to external networks is that an organization can achieve this internal restructuring without having to obtain an additional network number. With the Internetwork running out of network numbers, this is a great advantage.

Because the structure of the internal subnetworks is not visible to external networks, use of subnets results in an indirect improvement in network security.

Figure 7.9 shows the relationship between the different fields of an IP address and subnetworks that have been discussed so far. If the subnets are to be connected, routers must be used between them. Moreover, the routers must understand that subnetting is being used and how many bits of the hostid field are being used for subnets.

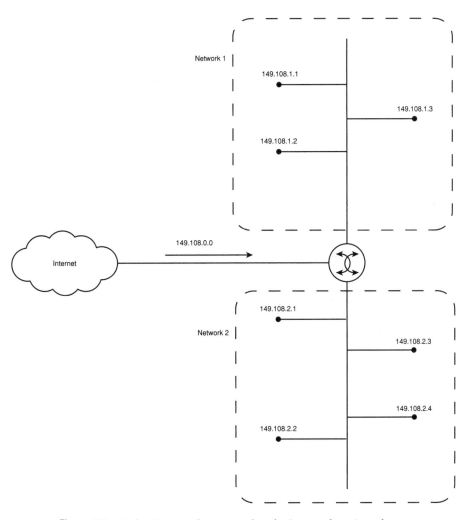

**Figure 7.8** A class B network connected to the Internet by using subnets.

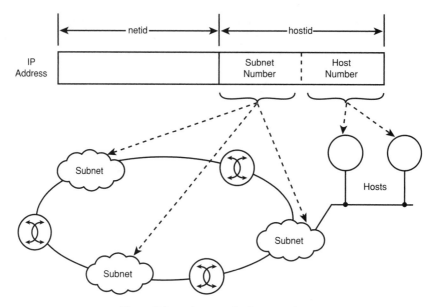

**Figure 7.9**   Subnets and subnet numbers.

The router in the example of Figure 7.8 must be made to understand that the hostid field of the IP address is to be treated specially—that is, a part of it used for the subnet number and the remaining part for the host number. This information is typically represented to the router as the subnet mask.

## Subnet Mask

The *subnet mask* is used by routers and hosts on a subnet to interpret the hostid field in such a way that they can determine how many bits are being used for subnetting. The subnet mask divides the hostid field into the subnet number and the hostnumber. The subnet mask is a 32-bit number whose value is formed by using the following rules:

- Ones (1s) in the subnet mask correspond to the position of the netid and subnet number in the IP address.

- Zeros (0s) in the subnet mask correspond to the position of the host number in the IP address.

Figure 7.10 shows an application of the previously stated rules. This figure shows a class B network number that is used for subnetting. Eight bits of the hostid field are being used for the subnet number. The resulting subnet mask is also shown in Figure 7.10. The subnet mask is a 32-bit pattern and is conventionally written in a dotted decimal notation form. Because a group of eight 1s corresponds to a decimal value of 255, the subnet mask of Figure 7.10 can be written in the following manner: 255.255.255.0

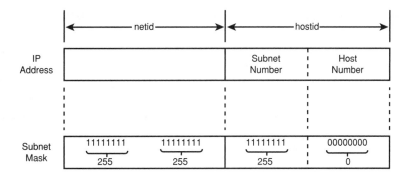

- 1s in the subnet mask correspond to netid and subnet number in the IP address

- 0s in the subnet mask correspond to host number in the IP address

**Figure 7.10**  Subnet mask representation.

If a subnet mask value of 255.255.0.0 is used for a class B address, this indicates that no subnetting is being used. A class B address has 16 bits of netid field. This netid field is accounted for by the first two 255s (255.255) in the 255.255.0.0 subnet mask value. The remaining value of 0.0 must correspond to the host number. There are no 1s in the subnet mask for the subnet number field, and therefore no subnetting is being used.

If the same subnet mask value of 255.255.0.0 is used for a class A address, it indicates that subnetting is being used. A class A address has 8 bits of netid field. This netid field is accounted for by the first 255 in the 255.255.0.0 subnet mask value. The remaining 255 must correspond to the subnet number, which is 8 bits long.

If a subnet mask value of 255.255.255.0 is used for a class C address, this indicates that no subnetting is being used. A class C address has 24 bits of netid field. This netid field is accounted for by the first three 255s (255.255.255) in the 255.255.255.0 subnet mask value. The remaining value of 0 must correspond to the host number. There are no 1s in the subnet mask for the subnet number field, and therefore no subnetting is being used.

If a subnet mask value of 255.255.0.0 is used for a class C address, this is an illegal value for subnet masks (you will learn later, however, that this value would be legal for creating *supernets*). A class C address has 24 bits of netid field but the first two 255s in the 255.255.0.0 account for only 16 bits of the netid. There should be at least another 255 to cover the remaining 8 bits of netid.

### New Subnet Number Options

Many router vendors now permit the use of all ones or all zeros for the subnet number. This has become increasingly popular due to the shortage of address space. An example of this would be using the mask 255.255.255.128 on a class C address to split it into two subnets. This topic is covered a bit later in the chapter.

The subnet mask value is usually required at the time you specify the IP address for a host or router. It can be expressed as the dotted decimal notation value seen in earlier examples.

A subnet number (the portion of the hostid field designated for subnetting) value of all 0 bits or all 1 bits is not permitted.

The subnet mask is usually stored in an internal configuration area in most operating systems. In Windows NT 5, the subnet number is stored in the following Registry entry:

```
HKEY_LOCAL_MACHINE\SYSTEM\CurrentControlSet\Services\Tcpip\Parameters\
➡Interfaces\netinterface
```

In Windows NT, the subnet number is stored in the following Registry entry:

```
HKEY_LOCAL_MACHINE\SYSTEM\CurrentControlSet\Services\netinterface\
➡Parameters\Tcpip
```

In retrospect, it might have been better if the designers of the subnet scheme had used an alternate representation different from the subnet mask to specify the number of bits to be used for subnetting. For instance, they could have specified that the subnet is to be represented by a single number called the *subnet bits*, which is the size of the subnet number field starting from the most significant part of the hostid field. Alternatively, the number of bits used for the network number and subnet number could be specified. This last scheme is used in many modern routers and is part of the *Classless Internet Domain Routing (CIDR) scheme*, which is typically used to combine several class C address destinations to a single routing entry.

If the TCP/IP software could determine the subnet mask values based on this information, this would have prevented several generations of network administrators becoming confused about subnet masks! The problem with subnet masks is that it often involves working with bit (or hex) patterns that most network administrators are unfamiliar with. For a systems programmer working in assembly or C/C++ languages, working with bit patterns is natural and easy, but for ordinary mortals such as network administrators it can be a daunting task.

## Subnet Masks in RFC Literature

Subnet masks are represented as a 3-tuple in the RFC literature:

```
{<network number>, <subnet number>, <host number>}
```

A -1 value is used to represent all 1s. For example, the subnet mask of 255.255.255.0 for a class B network is represented as the following:

```
{ -1, -1, 0}
```

The first -1 corresponds to all 1s for the *<network number>* value. The second -1 corresponds to all 1s for the *<subnet number>* value. The 0 corresponds to all 0s for the *<host number>* value.

## The IP Routing Algorithm

The IP routing algorithm discussed so far is described by the following steps. This algorithm takes into account the use of subnet masks discussed in previous sections.

Get the destination address field (*DestIPAddr*) of the IP datagram. From the *DestIPAddr*, determine the network prefix *NetPrefix*. For a class A network, the *NetPrefix* is the first byte of the *DestIPAddr*. For a class B network, the *NetPrefix* is the first two bytes of the *DestIPAddr*. For a class C network, the *NetPrefix* is the first three bytes of the *DestIPAddr*.

1. Get the destination address field (*DestIPAddr*) of the IP datagram. From the *DestIPAddr*, determine the network portion *NetPrefix* by doing a bitwise AND with the subnet mask listed in the routing table entry.

2. If *NetPrefix* matches the netid of any directly connected network, the destination host is on the directly connected network. In this case, perform direct delivery of the IP datagram. This may involve binding *DestIPAddr* to its physical address by using a protocol such as ARP. The IP datagram is encapsulated by the Data Link layer frame and sent on the directly attached network.

3. If there is no match in step 2, examine the routing table for a destination entry for *NetPrefix*. If such an entry is found, forward the IP datagram as indicated by the corresponding next hop router entry.

4. If there is no match in step 3, examine the routing table for a default entry: **0.0.0.0**. If such an entry is found, forward the IP datagram as indicated by the corresponding default router entry.

5. If there is no match in step 4, the IP datagram cannot be routed. Report a routing error to the upper-layer protocols.

# Routing on a Windows NT Server

To convert a Windows NT computer into a router, you must have at least two network adapters. If you are installing a network adapter card after Windows NT has already been installed, you must configure Windows NT to recognize the new network adapter.

After ensuring that network adapters are recognized by Windows NT, you must enable IP forwarding. Windows NT is now configured to act as a router between the interfaces.

If, in addition to acting as a simple forwarding router, you want Windows NT to actively participate in a routing protocol, you can enable the routing protocols discussed in the following sections.

## Configuring a New Network Adapter for Windows NT 5

After adding the network adapter and recording its settings, if any, perform the following steps to configure the new adapter for Windows NT 5:

1. Start the Hardware Wizard applet from the Control Panel.

2. When given an option to repair devices that aren't working, select No, I Want to Do Something Else and click Next.

3. Select the option to add new hardware.

4. Select the option to perform autodetection.

5. If autodetection succeeds, you will be informed about the new hardware that was detected. Verify that the correct network adapter was detected and follow prompts on the screen to complete the installation.

   If autodetection fails, you will be given a choice to proceed with the installation manually. Confirm that you want perform a manual installation.

   For manual installation, you will be shown a list of hardware types. Highlight Network Adapters Type and click Next. Select the manufacturer and the network adapter type, and click OK. Follow the prompts to complete the installation.

## Enabling IP Forwarding

After configuring at least two network adapter cards on the computer, perform the following steps to enable IP forwarding:

1. Start the Network applet from the Control Panel.

2. Select the Protocols tab.

3. Select TCP/IP Protocol and choose Properties.

4. Select the Routing tab (see Figure 7.11).

5. Check the Enable IP Forwarding check box.

6. Select OK. Close the Network applet and restart the computer.

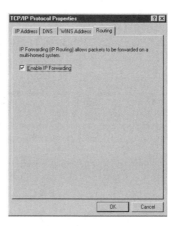

**Figure 7.11**   Routing tab.

# Building Efficient IP Networks Using Routers

If you want to build large networks that undergo frequent changes, it is important to know how to assign subnet numbers and host numbers efficiently so that as the networks change, there is a minimum amount of configuration that needs to be done.

The following sections discuss techniques for subnetting, variable-length subnet masks, and supernetting that will help you design more efficient networks using routers.

## Efficient Assignment of Subnet Numbers

In *subnetting*, the host part of the IP address is subdivided into two fields: the subnet number and host number. This gives the IP address a third level of hierarchy. Although this results in savings in routing and the reuse of a common network number prefix for subnets, it can result in inefficiency in the allocation of addresses. The inefficiency stems from the fact that a network administrator selects a subnet size to estimate the largest number of subnets and hosts that may be needed in the future. However, there is a way to select subnet number and host number values so as to give you maximum flexibility in changing the subnet mask, should you need to do so in the future, with a minimum impact on changing IP address assignments at each host in the subnets.

To get an intuitive understanding of this technique, consider Figure 7.12, in which the dotted line shows the boundary between the host number and the subnet number. This boundary is labeled as the subnet mask boundary, because to the left of this boundary the subnet mask consists of ones and to the right of this boundary it consists of zeros. If the subnet number and host number assignment is selected so that there are zeros near the subnet mask boundary, then moving the subnet mask boundary to the left or right will not alter the subnet and host number assignment; only the subnet mask will change. In fact, the subnet boundary mask can be moved as far left or as far right as possible, without changing the subnet and host number, until a value of 1 is encountered in the subnet or host number. This means that subnet numbers should be assigned with 1s in their leftmost position, and host numbers should be assigned with 1s in their rightmost position. The central region of the subnet mask should be filled with zeros as far as possible.

This assignment of subnet and host numbers is called *mirror image counting* because the subnet numbers and host numbers should be mirror images of each other.

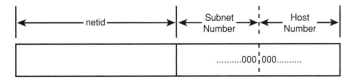

**Figure 7.12**  Efficient subnet mask assignment.

*Subnet number assignment:*

```
0          (reserved to mean "this subnet")
10
01
110
001
101
  :
  :
011...11
111...11   (reserved to mean "all subnets")
```

*Host number assignment:*

```
        0       (reserved to mean "this host")
       01
       10
      011
      100
      101
        :
        :
    11...110
    11...111        (reserved to mean "all hosts")
```

The technique on flexibility in assigning subnet numbers is described in detail in RFC 1219 on "On the Assignment of Subnet Numbers."

## Variable-length Subnet Masks

In the examples covered so far, the same subnet mask was used for a given network (for example, all subnets in a class B network have a subnet mask of 255.255.255.0). For a network address of 134.65.0.0 (a class B address), the subnet mask could be 255.255.255.0, which means that 8 bits of the host address field are used for subnetting. TCP/IP allows you to use different subnet masks for the same network address of 134.65.0.0. For example, a subdivided network of the network 134.65.0.0 could use a subnet mask of 255.255.255.192 while another uses a subnet mask of 255.255.255.0. When different subnet masks are used, there are restrictions on what combinations of host IP addresses and subnet masks can be used.

Suppose you want to divide a class C network (216.144.108.0) into three subnets with a maximum of 120 hosts on one subnet and a maximum of 60 hosts each on the other two subnets. What subnet mask can you use? The total number of hosts on the three subnets is 120 + 60 + 60 = 240 hosts. You can have 254 hosts in a class C network. This number is computed as 256 − 2 = 254; you subtract 2 for the reserved addresses of all 0s and all 1s. The number 256 arises because the maximum number of bit pattern combinations for an 8-bit field is $2^8 = 256$. It should be possible to have 240 hosts on a class C network. But when you decide to use a single subnet mask, you must accommodate the largest subnet possible, which in this case is the subnet with 120 hosts. There can be only one subnet mask for such a subnet:

11111111 11111111 11111111 **1 0000000**
255.255.255.128

The subnet number is the **1** in bold, and the host number is the seven zeros in bold. With one network bit and seven host bits, there are two subnets possible, each with a size of $2^7 - 2^1 = 128 - 2 = 126$ hosts. This type of subnet division can accommodate the subnet with 120 hosts, and one other subnet with 60 hosts but cannot accommodate the remaining 60-host subnet. This is because three subnets are needed and only two subnets are available. Actually, if you examine the subnet mask of 255.255.255.128, this is not legal as per the RFCs even though many commercial routers will permit this subnet. 255.255.255.128 is illegal for a class C network because the subnet number is 0 or 1—that is, all 0s or all 1s, which are not permitted for subnet numbers. However, as pointed out earlier, many commercial routers will permit this subnet mask.

You might say, let's use two bits for the subnet number which will then permit $2^2 =$ 4 subnets. The subnet mask then becomes the following:

11111111 11111111 11111111 **11 000000**
255.255.255.192

The subnet number is the **11** in bold, and the host number is the six zeros in bold. With six host bits, there are four subnets possible, each with a size of $2^6 - 2 = 62$ hosts. This type of subnet division can accommodate the two subnets with 60 hosts each. However, it cannot accommodate the remaining subnet with 120 hosts. This is because the subnet mask of 255.255.255.192 can accommodate only 62 hosts, which is much less than the desired 120 hosts on the subnet.

The previous example shows that a single subnet mask cannot be used for the class C network in some situations. What is needed is a way of dividing the class C network into subnets with 126 hosts, and dividing one of these subnets further into two subnets of $2^6 - 2 = 62$ hosts each. This technique is called *variable-length subnet mask (VLSM)* and is discussed in RFC 1878 on "Variable Length Subnet Table For IPv4."

Figure 7.13 shows an example of how variable-length subnet masks can be used. In this example, the subnet mask 255.255.255.128 is used to divide the class C network into two subnets of 126 hosts each. Then, the subnet mask 255.255.255.192 is used to divide one of the subnets into two subnets with 62 hosts each.

For your reference, Table 7.1 lists the number of hosts and subnets provided by commercial routers. Note that the "Number of Subnets" column includes the all -0s and all -1s combination, which is prohibited by RFCs but is permitted by many commercial routers.

### Using All Ones or Zeros for the Subnet

Some newer RFCs address the possible use of all 0s and all 1s for the subnet. This is still, strictly speaking, illegal, but these recent RFCs reflect actual usage.

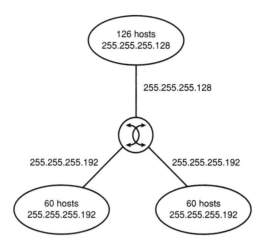

**Figure 7.13**   VLSM subnet mask example.

Table 7.1   **Capacity of Subnets for Class C Networks Permitted by Commercial Routers**

| Subnet Mask | Number of Subnets | Number of Hosts |
|---|---|---|
| 255.255.255.128 | 2 | 126 |
| 255.255.255.192 | 4 | 62 |
| 255.255.255.224 | 8 | 30 |
| 255.255.255.240 | 16 | 14 |
| 255.255.255.248 | 32 | 6 |
| 255.255.255.252 | 64 | 2 |

Not all routing protocols can handle different subnet masks used in a network. For example, the RIP (Routing Information Protocol) version 1 routing protocol does not handle a mix of different subnet masks for the same network address, and cannot be used in conjunction with variable subnet masks. If RIP were to be used with variable subnet masks, the network topology reported by RIP would not accurately reflect the network topology that you have set up. On the other hand, routing protocols such as OSPF (Open Shortest Path First), RIP version 2, and ISIS (Intermediate System to Intermediate System) enable routers to exchange subnet mask information for the interconnected networks, and can be used to support a mix of different subnet masks. However, despite the use of these protocols, VLSM is not as widely used for the following reasons:

■ IP address assignments for subnets must be grouped into blocks indicated by the VLSMs. Older IP address assignments must be changed, and this is not always easy.

- Some older networks use RIP version 1, which cannot support VLSM. Modern routing protocols, such as RIP version 2 and OSPF, allow subnet mask information to be exchanged.

- The VLSM technique is not well understood by many network administrators, and for this reason is seldom used. Many administrators have difficulty coping with subnet masks and subnetting. Better training and books such as this will hopefully address the problem.

# Installing and Configuring Routing Protocols

You must first install the Router service before you can configure the routing protocols. To accomplish this, complete the following steps:

1. Start the Network applet from the Control Panel.
2. Select the Services tab.
3. Select the Add button.
4. From the list of Network Services, select Router.
5. If the required files have already been installed, you are asked if you want to use the existing files. Otherwise, you must install the required files from the Windows NT distribution software.

   Select OK. If files are missing, you are asked to supply the distribution source.
6. You are asked to restart the computer before changes take effect. Select the option to restart the computer.

Next, you have the option to configure the routing protocols that you will be using. The following is a guideline for performing routing protocol configuration:

1. Select Programs, Administrative Tools, Routing, Remote Access Administrator.

   You should see the main Routing and RAS Admin screen (see Figure 7.14).
2. Click on IP Routing.

   You should see the Summary and Static Routes options (see Figure 7.15).
3. Right-click on the Summary option and select the Add Routing Protocol option.

   You should see the list of routing protocols that are available (see Figure 7.16)
4. The DHCP Relay Agent should be added to the router if the router is meant to forward BOOTP or DHCP request broadcasts. If you do not need this capability, you should not add the DHCP Relay Agent.

   The other two options are for adding OSPF or RIP-2 as routing protocols. OSPF is a link state protocol and the preferred protocol for many TCP/IP networks. RIP-2 is a distance vector protocol and is an older protocol. RIP-2 is an improvement of the classic RIP (version 1) protocol.

The configurations of these routing protocol options are described in the sections that follow.

**Figure 7.14**   Routing and RAS Admin screen.

**Figure 7.15**   Summary and Static Routes options.

## Configuring OSPF

If you double-click on the OSPF protocol option in Figure 7.14, you see the OSPF Configuration screen (see Figure 7.17).

The General tab in the OSPF Configuration screen is used to set the router identification. By default this is set to the IP address of the first network interface, which in this case is 199.245.180.20. The router identification can be any 32-bit number and is usually written using the dotted decimal notation.

You can use this General tab to enable the router as an autonomous system boundary router by checking the box labeled Enable Autonomous System Boundary Router. Large networks can be divided into routing domains known as *autonomous systems* (AS). Different autonomous systems can run different routing protocols. The different autonomous systems are connected using autonomous system boundary routers (ASBRs). ASBRs can run protocols such as Exterior Gateway Protocol (EGP) or Boundary Gateway Protocol (BGP) in addition to OSPF.

You can also use the General tab to select various logging options, as illustrated in Figure 7.17.

If you select the Areas tab, you see the options for configuring OSPF areas (see Figure 7.18). OSPF allows networks to be divided into areas so that hierarchical routing can be implemented with different areas. Each area is identified by a unique 32-bit number, also expressed in dotted decimal notation.

You can use the Add, Configure, and Delete buttons to add new area definitions, configure existing area definitions, or delete existing areas.

Figure 7.19 shows the configuration screen for a specific area. The backbone area has an area identification of 0.0.0.0 by default. Multiple areas are joined to the backbone area. Routers that connect OSPF areas to the backbone area are called *area border routers (ABRs)*. The backbone area must be configured to act as a backbone. If the backbone area becomes partitioned for geographical reasons, the different OSPF areas can be connected using virtual links.

You can enable clear text password for the area or disable authentication by not checking the box labeled Enable Clear-text Password.

**Figure 7.16**  Choice of routing protocols.      **Figure 7.17**  OSPF Configuration screen.

Figure 7.18   Configuring OSPF areas.

Figure 7.19   Configuring a specific OSPF area.

OSPF areas can be normal or stub areas. This can be set by checking or unchecking the option labeled Stub Area. In a stub OSPF area, the routers do not maintain link state information of routes external to the OSPF domain. This is because external route advertisements are not propagated through a stub area. In a stub area, all external routes are summarized by a default route that has a metric cost associated with it called the *stub metric*. The stub metric is the cost of the default route advertised to the stub area. If the Stub Area option is enabled in the configuration screen (refer to Figure 7.19), you can change the stub metric to a value other than 1, and also set the option to import summary advertisements.

If you select the Ranges tab in the configuration screen, you see the Range options shown in Figure 7.20. You can use this to set the address and mask pair that define a range of addresses that belong to the area.

If you select the Virtual Interfaces tab from the OSPF Configuration screen (see Figure 7.21), you can define the virtual link that can be used to connect two areas that no longer share a connection through a backbone.

The Transit area is the OSPF area through which a virtual link must pass. For example, if an OSPF backbone area had to be split for economic, geographical, or political reasons, then the OSPF area between the separated backbone serves as a transit area. Figure 7.22 shows the screen when the Add button is selected.

The following parameters on this screen are used to define the virtual link:

- The Virtual Neighbor Router ID defines the IP address of the router at the endpoint of the virtual link.

- The Transit Delay is an estimate of the number of seconds it takes to transmit the link state update information over this interface.

- The Re-transmit Interval is an estimate of the number of seconds between link state advertisements. The number should be significantly larger than the expected round-trip delay between any two routers on the attached network. Because it is difficult to estimate this time for a virtual link, it is better to use a large value and err on the side of caution.

- Hello Interval is used to select the number of seconds between OSPF Hello packets that are used to determine the status of the router links.

- Dead Interval specifies the number of seconds the neighbor routers will wait after they cease to hear the router's Hello packets before they declare that the router is down.

- If the Password is set, the two interfaces that define the endpoint of the virtual link must have the same password.

The last step to complete OSPF configuration is to specify the interfaces of the router on which the OSPF protocol is to run. You can do this by right-clicking on the OSPF option under IP Routing in the Router and Remote Access Administrator screen, and selecting Add Interface. You are shown a list of interfaces on which OSPF can be configured. Highlight the interface name and select OK.

You can optionally configure OSPF parameters on each interface by right-clicking on the interface name that has been added, and selecting the Configure Interface option.

## Configuring RIP 2

If you double-click on the RIP Version 2 for Internet Protocol option in Figure 7.16, you see the RIP for Internet Protocol Configuration screen (see Figure 7.23).

The General tab in the RIP for Internet Protocol Configuration screen is used to set the minimum number of seconds between triggered updates, which is set to a default value of 5 seconds. Triggered updates are sent when a change is detected in the routes rather than waiting to send the update at the next regular update interval. You can also use the General tab to select various logging options, as shown in Figure 7.23.

**Figure 7.20**  Specifying addresses and mask pairs for an area.

**Figure 7.21**  OSPF virtual link configuration.

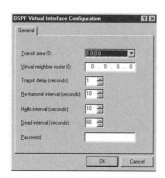

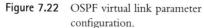

Figure 7.22  OSPF virtual link parameter configuration.

Figure 7.23  RIP for Internet Protocol configuration screen.

If you select the Security tab, you see the options for specifying which routers to use for receiving routing updates (see Figure 7.24). The default is to process announcements (routing table updates) from all routers. The other options are to process only announcements from the routers listed or discard all announcements from the routers listed. To maintain the list of routers, you can use the Add, Replace, and Delete buttons.

The last step to complete RIP configuration is to specify the interfaces of the router on which the RIP protocol is to run. You can do this by right-clicking on the RIP option under IP Routing in the Router and Remote Access Administrator screen, and selecting Add Interface. You are shown a list of interfaces on which RIP can be configured. Highlight the interface name and select OK.

You can optionally configure RIP parameters on each interface by right-clicking on the interface name that has been added, and selecting the Configure Interface option.

## Configuring DHCP Relay Agent

You can configure a DHCP relay agent on the Windows NT router so that this agent can forward BOOTP and DHCP broadcast requests across the router. DHCP is covered in Chapter 8, "DHCP Configuration and Management."

If you double-click on the DHCP Relay Agent option shown in Figure 7.16, you see the DHCP Relay Agent Configuration screen (see Figure 7.25).

You can use this configuration screen to add or remove the IP addresses of the DHCP servers that this router knows about.

The last step to complete DHCP Relay Agent configuration is to specify the interfaces of the router on which the relay agent is to run. You can do this by right-clicking on the DHCP Relay Agent option under IP Routing in the Router and Remote Access Administrator screen, and selecting Add Interface. You are shown a list of interfaces on which the DHCP Relay Agent can be configured. Highlight the interface name and select OK.

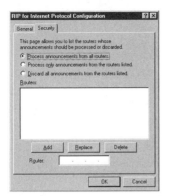

**Figure 7.24** RIP Security configuration.

**Figure 7.25** DHCP Relay Agent configuration screen.

You can optionally configure the DHCP parameters on each interface by right-clicking on the interface name that has been added, and selecting the Configure Interface option.

## Configuring Static Routes

You can add static routes by using the Routing and Remote Access Administrator screen. Under the IP Routing option in the main screen of the Routing and Remote Access Administrator, you find the Static Routes option. Right-click on the Static Routes option, and select the Add Static Route option. You will see the Static Route dialog box shown in Figure 7.26.

Use the screen shown in Figure 7.26 to specify the static route entry. The static route entry consists of the destination (network or host), the network mask (same as subnet mask), the gateway (forwarding router), and the metric (cost of going through that interface).

You can view the routing table by right-clicking on the Static Routes option, and selecting the View IP Routing Table option.

You can also configure and view static routes by using the `route` command.

To add a static route to a destination (144.19.0.0) through a router (199.245.180.10), with a metric cost of 2, you could use the following command:

```
route add 144.19.0.0 mask 255.255.0.0 199.245.180.10 metric 2
```

To delete a route for destination 198.23.4.0, you can use the following command:

```
route delete 198.23.4.0
```

To change the entry for a destination network (144.19.0.0) and specify a different router, such as 199.245.180.33, you can use the following command:

```
route change 144.19.0.0 199.245.180.33
```

To display a routing table, you can use the following command:

```
route print
```

**Figure 7.26**  Static Route dialog box.

You can also display the routing table by using the `netstat` command with a `-r` option:

```
netstat -r
```

## Viewing Routing Information

You can view routing and configuration information on a routing protocol or routing option by highlighting that option under IP Routing in Routing and Remote Access Administrator. When you select an option, you can view corresponding information on the right side of the panel.

If you have configured a routing protocol, you can right-click on its name in the Routing and Remote Access Administrator screen, and select View. For OSPF you see options to view areas, link state databases, neighbors, and virtual interfaces. For RIP 2, you can view the addresses, versions, bad packets, and bad routes of RIP neighbors.

If you right-click on a protocol name in the Routing and Remote Access Administrator screen, you can also see the option for configuring that routing protocol. The configuration options and screen for the routing protocols such as OSPF and RIP 2 are described in earlier sections.

You can view the protocol configuration information on each router interface by right-clicking on the interface name for the router and selecting the Configure Interface option.

## Changing Routing Protocols Preference Levels in Windows NT

Static routes have the highest priority amongst all routing methods. Static routes are never aged out because they are entered manually and the network administrator probably had a very good reason to add them in the first place. Static routes have a preference level of 1.

After static routes, the SNMP Set Routes command has the next level of priority at a preference level of 2. Next comes Routes Discovered Using OSPF, which has a preference level of 3. Lastly, Routes Discovered Using RIP has a preference level of 4.

You can change the default preference level through the Routing and Remote Access Administrator screen as follows:

1. Right-click on Summary under IP Routing.

2. Select Configure IP Parameters.

3. Select the Preference Levels tab. You should see the screen shown in Figure 7.27.

4. Highlight the protocol whose preference level you want to change.

5. Use the Raise Level or Lower Level button to raise or lower the preference level number.

Remember: Lower preference level numbers indicate higher priority given to routes discovered through that method in case of conflicting routing information received through other methods.

# Supernetting

The subnetting technique was devised in 1985 to make efficient use of IP address allocation for large networks. Subnetting works quite well for networks with large address spaces, such as class A or class B, but these network address formats are very popular and are rapidly being used up. Subnetting can also be used for class C addresses, but a class C address can support 254 hosts only. In many networks, subdividing a class C network may not be practical, when the number of hosts that need to be supported per subnet is more than 126.

Class A and class B addresses are rapidly being used up. This syndrome is called the ROADS (Running Out of ADdress Space) problem. While class A and class B network addresses are being used up, there is a sufficient number of class C addresses that are available. Large organizations that must support more than 254 hosts have to use several class C network addresses.

Suppose that an organization needs a class B address to support 65,534 hosts. If a class B address is not forthcoming from the InterNIC, how many class C addresses are needed to support 65,534 hosts? The answer is about 256. These 256 class C addresses can be assigned as a block. For example, the following class C address range supports the same number of addresses as a single class B address:

```
202.100.0.0  to  202.100.255.255
```

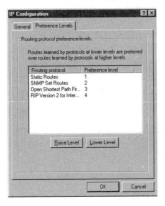

**Figure 7.27**  Routing protocol preference levels.

If you examine the range of bits that can vary in this class C address, you will see that there are 16 lower-order bits—the same number as for a class B address.

In *supernetting* or *supernet addressing*, a block of class C addresses, rather than a single class B network address, is assigned to create a virtual address class that is somewhere between a class C and a class B address class. This has the advantage of better address utilization. For example, if an organization must have a network of 8000 hosts, it is better to assign a block of 32 class C addresses rather than a single class B address. A class B address can support up to 65,534 hosts, but in this example, 65,534 − 8000 = 57,534 addresses are not utilized.

The supernetting technique is designed to be used by Internet Service Providers (ISPs) for Internet connectivity. Typically, only ISPs are allowed to obtain large address blocks of class C addresses. ISPs can then allocate smaller blocks of these class C addresses to other organizations that want to connect a large number of their computers to the Internet.

## Classless Internet Domain Routing (CIDR)

Allocating blocks of class C addresses prevents the rapid depletion of class B addresses. However, it requires additional routing table entries to be stored in routers. Since a block of 256 class C addresses is needed to support the same address space as a single class B address, a routing table must have 256 network address entries for each of the class C networks. This is an increase in the number of routing table entries by a factor of 256. If a router has 2 MB of memory for its routing table that uses class B addresses, then replacing these by class C addresses will require a memory of $2 \times 256 = 512$ MB!

The Classless Internet Domain Routing (CIDR) technique is used to summarize a block of class C addresses with a single routing table entry. This summarization results in a reduction in the number of separate routing table entries. The block of class C addresses is summarized by a routing table entry that consists of the following:

(*lowest address in block, supernet mask*)

The *lowest address in block* is the start of the address block, and the supernet mask specifies the number of class C addresses in the block. The *supernet mask*, also called the CIDR mask, contains ones for the common prefix for all the class C addresses, and zeros for the parts of the class C addresses that have different values. Consider the following CIDR routing table entry:

(200.1.160.0, 255.255.224.0)

The 200.1.160.0 and the CIDR mask 255.255.224.0 have the following bit representations:

**11001000 00000001 101**00000 00000000
**11111111 11111111 111**00000 00000000

The ones in the CIDR mask correspond to the following common prefix:
**11001000 00000001 101**

The zeros in the CIDR mask correspond to the varying part of the block of class C addresses. This means that the range of class C addresses are between the following lower- and upper-class C addresses:

11001000 00000001 10100000 00000000 = 200.1.160.0

11001000 00000001 10111111 11111111 = 200.1.191.255

Figure 7.28 illustrates the previous CIDR block of addresses.

How many class C addresses are there in this block of class C addresses? You can determine the total by noting the number of bits in the network portion of the class C address that can vary in the address range. There are five such bits shown in bold in the CIDR mask:

11111111 11111111 111**00000** 00000000

Therefore, the number of class C addresses in the range is $2^5 = 32$. Routes in a CIDR block can be summarized in a single router advertisement called an *aggregate*.

Table 7.2 shows the number of contiguous class C addresses that must be assigned for a given size of the network using CIDR. The number of contiguous class C addresses for CIDR must be a power of 2.

Another notation that is used for CIDR blocks is the following:

*lowest address in block/number of common prefix bits*

Table 7.2  **Number of Class C Addresses in CIDR for a Given Network Size**

| Network Size (# of Hosts) | Number of Class C Addresses |
| --- | --- |
| 254 | 1 |
| 255–508 | 2 |
| 509–1016 | 4 |
| 1017–2032 | 8 |
| 2033–4064 | 16 |
| 4065–8128 | 32 |
| 8129–16,256 | 64 |

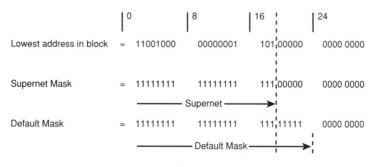

**Figure 7.28**  CIDR block.

The *number of common prefix bits* is the number of ones in the supernet mask. Thus the following are equivalent representations of the CIDR block:

(200.1.160.0, 255.255.224.0)

200.1.160.0/19

The default subnet mask of a class C address is 255.255.255.0. This indicates that hosts in a single class C address have 24 common prefix bits. Whenever the *number of common prefix bits* is less than 24 for a class C address, supernetting is being used.

Networks that are subsets of a CIDR block are said to be "more specific" relative to the CIDR block. The common prefix length of more specific addresses is greater than that of the CIDR block. The following shows an example of a CIDR block and a more specific route:

199.22.0.0/16          CIDR block with prefix length 16

199.22.176.0/20        More specific prefix of length 20

Routers that understand CIDR use the longest match to select a route. The CIDR mask is used to determine the number of prefix bits that are to be considered in the match. But if there is more than one route to the destination, the router selects the route with the longest prefix. Consider the example of the network shown in Figure 7.29, which has a router (R1) that receives two routing updates:

199.22.0.0/16 from router R2

199.22.176.0/20 from router R3

R1 selects the path through router R3 because it is the path with the longest prefix.

RFC 1519 on "Classless Inter-Domain Routing (CIDR): an Address Assignment and Aggregation Strategy" discusses the CIDR technique.

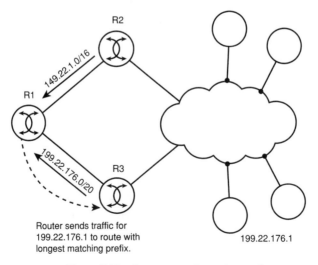

**Figure 7.29**  Longest match-routing prefix.

# 8

# DHCP Configuration and Management

I N LARGE NETWORKS, CONFIGURING TCP/IP PARAMETERS for each workstation can be a difficult and time-consuming task, particularly when the TCP/IP parameters, such as IP addresses and subnet masks, need to be changed. The changes can occur because of a major restructuring of the network or because the network has many mobile users with portable computers that can be connected to any of the network segments. The network connections can be direct physical connections or wireless connections. Because the TCP/IP parameters for computers depend on the network segment they connect to, appropriate values must be set up whenever a computer is connected to a different network segment.

Understanding the consequences of TCP/IP parameter changes requires knowledgeable network administrators. For TCP/IP internetworks, several auto-configuration protocols, such as Boot Protocol (BOOTP) and Dynamic Host Configuration Protocol (DHCP), have been developed by the Internet Engineering Task Force (IETF). A Windows NT Server can be configured as a DHCP server, which simplifies the configuration of TCP/IP devices (workstations, servers, routers, and so on) on the network. This chapter discusses the DHCP protocol and how it can be configured on a Windows NT Server. DHCP clients such as Windows 9x and Windows NT workstations must be configured to have knowledge of DHCP servers.

# Understanding the DHCP Protocol

DHCP can be used for dynamic configuration of essential TCP/IP parameters for hosts (workstations and servers) on the network. The DHCP protocol consists of two elements:

■ A mechanism for allocating IP addresses and other TCP/IP parameters

■ A protocol for negotiating and transmitting host specific information

The TCP/IP host requesting the TCP/IP configuration information is called the DHCP client, and the TCP/IP host that supplies this information is called a DHCP server. On a Windows NT network, the DHCP clients are Windows NT workstations or servers, but the DHCP server can only be a Windows NT Server.

## Understanding IP Address Management

DHCP uses the following three methods for IP address allocation:

■ **Manual allocation.** In the manual allocation method, the DHCP client's IP address is set manually by the network administrator at the DHCP server, and DHCP is used to convey to the DHCP client the value of the manually configured IP address.

■ **Automatic allocation.** In the automatic allocation method, no manual assignments of the IP address must be made. The DHCP client is assigned an IP address when it first contacts the DHCP server. The IP address assigned using this method is permanently assigned to the DHCP client and is not reused by another DHCP client.

■ **Dynamic allocation.** In the dynamic allocation method, DHCP assigns an IP address to a DHCP client on a temporary basis. The IP address is on loan or leased to the DHCP client for a specified duration. On the expiry of this lease, the IP address is revoked, and the DHCP client is required to surrender the IP address. If the DHCP client still needs an IP address to perform its functions, it can request another one.

The dynamic allocation method is the only one of the three methods that affords automatic reuse of an IP address. An IP address does not always have to be surrendered by the DHCP client on the expiry of the lease. If the DHCP client no longer needs an IP address, such as when the computer is being gracefully shut down, it can release the IP address to the DHCP server. The DHCP server then can reissue the same IP address to another DHCP client making a request for an IP address.

The dynamic allocation method is particularly useful for DHCP clients that need an IP address for temporary connection to a network. Consider, for example, a situation in which there are 300 users with portable computers on a network, and a class C address has been assigned to a network. This enables the network to have a maximum of 254 nodes on the network ($256 - 2$ special addresses = 254). Because computers connecting to a network using TCP/IP are required to have unique IP addresses, all of the 300 computers cannot be simultaneously connected to the network. If there are at most only 200 concurrent physical connections on the network, however, it is possible to use a class C address by reusing IP addresses that are not in use. Using DHCP's dynamic IP address allocation, IP address reuse is possible.

Dynamic IP address allocation is also a good choice for assigning IP addresses to new hosts that are being permanently connected, and where IP addresses are scarce. As old hosts are retired, their IP addresses can be immediately reused.

Regardless of which of the three IP address allocation methods is used, you can still configure IP parameters at a central DHCP server once, instead of repeating the TCP/IP configuration for each computer.

## The DHCP IP Address Acquisition Process

Upon contacting a DHCP server, a DHCP client goes through several internal states, during which it negotiates the use of an IP address and the duration of the use. The operation of how a DHCP client acquires the IP address can best be explained in terms of a *state transition diagram* (also called a *finite state machine*). Figure 8.1 shows the state transition diagram that explains the interaction between the DHCP client and DHCP server.

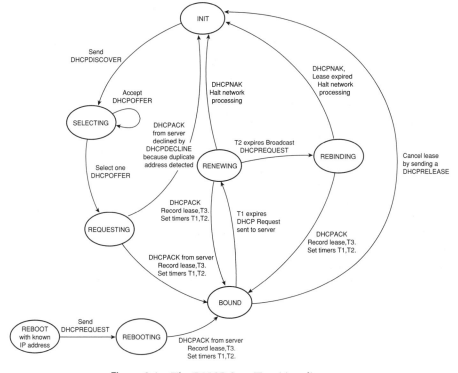

**Figure 8.1** The DHCP State Transition diagram.

When the DHCP client is first started, it begins in the INIT (initialize) state. At this point, the DHCP client does not know its IP parameters, and so sends a DHCPDISCOVER broadcast. The DHCPDISCOVER is encapsulated in a UDP/IP packet. The destination UDP port number is set to 67 (decimal), the same as that for a BOOTP server. This similarity occurs because the DHCP protocol is an extension of the BOOTP protocol. A local IP broadcast address of 255.255.255.255 is used in the DHCPDISCOVER packet. If DHCP servers are not on the local network, the IP router must have DHCP-relay agent support to forward the DHCPDISCOVER request to other subnetworks. DHCP-relay agent support is discussed in RFC 1542.

Before sending the DHCPDISCOVER broadcast packet, the DHCP clients wait for a random time interval between 1 and 10 seconds. This is done to prevent DHCP clients from starting at the same time; otherwise, simultaneous powerups will be attempted after power failures.

After sending the DHCPDISCOVER broadcast, the DHCP client enters the SELECTING state. In this state, the DHCP client receives DHCPOFFER messages from the DHCP servers that have been configured to respond to the DHCP client. The time period over which the DHCP client waits to receive DHCPOFFER messages is implementation dependent. The DHCP client must select one DHCPOFFER response if it receives multiple DHCPOFFER responses. After selecting a DHCPOFFER message from a server, the DHCP client sends a DHCPREQUEST message to the selected DHCP server. The DHCP server responds with a DHCPACK that includes the lease time.

The DHCP client may optionally perform a check on the IP address sent in the DHCPOFFER to verify if the address is not in use. On a broadcast network, the DHCP client can send an ARP request for the suggested IP address to see if there is an ARP response. An ARP response would imply that the suggested IP address is already in use, in which case the DHCPACK from the server is ignored and a DHCPDECLINE is sent, and the DHCP client enters the INIT state and tries again to get a valid IP address that is not in use. When the ARP request is broadcast on the local network, the client uses its own hardware address in the sender hardware address field of the ARP packet, but sets a value of 0 in the sender IP address field. A sender IP address of 0 is used, rather than the suggested IP address, so as not to confuse ARP caches on other TCP/IP hosts in case the suggested IP address is already in use.

When the DHCPACK from the DHCP server is accepted, three timer values are set, and the DHCP client moves into the BOUND state. The first timer, T1, is the *lease renewal timer*; the second timer, T2, is the *rebinding timer*; and the third timer, T3, is the *lease duration timer*. The DHCPACK always returns the value of T3, the lease duration. The values of timers T1 and T2 can be configured at the DHCP server, but if they are not set, default values are used based on the duration of the lease. The following shows the default values used for T1 and T2:

$$T1 = 0.5 \times T3$$
$$T2 = 0.875 \times T3$$

The actual times at which the timer values expire are computed by adding to the timer value the time at which the DHCPREQUEST that generated the DHCPACK response was sent. If the time at which the DHCP request was sent was T0, then the expiration values are computed as follows:

Expiration of T1 = T0 + T1

Expiration of T2 = T0 + T2

Expiration of T3 = T0 + T3

RFC 1541 recommends that a fuzz factor be added to timers T1 and T2 to prevent several DHCP clients from expiring their timers at the same time.

At the expiration of timer T1, the DHCP client moves from the BOUND state to the RENEWING state. In the RENEWING state, a new lease for the allocated IP address must be negotiated by the DHCP client from the DHCP server that originally allocated the IP address. If the original DHCP server does not renew the release, it sends a DHCPNAK message, and the DHCP client moves into the INIT state and tries to obtain a new IP address. If the original DHCP server sends a DHCPACK message, this message contains the new lease duration. The DHCP client sets its timer values and moves to the BOUND state.

If the T2 timer expires while waiting in the RENEWING state for a DHCPACK or DHCPNAK message from the original DHCP server, then the DHCP client moves from the RENEWING state to the REBINDING state. The original DHCP server may not respond because it or a network link is down. Note from the previous equations that T2 > T1, so the DHCP client waits for the original DHCP server for a duration of T2 – T1 to renew the release.

At the expiration of timer T2, a broadcast DHCPREQUEST is sent over the network to contact any DHCP server to extend the lease, and the DHCP client is in the REBINDING state. A DHCPREQUEST broadcast is sent because the DHCP client assumes, after spending T2 – T1 seconds in the RENEWING state, that the original DHCP server is not available, and the DHCP client tries to contact any DHCP server that is configured to respond to it. If a DHCP server responds with a DHCPACK message, the DHCP client renews its lease (T3), sets the T1 and T2 timers, and moves back to the BOUND state. If no DHCP server is able to renew the release after expiration of timer T3, the lease expires and the DHCP client moves to the INIT state. Note that by this time, the DHCP client has tried to renew the lease, first with the original DHCP server and then with any DHCP server on the network.

When the lease expires (when timer T3 expires), the DHCP client must surrender the use of its IP address and halt network processing with that IP address.

The DHCP client does not always have to wait for the expiration of the lease (timer T3) to surrender the use of an IP address. It could voluntarily relinquish control of an IP address by canceling its lease. A user with a portable computer may, for example, connect to the network. The DHCP server on the network might set the duration of the lease for one hour. Assume that the user finishes the network tasks in 30 minutes and now wants to disconnect from the network. As the user gracefully shuts down his or her computer, the DHCP client sends a DHCPRELEASE message to the

DHCP server to cancel its lease. The IP address that is surrendered is now available for use by another DHCP client.

If DHCP clients are run on computers that have a disk, the IP address that is allocated can be stored on the computer's disk, and when the computer reboots, it can make a request for the same IP address. This was shown in Figure 8.1 in the state labeled REBOOT with known IP address.

## DHCP Packet Format

The DHCP packet format is shown in Figure 8.2. The DHCP messages use a fixed format for all the fields except the options field, which has a minimum size of 312 octets. Readers who are familiar with the BOOTP protocol will recognize that with the exception of the flags field and the options field, the message formats for DHCP and BOOTP are identical. In fact, the DHCP server can be programmed to answer BOOTP requests.

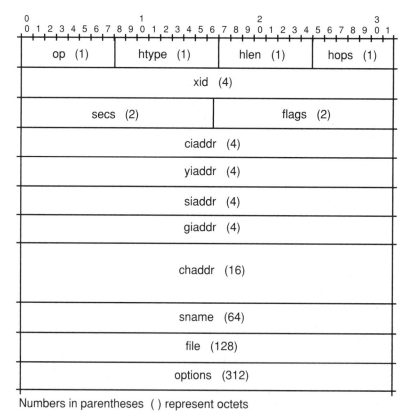

Numbers in parentheses ( ) represent octets

**Figure 8.2** DHCP packet format.

Table 8.1 gives an explanation of the fields used in a DHCP packet. Only the left–most bit of the DHCP options field is used (see Figure 8.3). The other bits in the options field must be set to 0.

Table 8.1 **DHCP Fields**

| Field | Octets | Description |
|---|---|---|
| op | 1 | Message operator code (message type). A value of 1 means it is a BOOTREQUEST message, and a value of 2 means it is a BOOTRE-PLY message. |
| htype | 1 | The hardware address type. The values are the same as those used for the ARP packet format. For example, a value of 1 is used for 10 Mbps Ethernet. |
| hlen | 1 | The hardware address length in octets. Ethernet and Token Ring hard-ware address length is 6 bytes. |
| hops | 1 | The DHCP client sets this to zero. This is used optionally by relay agents running on routers when they forward DHCP messages. When a DHCP message traverses a router, the hop field is incremented by 1. |
| xid | 4 | Transaction ID, which is a randomly generated number chosen by the DHCP client when it generates a DHCP message. The DHCP server uses the same Transaction ID in its DHCP messages to the client. The Transaction ID enables the DHCP clients and servers to associate DHCP messages with the corresponding responses. |
| secs | 2 | This field is filled by the DHCP client. It is the number of seconds elapsed since the client started trying to boot. |
| flags | 2 | The leftmost bit is used to indicate if this is a broadcast message (bit value of 1). All other bits must remain zero. |
| ciaddr | 4 | The DHCP client's IP address. It is filled by the DHCP client in a DHCPREQUEST message to verify the use of previously allocated configuration parameters. If the client does not know its IP address, this field is set to 0. |
| yiaddr | 4 | This is the DHCP client's IP address returned by the DHCP server. This is the field that is used to return the DHCP client's IP address. |
| siaddr | 4 | If the DHCP client wants to contact a specific DHCP server, it inserts the server's IP address in this field. The DHCP server's IP address might have been discovered in prior DHCPOFFER or DHCPACK messages returned by server. The value returned by the DHCP server may be the address of the next server to contact as part of the boot process. For example, this may be the address of a server that holds the operating sys-tem boot image. |
| giaddr | 4 | The IP address of the router that runs the relay agent. |
| chaddr | 16 | The DHCP client's hardware address. A value of 16 octets is used to allow different network hardware types. Ethernet and Token Ring use only 6 octets. |

*continues*

**Table 8.1   Continued**

| Field | Octets | Description |
|---|---|---|
| sname | 64 | An optional server host name if known by the DHCP client. It is a null-terminated string. |
| file | 128 | The boot file name. It is a null-terminated string. If the DHCP client wants to boot with an image of the operating system downloaded from a network device, it can specify a generic name, such as unix for booting a UNIX image in a DHCPDISCOVER. The DHCP server can hold more specific information about the exact operating system image needed for that workstation. This image name can be returned by a fully qualified directory-path name in the DHCPOFFER message from the DHCP server. |
| options | 312 | An optional parameters field. |

Most of the DHCP messages sent by the DHCP server to the DHCP client are *unicast* messages (messages sent to a single IP address). This occurs because the DHCP server learns about the DHCP client's hardware address in messages sent by the DHCP client to the server. The DHCP client can request that the DHCP server respond with a broadcast address by setting the leftmost bit in the options field to 1. The DHCP client responds with a broadcast address only if the client does not know its IP address yet. The IP protocol module in the DHCP client rejects a datagram it receives if the destination IP address in the datagram does not match the IP address of the DHCP client's network interface. If the IP address of the network interface is not known, the datagram is still rejected. The IP protocol module will, however, accept any IP broadcast datagram. Therefore, to ensure that the IP protocol module accepts the DHCP server reply when the IP address is not yet configured, the DHCP client requests that the DHCP server reply using broadcast messages instead of unicast messages.

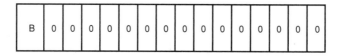

B = 1    Broadcast

B = 0    Unicast

**Figure 8.3**  DHCP options field.

The options field is variable in length, with the minimum size extended to 312 octets, so that the total minimum size of a DHCP message is 576 octets, which is the minimum IP datagram size a host must be prepared to accept. If a DHCP client must use larger messages, the client can negotiate this using the Maximum DHCP Message Size option. Because the sname and file fields are quite large and might not always be used, DHCP options can be further extended into these fields by specifying the Option Overload option. If present, the usual meanings of sname and file are ignored, and these fields are examined for options.

Options are expressed using the T-L-V (Type, Length, Value) format. Figure 8.4 shows that in DHCP, the option consists of a 1-octet Type field, followed by a 1-octet Length field. The value of the Length field contains the size of the Value field. The different DHCP messages themselves are expressed using a special Type value of 53.

The option values that describe the DHCP messages are shown in Figure 8.5.

# DHCP on a Windows NT Server

Now that you understand how DHCP works, you can better understand the parameter choices involved in installing, configuring, and administering DHCP servers. The following sections describe the procedures for maintaining and administering DHCP servers.

## Installing the DHCP Server on a Windows NT Server

Prior to the release of Windows NT Server 5, the DHCP Server had to be installed in a separate step as a service through the Network applet in the Control Panel. Starting with Windows NT Server 5, the DHCP Server service is automatically installed as part of Windows NT Server 5 installation. You can verify that the DHCP Server service is running by seeing it listed in the System Service Management screen. To view the System Service Management screen perform the following actions:

1. Select Programs.

2. Select Administrative Tools.

3. Select System Service Management.

4. Verify that the Microsoft DHCP Server service is running. By default this service is started automatically on startup.

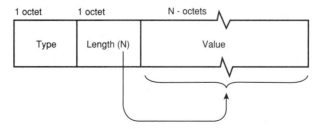

**Figure 8.4**  Option format of DHCP messages.

| | 1 octet | 1 octet | 1 octet |
|---|---|---|---|
| DHCPDISCOVER | 53<br>Type | 1<br>length | 1<br>value |
| DHCPOFFER | 53<br>Type | 1<br>length | 2<br>value |
| DHCPREQUEST | 53<br>Type | 1<br>length | 3<br>value |
| DHCPDECLINE | 53<br>Type | 1<br>length | 4<br>value |
| DHCPACK | 53<br>Type | 1<br>length | 5<br>value |
| DHCPNAK | 53<br>Type | 1<br>length | 6<br>value |
| DHCPRELEASE | 53<br>Type | 1<br>length | 7<br>value |

**Figure 8.5**   Option values for DHCP messages.

The DHCP server can be installed only on Windows NT Servers and not on Windows NT Workstations. Figure 8.6 shows a simple network configuration using Windows NT Server DHCP servers and Windows NT DHCP clients. Notice that if DHCP servers are separated by routers, the routers must be configured to forward BOOTP messages. Windows NT–based routers are configured to forward BOOTP messages using DHCP relay agents.

If the DHCP Server is not started, you can start it by right-clicking the Microsoft DHCP Server in the System Service Management screen and selecting Start. Alternatively, you can use the following command to start the DHCP Server:

```
NET START DHCPSERVER
```

## Configuring the DHCP Server

When Windows NT Server 5 network service is installed, you see an option added in the Administrative Tools under the DHCP Management program group. You can use the DHCP Management program to configure the DHCP server.

The following is an outline of the procedure for configuring a DHCP server by using DHCP Management:

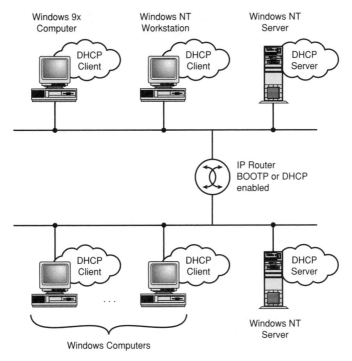

**Figure 8.6** Using Windows NT DHCP Servers.

1. Log on to the Windows NT Server as an administrator user.
2. Select Programs, Administrative Tools, DHCP Management.

   If this is the first time you have started the DHCP Manager, you should see that the DHCP Manager shows the local computer (see Figure 8.7).

   Subsequent to the first startup, the DHCP Manager screen shows the DHCP servers to which the DHCP Manager is connected, and their scopes.

3. Connect the DHCP Manager to another DHCP Server that you may be managing by selecting the Action menu, and choosing Add Server. If this Windows NT Server is the only computer that acts as a DHCP server, there is no need to connect to another DHCP server. The local DHCP server has the label Local Machine.

   If you decided to add a new DHCP server, you should see the Add New Server Wizard dialog box, which prompts you to enter the DNS name or IP address of the DHCP Server to add to the list (see Figure 8.8).

   You can add the DNS name if you have a DNS server on the network and your computer is configured to resolve DNS names. Otherwise, you should enter the IP address of the DHCP server. In the DHCP Server field, add the IP address of the DHCP Server you want to connect to. This should be the IP address of the DHCP Server you want to administer.

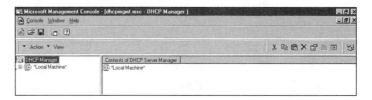

**Figure 8.7**   DHCP Management main screen.

**Figure 8.8**   Add New Server Wizard dialog box.

4. Select Next after specifying the DHCP server.

   The DHCP Server that you specified will be contacted. If the DHCP server cannot be contacted you have the option of adding it to the list anyway.

5. Select Finish to add the DHCP server to the list.

6. You should be back to the DHCP Manager screen showing the DHCP servers that have been added to the DHCP Server List (see Figure 8.9).

7. You must next define a *DHCP scope* (a grouping of DHCP client computers). You must create a DHCP scope for each IP subnetwork on your network. The DHCP scope defines parameters for that subnet, such as a subnet mask and lease duration values. The DHCP scope is identified by a DHCP scope name that is created at the time of defining the scope.

8. The instructions assume that you are configuring the local computer as the DHCP server. Right-click on the local computer in the DHCP Management screen and select New, Scope.

9. The Create Scope Wizard appears (see Figure 8.10). Specify a scope name that is meaningful for the group of DHCP clients in the scope. For example, you might choose a name based on the location of the DHCP clients or the type of use of the DHCP clients.

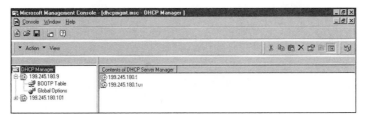

**Figure 8.9**  A new DHCP server added to DHCP Management screen.

**Figure 8.10**  Create New Scope Wizard.

10.  Select Next. You should see the screen for defining the range of addresses within the scope (see Figure 8.11). Use the From and To fields to enter the start and end of the IP addresses range for this address pool.

11.  Use the Length field to define the network prefix, which is the number of bits used for the network and subnet numbers. Alternatively, you can enter the subnet mask directly in the Mask field.

Figure 8.12 shows that the range of IP addresses is 199.245.180.1 to 199.245.180.254 with a subnet mask of 255.255.255.0. In this example, 199.245.180.0 and 199.245.180.255 have been excluded because these IP addresses have special meanings on TCP/IP networks.

12.  Select Next. You should see the screen for defining the exclusion range (see Figure 8.13). In the Exclusion Range group of fields, specify any IP addresses that are to be excluded from the IP address range pool that you specified in step 7. You might, for example, want to exclude IP addresses that are permanently assigned to certain TCP/IP hosts on the network or to non-DHCP clients, and are not to be part of the dynamically allocated IP address pool.

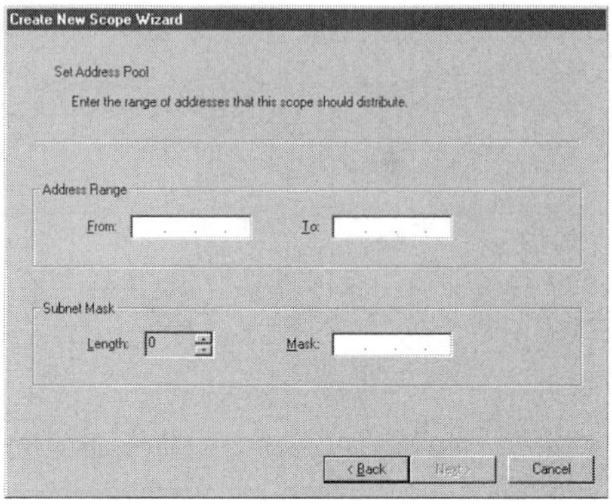

**Figure 8.11** Defining an address pool.

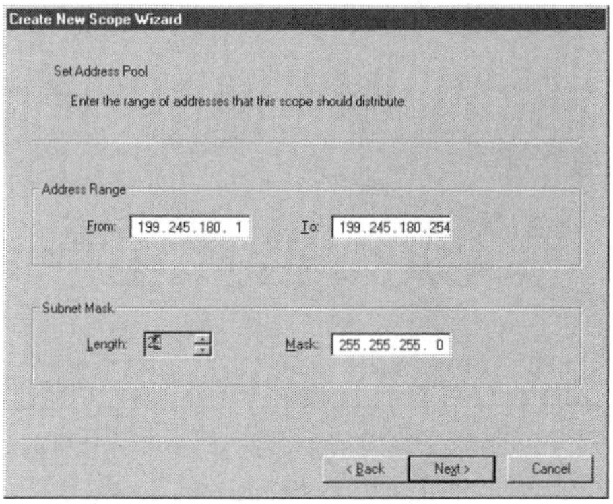

**Figure 8.12** Example of an address pool.

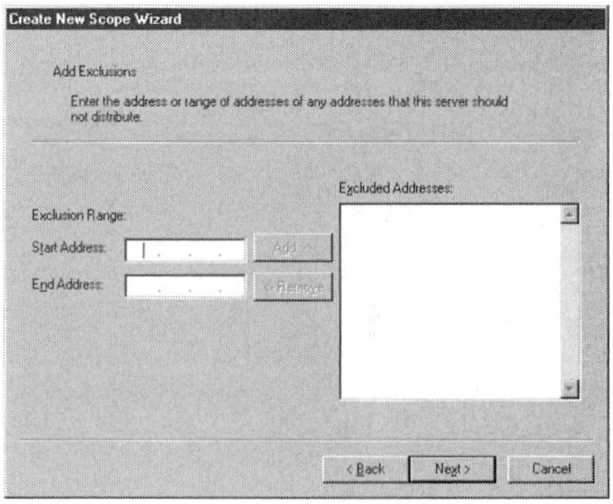

**Figure 8.13** Defining an exclusion range.

To define an exclusion range, enter the start IP address in the Start Address field and the end IP address in the End Address field, then choose the Add button. The excluded addresses are listed in the Excluded Addresses list box.

To exclude a single IP address, enter the address in the Start Address field and leave the End Address field blank. Next, choose the Add button.

Figure 8.14 shows a range of IP addresses that are excluded from the pool of IP addresses. IP addresses from 199.245.180.9 to 199.245.180.30, 199.245.180.102, 199.245.180.201, and 199.245.180.51 are excluded from the range of IP pool addresses 199.245.180.1 to 199.245.180.254.

13. Select Next. You should see the screen for defining the lease duration within the scope (see Figure 8.15). In the Lease Duration screen, you can specify a permanent lease by selecting the Unlimited option, or you can specify a lease of a limited duration.

   If you specify a limited duration lease, you can specify the value in days, hours, and minutes.

   Note that default values of the renewal timer and rebinding timers are calculated by the DHCP client based on the duration of the lease specified in the Lease Duration box. For a discussion on the lease timers, refer to the section "The DHCP IP Address Acquisition Process," earlier in this chapter. The default lease duration is 3 days. Using the Limited To option, you can specify a maximum lease of 999 days, 23 hours, and 59 minutes. If there is a large pool of IP addresses available and they are not likely to run out, you can set a high lease duration. But if there are only a few addresses available, you might need to set the lease duration for a shorter time, such as for just a few hours. If you limit the duration in this way, however, you run the risk of high network traffic caused by frequent renewal requests.

14. Select Next. You see a screen informing you that you need to add the scope options and activate the scope after this step.

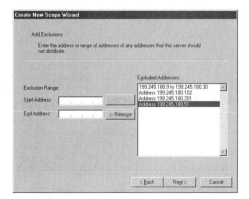

**Figure 8.14**  Example of an exclusion range.

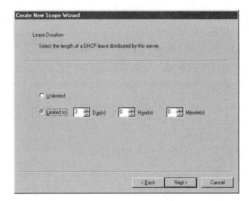

**Figure 8.15** Defining lease duration screen.

15. Select Finish to conclude the scope definition. You see the new scope name added to the DHCP Management screen.

16. Unless you want to further change the properties of the scope that you have created, you can make the scope active. Some of the properties of the scope that you can change are to enable dynamic update of DNS information with DHCP client addresses. To make the scope active, right-click on its name in the DHCP Management screen and select Activate.

## Enabling DNS and DHCP Synchronization

The DNS system is a distributed database that consists of resource records that define the symbolic name to IP address mappings, and other records defining DNS Servers, alias names, and mail exchangers. Mail exchangers are mail servers that receive mail on behalf of the specified domain.

DNS as it was originally defined assumed that IP addresses would be statically defined for hostnames and would not change dynamically. If an IP address of a host was changed, the resource record in the DNS configuration file would have to be changed manually, and the DNS software restarted to reflect this change.

In DHCP the IP address assignments for hostnames can change dynamically because IP addresses are leased from the pool of addresses in a DHCP scope on a first-come, first-served basis. To resolve names accurately using DNS, however, the resource records in the DNS database would have to be updated dynamically to reflect the new IP address assignments.

You can enable DNS and DHCP synchronization by editing the properties of a DHCP scope. You can accomplish this by performing the following actions:

1. Right-click on the DHCP scope name in the DHCP Management screen.

2. Select Properties. You see the scope properties screen (see Figure 8.16).

3. Select the Dynamic DNS tab. You see the screen for enabling DNS and DHCP synchronization (see Figure 8.17).

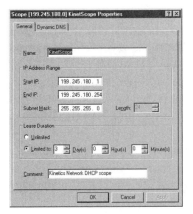

Figure 8.16   DHCP Scope Properties screen.

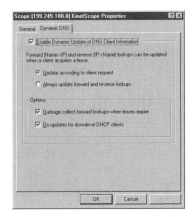

Figure 8.17   Dynamic DNS screen.

4. Check the box labeled Enable Dynamic Update of DNS Client Information. This enables forward and reverse DNS lookup resource records to be updated when the DHCP client acquires a lease.

5. If you enable Update According to Client Request, the DHCP server updates resource records in DNS only if the DHCP client makes the request. For a DHCP client to update the DNS, the client must be a dynamic DNS client. Currently only Windows NT Server 5, Windows NT Workstation 5, and Windows 98 or higher are capable of acting as dynamic DNS clients.

6. If you enable Always Update Forward and Reverse Lookups, the DHCP server updates address (A) and pointer (PTR) resource records in DNS when the DHCP client obtains a lease. The DNS server must be a dynamic DNS Server. Currently only Windows NT Server 5 or higher is capable of acting as a dynamic DNS server.

7. Enable Garbage Collect Forward Lookups when Leases Expire if you want the DHCP server to remove a client's address resource records (A) from the DNS zone database when the client's DHCP lease expires.

8. Enable Do Updates for Downlevel DHCP Clients if you want the DHCP server to perform updates of address (A) and pointer (PTR) resource records in the DNS zone database for DHCP clients that do not support dynamic DNS.

9. Select OK when you are done making your changes.

## Configuring DHCP Global Options

The DHCP options enable you to configure special classes of devices, such as DNS servers, routers, and so on. You can use the standard options defined in RFC 1542 or define new ones. Additionally, you can specify that the DHCP options are Global to all scopes or apply to a selected scope only. The DHCP options that you specify for a scope are included in the DHCPOFFER message sent by the DHCP Server to the DHCP Client. You can, therefore, use the DHCP options to configure a large number of TCP/IP parameters, such as those documented in RFC 1542.

1.  In the DHCP Manager screen, right-click on Global Options and select Configure Options. You should see the Global Options screen (see Figure 8.18). In the figure, option 003, the router option, is used to specify the default gateway/router.

2.  The Basic tab shows the Standard DHCP options. To enable the DHCP server to send this information on a DHCP client request, select the option by checking the box against the option name. You see additional fields that you can edit to complete the information for that option.

3.  Select the Advanced tab for showing some of the more advanced DHCP options (see Figure 8.19). As you enable a specific advanced option, you see additional fields that you can edit to complete the information for that option.

4.  Select the Custom tab to define additional options.

5.  Select OK when you are done making your changes.

## Configuring BOOTP Options

DHCP is designed to be an extension of BOOTP. BOOTP is used to supply the operating system image that the BOOTP client must download to boot itself. In addition, the server on which the operating system image resides is also specified.

Note that Windows NT 4.0 *does not* support BOOTP.

You can configure the DHCP server to supply the server and operating system image using the following steps:

**Figure 8.18**   Global Options screen.

**Figure 8.19**   DHCP Advanced options.

1. Right-click on the BOOTP Table option. Select New, and then select Boot Image. You should see a dialog box for entering the image name, file name, and file server on which the operating system image resides (see Figure 8.20).

2. Enter the image information and select Add.

3. Select Close when you are done adding the image name.

## Setting Default Options Globally

The DHCP options have a set of default values. For example, the 046 WINS/NBT Node Type DHCP option can have a value of 1 for B-node type, 2 for P-node type, 4 for M-node type, and 8 for H-node type. These node types are discussed in greater detail in Chapter 9, "TCP/IP Name Resolution Using WINS." You can change the default node type to any of these values.

To change the DHCP option values globally, perform the following actions:

1. Right-click on the IP address of the DHCP server in the DHCP Management screen. Select Set Default Options. You should see the Default Values screen (see Figure 8.21).

2. Select Option Class and Option Name to show the default value for that option. Edit the default value. For some values, such as an array of IP addresses, you will see a button labeled Edit Array. When you select this button you see the standard array editor.

3. To change the option type or name, select the Change button.

4. To add a new option type, select New. You can specify the option type, name, and comment for any new option that you define. The data type for the value of an option can also be set, and you can specify if this is a single value or an array of values.

**Figure 8.20**   Add BOOTP entry.

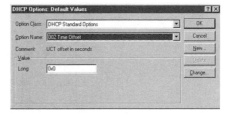

**Figure 8.21**   DHCP Option: Default Values screen.

## Defining a Super Scope on the DHCP Server

After you have defined more than one scope on the DHCP server, you can define a super scope whose members are the individual scopes. A *super scope* is a level of abstraction that allows several distinct scopes to be grouped under a single logical name. You may want to create a super scope consisting of several subnetworks in which each subnetwork is described by a scope. To define a super scope, perform the following steps:

1. Right-click on the DHCP server in the DHCP Management screen.

2. Select New, Superscope. You should see the Create New Superscope Wizard (see Figure 8.22).

3. Enter the super scope name and select Next. You should see the Select Scopes screen (see Figure 8.23).

4. Highlight the scopes that you want to add to the super scope and select Next.

5. Select Finish to confirm your choices.

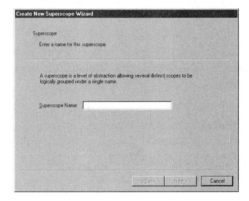

**Figure 8.22**   Create New Superscope Wizard.

**Figure 8.23**   Select Scopes dialog box.

## Viewing DHCP Server Information

This section discusses how you can view DHCP server information such as the following:

- Statistics for the entire DHCP server or selected scope
- Address Pools
- Active Leases
- Reservations
- Scope Options

To view statistics on the entire DHCP server, right-click the DHCP server name and select Show Statistics (see Figure 8.24).

To view statistics for a DHCP scope, right-click the DHCP scope name and select Show Statistics (see Figure 8.25).

To view the Address pools, Active leases, Reservations, or Scope Options, click on each of these options under the scope name. For example, the address pool for a scope name is shown in Figure 8.26.

## Configuring the DHCP Client on Windows NT

After configuring the DHCP server, you can configure the Windows NT computers on the network with DHCP clients that obtain the IP parameters from the DHCP server.

If you are installing the TCP/IP protocol for the first time on a Windows NT computer, enable the Obtain an IP Address from a DHCP Server Radio Button option in the Microsoft TCP/IP Properties dialog box's IP Address tab. If the TCP/IP protocol is already installed on the Windows NT computer, you can enable the DHCP client by performing the following steps:

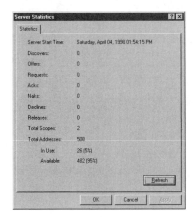

**Figure 8.24**  Show Statistics for entire DHCP server.

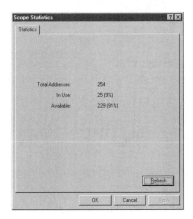

**Figure 8.25**  Show Statistics for a DHCP scope name.

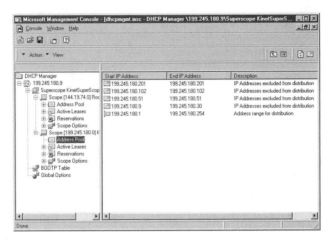

**Figure 8.26**   Address pool for a DHCP scope name.

1. Log on as the administrator user to the Windows NT computer.

2. Start the Network icon from the Control Panel.

3. In the Network dialog box, choose the Protocols tab and select the TCP/IP protocol, then click on the Properties button.

4. In the TCP/IP Properties dialog box that appears, check the Obtain an IP Address from a DHCP Server Radio Button option.

5. The IP Address, Subnet Mask, and Default Gateway fields in the dialog box are grayed out when you select DHCP, and the manually configured values are no longer displayed. If you choose Advanced, the Advanced IP Addressing dialog box indicates DHCP Enabled in the IP Addresses box. Select OK to return to the TCP/IP Properties IP Address tab.

6. Click on OK to return to the Protocols tab. Select OK again to close.

7. Select Yes to restart the computer for changes to take effect.

Note that if TCP/IP was already installed and certain values are defined in WINS servers or DNS servers, then this information will override any information provided via DHCP.

## Configuring DHCP Clients for Windows 9x

Windows 9x clients can act as DHCP clients and obtain TCP/IP parameter assignments from a DHCP server. To configure Windows 9x clients as DHCP clients, perform the following step:

1. From the Start menu, select Settings, and then Control Panel.

2. Click the Network icon from the Control Panel.

3. In the Network dialog box select the Configuration tab.

4. Highlight the TCP/IP to network interface binding and select the Properties button.

5. Select the IP Address tab in the TCP/IP Properties dialog box.

6. Check the Obtain an IP Address Automatically option button. This enables the computer to use DHCP to obtain TCP/IP parameter settings.

7. Select OK and close all windows opened in this procedure.

8. Select Yes to restart the computer for changes to take effect.

You can use certain commands to view information on DHCP lease expiration date/time and current IP address parameters. On a Windows NT computer, you can type the command `ipconfig /all` at the command prompt, whereas on a Windows 9x computer, you run the `winipcfg` application.

## Administering Client Leases on Windows NT Server

The IP addresses assigned by a DHCP server have an expiration date. The lease must be negotiated by the DHCP client as described in the earlier section "The DHCP IP Address Acquisition Process." You can monitor the lease duration and change settings for reserved IP addresses for DHCP clients. Reserving IP addresses for DHCP clients is discussed in the next section.

To manage client lease information, perform the following steps:

1. Log on to the Windows NT Server as an administrator user.

2. Start DHCP Managment.

3. Highlight the DHCP scope in the main screen and the Active Leases option.

4. The Active Leases dialog box displays the client IP address, name, type, and lease expiration.

5. To see details of a particular lease, right-click on it and select Properties.

Other options that you see when you right-click on a lease allow you to manage that lease.

## Reserving DHCP Client IP Addresses on Windows NT Server

Unless you have reserved an IP address for a DHCP client, an IP address is assigned dynamically by the DHCP server when the DHCP client sends a request for its IP

**Precedence of IP addresses**

IP addresses and static names specified in the WINS database take precedence over IP address assignments by a DHCP server. For such clients, create IP address reservations using the IP address defined in the WINS database.

parameter initialization. This IP address is chosen from a pool of available IP addresses. On a network with many DHCP clients, the IP address assigned to the DHCP client on restarting is likely to be different. For most DHCP clients, having a different IP address each time is not a problem. For some Windows NT and Windows 9x computers, however, it is important to reserve a specific IP address. You would, for example, need to reserve IP addresses in the following situations:

■ Windows NT domain controllers using the LMHOSTS file, which defines the IP addresses of the domain controllers for DNS Servers, SMTP, web servers, FTP servers, Gopher servers, and any servers that need to be identified in an external public DNS

■ Assignment by RAS servers to non-DHCP clients

■ Clients with static IP address assignments

DHCP servers do not communicate or synchronize information among themselves. If there are multiple DHCP servers in a DHCP scope, you must ensure that the IP addresses reserved for clients are identical on each DHCP server. Otherwise, DHCP servers will have a different view of which IP addresses are available for lease, and this can cause IP address conflicts.

The following is the procedure for reserving an IP address for a client:

1. Log on to the Windows NT Server as an administrator user.

2. Start DHCP Management.

3. Double-click on the DHCP scope name in the main screen and right-click on the Reservations option.

4. Select New, Reservation. You see the Add Reservation dialog box (see Figure 8.27).

5. Enter the IP address that you want to reserve in the IP Address field.

6. Enter a value in the Unique Identifier field to specify the MAC address for the DHCP client. On a Windows NT computer, you can determine the MAC address by using one of the following commands:

```
NET CONFIG WKSTA
NET CONFIG WORKSTATION
```

**Figure 8.27** Add Reservation dialog box.

You can also use `ipconfig /all` on NT machines or `winipcfg` on Win9x machines to view MAC addresses.

7. Enter the Windows NT computer name in the Client Name field. This is used for identification purposes only and does not affect the actual client computer name that is used.

8. Optionally, you can enter a text description of the client in the Client Comment field.

9. Specify whether the allowed client type is DHCP, BOOTP, or both.

10. Choose the Add button to add the reservation in the DHCP database.

11. Repeat steps 3–10 to add other client reservations.

12. After you finish adding client reservations, click on the Close button.

13. To enable the changes to take effect, restart the client computer for which you have reserved IP addresses.

To change an existing IP address reservation, you must first delete the existing reservation, then add the new reservation. You can delete the existing reservation by selecting Scope, Active Leases, then selecting the Properties button, followed by the Delete button. For details on managing active leases, refer to the earlier section "Administering Client Leases on Windows NT Server."

## Advanced Registry Parameter Configuration for DHCP

The DHCP parameters for the DHCP server that can be configured using the Registry Editor are kept under the following key (see Figure 8.28):

```
HKEY_LOCAL_MACHINE\SYSTEM\CurrentControlSet\Services\DHCPServer\Parameters
```

With the exception of the `RestoreFlag` value entry, changes made to the DHCP parameters require restarting the Windows NT computer before the changes take effect. Alternatively, you just stop and start the DHCP Server service for the changes to take effect.

Table 8.2 describes the DHCP parameter value entries. To change the DHCP parameters in the Registry, use the Registry Editor as described in Chapter 5, "Advanced TCP/IP Configuration Using the Registry and Perl."

The Registry parameters for the DHCP client are kept under the following key on the client computer:

```
HKEY_LOCAL_MACHINE\SYSTEM\CurrentControlSet\Services\DHCP\Parameter\
➥Options\option#
```

*option#* is the list of DHCP options that the client can request from the DHCP server. For each option, the following value entries are defined:

- `RegLocation`
- `OptionSize`

Table 8.2  **DHCP Server Value Entries in the Windows NT Registry**

| DHCP Value Entry | Description |
| --- | --- |
| APIProtocolSupport | Specifies the API protocol supported for the DHCP server. You can change this to ensure that computers running a supported protocol can access the DHCP server. The value entry has a data type of REG_ DWORD of values 0x1, 0x2, 0x4, 0x5, or 0x7, with a default of 0x1. The values have the following meanings: 0x1 = RPC over TCP/IP, 0x2 = RPC over named pipes, 0x4 = RPC over local procedure call (LPC) protocols, 0x5 = RPC over TCP/IP and RPC over LPC, and 0x7 = RPC over TCP/IP, named pipes, and LPC (all three API protocols). |
| BackupDatabasePath | Specifies the location of the backup data path where DHCP database files are backed up periodically. The value entry is of data type REG_EXPAND_SZ and has a default value of %SystemRoot%\system32\dhcp\backup. You should not use a network path because DHCP cannot access a network path for backup and recovery. |
| BackupInterval | Specifies the interval in seconds for backing up the database. The value entry is of type REG_DWORD. |
| DatabaseCleanupInterval | Specifies the interval for removing expired client records in the DHCP database. The value entry is of type REG_DWORD and has a default value of 0x15180 (86,400 seconds = 24 hours). |
| DatabaseLoggingFlag | Specifies whether to record the database changes in the DHCP transaction log file J50.LOG. The J50.LOG and related files are used for database recovery after a crash. The value entry is of type REG_DWORD and can have a value of 0 or 1. The default is 1, which means that database logging is turned on. Turning on database logging has an effect on system performance but increases the fault tolerance of the database. |
| DatabaseName | Specifies the file used to store the DHCP database information. The value entry is of type REG_SZ and has a default name of dhcp.mdb. |
| DatabasePath | Specifies the directory path under which the database files are created and opened. The value entry is of type REG_ EXPAND_ SZ and has a default name of %SystemRoot%\system32\dhcp. |
| RestoreFlag | Specifies whether to restore the database from the backup directory. The value entry is of type REG_ DWORD and has a value of 0 or 1. A value of 1 means restore, and a value of 0 means do not restore. The default value is 0. The flag is set to 0 automatically after a successful restore. |

**Figure 8.28**   DHCP parameters in the Registry.

- `OptionLocation`

- `KeyType`

Figure 8.29 shows the DHCP client parameters for DHCP option 44 (WINS/NBNS Servers). The value of the `RegLocation` parameter is shown in the String Editor dialog box because its full value is too large for the space in the right panel.

`RegLocation` is of type `REG_SZ` and specifies the location in the Registry where the option value is written when it is obtained from the DHCP server. The `?` character evaluates to the adapter name that the option value applies to.

`OptionSize` and `OptionValue` are meant to specify the size and location of the option. In the release of Windows NT that was tested these values are not set.

The `KeyType` specifies the type of Registry key for the option. It is of type `REG_DWORD` and has a default value of `0x7`.

**Figure 8.29**   DHCP Option 44 in the Registry Editor for a DHCP client.

## SNMP Parameters for Managing DHCP

The DHCP parameters can be managed by an SNMP manager. The DHCP MIB parameters and DHCP Scope group are described in Tables 8.3 and 8.4. The SNMP manager must have the capability to import these MIB objects that are specific to DHCP. The values shown in braces ({}) are the ASN.1 object IDs for the parameters. The labels, such as DhcpPar, DhcpScope, and so on, are ASN.1 macros that expand to an ASN.1 prefix value defined by Microsoft.

Table 8.3  **Windows NT DHCP MIB Parameters**

| Parameter | Description |
| --- | --- |
| ParDhcpStartTime | The DHCP Server start time. {ParDhcp 1} |
| ParDhcpTotalNoOfDiscovers | The total number of the DHCPDISCOVER messages sent. {ParDhcp 2} |
| ParDhcpTotalNoOfRequests | The total number of DHCPREQUEST messages sent. {ParDhcp 3} |
| ParDhcpTotalNoOfReleases | The total number of DHCPRELEASE messages sent. {ParDhcp 4} |
| ParDhcpTotalNoOfOffers | The total number of DHCPOFFER messages sent. {ParDhcp 5} |
| ParDhcpTotalNoOfAcks | The total number of DHCPACK messages sent. {ParDhcp 6} |
| ParDhcpTotalNoOfNaks | The total number of DHCPNAK messages sent. {ParDhcp 7} |
| ParDhcpTotalNoOfDeclines | The total number of DHCPDECLINE messages sent. {ParDhcp 8} |

Table 8.4  **Windows NT DHCP Scope Group Parameters**

| Parameter | Description |
| --- | --- |
| ScopeTable | The list of subnets maintained by the DHCP server. {DhcpScope 1} |
| sScopeTableEntry | The row in the scope table corresponding to a subnet. {ScopeTableEntry 1} |
| SubnetAdd | The subnet address. {sScopeTableEntry 1} |
| NoAddInUse | The number of IP addresses in use. {sScopeTableEntry 2} |
| NoAddFree | The number of free IP addresses that are available. {sScopeTableEntry 2} |
| NoPendingOffers | The number of IP addresses offers that are pending. {sScopeTableEntry 2} |

## Understanding the DHCP Database Files

The DHCP database files are kept by default in the `\%SystemRoot%\System32\dhcp`
directory. Figure 8.30 shows the contents of this directory.

The `DHCP.MDB` is the main DHCP database file. The `TMP.EDB` is a temporary file that
DHCP uses. The `J50.CHK`, `J50.LOG`, `RES*.LOG`, and `J50*.LOG` are transaction log files
used to recover from incomplete transactions in case of a system crash.

The DHCP database and related Registry value entries are backed up at periodic
intervals controlled by the Registry parameter `HKEY_LOCAL_MACHINE\SYSTEM\`
`CurrentControlSet\Services\DHCPServer\Parameters\BackupInterval`, which has a
default value of 15 minutes. The backed up files are kept by default in the
`HKEY_LOCAL_ MACHINE\SYSTEM\CurrentControlSet\Services\DHCPServer\Parameters\`
`BackupDatabasePath`. By default the backup database path is in the backup subdirectory under the `\SystemRoot\System32\dhcp` directory.

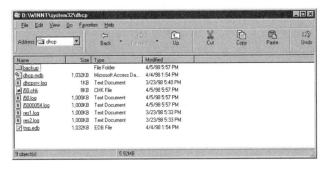

**Figure 8.30** DHCP database files.

# TCP/IP Name Resolution Using WINS

WINDOWS NT COMPUTERS REQUIRE THE USE of a computer name to uniquely identify the computer on the network. If the TCP/IP protocol is used, a unique IP address per network interface must be assigned in the computer. Although the TCP/IP protocol software uses IP addresses, users typically prefer using symbolic names, such as computer names, to identify the computers on the network. On TCP/IP networks, the mechanism of resolving computer names to their IP addresses is called *name resolution*.

This chapter discusses the name resolution methods used in Windows NT networks in general, with a special emphasis on how you can install and configure WINS name resolution on a Windows NT network.

## Overview of Windows NT Name Resolution Methods

Windows NT makes use of the following methods for name resolution:

- **WINS.** The WINS method uses Microsoft's name resolution server that runs on Windows NT Servers. Windows computers on the network can send name resolution requests to the WINS server. The WINS server contains a dynamic database that is used to map computer names to IP addresses. The WINS name resolution method can be used in conjunction with the broadcast name resolution method. WINS makes use of NetBIOS over TCP/IP mode of operation. This mode of operation is defined in RFC 1001/1002 as a p-node.

- **Broadcast Name Resolution.** The broadcast name resolution using NetBIOS over TCP/IP is another method that can be used in conjunction with WINS for resolving names. In the broadcast name resolution, computers use IP-level broadcasts to register their names. When a Windows NT computer starts up, it announces its name on the network. If a computer name already exists on the network, the computer with that name challenges attempts to register a duplicate name. The first computer on the network that registers its name, therefore, owns that name and must challenge attempts by other computers to use that name. The computer that owns the name responds to name queries for its registered name. This broadcast name resolution is defined in RFC 1001/1002 as b-node. The broadcast name resolution method generates a substantial amount of network traffic. In an improperly configured method, excessive broadcasts can lead to broadcast storms. Most routers are configured to reject broadcasts. This means that with an internetwork connected using routers, the routers will not forward the broadcasts. The broadcast name resolution method will therefore not work in an internetwork built using routers that reject broadcasts.

- **LMHOSTS file.** The LMHOSTS file on a Windows NT computer is used to specify NetBIOS computer name and IP address mappings. The LMHOSTS file syntax is compatible with the syntax of the HOSTS file that is used by Windows Socket applications. LMHOSTS is popular for use in small networks for providing name resolution. It also can be used in remote subnets where a WINS server might not always be available.

- **DNS.** The *Domain Name System (DNS)* is a distributed database of name services that provides a method of name lookup for computers connecting over a large network. Although WINS is specific to Microsoft networks, DNS can be used on all computer types, including Windows NT networks. DNS is a proven technology that is deployed and widely used on the Internet.

Windows NT Server 4 and later include a feature that provides DNS/WINS integration. This feature combines the universal reach of DNS and the convenience of WINS. DNS/WINS integration also provides WINS name resolution over the Internet. A DNS server on a Windows NT server can use WINS to resolve the host name of a Fully Qualified Domain Name (FQDN). This means that you can let WINS maintain a list of IP addresses dynamically. Your local DNS server will automatically refer to WINS for host name resolution.

# Understanding NetBIOS over TCP/IP Name Resolution

NetBIOS over TCP/IP is described in RFCs 1001 and 1002. These RFCs describe NetBIOS-to-IP address name resolution methods. These methods describe how

NetBIOS names are registered and resolved on the network. Name registration is the process used to define a unique name for each computer on the network. When a Windows NT computer starts, it attempts to register itself using the computer name that is stored in its Registry. Name resolution is the process of determining an IP address for a specific computer name. To provide flexibility in the NetBIOS-to-IP address name resolution, the following methods are defined:

- b-node. Uses only broadcasts to resolve names (also called the broadcast method)
- p-node. Uses only point-to-point communications with a name server to resolve names (also called the name query method)
- m-node. Uses b-node first, and if it fails, then p-node
- h-node. Uses p-node first, and if it fails, then b-node

These methods are discussed in greater detail later in this chapter.

You can change the node type of a computer by editing the following Registry entry:

```
HKEY_LOCAL_MACHINE\
```

The method used by a computer to resolve a name also is called its *node type*. Computers that use the broadcast method exclusively are called b-node types, for example, and computers that use only the name query method are called p-node types.

If DHCP is used to configure the IP parameters of a computer, their node types are defined by selecting the DHCP option 046 WINS/NBT Node Type for the DHCP scope on the DHCP server. This option is selected when configuring the DHCP server. Configuration of the DHCP server is discussed in Chapter 8, "DHCP Configuration and Management."

If a Windows NT client is manually configured with IP parameters (that is, DHCP is not used) and WINS servers are used for name resolution, the client uses NetBIOS over TCP/IP and the h-node name resolution method. That is, first p-node name queries are used to resolve computer names. If no WINS servers are on the network, NetBIOS over TCP/IP uses b-node broadcasts to resolve names.

Depending on how TCP/IP is configured on a Windows NT computer, the Windows NT computer also can use LMHOSTS files and DNS for name resolution. If the Enable DNS for Windows Name Resolution option is enabled, the HOSTS file will be checked before DNS is queried. The NETBT32.SYS module that implements NetBIOS over TCP/IP functionality supports name registration and resolution modes discussed in this chapter.

The different NetBIOS over TCP/IP methods of name resolution are discussed in further detail in the sections that follow.

## Understanding the *b-node* Method

The b-node method uses NetBIOS broadcast packets encapsulated in UDP/IP frames for name registration and resolution. Consider the example shown in Figure 9.1. If the Windows NT computer (NT1) wants to communicate with another Windows NT computer (NT2), it uses an IP-level–directed broadcast on the network. It then waits a specified time for NT2 to respond. If NT2 does not respond, by default the client (NT1 computer) will try the broadcast three times before it gives up. The default number of broadcast tries as well as the default time to wait for responses are controlled by the Registry entries `BcastNameQueryCount` and `BcastQueryTimeout`. If the name NT2 cannot be resolved, then the name resolution software on NT1 returns an error message.

While the `b-node` name resolution is simple and requires minimal configuration, several disadvantages are evident. Problems include the following:

- The broadcast packets can consume substantial amounts of network bandwidth.

- Routers usually are not configured to forward broadcast packets, meaning that `b-node` resolution fails for computers on network segments separated by routers.

The `b-node` method is suitable for small networks in which network bandwidth and broadcasts are not of as much concern as on larger networks.

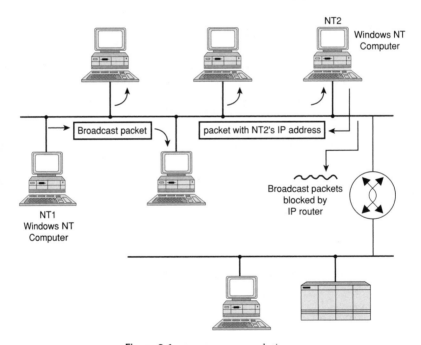

**Figure 9.1**　`b-node` name resolution.

## Understanding the *p-node* Method

The p-node method overcomes the limitation of the broadcast method by neither creating nor responding to broadcast requests. Windows NT computers are required to register themselves with the WINS server. The WINS server is a NetBIOS Name Server (NBNS) with Microsoft-specific enhancements.

In order for Windows NT computers to register themselves with the WINS server, you can provide an IP address of the WINS server when configuring the Windows NT TCP/IP protocol. Alternatively, you can also use DHCP to configure a client's WINS settings. Because all computers that use WINS must register themselves with the WINS server, the WINS server acts as a central database of computer names and their IP address mappings. The WINS server also ensures that no duplicate computer names exist on the network.

Figure 9.2 shows how the Windows NT computer NT1 uses the p-node method for discovering computer NT2's IP address. The computer NT1 is configured with the IP address of a WINS server on the network. Computer NT1 queries the WINS name server NTS about NT2's IP address. The name server NTS replies with the IP address of NT2. Computer NT1 then uses the IP address of NT2 to communicate with it directly. Because the name queries are sent to the WINS server, and all request/response packets are unicast packets, no broadcast traffic is generated for name resolution. Unlike the broadcast packets, the unicast packets are not blocked by IP routers and, therefore, p-node name resolution can be used in network segments separated by routers.

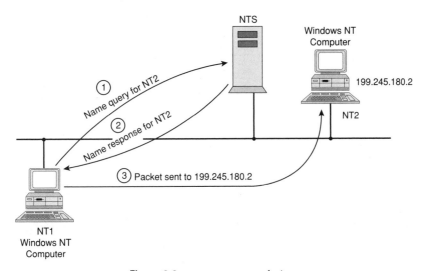

**Figure 9.2**  p-node name resolution.

While the p-node solves the broadcast-and-spanning-across-IP-routers problem (see Figure 9.3), it introduces the following concerns:

■ Computers on the network must be configured to know the address of the WINS server. If DHCP is used, this problem can be alleviated by defining the appropriate DHCP option for the WINS server's IP address. DHCP option settings are discussed in Chapter 8.

■ The WINS server introduces a single-point-of-failure problem. If the WINS server is down, or not accessible because of network faults, the computers that rely on the WINS server cannot resolve computer names. This problem can be alleviated by having multiple WINS servers and ensuring that the WINS database is replicated.

■ Note that in a mixed environment network in which clients may exist that do not support WINS, the p-node method cannot be used by these clients. In this case, the clients that do not have a setting for WINS will have to use the b-node method.

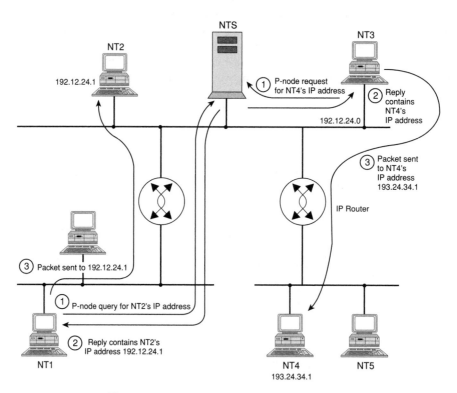

**Figure 9.3** p-node name resolution across routers.

## Understanding the *m-node* Method

The m-node method is a combination of the b-node and the p-node methods. In the m-node method, a computer first attempts registration and resolution using b-node. If b-node cannot resolve the computer name, it switches to the p-node method. Use of the b-node method generates broadcast traffic. This traffic, however, does not cross IP routers and is confined to the local network. For computers on the local network, the m-node method works the same as the b-node method (see Figure 9.4). If the computer is not found on the local network (for example, NT3 in Figure 9.5), the p-node, which crosses IP routers, is used to resolve the computer names.

The advantage of the m-node method is that computers on the local network segment can be reached via the b-node even if the WINS server is down or unreachable. This is because in networks in which local computers are accessed more often than remote computers, most computer names are resolved using the b-node.

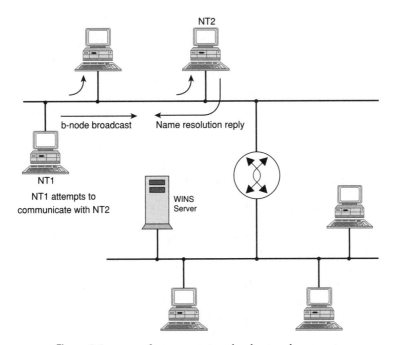

**Figure 9.4**   m-node for computers on local network segments.

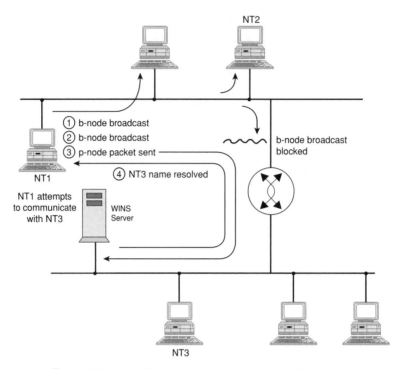

**Figure 9.5**   m-node for computers on remote network segments.

## Understanding the *h-node* Method

The h-node method is also a combination of the b-node and the p-node methods. In the h-node method, a computer first attempts registration and resolution using p-node. If p-node cannot resolve the computer name because the WINS server is down or unreachable, it switches to the b-node method. Unlike the m-node or b-node method, use of the p-node method first does not generate any initial broadcast traffic. If the p-node method fails to contact a WINS server, then the node tries to use the b-node method to resolve names. Because the b-node broadcast requests do not cross IP routers, remote computer names cannot be resolved. Local computer names, however, always can be resolved.

Because the h-node method uses the p-node method first, it avoids broadcast requests if the WINS server resolves the request. If the WINS server is down or unreachable, h-node uses b-node local broadcasts but continues to poll the WINS server. As soon as the WINS server comes back online, the h-node computers switch back to using p-node.

Figure 9.6 shows the operation of the h-node when the WINS server can be reached. In Figure 9.6 the use of broadcasts packets is completely avoided. Figure 9.7 shows the operation of the h-node when the WINS server cannot be reached. This figure shows that b-node broadcast packets are used as a last resort to resolve local computer names.

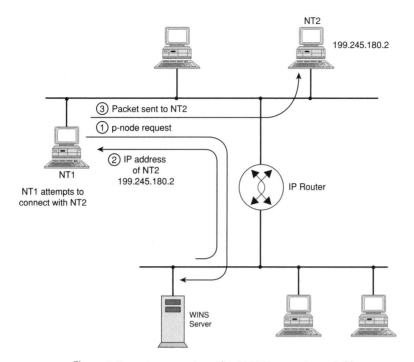

**Figure 9.6**  h-node operation when WINS server is reachable.

On a Windows network, the h-node can optionally be configured to use LMHOSTS after broadcast name resolution fails. Figure 9.8 shows the sequence of steps that will cause the LMHOSTS file to be used. In this figure, both the p-node and the b-node methods fail, and the LMHOSTS file is used as a last resort. The h-node method is the default method used if TCP/IP is configured manually and WINS server addresses are specified.

## Combining *b-node* with *LMHOSTS* Name Resolution

Except for the method shown in Figure 9.8, the b-node, m-node, and h-node methods described in RFCs 1001 and 1002 do not use the LMHOSTS file. Microsoft has added extensions to the standard b-node method that can use the LMHOSTS file. In the Microsoft extensions, if b-node fails to resolve the name, the LMHOSTS file is used to resolve names. Because b-node broadcasts cannot cross router boundaries, you can use the LMHOSTS file to resolve names for remote computers. The remote computers could be important servers and hosts, such as primary domain controllers and backup domain controllers, for a Windows NT domain. Windows NT uses the Microsoft extensions only if the WINS server is not specified for the Windows NT computer. Windows 3.11 for Workgroups and MS LAN Manager always use the b-node method with Microsoft extensions. Windows 9x will also use the b-node method unless the WINS server settings are specified as part of the TCP/IP properties.

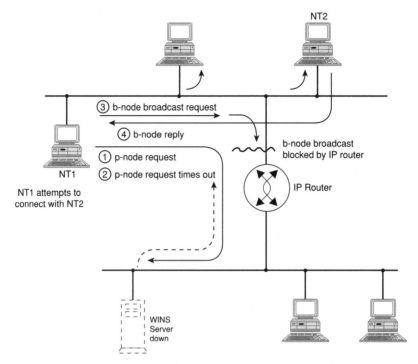

**Figure 9.7** h-node operation when WINS server is not reachable.

# The Windows Internet Name Service (WINS)

Microsoft's WINS server, which can be installed only on Windows NT Servers, is an implementation of the NetBIOS Name Server (NBNS) described in RFCs 1001 and 1002. The WINS server, however, adds extensions to the NBNS specification. One such extension is the interaction with DHCP. If DHCP is used to automatically generate IP addresses for Windows NT computers, the IP addresses assigned using DHCP are updated automatically in the WINS database.

## Name Resolution with WINS Servers

WINS uses a client/server architecture that consists of the WINS server and a WINS client. All Windows NT computers that have TCP/IP installed can be enabled to use the WINS client by specifying the IP address of the WINS server in the WINS Address tab of the Microsoft TCP/IP Properties dialog box (see Figure 9.9). To reach the Microsoft TCP/IP Properties dialog box, select TCP/IP in the Protocols tab of the Control Panel Network application and click on the Properties button. Figure 9.9 shows that a primary and secondary WINS server can be specified for a Windows NT network. As shown in Figure 9.9, the WINS Address tab also lets you enable the WINS/DNS integration described earlier in this chapter, as well as LMHOSTS lookup for IP addresses.

Windows 3.11 or Windows computers that are WINS-client enabled can also use the WINS server. Non-Microsoft clients that do not have a WINS client but are b-node compatible, as described by RFCs 1001 and 1002, still can access WINS servers through proxies. WINS proxies are Windows NT computers that listen for b-node broadcasts. The proxies contact the WINS server and return the reply to the computer that originated the b-node name query. Figure 9.10 shows the behavior of WINS proxies. Proxies are used for forwarding name query packets and verifying that duplicate computer names do not exist. Proxies do not, however, register b-node computer names with the WINS database. The proxy does not maintain its own names database. It can, however, cache the results of the name resolution for a period of time. If possible, the proxy resolves the name by looking up its cache.

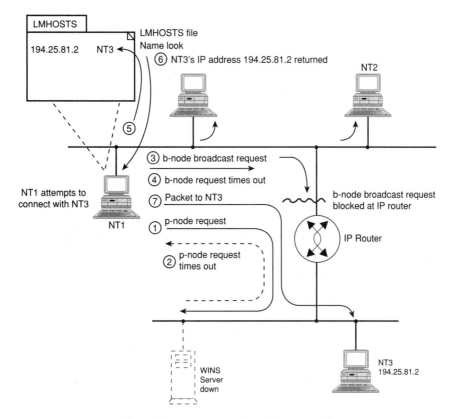

**Figure 9.8** h-node operation with LMHOSTS file.

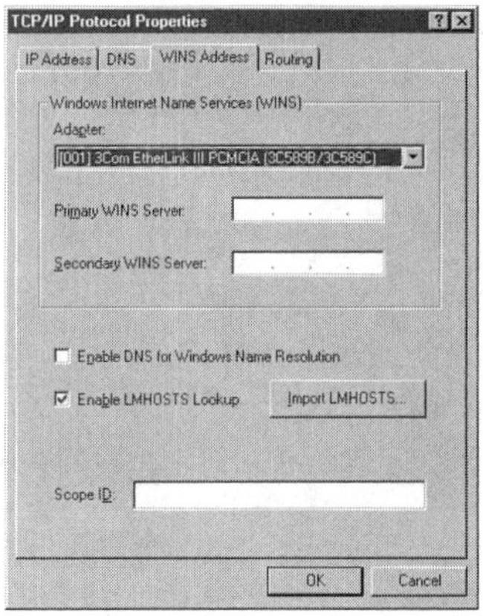

**Figure 9.9** The WINS Address tab in the Microsoft TCP/IP Properties dialog box.

If a Windows NT network does not have a WINS server, then the administrator must ensure that the user has a master browser on each network segment. This provision allows browsing on a network consisting of multiple network segments connected by routers. The master browser dynamically records a list of computer names on the network segment. Typically, this is done during the browse operation when the Network Neighborhood icon is clicked from the desktop. The list of computer names is returned to a browser client, such as another Windows NT computer. The master browser can be any Windows NT workstation or server. The master browsers also need entries for the domain controllers on other network segments in their LMHOSTS file.

If a WINS server is not specified in the TCP/IP configuration for a Windows NT computer, the computer registers its name by broadcasting name registration request packets using a directed broadcast on the local subnet, using UDP datagrams. The registration requests are sent to UDP port 137 (well-known port for NetBIOS name service). To resolve a computer name, the non–WINS computer sends b-node broadcast name query request packets on the local network. If the computer is on a remote network the b-*node* method fails. If the b-node method fails, the computer attempts to resolve the name by consulting the LMHOSTS file. Figure 9.11 shows this behavior when WINS is not enabled.

If a WINS server is specified in the TCP/IP configuration for a Windows NT computer, the computer first queries the WINS server. If the WINS server does not respond or is unable to resolve the name query, the name registration and query requests are broadcast via UDP datagrams in the h-node. The following steps describe the behavior in more detail:

**Transparent Browsing**

If a Windows NT network has WINS servers, browsing is provided transparently, even in situations in which the domain spans router boundaries, as long as there is a master browser on a network segment.

1. A name query request is sent to the WINS server. If the request originates from remote clients on another subnetwork, the request is forwarded by IP routers. The name query request is encapsulated in a UDP/IP datagram.

2. If the WINS server can resolve the name by consulting its database, the client attempts to establish a session to the IP address returned by WINS.

3. If the WINS server is unable to resolve the name, and if the Windows NT computer client is configured as an h-node, the client sends a b-node broadcast name query request packet.

4. If the b-node broadcast name query finally fails, the Windows NT computer client checks the local LMHOSTS file. The LMHOSTS file is only checked if that option is enabled in the TCP/IP setup.

## Name Registration Using WINS

Name registration is used to ensure that the computer's name and IP address are unique for each device. Name registration involves the following processes:

- **Name Registration.** The computer claims its name and IP address mapping.

- **Name Release.** The computer relinquishes control over its computer name and IP address mapping.

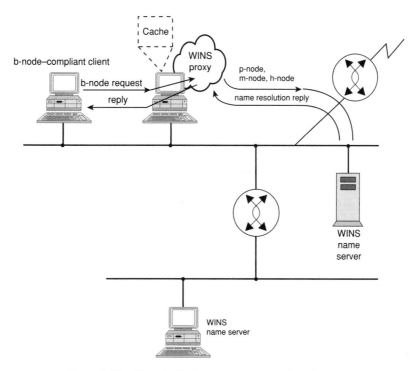

**Figure 9.10**  Use of WINS proxy to contact a WINS server.

■ **Name Renewal.** The computer name undergoes a timed re-registration.

The following sections describe the aforementioned processes.

### Name Registration

If a computer is configured to use a WINS server, its name registration request is sent directly to the WINS server. The WINS server examines the registration request and accepts or rejects it based on the information in its database. For instance, if the WINS database contains a different IP address for the computer name, the WINS server challenges the current computer name entry to determine whether that computer still claims the name. If the current computer name entry is valid, the WINS server rejects the name registration attempt. If no challenge to the new registration request is made, the WINS server accepts the registration request and adds it to its local database. The new registration is time-stamped, and an incremental unique version number and other information also are added. The version number is used to ensure that changes in a WINS database are propagated correctly to other WINS servers.

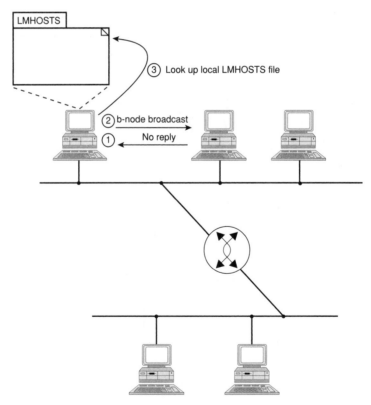

**Figure 9.11**  Windows NT name resolution for non-WINS computers.

If a computer is not configured to use a WINS server, its name registration request is broadcast to the local network. The broadcast packet contains the computer name and IP address. If another computer has previously claimed that name, this computer challenges the name registration, assuming that this computer still is active on the network. The challenge is sent in the form of a negative name registration response, which contests the registration name request. After receiving a negative name registration response, the computer should report an error. In the case of a Windows NT computer, this error also is recorded in the system event log, which can be viewed with the Event Viewer. If the registration attempt is not contested, the computer can use that name and IP address. Computers that have claimed a name must challenge duplicate name registration attempts and respond to name queries with the IP address of the computer.

## Name Release

When the computer is shut down, it releases its computer name and IP address mapping. Again, two situations occur: one in which the Windows NT computer is configured with a WINS server, and another in which it is not.

If a computer is configured to use a WINS server and the computer is shut down gracefully, then it sends a release message to the WINS server as part of the shutdown process. After receiving the release message, the WINS server marks the computer name entry in its database as released. If the entry continues to remain released for a period of time, the WINS server marks the entry as being extinct. This time period is called the *Extinction Interval*, and can be configured for the WINS server. The version number for this entry is updated so that the database changes are propagated among the WINS servers.

Extinct entries are held in the database for a period of time, called the *Extinction Timeout*, that is sufficiently long enough for all changes to have been propagated before the entry is scavenged (deleted) from the database. The last time an entry is scavenged, it is reported as a statistic parameter for a WINS server. The Extinction Timeout can be set for each WINS server.

If a WINS database entry is in the released state and a new registration request arrives that uses the same computer name, but a different IP address, then the WINS server registers the new computer name knowing that the old client has released that name because it is no longer being used.

If a computer is shut down abruptly, and another computer attempts to register the same computer name with a different IP address, the WINS server does not initially know of the shutdown and, therefore, seeks to verify whether the old registration still is valid by attempting to contact the old client. If the client still is shut down or has rebooted with a different IP address (in the case of a DHCP client, for example), then the WINS server allows the new registration attempt to succeed.

If a computer is not configured to use a WINS server, and the computer is gracefully shut down, it sends a directed broadcast datagram on UDP port number 138 (a well-known NetBIOS datagram port) to the subnet to release its name. Other

Windows NT computers that have cached the computer name must delete the computer name from their cache. If, during this shutdown period, the computer receives name query or registration packets specifying its name, it ignores the packets, enabling other computers to claim the computer name and IP address mapping.

### Name Renewal

When a WINS server registers a computer name, it returns to the WINS client a renewal time for the computer name, called the *Renewal Interval*. The client must re-register the computer name within the renewal time, or the WINS server will mark the name as released. A request to renew a computer name and IP address mapping is treated as a new name registration. The Renewal Interval can be configured for a WINS server. The client typically registers in half the value of the Renewal Interval.

By forcing computers to renew their registration, the WINS server ensures that its database does not contain old entries for computer names that were shut down abruptly.

The WINS server periodically verifies whether old names are still active. The time interval for performing this check is called the *Verify Interval*.

# Implementing WINS on a Windows NT Network

The previous sections have exposed you to the theory behind WINS servers. The following sections discuss how to implement a WINS server on a Windows NT network. Also covered are the configuration and administration of WINS servers, the configuration of replication partners, and the management of static mappings.

The WINS Server for Windows NT Server 5 is installed when the networking services are installed on the server, so no additional installation steps are required.

## Using the WINS Manager

The WINS Server is managed by using the Windows Internet Name Service, also called the WINS Manager. The Windows Internet Name Service option is created in the Administrative Tools program group during the installation of the Windows NT server. You can use the WINS Manager to view and configure parameters for any WINS server on the network. You can start the WINS Manager by selecting Start, Programs, Administrative Tools, Windows Internet Name Service.

Alternatively, you can use the following command:

```
START WINSADMN [WINServerIPaddress]
```

To start the WINS Manager on the local server, use the following command:

```
START WINSADMN
```

To start the WINS Manager for the server at 199.245.180.14, use the following command:

```
START WINSADMN 199.245.180.14
```

The following is a guided tour for showing you the features of the WINS Manager tool:

1. Log on as an administrator user. Start the WINS Manager according to one of the methods described earlier.

2. If the WINS server is running on the local computer, you will see the WINS server statistics (see Figure 9.12).

The basic statistics that are displayed in Figure 9.12 are as follows:

- **Server Start Time.** The time the WINS server service was started.
- **Database Initialized.** The time when this WINS database was first initialized. An administrator may initialize the database several times since the server was started.
- **Statistics Cleared.** The time when statistics for the WINS server were last cleared.
- **Last Replication Times.** The time when the WINS database was last replicated.
  - **Periodic.** The last time the WINS database was replicated based on the replication interval specified in the WINS Manager's Preferences dialog box (see the later section "Configuring WINS Preferences" for details on this dialog box).
  - **Admin Trigger.** The last time the WINS database was replicated because the administrator chose the Replicate Now button in the Replication Partners dialog box (see the later section "Configuring WINS Replication" for details on the Replication Partners dialog box).
  - **Net Update.** The last time the WINS database was replicated as a result of a network request. A network request is a push notification message that requests propagation.

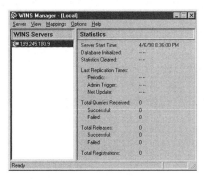

**Figure 9.12**  WINS Server statistics.

- **Total Queries Received.** The number of name query request messages received by this WINS server. The Successful status indicates how many names were successfully resolved, and Failed indicates the number of names the WINS server could not resolve.

- **Total Releases.** The number of messages received that indicate a NetBIOS application has shut itself down. Successful indicates how many names were successfully released, and Failed indicates how many names this WINS server could not release.

- **Total Registrations.** The number of name registration messages received from WINS clients.

3. If WINS is not running on the WINS server, when you start the WINS Manager, the Add WINS Server dialog box will appear.

   In general, to add other WINS servers in the list displayed on the left panel so you can administer them, choose Server, Add WINS Server.

   You should see the Add WINS Server dialog box (see Figure 9.13). You can only enter a WINS server that is available online. Figure 9.14 shows the Validate WINS Server dialog box that appears if you are unable to validate a WINS server.

4. To see detailed information about the current WINS server, choose Server, Detailed Information. The Detailed Information screen appears (see Figure 9.15).

   The meanings of the different detailed information parameters for WINS are explained in the following list.

   - **Last Address Change.** The time at which the last WINS database change was replicated.

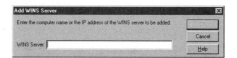

**Figure 9.13**   The Add WINS Server dialog box.

**Figure 9.14**   The Validate WINS Server dialog box.

**Figure 9.15**  Detailed Information on WINS Server.

■ **Last Scavenging Times.** The last times that the database was cleaned for specific types of entries.

  ■ **Periodic.** Indicates when the database was cleaned based on the renewal interval specified in the WINS Server Configuration dialog box (described in the following section).

  ■ **Admin Trigger.** Indicates when the database was last cleaned because the administrator chose the Initiate Scavenging option.

  ■ **Extinction.** Indicates when the database was last cleaned based on the Extinction interval specified in the WINS Server Configuration dialog box.

  ■ **Verification.** Indicates when the database was last cleaned based on the Verify interval specified in the WINS Server Configuration dialog box.

■ **Unique Registrations.** The number of name registration requests that this WINS server has accepted.

  ■ **Conflicts.** The number of conflicts encountered during registration of the unique computer names registered at the WINS server.

  ■ **Renewals.** The number of renewals received for unique computer names.

■ **Group Registrations.** The number of registration requests for groups that have been accepted by this WINS server.

  ■ **Conflicts.** The number of conflicts encountered during registration of group names.

  ■ **Renewals.** The number of renewals received for group names.

**Refreshing or Clearing the Statistics Screen**

The statistics screen is not automatically refreshed (refer to Figure 9.12). To refresh the statistics display, choose View, Refresh, or press F5. To clear the statistics counters, choose View, Clear Statistics.

## Configuring WINS Servers

Each WINS server can be configured for renewal, verification, and extinction intervals. Because the WINS server database is crucial for name resolution and registration, WINS servers can be configured with other servers as replication partners. Within a WINS replication partnership you can have a *pull partner* that pulls or fetches the database entries from its replica partner (see Figure 9.16). A *push partner* is a WINS server that *pushes* or sends update notification messages to its partner that the WINS database has changed (see Figure 9.17). As part of configuring a WINS server, you can specify the push and pull parameters for replicated servers.

The following is an outline of a procedure for configuring WINS servers:

1. Log on as administrator to the WINS server.

2. Start the WINS Manager.

3. Choose Server, Configuration.

   The WINS and Pull/Push Parameters appear in the WINS Server Configuration dialog box (see Figure 9.18).

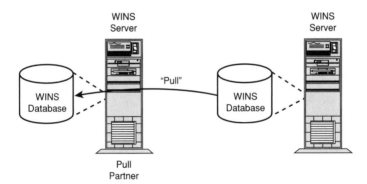

**Figure 9.16** A pull partner for replicated WINS databases.

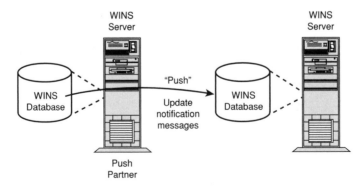

**Figure 9.17** A push partner for replicated WINS databases.

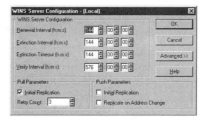

**Figure 9.18**  The initial WINS Server Configuration screen.

Use the screen in Figure 9.18 to specify the renewal, extinction, and verify parameters in hours, minutes, and seconds. The default settings of these timer values
are sufficient for most networks. You may want to use a smaller value such as 24
hours (or less) if new computers and network segments are being added daily,
which may happen during the initial growth phases of a network. If you make
the values *too* small, however, you will see an increase in network traffic caused
by the WINS operation:

- The Renewal Interval specifies that the client must re-register its name
  within this time period. The default setting is 96 hours (4 days). WINS
  clients will typically re-register and renew in half this time interval—that
  is, in 2 days.

- The Extinction Interval specifies the time interval between when an entry
  is marked as released and when it is marked as extinct. The default is 96
  hours (4 days).

- The Extinction Timeout is the time interval between when an entry is
  marked extinct and when the entry is finally scavenged from the database.
  The default is the same as the renewal interval (96 hours or 4 days by
  default).

- The Verify Interval is the time interval after which the WINS server must
  verify that old names it does not own are still active. The default is 576
  hours (24 days).

You should adjust the values of the interval timers based on your network
requirements. Take into account how often computer names and IP addresses
need to change and the amount of traffic generated by renewal, verification, and
extinction intervals.

4. Check the Initial Replication option in the Pull Parameters box, if you want the
   WINS server to pull replicas of new WINS database entries from its partners
   when the system is initialized, or when a replication-related parameter changes.
   In the Retry Count, specify how many attempts should be made if the pull
   operation does not succeed. Retries occur at the replication interval specified in
   the Preferences dialog box. If all the retries fail, WINS waits for a period of time,
   controlled in the Preferences dialog box, before starting replication again (see the

later section "Configuring WINS Preferences" for details on the Preferences dialog box). If the network is known to have some communication problems such as replicating over a slow or unreliable link, you may want to increase the Retry Count.

5. Check the Initial Replication option in the Push Parameters section, to send notification messages to the replica partners of the WINS database status when the system is initialized. To send notification messages about IP address changes to the replication partners, check the Replicate On Address Change option in the Push Parameters section. You may want to enable this option if you have network problems that might be caused by frequent IP address changes.

6. To see the Advanced options, choose the Advanced button.

Additional options appear for the WINS Server Configuration dialog box (see Figure 9.19).

The advanced options are explained here:

- The Logging Enabled option specifies whether logging of database changes to the transaction log file JET.LOG should be turned on. The transaction log file is used to recover from incomplete transactions in the database. This option is enabled by default. The transaction logging does take up disk space and a certain amount of processing overhead. It is, however, useful when troubleshooting because all changes in the WINS database are logged and can be traced. If troubleshooting and fault tolerance are not of concern, you can disable this option.

- The Log Detailed Events option specifies whether detailed information should be reported when events are logged. Logging detailed events consumes considerable system resources and should be turned off if you are tuning for performance. This option is disabled by default. The detail events can be viewed using the Event Viewer.

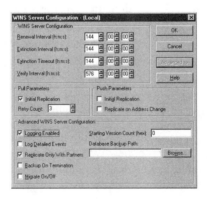

**Figure 9.19**   The WINS Server Configuration screen with advanced options.

■ The Replicate Only With Partners option specifies that replication will be performed only with WINS pull or push partners. If this option is not enabled, an administrator can ask a WINS server to pull from or push to a non-listed WINS server partner. This option is enabled by default.

■ The Backup On Termination option specifies that the database will be backed up automatically when WINS Manager is closed. This option is disabled by default.

■ The Migrate On/Off option specifies that static unique and multihomed (multiple network board) records in the database are treated as dynamic and overwritten when they conflict with a new registration or replica. Check this option if you are upgrading a non-Windows NT system to Windows NT. This option is disabled by default.

■ The Starting Version Count option specifies the starting version ID number for the database. Normally, you will not need to change this value unless the database becomes corrupted and needs a new start. In this case, set the Starting Version Count number to a number higher than that which appears as the version number counter for this WINS server on all the remote partners that have a replica of the WINS server's database records. The version number can be seen in the View Database dialog box in WINS Manager.

■ The Database Backup Path option specifies the directory where the WINS database backup files will be stored. WINS uses this directory to perform an automatic restoration of the database if the current database is found to be corrupted when WINS is started. You should not specify a network path for this field.

## Configuring WINS Replication

WINS servers can be configured in partnership among themselves so that they can replicate their databases. This ensures that the names registered on WINS servers are replicated to all WINS replication partners on the network. Replication changes are performed within the Replication Interval specified in the Preferences dialog box (see the later section "Configuring WINS Preferences" for details on the Preferences dialog box).

Replication is not performed indiscriminately among WINS servers on the network. Rather, you must explicitly specify WINS servers that are in a replication partnership. In the example in Figure 9.20, NTS2 and NTS5 have only one replication partner: NTS1. However, NTS1 has two replication partners: NTS2 and NTS5. NTS3 and NTS4 do not have any replication partners, and are therefore vulnerable to failure.

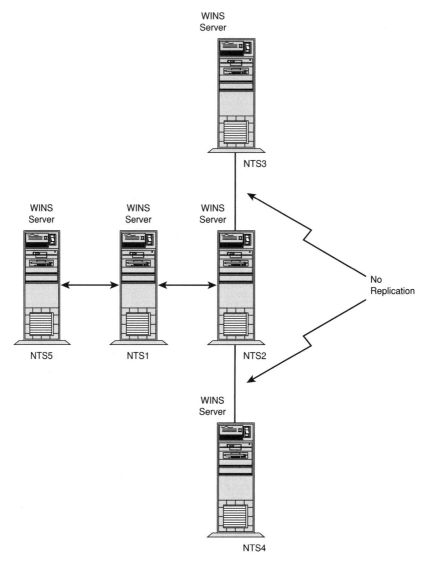

**Figure 9.20** A WINS server replication example.

As explained earlier, a WINS server can be configured as a push or a pull partner, or both. The pull partner gets its information by requesting and obtaining information from its push partner. A push partner sends notification changes to its pull partner. Version numbers associated with the WINS database records are used to decide the latest version of the information in the records.

Replication is initiated (*triggered*), when a WINS server polls another WINS server to get a replica. The polling can occur during WINS system initialization, at a specific time, and then repeat at the Replication Interval for periodic replication. Replication can also be triggered when a WINS server reaches an Update Count threshold set by the administrator. The server then notifies its pull partners that it has reached its threshold, and the other servers can then decide to pull replicas.

The following is an outline of how to configure replication partners for WINS servers:

1. Log on to the WINS server as an administrator user.

2. Start the WINS Manager.

3. Choose Server, Replication Partners.

   The Replication Partners dialog box appears (see Figure 9.21).

4. Click the Add button.

   The Add WINS Server dialog box appears (see Figure 9.22).

5. In the WINS Server field, enter the name or IP address of the WINS server that is a potential candidate to be added to the replicator list.

6. Click OK.

   If the WINS Server can be found, it will be added to the WINS Server list in the Replication Partners dialog box.

7. If you want to control which WINS servers are displayed in the Replication Partners dialog box, check or clear the following options in the WINS Servers To List box:

   ■ To display push partners for the current WINS server, enable the Push Partners option.

   ■ To display pull partners for the current WINS server, enable the Pull Partners option.

   ■ To display WINS servers that are neither push partners nor pull partners enable the Other option.

**Figure 9.21**   The Replication Partners dialog box.

**Figure 9.22**   The Add WINS Server dialog box.

8. From the WINS Server list in the Replication Partners dialog box, select the WINS server to be made a push or pull partner of the current WINS server.

9. Check either the Push Partner or Pull Partner option, or both, to specify the replication partnership with the current server, and click the corresponding Configure button(s).

   If the Pull Partner option is selected, you will see the Pull Partner Properties dialog box (see Figure 9.23).

   1. In the Start Time field of the Pull Partner Properties dialog box, enter the time when replication should begin.

   2. In the Replication Interval field of the Pull Partner Properties dialog box, enter the Replication Interval value. Enter smaller values in the Replication Interval if you expect frequent changes in the WINS database, but be aware that frequent replication will cause additional network traffic. If replication is being done over slow links, this may be of concern.

      If you want to use the values specified in the Preferences dialog box as the default settings, choose the Set Default Values button.

   3. Click OK in the Pull Partner Properties dialog box to return to the Replication Partners dialog box.

   If the Push Partner option is selected, you will see the Push Partner Properties dialog box (see Figure 9.24).

   1. In the Update Count field of the Push Partner Properties dialog box, specify a number for the additions and updates that are made to records in the WINS database that will result in a notification message being sent to the WINS partner that the changes need replication. If the push server is also acting as a pull server, replications that have been pulled from the partners are not part of the update count. The minimum value for Update Count is 20. You may want to increase this value if you want the WINS update to be done less frequently.

   2. If you want to use the values specified in the Preferences dialog box, choose the Set Default Value button.

   3. Click OK in the Push Partner Properties dialog box to return to the Replication Partners dialog box.

**Figure 9.23**  The Pull Partner Properties dialog box.

**Figure 9.24**  The Push Partner Properties dialog box.

10. You can send replication triggers for the partners you add immediately from the Replication Partners dialog box (refer to Figure 9.21). This option is useful if you have made substantial changes to the WINS database and want to replicate the database between the partners immediately, rather than waiting for the start time or replication interval.

    To send a replication trigger, select the WINS servers to which you want to send a replication trigger, and then choose the Push or Pull button, depending on whether you want to send the trigger to push partners or pull partners.

    If you want the selected WINS server to propagate the trigger to all its pull partners after it has pulled the latest information, set the Push With Propagation option. If the selected WINS server does not need to synchronize because it has the same or more up-to-date replicas than the source WINS server, it does not propagate the trigger to its pull partners.

    If Push With Propagation is not set, the selected WINS server will not propagate the trigger to its other partners.

11. If you need to start replication immediately, choose the Replicate Now button in the Replication Partners dialog box.

12. If you need to delete replication partners, select one or more servers in the WINS Server list in the Replication Partners dialog box, and then click the Delete button, or press Del.

    WINS Manager asks you to confirm the deletion if you have enabled Delete Confirmation in the Preferences dialog box.

## Configuring WINS Preferences

In the previous sections, the WINS Preferences dialog box was mentioned several times. This dialog box enables you to configure several global options for WINS administration.

The following is an outline of configuring WINS preferences:

1. Start the WINS Manager while logged on as an administrator user.

2. Choose Options, Preferences to open the Preferences dialog box (see Figure 9.25).

3. Click the Partners button to see all of the available preferences (see Figure 9.26).

**Figure 9.25**   Initial WINS Preferences dialog box.

**Figure 9.26**   WINS Preferences dialog box with all available options.

4. The Address Display section can be used to specify how you want address information to be displayed throughout WINS Manager. Your choices are computer name, IP address, computer name with IP address in parentheses, or IP address with computer name in parentheses. The kind of address display affects how a connection is made to the WINS server. For IP addresses, the connection is made via TCP/IP. For computer names, the connection is made via named pipes.

5. Enable the Auto Refresh option if you want the statistics in the WINS Manager window to be refreshed automatically at intervals specified in the Interval (Seconds) field.

6. Enable the LAN Manager-Compatible option if you want computer names to obey the LAN Manager naming convention. LAN Manager computer names are limited to 15 characters, as opposed to 16-character NetBIOS names used by applications such as Lotus Notes. In LAN Manager names, the 16th byte is used to indicate the device type: server, workstation, messenger, and so on. When this option is enabled, WINS adds and imports static mappings with 0, 0x03, and 0x20 as the 16th byte.

   For Microsoft Windows networks, you should follow the LAN Manager convention, and enable this option.

7. Enable the Validate Cache Of "Known" WINS Servers at Startup Time option if you want the WINS server to query the list of servers each time the WINS server starts, to find out if the servers in the list are available. Although this option updates the list of available servers, it can cause a slight delay in the startup of the WINS service.

**Refreshing WINS Statistics**

The statistics display is also refreshed whenever an action is initiated while you are working in WINS Manager or by pressing F5.

8. Enable the Confirm Deletion of Static Mappings & Cached WINS Servers option if you want a warning message to appear each time you delete a static mapping or the cached name of a WINS server.

9. In the Start Time field, enter the default value for the replication start time for new pull partners.

10. In the Replication Interval field, enter the time interval at which data replicas will be exchanged between the partners.

11. In the Update Count field, enter a number for the registrations and changes that will cause a replication trigger to be sent by this server when it is a push partner. The minimum value is 5.

12. After making the changes to the preference settings, click OK to save your changes.

## Creating Static Mappings

Not all TCP/IP hosts on your network are WINS enabled. Being *WINS enabled* means registering with a WINS server or obtaining name resolution information from the WINS server. For these TCP/IP hosts, you can create a permanent computer name/IP address mapping in the WINS database. Static mappings are created manually by the administrator for non–WINS-enabled computers and are not challenged or removed by the WINS protocols. The administrator can, of course, create, edit, import, or delete static mappings for any TCP/IP host.

The following is an outline of a procedure to view, add, and edit static mappings:

1. Start the WINS Manager while logged on as an Administrator user.

2. From the Mappings menu, choose Static Mappings.

   The Static Mappings dialog box appears (see Figure 9.27). If you have not assigned any static mappings, the Filter: None section will be empty.

3. To change the order in which the names are listed, select either of the following options:

   ■ Sort Static Mappings by IP Address

   ■ Sort Static Mappings by Computer Name

4. You can import static mappings by choosing the Import Mappings button or add static mappings by choosing the Add Mappings button. The import file should be in the format of an LMHOSTS file; it is an efficient method of importing a large number of hosts.

### DHCP IP Address Assignment and WINS Settings

If DHCP is also used on the network to assign IP addresses, a reserved IP address allocated by a DHCP server will override any WINS server settings. You should not assign static mappings to WINS-enabled computers.

**Figure 9.27**   The Static Mappings dialog box.

5. If you select the Add Mappings button to add static mappings, you will see the Add Static Mappings dialog box (see Figure 9.28).

6. In the Name field of the Add Static Mappings dialog box, enter the computer name that will have a static mapping. Computer names are represented in their UNC notation with two backslashes (\\) preceding them. If you do not type the two backslashes, WINS Manager will add them for you.

7. In the IP Address section of the Add Static Mappings dialog box, enter the IP address for the computer.

8. In the Type section, select the type of the static mapping. The meanings of the different types are described here:

   ■ Unique is for computer names that are unique in the database, with one address per name.

   ■ Group is used for computers on a subnet. It does not store addresses for individual members. A group can be defined for any subnet and can be registered with more than one WINS server. If the WINS server receives a name resolution query for the group name, it resolves it to the limited broadcast address 255.255.255.255. The WINS client will then use 255.255.255.255 as the destination address in the datagram sent to the group name. This will result in a local broadcast on the subnet. The group name is renewed when any member of the group renews the group name. The group's time stamp shows the last time for any change received for the group.

**Immediacy of Changes to Static Mappings**

Note that changes you make to the static mappings are effective immediately—you cannot cancel changes because there is no Cancel button. To correct an error, you must manually delete the entry and then add it again.

**Figure 9.28**    The Add Static Mappings dialog box.

- Domain Name is a group of up to 25 NetBIOS names that have 0x1C as the 16th byte. Each group member must renew its name individually. If you try to register more than 25 names, the WINS Manager overwrites a replica address in the group. If no replica address is present, WINS Manager overwrites the oldest entry.

- Internet Group is a group of up to 25 NetBIOS names and IP addresses. A character space (0x20) is appended to the group name. You can override the default 0x20 16th byte by placing a different character in brackets at the end of the Internet group name; however, you can't use the character 0x1C, which is reserved for domain name groups (see the preceding entry).

  Name registrations received for the Internet groups are stored with their actual IP address rather than the subnet broadcast address. In addition, a time stamp and owner ID are stored with the actual IP address. The owner ID indicates the WINS server registering that address. If the Internet Group name has fewer than 25 members, dynamically registered names can be added to the Internet Group. If the Internet Group already has the maximum 25 members, WINS looks for and removes a member registered by another WINS server (replica member) and adds the new member. If there are no replica members—that is, all the 25 members are owned by this WINS server—the oldest member is replaced by the new one.

  WINS gives members in an Internet Group name that registered with it precedence over remote members. This means that the Internet Group name always contains the geographically closest Windows NT Server computers. WINS resolves a query for the Internet Group name by returning the 24 closest Windows NT Server computers in the domain plus the domain controller. The Internet Group Name can also be used to discover a Windows NT Server in a domain when a Windows NT computer needs a server for pass-through validation. Note that the Internet Group Name list is static and does not accept dynamic updates from WINS-enabled computers.

- Multihomed is used for computers with multiple network cards or multiple IP addresses bound to NetBIOS over TCP/IP. A multihomed computer can register its IP addresses at different times by sending a special name registration packet. A multihomed group name can contain up to 25 IP addresses. New registration requests received for a multi-homed group that already has reached its limit of 25 computers will result in replica addresses being overwritten first; if no replicas are present, then the oldest registered name is overwritten.

Note that when the Internet Group or Multihomed group is selected, additional controls are added to the Add Static Mappings dialog box to add multiple IP addresses.

Table 9.1 summarizes the different types of NetBIOS names that are distinguished by the 16th character. You can view the NetBIOS names registered on a computer by using the `nbtstat -n` command.

9. After adding a computer name and IP address and selecting the type in the Add Static Mappings dialog box, choose the Add Mappings button, and repeat the previous steps for adding additional names.

Another method of adding static entries is to import them from the file containing the computer name/IP address mappings. The file that contains these mappings must have the format of the LMHOSTS file. However, group names and multihomed

Table 9.1  **NetBIOS Computer Names**

| Character Ending a NetBIOS Name | Description |
| --- | --- |
| 0x1E | This is a group name. Browsers broadcast to this name and listen on it to elect a master browser. The broadcast is done on the local subnet using the limited broadcast address 255.255.255.255 and should not cross routers. WINS always returns the limited broadcast address 255.255.255.255 when resolving a group name. |
| 0x1D | Clients resolve this name to access the master browser for server lists. There is one master browser per subnet. |
| 0x1C | This refers to the Domain name group. |
| 0x20 | This refers to the Internet Group. Each member of the group must renew its name individually or be released. The Internet Group has a maximum of 25 names. WINS returns a positive response for a dynamic regis tration of a static Internet Group name, but the address is not added to the list. When a static Internet Group name is replicated, which clashes with a dynamic Internet Group name on another WINS server, the members of the group are merged, and the Internet Group name is marked as static. |

names can be added only by interactively entering them in the Add Static Mappings dialog box:

1. To import a file containing static mappings, choose the Import Mappings button in the Static Mappings dialog box.

2. You should see the Select Static Mapping File dialog box. Use this dialog box to select the mappings file, and select OK.

With the exception of the #DOM keyword used in the LMHOSTS file, all other keywords are ignored. If there is a #DOM entry in the file, an Internet Group name is created and the address is added to the group. Figure 9.29 shows the result of importing an LMHOSTS file.

To edit a static mapping, select the mapping you want to change and choose the Edit Mapping button in the Static Mappings dialog box. Alternatively, double-click on the mapping entry in the list (see Figure 9.30).

You can change the IP address in the mapping, but you can only view the Computer Name and Mapping Type values. To change the Computer Name or Mapping Type, you must delete the entry and create a new mapping entry. After making changes in the Edit Static Mapping dialog box, click OK to save your changes.

To delete a mapping entry, select it in the Static Mappings dialog box, and click the Delete Mapping button or press the Del key.

To limit the range of IP addresses or computer names displayed in the dialog boxes, click the Set Filter button. The Set Filter dialog box appears (see Figure 9.31).

In the Computer Name and IP Address fields, use an asterisk (*) for portions of computer names and IP addresses. For example, to only see computer names on subnet 144.19.74.0, use this notation:

```
144.19.74.*
```

To see only computer names beginning with the letters KNT, use this notation:

```
\\KNT*
```

After defining the filter, click OK.

To cancel a filter, click the Clear Filter button in the Static Mappings dialog box.

**Figure 9.29**   Static Mappings from importing an LMHOSTS file.

**Figure 9.30**   Edit Static Mapping dialog box.

**Figure 9.31**   The Set Filter dialog box.

## Managing the WINS Database

The WINS database files are stored in the \\*systemroot*\\SYSTEM32\\WINS directory. Table 9.2 describes the WINS database files.

### Scavenging the WINS Database

The WINS database should be periodically cleared of old entries and backed up. The periodic cleaning up of the WINS database is called *scavenging* in the Microsoft literature. Scavenging is done automatically at times set by the Extinction Timeout interval defined in the WINS Server Configuration dialog box (refer to Figure 9.18).

You can also scavenge the WINS database manually. To scavenge a database, select Initiate Scavenging from the Mappings menu.

You will see a message that the scavenging command has been queued. Table 9.3 explains the state of database information before and after scavenging.

Table 9.2   **WINS Database Files**

| Filename | Description |
| --- | --- |
| WINS.MDB | This is the WINS database file. |
| J50.*,RES*.LOG | This file contains a log of all transactions performed on the WINS database. The file is used by WINS to recover from incomplete transactions. |
| WINSTMP.MDB | This is a temporary file that WINS creates. The file may remain in the WINS subdirectory after a system crash. |

Table 9.3   **Scavenging Status**

| State Before Scavenging | State After Scavenging |
| --- | --- |
| Active names with Renewal interval expired | Marked released |
| Released names with Extinct interval expired | Marked extinct |
| Extinct names with Extinct timeout expired | Deleted |
| Replicas of extinct names with Extinct timeout expired | Deleted |

| State Before Scavenging | State After Scavenging |
| --- | --- |
| Replicas of active names with Verify interval expired | Revalidated |
| Replicas of extinct or deleted names | Deleted |

## Compacting the WINS Database

If the WINS server has been active for a long time, the database can grow in size. You can compact the database to improve the WINS performance. To compact the WINS database, perform the following steps:

1. Stop the WINS server so that you can compact the database files. You can perform this by using the System Service Management option in the Administrative Tools group, or by using the command `net stop wins`.

2. Run the `Jetpack.exe` program (kept in the `\systemroot\SYSTEM32 directory`).

3. Restart the WINS service with the `net start wins` command or use the System Service Management option in the Administrative Tools group to start WINS.

## Backing Up the WINS Database

After the WINS database has been scavenged and compacted using the steps outlined in the previous section, you can back up the WINS database. The WINS Manager includes backup capabilities for the WINS database. You must specify a backup directory for the WINS database. The WINS server then performs complete database backups every 24 hours using the specified directory.

The following is an outline for configuring the WINS backup:

1. Start the WINS Manager while logged on as an Administrator user.

2. Select Backup Database from the Mappings menu.

   The Select Backup Directory dialog box appears. Use this dialog box to specify the location of the backup directory. For example, this could be the WINS subdirectory.

3. After you select the backup directory and click OK, WINS creates a backup subdirectory named `wins_bak` that contains the backed-up database files.

You should also periodically back up the WINS Registry entries for the WINS server. A brief outline of the procedure for backing up the WINS Registry information is presented here for your convenience.

1. Run `REGEDT32.EXE`.

2. Select the following key:
   ```
   HKEY_LOCAL_MACHINE\SYSTEM\CurrentControlSet\Services\WINS
   ```

3. Select Save Key in the Registry menu.

4. Specify the path where you backup the WINS Registry Key.

### Viewing the WINS Database

You can view the current active and static mappings in the WINS database by following these steps:

1. Start the WINS Manager while logged on as an Administrator user.

2. Select Mappings, Show Database from the WINS Manager screen.

   The Show Database dialog box appears (see Figure 9.32).

3. Select the Show Only Mappings from Selected Owner option button to view the mappings in the database for a specific WINS server that you have selected from the Select Owner list box.

   Or, select Show All Mappings to see all mappings for all servers in the Select Owner list box.

4. Select a Sort Order option to sort by IP address, computer name, time stamp for the mapping, version ID, or type. The default is to sort by computer name.

5. To view only a range of mappings, choose the Set Filter button. To cancel a filter setting, choose the Clear Filter button.

6. Use the scroll bars in the Mappings box to view entries in the database. Then click Close when you are finished viewing.

In the Mappings list (see Figure 9.32), you see the following information for each record in the WINS database:

- The Computer name, which is the NetBIOS name for the computer.

- The IP address—that is, the assigned Internet Protocol address.

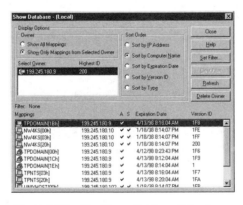

**Figure 9.32**   The Show Database dialog box.

- The A or S indicator, which indicates whether the mapping is Active (dynamic) or Static.

- The Expiration Date, which shows when the mapping is scheduled to expire.

- The Version ID, which is a unique hexadecimal number assigned by the WINS server during name registration. The Version ID is used by the server's pull partner to find new and changed records.

You can delete a record by highlighting it and clicking the Delete Owner button.

## Advanced Registry Parameters for WINS

The WINS parameters for the WINS server that can be configured using the Registry Editor are kept under the following key:

HKEY_LOCAL_MACHINE\SYSTEM\CurrentControlSet\Services\WINS

If a parameter is not listed in the Registry, its default value is assumed.

The DbFileNm value entry is of data type REG_EXPAND_SZ, and has a default value of %SystemRoot%\system32\wins\wins.mdb. This value entry specifies the full path name for the WINS database file.

The DoStaticDataInit value entry is of data type REG_DWORD and has a value of 0 or 1. The default value is 0, which means that the WINS server does not initialize its database. If this parameter is set to 1, the WINS server reads one or more files listed under the \Datafiles subkey to initialize its database. This initialization occurs when WINS is started or whenever a change is made to one or more values of the \Parameters or \Datafiles keys.

Table 9.4 lists the parameters, most of which can be set from the WINS Server Configuration dialog box (refer to Figure 9.18).

The Wins\Partners Registry key has two subkeys: Pull and Push. Under these subkeys are the IP addresses of all push and pull partners of the WINS server.

Table 9.4 **Registry Parameters Set in the WINS Server Configuration**

| Registry Parameter | WINS Server Configuration Option |
| --- | --- |
| LogDetailedEvents | Log Detailed Events |
| LogFilePath | Not Specified |
| LoggingOn | Logging Enabled |
| RefreshInterval | Renewal Interval |
| RplOnlyWCnfPnrs | Replicate Only With Partners |
| TombstoneInterval | Extinction Interval |
| TombstoneTimeout | Extinction Timeout |
| VerifyInterval | Verify Interval |

A push partner's IP address, listed under the `Partners\Pull` subkey, has the `MemberPrec` value entry. The `MemberPrec` value entry is of data type `REG_DWORD`, has a value of `0` or `1`, and specifies the order of precedence for this WINS partner. The default is `0`, which indicates low precedence. A value of `1` indicates high precedence. Dynamically registered names have a high precedence. Set the value to `1` if the WINS server is serving a nearby location.

Under the `Partners\Pull` subkey are defined the `InitTimeReplication` and `CommRetryCount` value entries. These correspond to the Initial Replication option and the Retry Count field in the WINS Configuration dialog box.

Under the `Partners\Pull\IpAddress` subkey are defined the `SpTime` and `TimeInterval` value entries. These correspond to the Start Time for pull partners and Replication Interval in the WINS Preferences dialog box.

Under the `Partners\Push` subkey are defined the `InitTimeReplication` and `RplOnAddressChg` value entries. These correspond to the Initial Replication option and the Replicate on Address Change option in the WINS Configuration dialog box.

Under the `Partners\Push\IpAddress` subkey is defined the `UpdateCount` value entry. This corresponds to the Update Count field in the WINS Preferences dialog box.

## SNMP Parameters for WINS

The WINS parameters can be managed by an SNMP manager. The WINS MIB parameters are described in Tables 9.5 to 9.9. The parameters are grouped in separate tables by their SNMP group. Most of the management tasks for the WINS server can be performed by reading or writing to the SNMP MIB objects defined in these tables. Table 9.9 is particularly interesting, because it can be used to trigger management actions such as sending push notification messages, initiating scavenging of a WINS database, and so on.

The SNMP manager must have the ability to import these MIB objects that are specific WINS parameters. The values shown in braces ({}) are the ASN.1 object IDs for the parameters. The labels such as `Par`, `Datafiles`, `Pull`, and so on, are ASN.1 macros that expand to an ASN.1 prefix value defined by Microsoft.

Table 9.5   **Windows NT WINS MIB Parameters**

| Parameter | Description |
| --- | --- |
| ParWinsStartTime | WINS start time. {Par 1} |
| ParLastPScvTime | Most recent time stamp at which a planned scavenging took place. {Par 2} |
| ParLastATScvTime | Most recent time stamp at which scavenging took place as a result of administrative action. {Par 3} |
| ParLastTombScvTime | Most recent time stamp at which extinction scavenging took place. {Par 4} |

| Parameter | Description |
|---|---|
| ParLastVerifyScvTime | Most recent time stamp at which revalidation of old active replicas took place. {Par 5} |
| ParLastPRplTime | Most recent time stamp at which planned replication took place. {Par 6} |
| ParLastATRplTime | Most recent time stamp at which administrator-triggered replication took place. {Par 7} |
| ParLastNTRplTime | Most recent time stamp at which network-triggered replication occurred. Network-triggered replication occurs as a result of an update notification message from a Push partner. {Par 8} |
| ParLastACTRplTime | Most recent time stamp at which address change-triggered replication occurred. Address change-triggered replication occurs when the IP address changes because of a new registration. {Par 9} |
| ParLastInitDbTime | Most recent time stamp at which static entries in the local WINS database were generated by importing from data files. {Par 10} |
| ParLastCounterResetTime | Most recent time stamp at which the local counters were initialized to zero. {Par 11} |
| ParWinsTotalNoOfReg | Number of registrations received. {Par 12} |
| ParWinsTotalNoOfQueries | Number of queries received. {Par 13} |
| ParWinsTotalNoOfRel | Number of releases received. {Par 14} |
| ParWinsTotalNoOfSuccRel | Number of releases that succeeded. {Par 15} |
| ParWinsTotalNoOfFailRel | Number of releases that failed because the address of the requester did not match the address of the name. {Par 16} |
| ParWinsTotalNoOfSuccQueries | Number of queries that succeeded. {Par 17} |
| ParWinsTotalNoOfFailQueries | Number of queries that failed. {Par 18} |
| ParRefreshInterval | Renewal interval in seconds. {Par 19} |
| ParTombstoneInterval | Extinct interval in seconds. {Par 20} |
| ParTombstoneTimeout | Extinct timeout in seconds. {Par 21} |
| ParVerifyInterval | Verify interval in seconds. {Par 22} |
| ParVersCounterStartVal_ ➡LowWord | The value of the low word of the version counter that WINS should start with. {Par 23} |
| ParVersCounterStartVal_ ➡HighWord | The value of the high word of the version counter that WINS should start with. {Par 24} |
| ParRplOnlyWCnfPnrs | Specifies if replication is allowed with nonconfigured partners. A non-zero value specifies that replication will be done only with partners listed in the Registry. {Par 25} |
| ParStaticDataInit | Specifies if static data should be read in at initialization and reconfiguration time. {Par 26} |

*continues*

Table 9.5 **Continued**

| Parameter | Description |
|---|---|
| ParLogFlag | Specifies whether logging should be done. {Par 27} |
| ParLogFileName | Specifies the path to the log file. {Par 28} |
| ParBackupDirPath | Specifies the path to the backup directory. {Par 29} |
| ParDoBackupOnTerm | Specifies if WINS should perform a database backup upon exit. {Par 30} |
| ParMigration | Specifies whether static records in the WINS database should be treated as dynamic records during conflict with new name registrations. Values can be 0 for NO or 1 for YES. {Par 31} |

Table 9.6 **Windows NT Datafiles Group MIB Parameters**

| Parameter | Description |
|---|---|
| DFDatafilesTable | The list of datafiles specified under the \Datafiles key in the Registry. The files are used for static initialization of the WINS database. {Datafiles 1} |
| dDFDatafileEntry | Data file name record. {DFDatafilesTable 1} |
| dFDatafileIndex | Index into the datafiles table. {dDFDatafileEntry 1} |
| dFDatafileName | Name of the datafile used for static initialization. {dDFDatafileEntry 2} |

Table 9.7 **Windows NT Pull Partner Group MIB Parameters**

| Parameter | Description |
|---|---|
| PullInitTime | Specifies if pull should be done at WINS start and at reconfiguration. Modifying pull or push group's MIB variable constitutes a reconfiguration. {Pull 1} |
| PullCommRetryCount | Specifies the retry count in case of communication failure during a pull replication. {Pull 2} |
| PullPnrTable | List of partners for performing a pull replication. {Pull 3} |
| pPullPnrEntry | The row corresponding to a partner. {PullPnrTable 1} |
| PullPnrAdd | The IP address of the remote WINS partner. {pPullPnrEntry 1} |
| PullPnrSpTime | The time at which pull replication should occur. {pPullPnrEntry 2} |
| PullPnrTimeInterval | The time interval for pull replication. {pPullPnrEntry 3} |
| PullPnrMemberPrec | The precedence to be given to members of the group pulled from the WINS. The precedence of locally registered members |

| Parameter | Description |
|---|---|
| | of a group is greater than that of any replicas. {pPullPnrEntry 4} |
| PullPnrNoOfSuccRpls | The number of times replication was successful with WINS after startup or reset of counters. {pPullPnrEntry 5} |
| PullPnrNoOfCommFails | The number of times replication was unsuccessful with the WINS because of communication failure. {pPullPnrEntry 6} |
| PullPnrVersNoLowWord | The value of the low word for the highest version number found in records owned by this WINS. {pPullPnrEntry 7} |
| PullPnrVersNoHighWord | The value of the high word for the highest version number found in records owned by this WINS. {pPullPnrEntry 8} |

Table 9.8  **Windows NT Push Partner Group MIB Parameters**

| Parameter | Description |
|---|---|
| PushInitTime | Specifies if a push notification message should be sent at WINS startup. {Push 1} |
| PushRplOnAddChg | Specifies if a notification message should be sent when an address changes. {Push 2} |
| PushPnrTable | Specifies WINS partners with which push replication is to be initiated. {Push 3} |
| pPushPnrEntry | The row corresponding to the WINS partner. {PushPnrTable 1} |
| PushPnrAdd | IP address of the WINS partner. {pPushPnrEntry 1} |
| PushPnrUpdateCount | Number of updates that should trigger a push notification message. {pPushPnrEntry 2} |

Table 9.9  **Windows NT Command Group MIB Parameters**

| Parameter | Description |
|---|---|
| CmdPullTrigger | When set, it causes the WINS to pull replicas from the remote WINS server identified by the IP address. {Cmd 1} |
| CmdPushTrigger | When set, it causes WINS to send push notification message to the remote WINS server identified by the IP address. {Cmd 2} |
| CmdDeleteWins | When set, it causes all information pertaining to a WINS server to be deleted from the local WINS server. This command could be used when the owner-address mapping table is nearing capacity. {Cmd 3} |
| CmdDoScavenging | When set, it causes WINS to initiate scavenging. {Cmd 4} |

*continues*

Table 9.9 **Continued**

| Parameter | Description |
|---|---|
| CmdDoStaticInit | When set, WINS will perform static initialization using the file specified as the value. When set to 0, WINS will perform static initialization using the files specified in the Registry. {Cmd 5} |
| CmdNoOfWrkThds | Reads the number of worker threads in WINS. {Cmd 6} |
| CmdPriorityClass | Reads the priority class of WINS. {Cmd 7} |
| CmdResetCounters | Resets the WINS counters. {Cmd 8} |
| CmdDeleteDbRecs | When set, it causes only the data records pertaining to a WINS server to be deleted from the local WINS server. {Cmd 9} |
| CmdDRPopulateTable | Gets records of a WINS server whose IP address is provided and uses it to generate the WINS database. {Cmd 10} |
| CmdDRDataRecordsTable | The table that stores the WINS data records. The records are sorted by computer name; the table is cached for a time period. To regenerate the table, set the CmdDRPopulateTable MIB variable. {Cmd 11} |
| CmdDRRecordEntry | This is the data record owned by the WINS server whose IP address was specified in the CmdDRPopulateTable command. {CmdDR Data RecordsTable 1} |
| CmdDRRecordName | Name in the record. {cCmdDRRecordEntry 1} |
| CmdDRRecordAddress | The addresses of the mapping record. If the record is a multi-homed record or an Internet group, the addresses are returned sequentially in pairs, in which each pair consists of the address of the owner WINS server followed by the address of the computer or of the Internet group member. The records are always returned in network byte order. {cCmdDRRecordEntry 2} |
| CmdDRRecordType | The type of the record: unique, multi-homed, group, or Internet group. {cCmdDRRecordEntry 3} |
| CmdDRRecordPersistenceType | Specifies whether the mapping record is static or dynamic. {cCmdDRRecordEntry 4} |
| CmdDRRecordState | Specifies the state of the record: active, released, or extinct. {cCmdDRRecordEntry 5} |
| CmdWinsVersNoLowWord | The value of the low word of the version number counter of the record. {Cmd 12} |
| CmdWinsVersNoHighWord | The value of the high word of the version number counter of the record. {Cmd 13} |

# 10

# TCP/IP Name Resolution Using DNS

T HE *DOMAIN NAME SYSTEM (DNS)* IS a hierarchical, distributed naming system that is commonly used in most TCP/IP networks. DNS is also used as the primary name service on the Internet. The Windows NT Server can be configured to act as a DNS Server. This chapter discusses creating name servers and delegating subdomains. It teaches you how to integrate DNS and WINS, as well as troubleshoot name services. It also touches on some security issues. The graphical DNS Admin serves as your main tool for setting up and configuring your DNS Server, although you can use BIND-style text files if you prefer.

One feature in Windows NT Server is the capability to configure the NT Server as a Domain Name System (DNS) Server. The NT DNS name server is unique in two respects:

- You can integrate it with WINS, which enables the IP name database to be updated dynamically as NetBIOS names are registered.
- It comes with a DNS Admin utility, a simple Windows-based front-end for graphically managing all aspects of DNS.

## What Is DNS?

DNS is a distributed database designed to provide mappings between host names and IP addresses (and a few other things discussed later in the chapter). Given a computer name, a DNS Server returns that computer's IP address or some other requested information. The distributed structure of the DNS database results from different name servers having authority over different parts of the name tree.

This distributed structure of the DNS database is critical to the success of the Internet. Distributing the Internet's name services reduces the work load on any one server, while introducing a naming hierarchy that gives administrators flexibility in choosing their hostnames. This means that administrators no longer have to worry about whether someone outside their domain may have already claimed a particular hostname.

Relying on a single person or organization to maintain an authoritative hosts file could not scale as quickly as the Internet was growing. The file itself did not provide for any naming hierarchy, which created a problem with name collisions. The hosts file was growing quickly, and had too much information for computers to process efficiently. Perhaps worst of all, because the hosts file on a computer was static, copies were always out of date. People constantly wanted to download the latest hosts file, but all the updates being sent for, in addition to the master copy, were creating such an administrative burden that even the master copy was out of date.

The Internet community solved this problem by creating the Domain Name System (DNS).

# Do You Need DNS?

Before configuring a DNS Server, you need to decide whether it is a good idea for you to maintain one. Often, Internet service providers maintain DNS services for a small fee. Utilizing their services is especially appropriate if you have a small network. You may want to maintain your own DNS Server if any of the following circumstances apply:

- You have your own Internet domain name, and would like to create and delegate subdomains within it.

- You need DNS services under local control for increased flexibility.

- You are running a firewall that hides at least some of your organization's internal names from the outside.

## Preliminary Tasks

To configure a DNS Server, several things are necessary. You need to decide where in the domain hierarchy you want to fall so you can register with your parent domains. One domain is used for the name-to-IP address mapping, and the other domain (IN-ADDR.ARPA) is used for IP address-to-name mapping. Your Internet service provider will usually supply you with this information. If for some reason they don't, contact the InterNIC, the Internet Network Information Center, at `http://www.internic.net/`.

Except for its interaction with WINS and DHCP (discussed in Chapter 8, "DHCP Configuration and Management"), DNS is not a dynamic service and must be configured manually. Plan your DNS name space carefully; a good design saves you a lot of trouble later. To keep administrative overhead down, you want to make as few changes as possible over time. Owing to DNS's hierarchical database structure, the upper levels of your domain name space are particularly important, and you want to keep them as fixed as possible—if your organization reorganizes frequently, for example, consider staying away from using organizational names for your subdomains and instead use regional names.

If you have more than a few hundred hosts, you should distribute them relatively evenly throughout your network so that they lie in different zones and subdomains. This helps prevent the zones from becoming too large. A network design that includes large zones and little distribution is likely to have congestion problems from zone transfers that occur when the secondary name servers obtain the updated information from the primaries.

It is important that a DNS Server be running at all times to maintain Internet connectivity. It is recommended, therefore, that you set up at least one secondary server in addition to your primary DNS Server. In some cases, you may need several DNS Servers, although it is not considered good practice to advertise more than seven of them as authoritative. The secondary server(s) will obtain updates from the primary server periodically. You may want to have a DNS Server for each network or subnet in your organization so that if a router fails you can still resolve names of local systems. Often an Internet service provider will be able to act as a secondary server for you, which helps to minimize network traffic on your network—all outside queries are resolved outside your network.

## Installing DNS Services on a Windows NT Server

Installing DNS Services for Windows NT Server is simple. You must be running at least Windows NT Server 4 or later. The discussion in this section applies to Windows NT Server 5.

### Configuring the Server

When you install the Windows NT Server 5, the DNS Management option is installed in the Administrative Tools group. You must have the TCP/IP protocol installed if you plan to set up DNS. Follow these steps to configure the DNS Server:

1. Log on as an Administrator or equivalent user and make sure that the Windows NT installation CD is in the CD-ROM drive.

2. Select Start, Programs, Administrative Tools, DNS Management.

3. If this is the first time you are configuring the DNS Server you will see a message asking you if you want to configure the server. Select Yes.

   You should see the Configure New Server Wizard (see Figure 10.1).

4. Select Next. You will see a screen for selecting the type of DNS Server (see Figure 10.2). You can select a private DNS for a private network not connected to the Internet. Or you can select an Internet DNS for a server that is connected to the Internet directly or through a firewall. For Internet DNS, the server will use Internet root servers, whereas for a private DNS, the server will use private root servers. The following steps assume that you have selected a private DNS.

5. Select Next. You will see a screen for selecting the root server type (see Figure 10.3). If you select the Make this Server a Root Server option, the root server data file is created for this server. If you select Do Not Make this Server a Root Server you will have to enter the IP address of a root server on the network. The following steps assume that you are making this server a root server.

6. Select Next. You will see a screen for adding a forward lookup zone (see Figure 10.4). You can add a forward lookup zone now or later. The following steps assume that you are adding a forward lookup zone.

7. Select Next. You will see a screen for selecting the DNS Server type (see Figure 10.5). The server type choices are Primary, Primary DS, and Secondary:

   - Primary servers are used to create a master copy of an entirely new zone. Primary servers are read/write.

   - Primary DS (Directory Service) servers are used to create a master copy of an entirely new DS integrated zone. Primary DS servers are read/write.

   - Secondary servers are used to create a replica of an existing zone. Secondary servers are read-only.

The following steps assume that you have selected a Primary server.

**Figure 10.1**   Configure New Server Wizard.

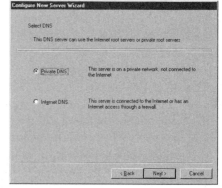

**Figure 10.2**   Select DNS Server type.

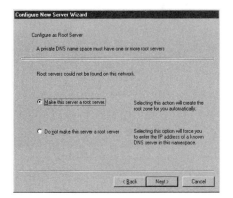

**Figure 10.3** Configure as root server screen.

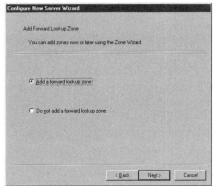

**Figure 10.4** Configure as forward lookup server screen.

8. Select Next. You will see a screen for entering the name of the zone root name (see Figure 10.6). Enter the zone root name. This is usually a name that has been registered with the InterNIC. For example, if your company is XYZ and you have registered this with the InterNIC under the COM domain, you can then use XYZ.COM as the zone root name.

9. Select Next. You will see a screen for entering the name of the zone file (see Figure 10.7). You can create a new file or import a data file. You can also store the zone data information in the Active Directory rather than in text files. The data files are text files using a syntax defined in RFCs 1034 and 1035. The data files may already have been created on the DNS implementations for UNIX systems. The most popular and widely used DNS implementation for UNIX is BIND (Berkeley Internet Name Domain) and the data files describing the zone information are called *zone data files* or *BIND files*.

10. Select Next. You will see a screen for adding reverse lookup (see Figure 10.8). You can add reverse lookup zone now or later. The following steps assume that you have selected the option to add reverse lookup zones. Reverse zone lookups are used to return the result of reverse DNS queries. A reverse DNS query submits an IP address to DNS and expects to see a symbolic name corresponding to the IP address. This is the reverse of normal DNS queries, in which symbolic names are submitted to DNS and an IP address that the symbolic name maps to is returned by DNS.

11. Select Next. You will see a screen for selecting the DNS Server type (refer to Figure 10.5). The server type choices are Primary, Primary DS, and Secondary, which have been discussed earlier. However, the server type you are now defining is for the reverse zone lookup.

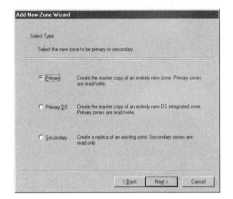

**Figure 10.5** Select Server type screen.

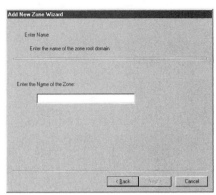

**Figure 10.6** Zone root name screen.

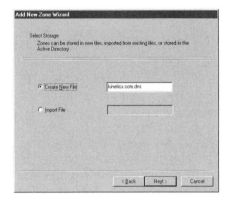

**Figure 10.7** Select storage screen.

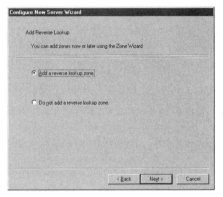

**Figure 10.8** Add reverse lookup screen.

12. Select Next. You will see a screen for entering the name of the zone root name (see Figure 10.9) for the reverse lookup. You can enter the subnet ID for the reverse lookup zone or you can enter another name for the zone root name. For example, if you enter 199.245.180 as your subnet ID, then the name of the zone becomes 180.245.199.in-addr.arpa.

13. Select Next. You will see a screen for entering the name of the reverse zone file (see Figure 10.10). You can create a new file or import a data file.

14. Select Next. You will see the final configuration screen, which summarizes the choices you have made (see Figure 10.11).

15. Select Finish to complete the configuration. You will see the DNS Admin screen with the name of the server on which you have configured DNS.

16. If you click on the DNS Server name in the DNS Admin screen, you will see the zone names that you have created on the server (see Figure 10.12).

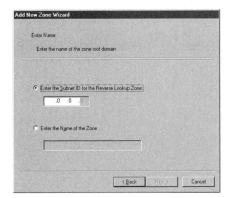

Figure 10.9    Enter reverse lookup zone name screen.

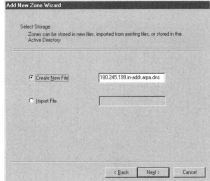

Figure 10.10    Creating reverse lookup zone file screen.

### DNS Database Files

The DNS database files are created as text files in the manner of the text configuration files created for the BIND (Berkeley InterNet Domain) implementation. BIND is the most popular DNS implementation on the Internet and is traditionally implemented on UNIX systems.

You can configure DNS on Windows NT server by directly editing these files. The configuration files have the same format as that for UNIX systems. So if you are familiar with BIND configuration files on UNIX systems, you can edit these files directly.

When you initially configure DNS using the procedure outlined in the previous section, the following database files are created in the `\%Systemroot%\system32\DNS` directory:

- `root.dns`
- `cache.dns`
- `zonedata.dns`
- `reversesubnetid.in-addr.arpa`

The following are skeleton database file examples of the previously listed DNS data files.

Here is the sample `root.dns` file:

```
;

;   Database file root.dns for . zone.

;       Zone version:  3

;
```

**Figure 10.11**   Final configuration screen.

**Figure 10.12**   DNS Admin screen showing zone names.

```
@                           IN  SOA (

                            tpnts.siyan.com.   ; primary DNS Server
                            administrator.siyan.com.   ; zone admin e-mail
                            3              ; serial number
                            3600           ; refresh
                            600            ; retry
                            86400          ; expire
                            3600           ) ; minimum TTL


;
;  Zone NS records
;

@                           NS   tpnts.siyan.com


;
;  Zone records
;



;
;  Delegated sub-zone:  0.in-addr.arpa.
;
0.in-addr.arpa             NS   tpnts.siyan.com
;  End delegation


;
;  Delegated sub-zone:  127.in-addr.arpa.
```

```
;
127.in-addr.arpa          NS    tpnts.siyan.com
;  End delegation


;
;  Delegated sub-zone:  180.245.199.in-addr.arpa.
;
180.245.199.in-addr.arpa NS    tpnts.siyan.com
;  End delegation


;
;  Delegated sub-zone:  255.in-addr.arpa.
;
255.in-addr.arpa          NS    tpnts.siyan.com
;  End delegation


;
;  Delegated sub-zone:  kinetics.com.
;
kinetics.com              NS    tpnts.siyan.com
;  End delegation

tpnts.siyan.com           A    199.245.180.9
```

Here is the sample cache.dns file:

```
;

;    cache.dns -- DNS CACHE FILE


;


;    Initial cache data for root domain servers.


;


;    YOU SHOULD CHANGE:


;    -> Nothing if connected to the Internet.  Edit this file only when
;       updated root name server list is released.
;           OR
;    -> If NOT connected to the Internet, remove these records and
►replace
;       with NS and A records for the DNS Server authoritative for the
;       root domain at your site.
;
;    Note, if you are a root domain server, for your own private intranet,
;    no cache is required, and you may edit your boot file to remove
```

```
;   it.
;


;
;       This file holds the information on root name servers needed to
;       initialize cache of Internet domain name servers
;       (e.g. reference this file in the "cache  .  <file>"
;       configuration file of BIND domain name servers).
;
;       This file is made available by InterNIC registration services
;       under anonymous FTP as
;           file                    /domain/named.root
;           on server               FTP.RS.INTERNIC.NET
;       -OR- under Gopher at     RS.INTERNIC.NET
;           under menu              InterNIC Registration Services (NSI)
;             submenu               InterNIC Registration Archives
;           file                    named.root
;
;       last update:    Aug 22, 1997
;       related version of root zone:    1997082200
;
;
; formerly NS.INTERNIC.NET
;
.                           3600000   IN  NS    A.ROOT-SERVERS.NET.
A.ROOT-SERVERS.NET.         3600000       A     198.41.0.4
;
; formerly NS1.ISI.EDU
;
.                           3600000       NS    B.ROOT-SERVERS.NET.
B.ROOT-SERVERS.NET.         3600000       A     128.9.0.107
;
; formerly C.PSI.NET
;
.                           3600000       NS    C.ROOT-SERVERS.NET.
C.ROOT-SERVERS.NET.         3600000       A     192.33.4.12
;
; formerly TERP.UMD.EDU
;
.                           3600000       NS    D.ROOT-SERVERS.NET.
D.ROOT-SERVERS.NET.         3600000       A     128.8.10.90
;
; formerly NS.NASA.GOV
;
.                           3600000       NS    E.ROOT-SERVERS.NET.
E.ROOT-SERVERS.NET.         3600000       A     192.203.230.10
```

```
;
; formerly NS.ISC.ORG
;
.                               3600000        NS      F.ROOT-SERVERS.NET.
F.ROOT-SERVERS.NET.             3600000        A       192.5.5.241
;
; formerly NS.NIC.DDN.MIL
;
.                               3600000        NS      G.ROOT-SERVERS.NET.
G.ROOT-SERVERS.NET.             3600000        A       192.112.36.4
;
; formerly AOS.ARL.ARMY.MIL
;
.                               3600000        NS      H.ROOT-SERVERS.NET.
H.ROOT-SERVERS.NET.             3600000        A       128.63.2.53
;
; formerly NIC.NORDU.NET
;
.                               3600000        NS      I.ROOT-SERVERS.NET.
I.ROOT-SERVERS.NET.             3600000        A       192.36.148.17
;
; temporarily housed at NSI (InterNIC)
;
.                               3600000        NS      J.ROOT-SERVERS.NET.
J.ROOT-SERVERS.NET.             3600000        A       198.41.0.10
;
; housed in LINX, operated by RIPE NCC
;
.                               3600000        NS      K.ROOT-SERVERS.NET.
K.ROOT-SERVERS.NET.             3600000        A       193.0.14.129
;
; temporarily housed at ISI (IANA)
;
.                               3600000        NS      L.ROOT-SERVERS.NET.
L.ROOT-SERVERS.NET.             3600000        A       198.32.64.12
;
; housed in Japan, operated by WIDE
;
.                               3600000        NS      M.ROOT-SERVERS.NET.
M.ROOT-SERVERS.NET.             3600000        A       202.12.27.33
; End of File
```

Here is the sample zonedata.dns file:

```
;
;   Database file kinetics.com.dns for kinetics.com zone.
```

```
;       Zone version:  1

;

@                               IN   SOA  (

                                tpnts.siyan.com.   ; primary DNS Server

                                administrator.siyan.com.   ; zone admin e-mail
                                1            ; serial number
                                3600         ; refresh
                                600          ; retry
                                86400        ; expire
                                3600       ) ; minimum TTL


;
; Zone NS records
;

@                               NS   tpnts.siyan.com.


;
; Zone records
;
```

Here is the reversesubnetid.in-addr.arpa file:

```
;

; Database file 180.245.199.in-addr.arpa.dns for 180.245.199.in-addr.arpa
➡zone.

;       Zone version:  1
;

@                               IN   SOA  (
                                tpnts.siyan.com.   ; primary DNS Server
                                administrator.siyan.com.   ; zone admin e-mail
                                1            ; serial number
                                3600         ; refresh
                                600          ; retry
                                86400        ; expire
                                3600       ) ; minimum TTL


;
; Zone NS records
;
```

```
@                         NS    tpnts.siyan.com.


;
;  Zone records
;
```

## Upgrading from NT 3.51

If you currently are running NT Server version 3.51 with the DNS Server from Microsoft's 3.51 Resource Kit and you want to upgrade to version 4 with its included DNS Server, use `REGEDT32.EXE` to delete all the DNS-related Registry entries before beginning the upgrade process.

After your upgrade to Windows NT Server completes, configure DNS following the steps listed in the earlier section "Configuring the Server."

## Migrating from a BIND-Based DNS Server

BIND still is the most widely used name server program; it is part of most UNIX distributions. If you currently run a BIND DNS Server on another platform and want to transfer those duties over to NT, you can do so by copying the BIND database files into the directory `%Systemroot%\system32\DNS` after installing (but before starting) DNS. To use WINS and NBSTAT for integrated NetBIOS name resolution, you need to edit the `in-addr.arpa` file in the `%Systemroot%\system32\DNS` directory to include these options. The `in-addr.arpa` file contains the reverse lookup information mapping IP addresses to host names for DNS. Open the `in-addr.arpa` file from the DNS directory into a text editor such as WordPad. The relevant sections of the file resemble the portion given here:

```
;
;  arpa-192.rev
;
;  Reverse lookup file for 29.5.192.in-addr.arpa. domain.
;
;  This file provides address to name matching (reverse lookup)
;  for addresses 192.5.29.?.
;
;
;  Note that all domain names given in this file, which are not
;  terminated by a "." and hence fully qualified domain names (FQDN),
;  are implicitly appended with "29.5.192.in-addr.arpa."
;
;  Examples:
;      "6"  =>  6.29.5.192.in-addr.arpa.
;
;  If a name outside of "29.5.192.in-addr.arpa." is required, then it
;  must be explicitly terminated with a dot, to indicate that it is a
;  FQDN.
```

```
;
;   Example:
;       "7.30.5.192.in-addr.arpa."  =>  7.30.5.192.in-addr.arpa.
;


;
;
;   NBSTAT Record
;
;   The NBSTAT RR is specific to Windows NT and may be attached ONLY
;   to the zone root of a reverse lookup domain.
;
;   Presence of an NBSTAT record at the zone root instructs the name
➥server
;   to use a NetBIOS node status request for any reverse lookup
;   requests for IP addresses which are NOT given in PTR records below.
;
;   Examples:
;
;   1) A query for 135.29.5.192.in-addr.arpa. (192.5.29.135)
;       192.5.29.135 has a PTR record below, so DNS Server responds
;       with the PTR record without NBSTAT lookup.
;
;   2) A query for 206.29.5.192.in-addr.arpa. (192.5.29.206)
;       192.5.29.206 is within the 29.5.192.in-addr.arpa zone, but
;       there is no PTR record for it in this zone file.
;       DNS will issue an NBSTAT query to 192.5.29.206.
;       If a response is received, the host name in the response will be
;       appended to the result domain in the NBSTAT record and used
;       as the host name corresponding to 192.5.29.206.  The PTR
;       record will be cached and a response sent to the client.
;       If a response is NOT received, the DNS Server responds to
;       the client with a name error.
;
;   3) A query for 29.5.192.in-addr.arpa. (192.5.29)
;       192.5.29 is within the 29.5.192.in-addr.arpa zone, but is NOT
;       an IP address.  Hence no NBSTAT lookup is done, and the server
;       responds with a name error.
;

;
;   NBSTAT and zone transfer:
;
;   The MS DNS Server will configure NBSTAT information as a resource
;   record to allow it to be transferred to MS DNS secondary servers.
;
```

```
;    If you have MS DNS secondaries, and want them to use exactly the
;    same NBSTAT info as the primary server, then omit the LOCAL flag
;    in the NBSTAT record.
;
;    If you have UNIX secondaries, or MS secondaries using different
;    NBSTAT information, then use the "LOCAL" flag after the "NBSTAT"
;    flag and the NBSTAT information will NOT be considered part of the
;    zone's resource records and will NOT be sent in the zone transfer.
;
;
;    YOU SHOULD CHANGE:
;        - Change the resulting domain that should be appended to
;          names found with NBSTAT lookup.
;        - Uncomment the line with LOCAL flag, if NBSTAT information should
;            not be transferred as part of the zone data.
;        - Uncomment the line without the LOCAL flag, if NBSTAT information
;            should be transferred to MS DNS secondaries.
;            OR
;        - Leave this line commented out, if NBSTAT lookup not desired.

;@   IN   NBSTAT          place.com.
;@   IN   NBSTAT   LOCAL  place.com.
```

To enable NBSTAT, uncomment the NBSTAT line by removing the semicolon (;) in front of it. If you want to use WINS, make certain that you list your WINS servers in the PTR section.

# Managing DNS

You can manage the Microsoft DNS Server's database directly by using any text editor to edit the files. Doing so may come naturally to you if you have worked with UNIX's BIND before, but most people prefer the graphical environment of Microsoft's DNS Admin.

Database files that contain the server's resource records need to be in the %Systemroot%\system32\DNS directory. Sample database files are in the %Systemroot%\system32\DNS\Samples subdirectory; you can use those as a guide.

The Microsoft DNS Admin operates like the WINS Manager or the DHCP Manager programs. DNS Admin stores the DNS BOOT file information in the Windows NT Registry.

The DNS database files in the %Systemroot%\system32\DNS folder are read when the Microsoft DNS Server initializes. If you use a text editor to make changes to those files, you have to stop and restart the DNS Server before your changes can take effect. If you use the DNS Admin to maintain your DNS databases, it automatically communicates changes to the DNS Server without requiring it to shut down and restart.

The DNS Admin program is in the Administrative Tools folder. To open it, choose Programs from the Start menu. Select Administrative Tools. Click on the DNS Admin icon to start the DNS Admin.

As you make changes with the DNS Admin, those changes write to the appropriate DNS database files periodically. At any point, you can force the DNS Admin to update the files on the DNS Server. Choose DNS, Update Server Data Files. All the files are immediately updated. The files update at regular intervals as well as when the DNS Server or the DNS Admin is shut down.

You can use the DNS Admin program to create and manage the following:

- **Servers.** See the following section, "Servers."

- **Zones.** See the later section "Understanding Zones."

- **Records.** See the later section "DNS Resource Records."

- **Domains.** See the later section "Domains."

- **WINS Integration.** See the later section "WINS Integration."

- **Special options.** See the later section "Special Options."

## Servers

The following sections deal with various procedures you can perform involving servers, including adding and removing servers in a DNS Admin list and viewing server statistics.

### Adding and Removing Servers in the DNS Admin List

You need to add each DNS Server you are running to the DNS Admin list, including secondary servers. Follow these steps:

1. Right-click on the DNS Admin folder in the DNS Admin window, and select Connect To Computer.

2. Type the name or IP address of the server you want DNS Admin to manage.

3. Click OK.

Under the Server List, the Microsoft DNS Admin displays a server icon for each configured DNS Server. The status of each server is indicated graphically on each server's icon. A green light indicates that the server is running and that the DNS Admin can connect to it. If a red X superimposes the icon, the DNS Admin cannot connect to the DNS service on that server. In that case, an error message displays in the bottom-right corner of the DNS Admin box when the server is selected.

To remove a server from the list, highlight it and press the Delete key.

### Effect of Removing/Reinstalling DNS Server on Data Files

If you remove and reinstall the DNS Server, it will not replace your existing BOOT, CACHE, or other database files. If you want new copies of these files, rename or move your old ones before you reinstall DNS Server.

### Viewing Server Statistics

The server statistics keep track of various activities, such as the number of UDP queries and responses, TCP client connections, reverse lookups, and WINS lookups (see Figure 10.13).

To view the statistics, right-click on the icon of the server in which you're interested. Select Properties and then the Statistics tab. Table 10.1 lists some of the information in the Server Statistics screen and tells what they measure.

Table 10.1  **Server Statistics**

| Statistic | What It Measures |
| --- | --- |
| Udp Queries | Increments each time the DNS Server receives a DNS name resolution request over UDP |
| Udp Responses | Increments each time the DNS Server sends a reply using UDP |
| Tcp Client Connections | Increments each time another system opens a TCP connection to the DNS port on the server |
| Tcp Queries | Increments each time the DNS Server receives a DNS name resolution request over TCP |
| Tcp Responses | Increments each time the DNS Server sends a reply using TCP |
| Recursive Lookups | Increments each time the DNS Server needs to query other servers to satisfy a client's request for recursion |
| Recursive Responses | Increments each time the DNS Server replies to a client's recursive request |

**Figure 10.13**   DNS Statistics.

| WINS Forward Lookups | Increments each time a WINS name-to-IP address mapping is requested |
|---|---|
| WINS Forward Responses | Increments each time a WINS name-to-IP address mapping request receives a reply |
| WINS Reverse Lookups | Increments each time an IP address-to-WINS name mapping is requested |
| WINS Reverse Responses | Increments each time a WINS name-to-IP address mapping receives a reply |
| Master Zone Notify Sent | Indicates the number of master zone transfer messages that were sent in response to secondary zone transfer requests |
| Secondary Zone Notify Received | Indicates the number of secondary zone transfer requests that were received |
| Master Zone Axfr xxxxx | Master zone address transfers for address records for the specified state xxxxx |
| Secondary Zone Axfr xxxxx | Secondary zone address transfers for address records for the specified state xxxxx |

## Understanding Zones

A *zone* contains one or several domains. A zone also may contain subdomains. A zone is authoritative for all the DNS information within the domains and subdomains that it contains. If a subdomain is delegated, the DNS Servers to which it is delegated hold the authoritative zone for that subdomain.

The two types of zones are as follows:

- Primary
- Secondary

A *primary* zone has its own SOA (Start of Authority) resource record (see the later section "DNS Resource Records" for details). Primary zones depend directly on the information configured in the DNS database files.

**Standard Files Created by DNS Server**

As part of its internal setup, the NT DNS Server automatically adds three reverse lookup zones for mapping IP addresses to DNS host names. These zones are as follows:

- 0.in-addr.arpa
- 127.in-addr.arpa
- 255.in-addr.arpa

The 127.in-addr.arpa serves for the standard loopback interface. The reverse lookup zones are part of the in-addr.arpa domain and are added for each DNS Server in the Server List. These reverse lookup zones serve performance purposes and you shouldn't edit or delete them.

*Secondary* zone name servers rely on information they get from another name server, generally a primary name server. The secondary zone name server gets its information from a zone transfer.

## Creating a Primary Zone

Follow these steps to create a primary zone:

1. Click on the server icon that represents the name server for the new zone.
2. Right-click on the right panel and select Create a New Zone.
3. In the Add New Zone Wizard dialog box, choose Primary.
4. Click on the Next button and select the lookup method for the zone (forward or reverse).
5. Click on the Next button, and enter the zone name.
6. Click on the Next button, and enter the zone file name for the database.
7. Click on the Next button.
8. Click on the Finish button.

The new zone is added to your server with an SOA record and an A record (see the later section "DNS Resource Records" for information on resource records).

## Creating a Secondary Zone

A secondary zone is a read-only copy of an existing zone. Its main role is to serve as a backup for the primary zone. A secondary zone can help load-balance as well as help minimize network traffic if it bypasses the need to use a router to access the primary zone. Select a different server for the secondary zone from the name server for the primary zone. A given server can be the name server for a primary zone, however, and a different secondary zone at the same time.

1. Click on the server icon.
2. Right-click on the right panel and select Create a New Zone.
3. In the Add New Zone Wizard dialog box, choose Secondary.

### Viewing Information for a Particular Zone

You can see information for a particular zone in the right panel of the DNS Admin by clicking on that zone's icon.

4. Click on the Next button and select the lookup method for the zone (forward or reverse).

5. Click on the Next button, and enter the zone name.

6. Click on the Next button, and enter the IP address of the IP Master and click on the Add button. The IP Master is the IP address of one or more DNS Servers to copy the zone from.

7. Click on the Next button.

8. Click on the Finish button.

### Creating a Primary Zone in the *in-addr.arpa* Domain

The `in-addr.arpa` domain is a special domain used in the exact opposite way of other domains. Rather than look up a name and return an IP address, it looks up an IP address and returns a hostname. This zone must be coordinated with the authoritative zone for the computer names in your domain name space. If your regular name domain and your `in-addr.arpa` domain are not synchronized, many servers on the Internet will deny access.

1. In the Server List, click on the server icon.

2. Right-click on the right panel and select Create a New Zone.

3. In the Add New Zone Wizard dialog box, choose Primary.

4. Click on the Next button and select the Reverse Lookup method for the zone.

5. Click on the Next button, and enter the subnet ID for the reverse lookup zone. This will automatically create the subnet ID reverse zone filename based on the subnet ID that you enter.

6. Click on the Next button, and enter the zone filename for the database or accept the default.

7. Click on the Next button.

8. Click on the Finish button.

Computers outside of your network will need to reach this zone to verify that you are who you say you are by doing reverse lookups. To enable this, you need to register it with its parent domain, `in-addr.arpa`. Normally, the organization from which you received your network number(s), either an IS department or an ISP, handles setting up this delegation if you request it. Unless you have your own network number and at least two name servers, you will not be delegated an `in-addr.arpa` domain. If you have had your numbers for a long while and never registered them, you may need to contact the InterNIC directly. The DNS Resources Directory on the World Wide Web

**Defining an IP Master**

The IP master is a name server from which a secondary zone can get its zone information and updates. You can configure several IP masters if necessary.

has registration information along with a great deal of other useful information:

`http://www.dns.net/dnsrd/`

### Adding a New Host to a Primary Zone

Follow these steps to add a new host to a primary zone:

1. Click on either the Forward Lookup Zones or Reverse Lookup Zones.
2. Right-click on the zone name.
3. Select New, Host.
4. Type the host name and its IP address (see Figure 10.14).
5. If you want to automatically create the PTR record for reverse lookups, enable the Create Associated PTR Record check box.
6. Click on the Add Host button.

You can add as many hosts as you want at this point. Every host that is reachable from the Internet should have at least an A record and a PTR record (see the next section for details on these records). The new host and its IP address appear in the zone information window as an address (A) record.

## DNS Resource Records

Each set of information stored in the DNS database is referred to as a *resource record*. The essential ones are as follows:

- Name Server (NS)
- Address (A)
- Start of Authority (SOA)
- Pointer (PTR)
- Mail Exchange (MX)

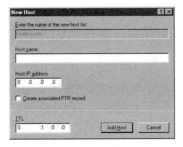

**Figure 10.14** Dialog box for adding a new host.

Many other record types exist, only a few of which are you likely to ever have reason to use (like the CNAME record). Some of the other record types are experimental; others just aren't widely used. Table 10.2 summarizes the various resource records and the information they contain. Resource records are covered in more detail later in this chapter.

### Adding a New Record

1. Right-click on the zone or domain to which you want to add the record.
2. Choose New, Other Record. You will see the Record Type dialog box (see Figure 10.15).
3. From the Select Record Type list, select a type of resource record, such as MX, A, or CNAME.
4. Type the required information and click OK.

Many of the resource records are experimental, and not essential for DNS services. Several records are highly important: the address record (A), the pointer record (PTR), the mail exchange record (MX), the canonical name record (CNAME), and the start of authority record (SOA). The following sections provide a description of the records and the role of each.

### Address (A) Record

The A record maps a host computer or another network device name to an IP address in a DNS domain, and contains three fields:

- **Domain.** Enter the name of the domain that contains the host.
- **Hostname.** Enter the name of a computer or network device.
- **Host IP Address.** Enter the address of the host.

The hostname combined with the domain name comprise a fully qualified domain name (FQDN). The DNS Admin automatically generates the A record when you add a new server, host, or domain.

Table 10.2 **Most Widely Used DNS Resource Records**

| Record Name | Description |
| --- | --- |
| A (Address) | Maps a host computer or another network device name to an IP address in a DNS zone |
| CNAME (Canonical name) | Creates an alias for the specified hostname |
| MX (Mail exchange) | Identifies a mail exchange server for a host computer |
| NS (Name server) | Identifies the DNS name server(s) for the DNS domain |
| PTR (Pointer) | Maps an IP address to a hostname in a DNS reverse zone |
| SOA (Start of authority) | Indicates that this DNS name server is the best source of information for the data within this DNS domain |

**Figure 10.15**  Record Type dialog box.

### AFS Database (AFSDB) Record

The AFSDB record (originally from Andrew File System) provides the location of an AFS cell database server or a DCE (Distributed Computing Environment) cell's authenticated name server. In addition to the domain name and the optional host name, you need to provide the Server DNS Name—which is the DNS name for the AFS cell database server or the DCE name server—and then select the type of server. Choose AFS Cell Database Server or choose DCE Name Server. Relatively few networks have these.

### Canonical Name (*CNAME*) Record

The `CNAME` record creates an alias for the particular hostname. You can use `CNAME` records to hide the implementation details of your network from the clients that connect to it. For alias names, you can use shortened forms of the hostnames. The hostname `public1.business.com`, for example, might have an alias of `www.business.com`. The three fields required in the DNS database for this type of record are as follows:

- **Alias Domain.** Enter the domain in which the alias host exists.
- **Alias Name.** Enter the canonical name, such as `www`....
- **For Hostname.** Enter the hostname (as specified in the Address record) it represents. This is the host's "real" name.

### Hardware Information (*HINFO*) Record

The `HINFO` record identifies a host's hardware type and operating system. The Internet standard abbreviations for identifying the operating system of a host are published in the Assigned Numbers RFC (RFC 1700 at the time of this writing) under the System Names List. Abbreviations for the hardware type of hosts also are defined in the Assigned Numbers RFC. The CPU Type identification number is in the Machine

Names List. For a small sample of the types specified in the Assigned Numbers RFC, see the following lists. The names are up to 40 characters long and can contain upper-case letters and digits, including hyphens (-) and slashes (/). The name must begin with a letter and end with a letter or digit.

Here are some of the operating system codes for DNS HINFO records as per the RFC 1700 Standard:

| | | |
|---|---|---|
| APOLLO | OPENVMS | TANDEM |
| AIX/370 | OS/2 | UNIXDOMAIN |
| PCDOS | UNIX-BSD | |
| DOS | SCO-OPEN-DESKTOP-2.0 | UNIX-PC |
| INTERLISP | SCO-OPEN-DESKTOP-3.0 | UNKNOWN |
| ITS | SCO-UNIX-3.2V4.0 | VM |
| LISP | SCO-UNIX-3.2V4.1 | VM/370 |
| MSDOS | SCO-UNIX-3.2V4.2 | VMS |
| MULTICS | SUN | WANG |
| MVS | SUN-OS-3.5 | WIN32 |
| NONSTOP | SUN-OS-4.0 | X11R3 |

Here are the CPU codes for DNS HINFO records:

| | | |
|---|---|---|
| APOLLO | IBM-RS/6000 | SUN-4/200 |
| APPLE-MACINTOSH | INTEL-386 | SUN-4/390 |
| APPLE-POWERBOOK | M68000 | SYMBOLICS-3600 |
| CRAY-2 | MAC-II | UNKNOWN |
| DECSTATION | MAC-POWERBOOK | VAX |
| DEC-VAX | MACINTOSH | VAX-11/725 |
| DEC-VAXCLUSTER | MICROVAX | VAXCLUSTER |
| DEC-VAXSTATION | PDP-11 | VAXSTATION |
| IBM-PC/AT | SILICON-GRAPHICS | |
| IBM-PC/XT | SUN | |

## Integrated Services Digital Network (ISDN) Record

The ISDN record maps the hostname to an ISDN address. The ISDN phone number also can include the Direct Dial In (DDI) number. An ISDN subaddress is optional. ISDN records have several possible uses. The ISDN resource records can provide simple documentation of the correct addresses to use in static configurations of ISDN dial-up applications. In the future, they also may be used automatically by Internet routers.

### Mailbox (*MB*) Record

The MB record identifies a mailbox for the indicated host. You must provide the mailbox name and the FQDN of the host that contains the mailbox. This record type is considered experimental and should not be used unless you are part of the Internet experiment.

### Mailgroup (*MG*) Record

The MG record identifies a mailbox that is a member of the group mailing list in the given DNS domain name. You must type the mailbox name as a FQDN. This record type is considered experimental and should not be used unless you are part of the Internet experiment.

### Mail Exchange (*MX*) Record

An MX record indicates the hostname of a server that will process or forward mail for a given domain or host. The hostname of the mail exchanger must be a FQDN. The MX record format consists of the following fields:

- **For Domain.** Enter the host or domain name for which the mail exchanger will process mail.
- **Mail Exchange Server DNS Name.** Enter the FDQN of the mail exchange server.
- **Preference Number.** Enter the preference number of that particular mail exchanger.

The *preference number* is a number from 0 to 65,535 that indicates the mail exchange server's priority with respect to the other mail exchange servers for that destination. Lower preference numbers have higher priority, the highest priority being a preference number of 0. The absolute value of the preference is not significant except in relation to other mail exchangers for the same destination. A mailer attempts delivery to the mail exchange server with the lowest preference number first. If delivery fails, the mail exchange server with the next highest preference number is tried next. If two or more

---

**Security Issues in Using HINFO Records**

Some people choose not to provide this on publicly accessible DNS Servers because it reveals information about a computer system that might make it easier for someone to break into a system, perhaps by
attacking known security flaws for a particular system type. If you do use HINFO records, be sure to
keep up with CERT security advisories for your systems.

mail exchange servers share the same preference number, the mailer must decide which one to try first. The order it decides is not specified in the RFCs but rather is implementation-dependent. For example, the order could be based on a random choice. All mail exchange servers with a given preference number are tried before the mailer moves up to the next highest preference number, however. One normally uses a preference of 10 for the best mail server, with less preferred mail exchangers identified at 20, and then 30, or some similar scheme. Doing so enables you to insert a new mail exchanger between or before your existing mailers if needed.

Mail Exchange lookups are not recursive. After an MX record identifies the best destination for mail to a host, the only other lookup performed is for the A record of the mail exchanger. MX records for the mail exchanger itself are ignored unless the mail is addressed directly to that particular mail exchanger.

### Mail Information (*MINFO*) Record

The MINFO record provides information about a mailing list or mailbox. It has two fields:

- **Responsible Mailbox DNS**. Contains the FQDN of the mailbox that is responsible for the mailing list identified in the resource record.

- **Error Mailbox DNS**. Contains the FQDN of the mailbox that is to receive error messages related to the mailing list.

Although you can associate these records with a simple mailbox, they usually are used with a mailing list that uses different mailing addresses for administrative matters, such as subscriptions (usually the responsible mailbox), and for error messages, such as mail not deliverable (the error mailbox).

### Mail Rename (*MR*) Record

The MR record renames a given mailbox. Type the FQDN of the new mailbox name in the Replacement Mailbox DNS Name field. You can use an alias name if a mailbox is moved from one host to another. This record type is considered experimental and should not be used unless you're part of the Internet experiment.

### Name Server (*NS*) Record

The NS Record identifies an authoritative DNS Server for the DNS domain. You should always have at least two of these for any domain. An NS record has two fields:

- **For Domain.** Enter the domain name.

- **Name Server DNS Name.** Enter the authoritative server name (which should refer to an A record).

### Pointer (*PTR*) Record

Pointer records map an IP address to a hostname in the DNS reverse lookup domain (`in-addr.arpa`). You use the IP Address and Host DNS Name fields. You can have the DNS Admin automatically create the associated `PTR` records for the hosts for which you create address records by enabling the Create Associated `PTR` Record option when you enter the A record. Use the FQDN for the hostname if you create these records manually. If you use the DNS Admin to create these records, just type the IP address of the host; DNS Admin automatically appends `in-addr.arpa` to the IP address for you.

### Responsible Person (*RP*) Record

The `RP` record indicates who is responsible for the device identified by the specified DNS name. Although the `SOA` record indicates who is responsible for a zone and gives the best point of contact for DNS-related issues, different people usually are in charge of various hosts within a domain. The `RP` record enables you to indicate who should be contacted if a problem arises associated with something that has a DNS name. Typical problems might be that an important server has become unavailable or that another site is noticing suspicious activity from a host.

An `RP` record requires an email address and the FQDN to check for text records with more information. The email address is in standard DNS domain name format, with a period for the "at" symbol (@) used in most email addresses. The DNS text reference is a DNS domain name that acts as a pointer to a `TXT` resource record. You can use the Text resource record to which the `RP` record points to provide free-format information about the contact, such as full name and phone or pager number.

### Route Through (*RT*) Record

The `RT` record identifies an intermediate host that routes packets to a destination host that does not have direct connectivity itself. The Intermediate Host DNS Name must be a FQDN of an intermediate host that will accept packets for the destination. An intermediate host functions like a mail exchange server, in that there can only be one level of indirection, which means that the path to an intermediate host cannot be through another intermediate host.

### Start of Authority (*SOA*) Record

An `SOA` record indicates that this DNS name server is the best source of information for the data within this DNS domain. `SOA` records (see Figure 10.16) serve to identify the email contact for the zone, to identify that changes have been made to a zone's

---

**Security Issues in Maintaining PTR Records**

Many Internet sites deny access to computers that do not have matching Address and Pointer records as a security measure, so be sure to keep your PTR records synchronized with your A records.

database file, and to set timers on how often other servers update their copies of the zone information.

You can access the SOA record for each primary zone by clicking on the zone and choosing Properties. The Primary Name Server DNS Name field contains the name of the server host that acts as the original or primary source of data for this DNS zone.

The Serial Number field contains the serial number, which controls DNS zone transfers between primary and secondary DNS name servers. The secondary name server contacts a primary name server periodically and requests the serial number of the primary's zone data. If the primary zone's serial number is larger than the secondary's, the secondary's zone data is out of date and the secondary transfers a new copy of the zone data from the primary. The Microsoft DNS Server attempts to notify secondaries when changes occur, but older versions of BIND may not accept such invitations to refresh their data.

The number in the Refresh Interval field specifies how often the secondary DNS name servers check the zone data of the primary. The default refresh interval is three hours; if your secondaries accept notification of changes, you can safely increase it to a long value (a day or more) to reduce the polling. This is particularly valuable over slow or on-demand lines.

The Retry Interval field determines how often a secondary server should try to reconnect after a failed connection. The Retry Interval usually is shorter than the Refresh Interval. The default value is 60 minutes.

The Expire Interval field refers to the amount of time for which the secondary server's data is good. If a secondary DNS name server fails to contact the primary DNS name server, the secondary's data may be invalid. The secondary server stops responding to queries about the data after the expire time uses up. The default value is three days, and it must exceed both the minimum and retry values.

**Figure 10.16**   SOA record.

The Minimum TTL (Time-to-Live) has the greatest effect on DNS traffic. It controls how long a receiving server can cache the data. Each query response is sent with a TTL value. The default value is 24 hours. If you anticipate making major changes to your DNS zone, you should temporarily set this to a shorter interval, such as one hour, and then wait the previous minimum value before making your changes. After you verify the correctness of your changes, you should return the TTL to its previous value. Following this procedure enables your changes to propagate through the Internet much more efficiently and reduces the time during which stale DNS data may lurk in other servers' caches.

### Text (*TXT*) Record

The TXT record contains information in straight text form, often a name and phone number of a contact or other relevant information. The text string must be less than 256 characters in length.

### Well Known Service (*WKS*) Record

The WKS record describes the services provided by a particular protocol on a particular interface, identified by the IP address. The services include Telnet and FTP. The Access Protocol indicates the protocol for the available service. This record generally isn't used and should be avoided (RFC 1123).

### *X25* Record

The X25 record is similar to the A Resource Record, but maps the host name to an X.121 address rather than an IP address. X.121 addresses are the standard form of addresses for X.25 networks. The PSDN (Public Switched Data Network) address begins with the four-digit DNIC (Data Network Identification Code) specified in X.121—guidelines established by the International Telephone and Telegraph Consultative Committee. Do not use the national prefixes as part of the address. The X25 resource record is designed for usage in conjunction with the RT (route through) resource record.

## Domains

This section focuses on activities related to domains, such as creating a domain within a primary zone.

To create a domain within a primary zone, perform the following actions:

1. Right-click on the zone under a server.

2. Select New, Subdomain.

3. Type the name of the new domain and click OK.

### Creating and Delegating Subdomains

If you create but do not delegate a subdomain, WINS cannot resolve names in that subdomain. You should, therefore, always delegate subdomains when trying to achieve integration between DNS and WINS. For more information on resolving WINS names, see the next section, "WINS Integration."

To delegate a subdomain, follow these steps:

1. From the DNS Admin Server List, select the server that will be authoritative for the new subdomain. It can be the same server you are delegating from or a different server.

2. Create the subdomain as a new primary zone on the authoritative server.

3. Add the appropriate resource records, such as A, CNAME, and MX, to the new zone. See the earlier section "DNS Resource Records" for details on creating the different types of resource records.

4. If you want to use WINS Lookup, click on the zone and choose Properties.

5. Select the WINS Lookup tab and enable the Use WINS Resolution check box.

6. Type the IP addresses of the WINS Servers, and then click OK.

7. In the Server List, double-click on the zone icon of the parent domain.

8. Delete all records that now belong to the new subdomain.

9. Type the name of the new subdomain that you just created.

10. Right-click on the newly created subdomain icon (the one under the parent's primary zone icon), and then select Properties, and the Name Servers tab.

11. Click Add. Enter the name of the server for the new subdomain in the Server Name box, and its IP address in the Name Server IP Address, and then click OK.

12. Right-click on the zone name. Select New, Other Record and select the A Record. Type the name of the server for the new subdomain (the same name that you used in the previous step) in the Hostname field, type its corresponding IP address in the Host IP Address field, and then click OK.

13. Choose DNS, Update Server Data Files.

## WINS Integration

WINS is a dynamic name resolution system that relies on each workstation to register its own name and IP address. This is an automatic service in workstations that run Windows 95 or Windows NT. If you disable this function or turn off the computer, DNS cannot use WINS to resolve that computer's name. Note that WINS only resolves names that are direct children of the primary, or zone root, domain. In other words, hostnames in subdomains cannot be resolved by DNS unless those subdomains are delegated, in which case they are in their own primary domain. Consequently, putting the WINS hosts in one zone (if possible) is easiest.

Your DNS Server also can act as a WINS server, or it can point to a different WINS server. Only Windows NT DNS Servers can query a WINS database to resolve dynamically learned names at this time. The differences between WINS and DNS are shown in Table 10.3.

You can configure non-NetBIOS hosts to query the Windows NT DNS Server for all names in the zone that use WINS for lookups. If the dynamic portion of the network exists in several zones, you can set up one Windows NT DNS Server as the primary master name server for each of those zones, or you can give each of those zones its own Windows NT DNS Server.

### Enabling WINS Lookup in a Zone Root Domain

Follow these steps to enable WINS lookup in the zone root domain:

1. In the Server List, click on the primary zone icon and choose Properties.
2. Select the WINS tab (see Figure 10.17).
3. Enable the Use WINS Resolution check box.
4. Under WINS Servers, add one or more IP addresses for the WINS Servers on your network.

You can click on the Advanced button if you want to change the settings, such as if your network uses a NetBIOS scope or if you need to alter the default timeout values.

### Enabling WINS Reverse Lookup in an *in-addr.arpa* Zone Root Domain

This is a feature of the Microsoft DNS Server that became necessary so that WINS-learned names could access resources that performed reverse lookups.

1. In the Server List, click on the `in-addr.arpa` primary zone icon, then choose Properties.
2. Select the WINS-R tab (see Figure 10.18).
3. Enable the Use WINS Reverse Lookup check box.
4. In the Domain Name to Be Appended to Reverse Lookup text box, type the default domain name to append to responses that WINS returns.
5. If you need to alter the default timeout values, click on the Advanced button.

Table 10.3  **Comparing WINS and DNS**

| WINS | DNS |
| --- | --- |
| Resolves NetBIOS IP addresses | Resolves hostnames to IP names to addresses. |
| Flat and dynamic structure | Hierarchical and static structure. |
| Supports DHCP | Supports TCP/IP applications that require more information than the hostname and IP address. DHCP dynamic update is possible with Windows NT Server 5 and higher. |

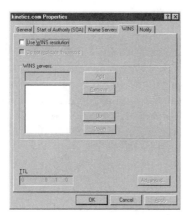

**Figure 10.17**   WINS tab.

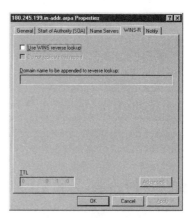

**Figure 10.18**   WINS-R tab.

## Special Options

This section takes a look at some less easily categorized areas, such as selectively enabling DNS on a multihomed server, or specifying a boot method for a DNS Server.

### Selectively Enabling DNS on a Multihomed Server

Note that DNS can operate on all the network adapters of a multihomed server if you don't specify any particular IP addresses. This normally is a primary reason to install multiple network interfaces in a DNS Server, but sometimes you may want to specify which interfaces will accept DNS queries. If that's what you need to do, follow these steps:

1. In the Server List, right-click on the server icon.
2. Select Properties and the Interfaces tab.
3. In the DNS Server IP Addresses section (see Figure 10.19), type the IP addresses for each network adapter that you want to enable for DNS traffic.

### Specifying a Boot Method for a DNS Server

To specify a boot method for the DNS Server, perform the following steps:

1. In the Server List, right-click on the server icon.
2. Select Properties and the Advanced tab (see Figure 10.20).
3. In the Boot Method field, select the Boot From Registry or Boot From BootFile option.

If you boot from the Registry, the Microsoft DNS Server doesn't consult its BOOT file for configuration information, but rather, uses the information in the

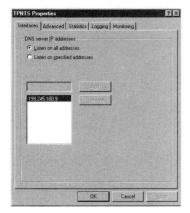

**Figure 10.19**    Interfaces tab.        **Figure 10.20**    Advanced tab.

Registry. If you make changes to the BOOT file that you want to use, you need to be sure to set the Boot Method to Boot from BootFile.

### Setting the Primary Zones to Notify the Secondary Zones of Changes

Follow these steps if you want to have the primary zones notify the secondaries of changes:

1. In the Server List, right-click on the primary zone icon.

2. Choose Properties and then the Notify tab.

3. In the Notify List, type the IP addresses of the secondaries.

You would want to make this arrangement if your secondaries are running the Microsoft DNS Server, version 4.9.3 or later of BIND, or some other implementation that supports notification of secondaries after changes are made to the primary.

### Modifying the Cache

The cache contains a list of root name servers for the Internet. If you're not connected to the Internet, and so have commented out the cache line in the Boot file, you do not have a cache icon in the DNS Admin server list.

You only have to modify the cache when the root name servers change, which is infrequently. You should plan to check the InterNIC for an updated list about once a year.

1. From the DNS Admin Server List, click on the Cache icon.

2. Right-click on the record that you need to change, and then choose Properties.

3. For an NS record, type the new name. For an A record, type the new IP address.

The only valid resource records for the cache are the Name Server (NS) and Address (A) Records.

# Security Issues

As convenient as you might find being able to access the Internet and other places outside your network, you may not want to let just anyone into your network. The most common packet filters on routers and proxy servers are for specific applications, such as Telnet, FTP, and web browsers.

You can take several precautions with DNS to minimize your network's exposure. Some of the most common include configuring your publicly accessible servers to perform reverse lookups to keep out computers that are misrepresenting their identities, and restricting zone transfers to authorized secondaries only.

Using reverse lookups is something that you generally must configure for each individual service (FTP or Telnet, for example), but the rationale is fairly obvious. If an unauthorized system is configured to use the same name as a trusted system's, but the name derived from a DNS reverse lookup using `in-addr.arpa` does not match, the system may be an impostor and should be denied access. If you provide a public and anonymous service, this matter isn't particularly relevant, but if you need to restrict access based on the hostname, it's definitely worthwhile.

If you decide to hide some of your internal hosts behind a firewall, you may decide to implement a "split-brain" approach to DNS (a DNS configuration that involves having primary servers that have different information on both sides of a firewall). The server outside the firewall has limited information about the network on the inside—it typically knows about only a few internal hosts (such as web servers and mail servers) that are permitted through the firewall but has full connectivity to the rest of the Internet. The DNS Server on the inside has access to full information about all the computers within the firewall, but is configured to ask the DNS Server on the other side of the firewall about anything outside of the local name space. This arrangement enables computers inside the firewall to perform DNS lookups on the entire Internet, but keeps anyone outside the firewall from learning about what is inside.

To implement a split-brain configuration, set both the DNS Servers as primary masters and have the one inside the firewall use Forwarders to contact the one outside the firewall as needed. Implement some form of restricted access between them (like a specific-host-to-specific-host router filter that allows only DNS traffic).

## Controlling Which Secondaries Have Access to the Primary

Restricting zone transfers to only authorized secondaries is useful because it hides the details of your internal network from outsiders. Enabling people to easily learn about all of a network's hosts can divulge enough information to prospective computer crooks that let them know breaking in might prove sporting, interesting, or downright profitable.

To restrict zone transfers, follow these steps:

1. Right-click on the primary zone icon.

2. Choose Properties.

3. In the Notify tab, add the IP addresses of the secondaries that have permission to access the primary.

4. Click on Only Allow Access from Secondaries Included on Notify List.

After you make any changes in the DNS Admin, you need to update the server data files by choosing Update Server Data Files from the DNS Admin menu. Otherwise, the DNS database can't write the current information to its configuration files immediately, and the information can end up lost if the system crashes before the next regularly scheduled update.

# DNS Troubleshooting

If the DNS Admin will not run, seems to have incorrect data, or indicates an unreachable server, you may need to diagnose the problem. The two best troubleshooting tools for this purpose are NsLookup and the Event Log. The following sections describe these tools.

## NsLookup

Nslookup is a command-line tool that serves as the main diagnostic tool for DNS. As with DNS, you must have TCP/IP installed before you can use it. Nslookup is to DNS what PING is to general IP connectivity: the first tool you turn to for testing. It queries DNS name servers and shows you the results it receives, optionally in excruciating detail. The query length must be less than 256 characters. You can interrupt it at any point by pressing Ctrl+C. To leave NsLookup, type **exit**. All unrecognized commands are interpreted as computer names, and it sends queries to its default server to try to look them up as domain names. NsLookup has two modes: interactive and non-interactive. Use the interactive mode when troubleshooting problems, so you can easily perform multiple queries.

Following is a list of NsLookup commands in interactive mode:

- help
- exit
- finger
- ls
- lserver
- root
- server
- set
- view

To use NsLookup for a command-line query, type the `nslookup` command at the command prompt as follows:

1. Type the name or IP address of the computer you are looking up. (If the computer isn't in the same domain as the name server, type a period after the computer name.)

2. If you want to specify a DNS name server, type its name or IP address. If you leave it blank, NsLookup uses the default name server.

The following sections look at each of the NsLookup interactive mode commands in turn. Consider it a kind of reference section. Each section summarizes the command and furnishes a syntax line.

### help

The `help` command displays a brief summary of NsLookup commands. The question mark (?) is a synonym for the `help` command.

```
help | ?
```

### exit

Type this command to exit `nslookup`.

```
exit
```

### finger

The `finger` command connects with the finger server on the current computer. The current computer is defined when a previous lookup for a computer was successful and returned address information (see the later section "`set q[uerytype] or set type`").

```
finger [username] [> filename] | [>> filename]
```

### ls

Use the `ls` command to list information for a DNS domain. The default information consists of computer names and their IP addresses. You can direct the output to a file. Hash marks separate every 50 records. Table 10.4 lists and describes various options you can use with the `ls` command.

```
ls [option] dnsdomain [> filename] | [>> filename]
```

Table 10.4 *ls* **Options**

| Option | Description |
|--------|-------------|
| -t | Lists all records of the specified type (see the later section "set q[uerytype] or set type") |
| -a | Lists aliases of computers in the DNS domain (same as -t CNAME) |
| -d | Lists all records for the DNS domain (same as -t ANY) |
| -h | Lists CPU and operating system information for the DNS domain (same as -t HINFO) |
| -s | Lists well-known services of computers in the DNS domain (same as -t WKS) |

Specify the DNS domain for which you want information after the option and the filename in which to save the output. You can use the > and >> characters to redirect the output in the usual manner.

Here is a sample ls request and its response:

```
> ls hq.mycompany.com
res_mkquery(0, hq.mycompany.com, 1, 252)
[nameserver1.hq.mycompany.com]
 hq.mycompany.com.              server = mailer.hq.mycompany.com
 mailer.hq.mycompany.com.       10.132.13.2
 hq.mycompany.com.              server = nameserver1.hq.mycompany.com
 nameserver1.hq.mycompany.com.  10.132.40.80
 hq.mycompany.com.              server = sal.hq.mycompany.com
 sal.hq.mycompany.com.          10.132.13.25
 hq.mycompany.com.              10.132.13.2
 bill.hq.mycompany.com.         10.132.70.3
 database.hq.mycompany.com.     10.132.13.248
 mary.hq.mycompany.com.         10.132.29.4
```

### *lserver*

The lserver command uses the local DNS Server to look up the information about the specified DNS Server, and then changes the default server to the one specified as its argument. This command is useful if you have changed your default server to one that no longer responds, and you only know the DNS name of others that may still be working.

```
>lserver <name>
```

### *root*

The current default server for the root of the DNS domain name space is ns.nic.ddn.mil. You can change the default server for the root by using the set root command. The lserver ns.nic.ddn.mil command accomplishes the same thing.

```
>root
```

*server*

The `server` command uses the current default server to look up the information about the specified DNS Server, and changes to the specified server as the new default server.

```
>server <name>
```

*set*

The `set` command has many subcommands. It changes settings that affect how lookups function. Here is a list of the possibilities:

- `set all`
- `set cl[ass]`
- `set [no]d2`
- `set [no]deb[ug]`
- `set [no]def[name]`
- `set do[main]`
- `set [no]ig[nore]`
- `set po[rt]`
- `set [no]rec[urse]`
- `set q[uerytype]`
- `set ty[pe]`
- `set ret[ry]`
- `set ro[ot]`
- `set [no]sea[rch]`
- `set srchl[ist]`
- `set ti[meout]`
- `set [no]v[c]`

*set all*

Use the `set all` command to get the current NsLookup configuration settings, such as information about the default server and type of queries being performed.

Here is a sample:

```
> set all
Default Server:  nameserver1.hq.mycompany.com
Address:  10.132.40.254f

Set options:
    nodebug         defname         search          recurse
```

```
nod2            novc            noignoretc      port=53
querytype=A     class=IN        timeout=6       retry=4
root=ns.nic.ddn.mil.
domain=hq.mycompany.com
srchlist=hq.mycompany.com
```

### set cl[ass]

You can change the protocol to the following types:

- **IN.** Internet class
- **CHAOS.** Chaos class
- **HESIOD.** MIT Athena Hesiod class
- **ANY.** Any of the above

The default is the Internet class, and you aren't likely to need any of the other classes; they're not widely used.

```
set class=value
```

### set [no]d2

This command controls the exhaustive debugging mode. nod2 turns the mode off. When on, the fields of every packet are printed. The default is nod2.

```
set [no]d2
```

### set [no]deb[ug]

You can turn debugging on or off. With debugging on, more information is printed about the packet sent to the server and the resulting answer. The default is nodebug.

```
set nodebug
```

Here is part of a sample:

```
- - - - - - - - - - -
Name:    nameserver2.hq.mycompany.com
Address: 10.132.13.251

> set debug
> nameserver2
Server:  nameserver1.hq.mycompany.com
Address: 10.132.40.80

res_mkquery(0, nameserver2.hq.mycompany.com, 1, 1)
- - - - - - - - - - -
SendRequest(), len 40
    HEADER:
        opcode = QUERY, id = 5, rcode = NOERROR
```

```
        header flags:  query, want recursion
        questions = 1,  answers = 0,  authority records = 0,  additional
= 0

    QUESTIONS:
        nameserver2.hq.mycompany.com, type = A, class = IN

- - - - - - - - - - - -
- - - - - - - - - - - -
Got answer (56 bytes):
    HEADER:
        opcode = QUERY, id = 5, rcode = NOERROR
        header flags:  response, auth. answer, want recursion, recursion
↪avail.
        questions = 1,  answers = 1,  authority records = 0,  additional
= 0

    QUESTIONS:
        nameserver2.hq.mycompany.com, type = A, class = IN
    ANSWERS:
    ->  nameserver2.hq.mycompany.com
        type = A, class = IN, dlen = 4
        internet address = 10.132.13.239
        ttl = 3600 (1 hour)

- - - - - - - - - - - -
Name:    nameserver2.hq.mycompany.com
Address:  10.132.13.239
```

### set [no]def[name]

Setting the `defname` appends the default DNS domain name to a single-component lookup request, one that contains no periods. The default is `defname`.

```
set defname
```

### set do[main]

You can change the default DNS domain to the name specified. Some search options append the default DNS domain name to a lookup request. The default is from the hostname.

```
set domain=name
```

### set [no]ig[nore]

If you set `ignore`, NsLookup ignores packet truncation errors. The default is `noignore`.

```
set noignore
```

### set po[rt]

To change the DNS name server port from the default TCP/UDP port 53, `set port` must specify a different port number. For more information on port number values, see Table 10.5.

```
set port=number
```

### set [no]rec[urse]

If the DNS Server doesn't have the information requested, the `recurse` setting tells the DNS name server to query other servers. The default is to `set recurse`.

```
set recurse
```

### set q[uerytype] or set ty[pe]

This command changes the type of query. RFC 1035 has more information about different information types. The default query is for address information (A). Table 10.5 summarizes the values used with the `set q[uerytype]` command.

```
set querytype=value
```

If NsLookup doesn't display the information you requested, it usually prints an error message. The following section lists common error messages, explaining their meanings and suggesting some possible solutions.

Table 10.5  **Value Parameters for Query Type**

| Value | Description |
|-------|-------------|
| A | Computer's IP address |
| ANY | All types of data |
| CNAME | Canonical name for an alias |
| GID | Group identifier of a group name |
| HINFO | Computer's CPU and operating system type |
| MB | Mailbox domain name |
| MG | Mail group member |
| MINFO | Mailbox or mail list information |
| MR | Mail rename domain name |
| MX | Mail exchanger |
| NS | DNS name server for the named zone |
| PTR | Computer name if the query is an IP address; otherwise, the pointer to other information |
| SOA | DNS domain's start-of-authority record |
| TXT | Text information |
| UID | User ID |
| UINFO | User information |
| WKS | Well-known service description |

*set ret[ry]*

If a reply is not received in a certain amount of time, the request is re-sent. By changing the retry value, you change the number of times a request is re-sent before giving up. The default is four.

```
set ret[ry]=number
```

*set ro[ot]*

You can change the name of the root server by specifying a different computer name. The default setting is = ns.nic.ddn.mil.

```
set root=<server>
```

*set [no]sea[rch]*

When search is set and the request contains at least one period but does not end with a trailing period, NsLookup appends the DNS domain names in the DNS domain search list to the request until an answer is received. The default is search.

```
set search
```

*set srchl[ist]*

You can use a searchlist in a different domain by changing from the default search-list. You can list up to six names, which you must separate using slashes. This command overrides the set domain command. To display the list, use the set all command. The default searchlist is based on the hostname.

```
set srchlist=name1/name2/...
```

For example, the following command sets the DNS domain to mfg.widgets.com and the searchlist to the three specified domain names:

```
set srchlist=mfg.widgets.com/mrp2.widgets.com/widgets.com
```

*set ti[meout]*

The timeout governs the waiting time (in seconds) for a reply. If the reply doesn't come within the specified time, the request is sent again with a wait period double the initial timeout value. The default is five seconds.

```
set timeout=number
```

*set [no]v[c]*

This command sets a virtual circuit when sending requests to the server. The default is [no]v[c].

```
set novc
```

*view*

You can use the `view` command to sort and list the output file of previous `ls` command(s).

```
>view <filename>
```

## Error Messages

The following are explanations of some of the error messages that you may encounter when using NsLookup:

Message: **Timed out**

- Description: Server failed to respond in a certain amount of time.

- Suggestions: Ping the server to make certain that it's alive. Look for general network connectivity problems, such as misconfigured default gateways or subnet masks. If the server responds to pings but doesn't answer DNS queries, make certain that its DNS Service is configured correctly. Check the NT Server Event Log for messages related to DNS Server problems. Increasing the timeout would help for servers in remote locations.

Message: **No response from server**

- Description: DNS is not running on the server. The server responded with an ICMP port unreachable message to inform you that it isn't providing DNS services.

- Suggestions: Check the services list in Control Panel to verify that DNS Server isn't running. Check the NT Server Event Log for messages related to DNS Server problems. Either configure and start the DNS service, or select a different server for your queries.

Message: **No records**

- Description: The DNS Server doesn't have the records of the requested type.

- Suggestions: Use the DNS Admin to view the DNS database to see what records are available. Use a text editor to check that the DNS database files in `%Systemroot%\system32\DNS` have the records that you seek. Check the Event Log to see if DNS found errors while loading the files.

Message: **Format error**

- Description: The request packet isn't in the proper format.

- Suggestions: The error could indicate that you're querying an old version of a DNS Server, or it might indicate packet corruption in the network.

Message: **Server failure**

- Description: There is an internal inconsistency in the DNS database.

- Suggestions: Check for typographical errors in the DNS database files, especially in the IP addresses.

Message: **Connection refused** or **Network is unreachable**

■ Description: Connection to the server could not be made.

■ Suggestions: Make certain that the link between you and the server is viable by using ping and tracert.

Message: **Refused**

■ Description: DNS name server refused to service the request.

■ Suggestions: Make certain that your query went to an interface accepting DNS queries. Check whether the server is configured to use only certain interfaces.

## Other Diagnostic Utilities

Another very helpful diagnostic tool is the Event Log. It can help identify many different kinds of startup problems. Open the Event Viewer by double-clicking on the Event Viewer icon in the Administrative Tools program group.

You can configure the Event Log with several different options. Make certain that the System is checked in the Log menu. The following sections enumerate possible problems that the Event Log can identify.

### Network Adapter Not Responding

Check that it is seated well with a network cable plugged in. Check that it is configured correctly, particularly for correct IRQ, memory, and I/O address. Make certain that it is using the correct driver.

### DNS Failed To Start

Check that there is a Boot and Cache file in the DNS directory, or appropriate entries in the NT Registry under the DNS hive. Check that TCP/IP is installed. Check that the server has enough system resources with the Performance Meter.

### Incorrect Data in Boot or Cache File

Check for a typographical error in the Boot or Cache file. Make certain that all necessary trailing periods are present.

# 11

# Network Management for Microsoft Networks Using SNMP

T CP/IP NETWORKS USE A STANDARD MANAGEMENT PROTOCOL called *Simple Network Management Protocol* (*SNMP*). The SNMP protocol is widely used in the industry. While SNMP was developed as a solution for network management on TCP/IP networks, it is not limited to TCP/IP networks. The SNMP protocol can be run on other transport protocols such as IPX, AppleTalk, and OSI.

Windows 9x and Windows NT Workstations and Servers can be configured with an SNMP agent. This SNMP agent is automatically installed when the TCP/IP protocol is installed for Windows NT version 5 and later. For Windows NT Server 4 and earlier, you can add the SNMP agent for Windows NT as a seperate step. After you configure the SNMP agent, the Windows station management variables can be accessed and set from a central SNMP Network Management Station.

In this chapter, the fundamental concepts of SNMP are reviewed. These concepts apply to SNMP implementations on any platform including Microsoft operating system platforms. Before discussing SNMP a model for network management is presented. This model describes the goal of network management and is applicable for most modern network management protocols including SNMP.

**Obtaining the Network Management System Software**

Windows 9x and Windows NT ships only with the SNMP agent software and not with the Network Management System software. However, a number of SNMP vendors supply the Network Management System software.

# A Model for Network Management

Figure 11.1 shows a model for network management. In this model, the network consists of several devices that have a management *agent* running in them. The management agent has knowledge of the device parameters it runs on. Some of the device parameters are specific to the device that is managed. For instance, router devices will have parameters that describe the routing table. All devices can be expected to have some common parameters such as the name of device, how long the device has been active (*up time*), and so on.

Figure 11.1 shows that the agents can be managed by a special device called the *Network Management Station (NMS)*. The Network Management Station can issue specific requests to a device for information about its network parameters. The agent for the device will receive these requests, and send back the requested information. The Network Management Station, upon receiving the reply, knows the value of the requested parameters. It can use this information to deduce information on the state of the device and whether the device requires attention.

It might also be important to prevent an unauthorized Network Management Station from obtaining information on the devices on the network. This requires that some authentication scheme be implemented that will prevent unauthorized access.

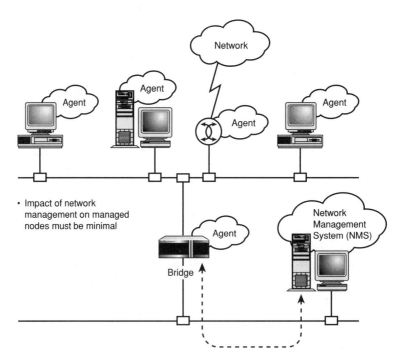

**Figure 11.1**   Model for network management.

Figure 11.2 shows the goal of network management. The network is shown as a "cloud" that has both input and output. The network *input* is the shared data and the activity generated by users of the network. The network *output* is the increased efficiency that results from information sharing. The network is subject to disturbances in the form of computers, devices and network links becoming inoperational. The goal of network management is to monitor the status of the network, and use control mechanisms to achieve the desired output (increased efficiency) despite the network disturbances.

The mechanisms used for monitoring and controlling the network should be such as to have a minimal impact on the network. In other words, the protocols used to collect information should not impact the performance of the network and the devices that are managed. If the network management mechanism uses up most of the network bandwidth, very little will be available for the network users. In this case the network traffic will be disrupted or the network will slow down because user network traffic must compete with network management traffic for bandwidth. The network agents running on the devices should not consume a great deal of processing power on their devices; otherwise, the device may not be able to perform its normal functions in the desired time.

## The Managed Node

The device that is being managed by the Network Management Station is called the *managed node*. The managed node (see Figure 11.3) has parameters that the Network Management Station can *query* and obtain values for. A *management protocol* is used as the means to establish communications between the Network Management Station and the managed node and send queries and receive responses. An example of this management protocol is SNMP (Simple Network Management Protocol).

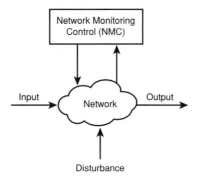

**Figure 11.2**    The goal of network management is to achieve desired output with minimum disturbance to the network.

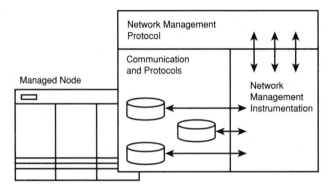

- Management protocol permits monitoring and control of the managed node
- Management instrumentation provides access to internal data structures of the managed node

**Figure 11.3** The managed node.

The management protocol interfaces with the *network management instrumentation* within the managed node. The management instrumentation has internal knowledge of the parameters and memory locations within the managed node. When a query is received through the management protocol, such as SNMP, the network management instrumentation receives the request and accesses the managed node's parameters. The results are reported back to the Network Management Station by the management instrumentation by using the network management protocol.

There has been considerable activity in the development of SNMP and MIBs (see the following section) for various devices. The following are some of the more recent and relevant RFCs as they pertain to SNMP:

- **RFC 2021 PS.** S. Waldbusser, "Remote Network Monitoring Management Information Base Version 2 using SMIv2," 01/16/1997. 130 pages, .txt format.

- **RFC 2012 PS.** K. McCloghrie, "SNMPv2 Management Information Base for the Transmission Control Protocol," 11/12/1996. 10 pages, .txt format, updates RFC1213.

- **RFC 1910 E.** G. Waters, "User-based Security Model for SNMPv2," 02/28/1996. 44 pages, .txt format.

- **RFC 1909 E.** K. McCloghrie, "An Administrative Infrastructure for SNMPv2," 02/28/1996. 19 pages, .txt format.

**Managed Node versus Managed Device**

In the discussion on SNMP, the managed node is often called the *managed device*. These terms are used interchangeably in this chapter.

- **RFC 1907 DS.** J. Case, K. McCloghrie, M. Rose, S. Waldbusser, "Management Information Base for Version 2 of the Simple Network Management Protocol (SNMPv2)," 01/22/1996. 20 pages, .txt format, obviates RFC1450.

- **RFC 1757 DS.** S. Waldbusser, "Remote Network Monitoring Management Information Base," 02/10/1995. 91 pages, .txt format, obviates RFC1271.

- **RFC 1451 PS.** J. Case, K. McCloghrie, M. Rose, S. Waldbusser, "Manager to Manager Management Information Base," 05/03/1993. 36 pages, .txt format.

- **RFC 1446 PS.** J. Galvin, K. McCloghrie, "Security Protocols for Version 2 of the Simple Network Management Protocol (SNMPv2)," 05/03/1993. 51 pages, .txt format.

## Management Information Base (MIB)

The parameters in the managed node are called *management objects*. The set of these management objects is called the Management Information Base (MIB). The MIB can be conceptually regarded as a database. The objects in the MIB, also called *variables*, have a number associated with them that is used to uniquely identify the object. This number is called the *object id*. The *object id* is based on a hierarchical numbering scheme and allows the variable in the MIB to be *ordered*. The ordering of the variables means that given an object id for a variable, you can determine the "next" variable that follows. The ordering of the MIB variables is conceptually similar to the indexing that orders records in a database.

A MIB variable also includes a status flag indicating whether the variable is read-only or has read-write access.

A certain set of standard MIB variables exists for the different protocol elements of TCP/IP. These MIB variables deal with parameter values for IP, ICMP, TCP, SNMP, EGP (Exterior Gateway Protocol) and Address Translation tables.

Data-link interfaces such as Ethernet, Token-Ring, SMDS, and ATM have their own set of MIB variables. It is even possible for a vendor of a special device to have MIB variables specific to that device. MIB variables that are specific to a vendor's device are called *proprietary MIBs*. There are interface mechanisms that enable an SNMP manager to take a description of a proprietary MIB and *compile* it to so that it becomes part of the MIB variables known to the SNMP Manager. For example, many of the Windows NT specific parameters such as those for DHCP and WINS have their own MIB definitions. These Windows NT–specific parameters can be monitored and controlled using a Network Management Station.

## The Management Paradigm in SNMP

The Network Management Station for SNMP is called the SNMP Manager. The SNMP Manager uses a management paradigm that is called the *remote debugging* paradigm (see Figure 11.4). In this paradigm, the SNMP Manager is similar to a programmer at a workstation debugging programs from a remote location. Such a hypothetical programmer would be interested in reading the values of variables in the program and changing the values of certain critical variables. Likewise, the SNMP Manager should be able to read and update values of MIB variables on the managed devices. The SNMP Manager should be able to perform the following actions:

- Read or read-write of MIB variables
- Trap-directed polls
- Simple traversal of variables in the managed node

When an exceptional condition occurs at a managed device, such as failure of a link or a critical change in status of a device, the managed device sends a *trap* SNMP message to the SNMP Manager. The trap message contains an indication of the event that caused the generation of the message. It is up to the SNMP Manager to respond to the trap message. The SNMP Manager can simply log the message in a trap log file, or take more extensive action. The SNMP Manager can, for instance, request additional information from the device that generated the trap message. The additional information can be obtained through read requests for specific MIB variables. If the SNMP Manager is programmed for control of the device, it can issue a write request to modify the value of a MIB variable.

All control actions within SNMP occur as a "side effect" of modifying a MIB variable. For example, if a device is to be powered-off remotely from an SNMP Manager, the SNMP Manager could send a write request to modify a MIB variable called the

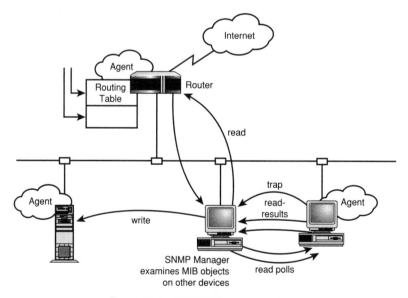

**Figure 11.4** SNMP Manager paradigm.

`ifPowerOn` variable. The managed device can be programmed so that the `ifPowerOn` variable causes the following side effect: the value of the variable is normally `1`; if the value is `0`, the device will be powered off. The managed device, upon sensing a value of `0` in its `ifPowerOn` variable, can initiate a device shutdown.

Because the MIB variables are ordered according to their object identifiers, the SNMP manager can traverse all the variables in the device using an SNMP command called `GetNext`. This is called a *simple traversal* of the MIB.

Because SNMP uses side effects to initiate control actions, the SNMP commands consist of only the following:

- `Get` (Read a MIB variable)
- `Set` (Write a MIB variable)
- `GetNext` (Return the next MIB variable)
- `Trap` (Sent to SNMP manager to report exceptional conditions)

Note that the terms *trap* and *event* are synonymous because the occurrence of an SNMP event generates an SNMP trap message.

## SNMP Commands and Protocols

Figure 11.5 shows the SNMP commands and the transport and protocols SNMP depends on. The SNMP Manager can issue any of the following commands:

- `Get`
- `GetNext`
- `Set`

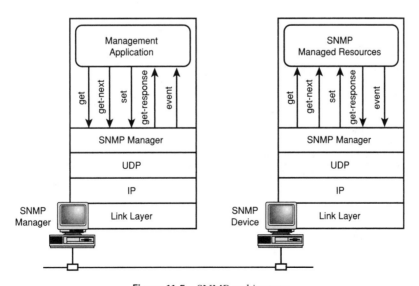

**Figure 11.5** SNMP architecture.

These commands are sent using the UDP/IP protocols to the SNMP agent. The SNMP agent can send a GetNext_Response SNMP command in reply to the SNMP Get request or GetNext request from the SNMP Manager. The SNMP Set command from the SNMP Manager is not explicitly acknowledged. In other words, there is no such command as a Set_Response command sent from the SNMP agent to the SNMP Manager. The trap events are sent from the SNMP agent to the SNMP Manager when exceptional conditions occur in the managed device.

## SNMP Traps

When an unusual condition occurs in the SNMP device, the SNMP agent alerts the SNMP Manager through SNMP traps. Figure 11.6 shows a sample network showing some of the trap messages that can be generated by SNMP agents.

The EGP protocol was at one time widely used on the Internet. Its inclusion as an SNMP trap message is to support those sites that may still be using it. The SNMP agent must be configured to send trap messages to an SNMP Manager station. Table 11.1 summarizes the different SNMP trap messages that can occur.

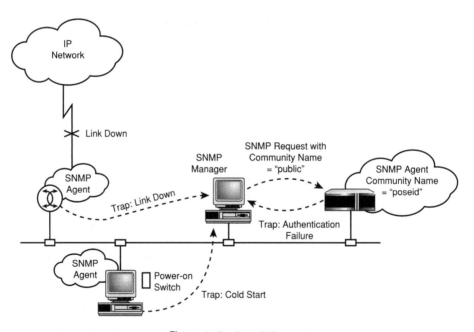

**Figure 11.6**   SNMP Traps.

**Table 11.1  SNMP Trap Messages**

| Parameter | Description |
| --- | --- |
| Link up or link down | When a network interface on the managed device fails, a `link down` trap message is generated; if the network interface comes back to life, a `link up` trap message is generated. |
| Cold start or warm start | When an SNMP agent starts, a `cold start` trap message is generated. If the SNMP initializes its table, a `warm start` trap message is generated. |
| Authentication failure | When an SNMP agent receives an SNMP request with a community name that does not match the community name the device is configured with, an `authentication failure` trap message is generated. |
| Loss of EGP neighbor | When an SNMP agent cannot communicate with its EGP (Exterior Gateway Protocol) neighbor, a `loss of EGP neighbor` trap message is generated. |

On a NetWare network, any of these trap messages can occur except for the `loss of EGP neighbor` trap.

# SNMP Object Identifiers and Messages

The following sections discuss the structure of SNMP messages. In this treatment, only the widely used SNMP version 1 message structure is discussed. SNMP version 2 currently is not widely used.

Many SNMP messages and replies contain the name of the MIB object whose value is being sought. Before discussing the SNMP message structure, the names used to describe MIB objects are discussed.

### SNMP Versions 1, 2 and 3

SNMP version 2 provides for better authentication and a more uniform syntax for SNMP messages, in which trap messages are similar to other messages. SNMP version 2 provides better support for non-TCP/IP protocols and mechanisms for communication between SNMP manager stations. SNMP version 2 defines a new get_bulk SNMP message that is used to make a request for all of the MIB variables in a device. This is an improvement over SNMP version 1, in which repeated get_next messages must be sent to read all of the MIB variables for a device. SNMP version 2 had not been widely implemented because of acrimonious disagreements over the standard between the major authors of SNMP. SNMP version 3 is expected to resolve these differences. SNMP version 3 is expected to include support for IP version 6, the replacement for the current IP protocol, called IP version 4.

## MIB Object Identifiers

In SNMP, MIB objects are given a unique object identifier consisting of a sequence of numbers separated by a period (.). These sequences of numbers are read from left to right and correspond to nodes of the object name tree. Figure 11.7 shows a partial object name tree that shows the object identifiers for the MIB objects sysDescr and sysLocation. The topmost nodes in the tree represent different committees and high-level organizations responsible for the composition of the name underneath its tree branch. The following topmost nodes are defined:

- ccitt(0). The nodes under the ccitt(0) branch are administered by the International Telegraph and Telephone Consultative Committee.

- iso(1). The nodes under the iso(1) branch are administered by the International Organization for Standardization and the International Electrotechnical Committee (ISO/IEC).

- joint-iso-ccitt(2). The nodes under the joint-iso-ccitt(1) branch are jointly administered by the International Telegraph and Telephone Consultative Committee, the International Organization for Standardization, and the International Electrotechnical Committee.

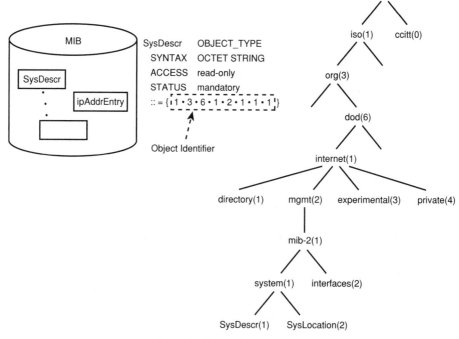

**Figure 11.7** Object name tree.

Network management is defined under the iso(1) tree branch. Under this tree branch are a number of subordinate organization definitions. Network Management falls under the org(3) node.

Under the org(3) node are a number of subordinate organizations. Network Management falls under the dod(6) node for the Department of Defense (DoD).

Under the dod(6) node are a number of subordinate networks. Network Management falls under the internet(1) node for the Internet.

Under the internet(1) node are a number of subordinate nodes representing different standardization efforts in the area of directory, management, experimental and private MIBs. Network Management objects that have been standardized fall under the mgmt(2) node.

Under the mgmt(2) node are a number of subordinate nodes representing different standardization efforts. Network Management objects that have been standardized fall under the mib-2(1) node.

Under the mib-2(1) node are a number of subordinate nodes representing groupings of MIB variables. Figure 11.7 shows the system(1) and interfaces(2) MIB variable groupings.

Under the system(1) node are shown the two MIB variables: sysDescr(1) and sysLocation(2). The object identifiers for these variables are defined by enumerating the node numbers starting from the top of the object name tree to the MIB variable object. These numbers are written from left to right and are separated by periods. Therefore, the object identifiers for these MIB variables have the following names:

sysDescr:       1.3.6.1.2.1.1.1

sysLocation:    1.3.6.1.2.1.1.2

Notice that there is a natural ordering of the MIB variables. The "next" variable after sysDescr is sysLocation because the last number in the object identifier representation changes from 1 to 2.

## SNMP Messages

SNMP message formats are variable in length and are complex. A subset of the ASN.1 (Abstract Syntax Notation, version 1) language is used to describe the SNMP message structure. ASN.1 is a fairly intuitive language, although its rigorous definition is beyond the scope of this book. As an example of the intuitive nature of this language, consider the following, which describes the structure of an Ethernet frame using ASN.1:

```
Ethernet-Frame ::= SEQUENCE {
destAddr        OCTET STRING (SIZE(6)),
srcAddr         OCTET STRING (SIZE(6)),
etherType       INTEGER (1501..65535),
data            ANY(SIZE(46-1500)),
crc             OCTET STRING(SIZE(4))
}
```

Note that the information following the double colon (::=) defines the variable listed before the double colon—in this case, Ethernet-Frame. The SEQUENCE {} represents an ordered list of items inside the braces ({}). The ordered list is the fields of the Ethernet frame, such as the destination address, source address, Ethernet type, data, and CRC.

The type of each field is named immediately after the name of the field variable. For example, destAddr and srcAddr are each defined as the type OCTET STRING, which defines a data type taking 0 or more octets as its value. Each octet in the octet string can vary in value from 0 to 255. The size of the octet string is placed after the OCTET STRING type.

etherType is defined to be an INTEGER that is an integer value of arbitrary size and precision. The (1501..65535) placed immediately after the INTEGER defines its size.

The data field is of type ANY, and is between 46 and 1500 octets long.

The crc field is a 4-octet OCTET STRING.

Using the ASN.1 notation, all SNMP messages can be considered to have the following format:

```
SNMP-message ::= SEQUENCE {
version INTEGER {version-1(1)},
community OCTET STRING,
data ANY}
```

This message format is shown in Figure 11.8, which explains the meanings of the fields.

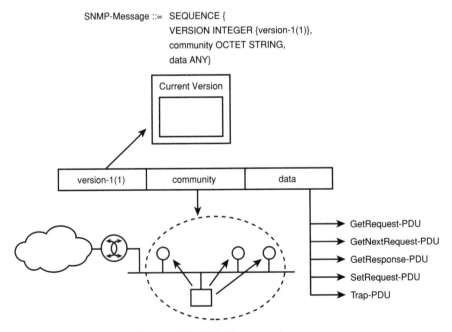

**Figure 11.8** SNMP message format.

`version` is the version number of the message format. `community` is a string value that is sent in every SNMP message. An agent receiving an SNMP message checks the community name against its configured community name value. If there is a match, the operation requested in the SNMP message is performed. If there is no match, the SNMP agent sends an SNMP trap message indicating authentication failure. This is a very simple authentication scheme because the community name is like a password. The problem with this authentication scheme is that the password is not encrypted and is sent in the clear.

Note that in most SNMP implementations, including the one in Windows NT, the SNMP agent will only send an authentication failure if it is configured to do so.

The `data` field represents the details of the different SNMP messages such as the `GetRequest`, `GetNextRequest`, `GetResponse`, `SetRequest`, and `Trap`. The format of these message types is described in Figures 11.9 and 11.10.

# SNMP Support for Windows NT

Although SNMP has its origins on TCP/IP networks, it has been adapted for use over IPX, DECNET, and OSI protocols. On a Windows NT network, SNMP is typically used over the TCP/IP protocol.

Windows NT computers include support for SNMP and define MIB objects for Windows NT, DHCP, and WINS servers. The following sections discuss installation and configuration of basic SNMP services.

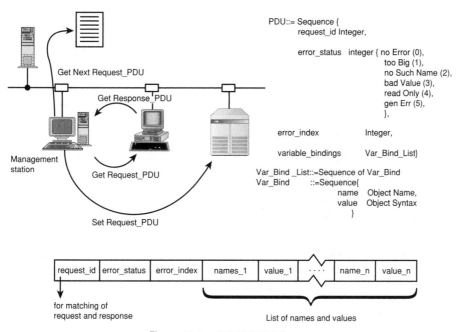

Figure 11.9   SNMP PDU format.

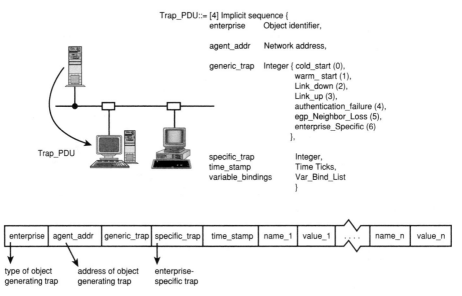

**Figure 11.10** Trap PDU format.

## Installing SNMP on Windows NT

Normally, the SNMP agent is installed on the NT computer at the time you install and configure the TCP/IP protocol. This is true if you are running Windows NT Server 5 and later. For Windows NT Server 4 and earlier, you can add the SNMP agent for Windows NT as a separate step. In case the SNMP agent is not installed, you install the SNMP service by adding the SNMP Service option in the Windows NT Network Services dialog box.

The following is an outline of the procedure for installing SNMP on Windows NT if you have not installed it on the computer. To install SNMP, you must have the TCP/IP protocol installed.

1. Log on to the Windows NT Server as an Administrator user.

2. Double-click the Network icon in the Control Panel.

3. Choose the Services tab from the Network dialog box.

4. Click the Add button.

5. Highlight the SNMP Service option and choose OK.

    You should see a dialog box prompting you for the path of the distribution files. If you have a CD-ROM on the Windows NT Server, the path contains the path to the CD-ROM distribution files.

6. Ensure that you have the appropriate distribution media in the install device and click Continue.

    You should see a status of the copy operation as files are copied. At the end of the file copy, the SNMP Service Properties dialog box appears.

7. You must reboot for changes to take effect.

The following sections discuss configuring various SNMP properties.

### Configuring the SNMP Agent

All SNMP devices have MIB values for information on the contact, location, and type of service. You can specify these values by configuring the SNMP agent running on the Windows NT computer.

The following is an outline of the procedure for configuring SNMP agents in Windows NT version 5 and later:

1. Log on to the Windows NT Server as an Administrator user.

2. Select Start, Programs, Administrative Tools, SNMP Service (see Figure 11.11).

3. Choose the Agent tab in the SNMP Properties dialog box, if this is not already selected.

4. In the Contact field, enter the name of the person or organization responsible for the Windows NT computer. For example, if Bob Smith is the owner or administrator responsible for the Windows NT computer, you can enter his name here.

5. In the Location field, enter the location of the Windows NT computer. For example, if the Windows NT computer is on the 3rd floor of the Financial Services building you can enter a value of "Floor #3, Financial Services Bldg".

6. In the Service box, select all options that apply to the Windows NT computer.

   - Choose the Physical option if the Windows NT computer manages a physical device, such as a repeater (Windows NT can be used as an embedded system).

   - Choose the Applications option if the Windows NT computer runs TCP/IP applications, such as FTP. This option should be selected for all Windows NT computers.

   - Enable the Datalink/Subnetwork option if the Windows NT computer manages a datalink device, such as a bridge or TCP/IP subnetwork.

   - Select the Internet option if the Windows NT computer acts as a router (also called *IP gateway*).

   - Check the End-to-End option if the Windows NT computer acts as a host (called *end-system* in the OSI model). This option should be selected for all Windows NT computers.

7. You can choose OK on successive screens to complete the SNMP service configuration, or go on to the next tab, Traps, discussed in the following section.

### Configuring SNMP Traps

To configure SNMP traps, follow these steps:

1. Use the steps described in the previous section, "Configuring the SNMP Agent," to access the SNMP Services.

2. Select the SNMP Properties Traps tab, which identifies the communities and trap destinations (see Figure 11.12).

   Community names are used for authentication purposes. An SNMP agent responds to an SNMP command only if the command includes a community name of which it is aware. In other words, the community name acts as a simple password scheme.

   When the Windows NT SNMP service receives a request for information that does not contain a valid community name and does not match an accepted host name for the service, the SNMP service sends an authentication-failure trap message to the trap destinations for the community name.

3. To add community names that the Windows NT computer knows about, enter the community name in the Community Names field and click the Add button. When the Windows NT computer sends trap messages, it includes the community name in the SNMP packet when the trap is sent. To delete a community name, highlight it and click the Remove button.

   You can use any alphanumeric characters for community names. Community names are case-sensitive. All hosts typically belong to the community name public, which is the standard name for the common community of all hosts.

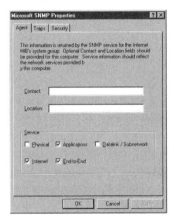

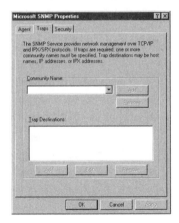

**Figure 11.11**  Microsoft SNMP Properties.    **Figure 11.12**  SNMP Traps configuration.

4. In the Trap Destination box, you enter the trap destinations for a selected community name that receives trap messages. Trap destinations are specified by listing the IP address of hosts (usually SNMP Managers) that receive the trap messages by the SNMP service running on the Windows NT computer.

5. To enter trap destinations, highlight the community name to which you want the Windows NT computer to send traps. Next, enter the IP address or IPX address of the host in the IP Host/Address Or IPX Address field. Click the Add button to add to the list of trap destinations. To delete a trap destination from the list, highlight it and click the Remove button.

### Configuring SNMP Security

Windows NT SNMP Services enables you to specify the community names and hosts that the Windows NT computer will accept requests from. You also can specify whether to send an authentication trap when the Windows NT computer receives an unauthorized community in an SNMP command.

The following is an outline of the procedure for configuring SNMP security on Windows NT:

1. Use the steps described in the previous section "Configuring the SNMP Agent" to access the SNMP Services.

2. Select the SNMP Security tab, which identifies the security related parameters (see Figure 11.13).

3. If you want to enable the sending of SNMP trap messages for unsuccessful authentications, set the Send Authentication Trap option (see Figure 11.13); otherwise, clear the check box for this option. The default is to send authentication trap messages on unsuccessful authentication attempts.

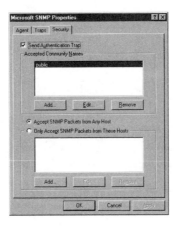

**Figure 11.13**  SNMP Security.

4. In the Accepted Community Names list, enter the community names from whom the Windows NT computer accepts requests. By default, requests that have the community name `public` are always accepted, which is why you see the community name `public` already listed in Figure 11.13. To add additional community names, enter the community name in the Accepted Community Names field, and click the Add button. To remove a community name from the Accepted Community Names list, highlight it and click the Remove button.

5. You can select an option to accept SNMP packets from any host or only from specified hosts.

   If the Accept SNMP Packets from Any Host option is selected, SNMP packets are not rejected on the basis of their address. This option is selected by default.

   If the Only Accept SNMP Packets from These Hosts option is selected, SNMP packets are filtered based on their source address. Only those SNMP packets that are from the hosts listed are accepted; all other SNMP packets are rejected. In the Only Accept SNMP Packets from These Hosts box, enter the host name, IP, or IPX address of the hosts from which the Windows NT computer accepts SNMP requests. Next, click the Add button to add to the list of accepted hosts. To delete an entry in the host list, highlight it and click the Remove button.

6. Choose OK on successive screens to complete the SNMP Service Configuration.

# Accessing the Internet Using RAS and PPTP

**W**INDOWS NT SERVER AND WORKSTATION include a copy of Remote Access Services (RAS), which can be used to connect a Windows NT computer and other workstations to a Windows NT network from a remote location. This capability is particularly useful for mobile users who need to connect to their corporate network. LAN users commonly use RAS to dial out and access services on other networks. And recently, RAS has become popular with Internet service providers as a means of supporting PPP connections. This chapter discusses the features of the Windows NT Remote Access Services and provides procedures on how to install and configure these services. Also discussed are the IP routing capabilities of the RAS server and Virtual Private Networks (VPNs).

## Overview of Remote Access Services (RAS)

RAS enables remote users to connect to a Windows NT computer using dial-up lines, a WAN link, or a protocol such as ISDN. Figure 12.1 illustrates how RAS can be used. The remote access clients can be Windows, Windows for Workgroups, Windows 9x, MS-DOS, or LAN Manager RAS clients. Although a Windows NT Workstation can be used as a RAS server, the RAS server is typically a Windows NT Server that supports up to 256 remote RAS clients. If a Windows NT Workstation is used as a RAS server, it can support only one remote RAS client.

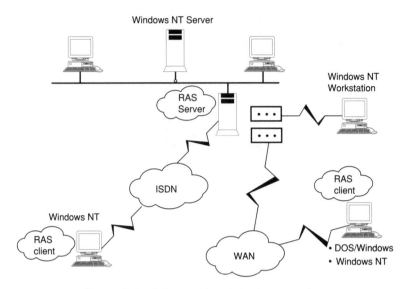

**Figure 12.1**   A Remote Access Services example.

The RAS client and RAS server software is bundled with the Windows NT distribution software. It is not, however, automatically installed when you install the Windows NT operating system. You must install and configure the RAS software in a separate step. See the section "Installing RAS Server" later in this chapter.

To access a RAS server from DOS workstations, you must be running Microsoft Network Client for MS-DOS in the full redirector mode.

The Windows NT RAS client uses the authentication and security features of Windows NT to log on to the Windows NT network. The RAS client users log on to the network as if they were logging on through a LAN connection. For additional security, Windows NT clients can encrypt data using the RSA encryption.

The physical connections and the protocols between the RAS client and the RAS server are discussed in the following sections.

## RAS Physical Connection Options

You can connect the RAS client to the RAS server over any of the following options:

- Phone lines
- ISDN
- X.25
- RS232C null modem

These options are discussed in the following sections.

Windows NT Server version 5 also provides Multilink. *Multilink*, a new feature based on the IETF standard RFC 1717, lets you increase your bandwidth by combining different communication paths into a single connection. A multilink connection can include both analog modem paths and digital paths (such as ISDN).

### Phone Lines

Phone lines are still the most ubiquitous means of creating a physical connection between the RAS client and the RAS server. Most phone lines are analog lines, and therefore a modem is required at the client and the server to convert the digital signals used by the RAS computers to analog signals used by the phone lines.

Windows NT provides compatibility with more than 200 different types of modems. To ensure compatibility between the modems for the RAS client and the server, your modems should comply with the same modem protocol standard or, even better, be of the same make and model. The modem standards that are widely used are the V.34 (which operates at 28.8 Kbps), the V.34bis (which operates at 33.6 Kbps), and the V.90 (which operates at 56 Kbps).

Microsoft publishes a hardware compatibility list that describes the modems that have been tested. If your modem is not supported, you can configure Windows NT to support your modem by editing the MODEMS.INF file. You can also choose a modem from the list that your unlisted modem can emulate or is compatible with. Details for configuring the MODEMS.INF file are described in Appendix E of the Microsoft manual *Microsoft Windows NT: Remote Access Service*.

### ISDN

Many parts of the world support access to remote locations through Integrated Services Digital Network (ISDN). The ISDN line is installed at the customer premises, usually by the local phone company. You need an ISDN card in the Windows NT computer to connect to the ISDN line. Figure 12.2 shows an example of the range of services that can be connected with an ISDN network.

ISDN services have many classifications, two of which are the Basic Rate Interface (BRI) and the Primary Rate Interface (PRI). The BRI provides two digitized channels for user information at 64 Kbps each, and one data channel for signal control purposes. The 64 Kbps channels are referred to as the B (Bearer) channels, and the data-signaling channel is called the D channel. For this reason, the BRI is often said to provide 2B + D channels. For BRI, the D channel operates at 16 Kbps. The BRI is typically used to provide access to an ISDN central office for residential customers.

The PRI provides 23 B channels operating at 64 Kbps, and one D channel operating at 64 Kbps. The PRI provide 23B + D channels.

With BRI services you can transmit data up to 128 Kbps; with PRI you can transmit up to 1.544 Mbps over a T1 line. In PRI service, because one channel is used for the D channel, this leaves 23 B channels for data or 1472 Kbps (64 × 23). These data rates are larger than those available through most modems and therefore are very attractive.

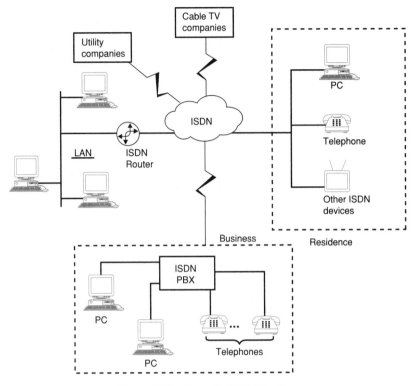

**Figure 12.2** Example ISDN Services.

### X.25

The X.25 protocols are used to implement a packet-switched network (PSN). The X.25 protocols describe the first three layers of the OSI model, although if some X.25 options are enabled, some functionality of layer 4 (transport layer) of the OSI model also is implemented.

RAS clients and servers interface with the X.25 network through a Packet Assembled Disassembler (PAD) device (see Figure 12.3). The PAD is provided by the X.25 provider (Sprintnet, Infonet, PSS, and so on). Some companies such as Hewlett-Packard, DEC, and IBM maintain their own private X.25 networks. The Windows NT computers must have an X.25 card installed (an X.25 device cannot just be connected to the serial port).

The connections to the PAD can be dial-up connections that are established for only the duration of the call. Dial-up connections are therefore suitable for occasional access to the remote computers. If you need permanent access to remote computers, it is preferable to have a direct X.25 connection. As you might expect, the direct connection is equivalent to the leased line connection and is therefore more expensive. X.25 PADs can provide both types of connections.

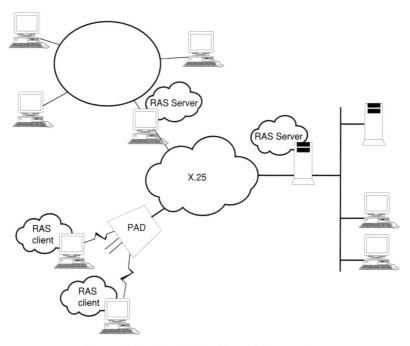

**Figure 12.3**  Using RAS with an X.25 network.

The RAS also supports X.25 smart cards. X.25 smart cards act as modem cards and have a PAD embedded in the card itself. The smart card appears to the Windows NT computer as several communication ports attached to the PADs. Figure 12.4 shows an example of RAS using X.25 smart cards. Table 12.1 shows the X.3 parameters that must be set for the PAD and the X.25 card interface for X.25 RAS connections to work properly.

### RS-232C Null Modem

If a network attachment is not available between two computers, you can physically connect them by using an RS-232 null-modem cable.

The RS-232C null-modem cable provides a direct point-to-point attachment between the two computers through a specially prepared cable (see Figure 12.5). The null-modem cable connects to the serial ports of both computers. Physical modems are eliminated when this special cable is used, and hence the name null modem is used for the cable.

Null-modem cables can be purchased or specially built. If you have to build null-modem cables for RAS connections, use Tables 12.2 and 12.3 as a reference for building a 9-pin or 25-pin null-modem cable.

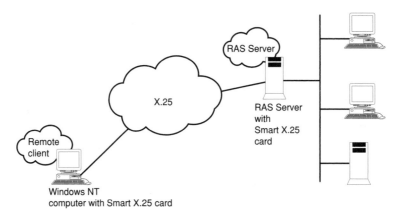

**Figure 12.4** Smart X.25 cards used by RAS.

Table 12.1 **X.3 Configuration Parameters for X.25 PADs Used with Windows NT RAS**

| Parameter Number | X.3 Parameter | Value |
| --- | --- | --- |
| 1 | PAD Recall | 0 |
| 2 | Echo | 0 |
| 3 | Data Forward Char. | 0 |
| 4 | Idle Timer | 1 |
| 5 | Device Control | 0 |
| 6 | PAD Service Signals | 1 |
| 7 | Break Signal | 0 |
| 8 | Discard Output | 0 |
| 9 | Padding after CR | 0 |
| 10 | Line Folding | 0 |
| 11 | (Not set) | N/A |
| 12 | Flow Control | 0 |
| 13 | Linefeed Insertion | 0 |
| 14 | Passing after LF | 0 |
| 15 | Editing | 0 |
| 16 | Character Delete | 0 |
| 17 | Line Delete | 0 |
| 18 | Line Display | 0 |
| 19 | Editing PAD Srv Signals | 0 |
| 20 | Echo Mask | 0 |
| 21 | Parity Treatment | 0 |
| 22 | Page Wait | 0 |

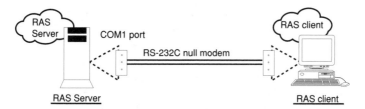

**Figure 12.5** RAS connections using a null-modem cable.

Table 12.2  **9-pin Null-Modem Pin-Out Connections for RAS Connections**

| Called Host Pin | Calling Host Pin | Signal |
|---|---|---|
| 3 | 2 | Transmit data |
| 2 | 3 | Receive data |
| 7 | 8 | Request to Send |
| 8 | 7 | Clear to Send |
| 6, 1 | 4 | Data Set Ready and Carrier Detect |
| 5 | 5 | Signal Ground |
| 4 | 6, 1 | Data Terminal Ready |

Table 12.3  **25-pin Null-Modem Pin-Out Connections for RAS Connections**

| Called Host Pin | Calling Host Pin | Signal |
|---|---|---|
| 3 | 2 | Transmit data |
| 2 | 3 | Receive data |
| 4 | 5 | Request to Send |
| 5 | 4 | Clear to Send |
| 6, 8 | 20 | Data Set Ready and Carrier Detect |
| 7 | 7 | Signal Ground |
| 20 | 6, 8 | Data Terminal Ready |

## RAS Protocol Options

The protocols that are used over the physical connections outlined in the previous section are the Serial Line Interface Protocol (SLIP), Point-to-Point protocol (PPP), and the Microsoft RAS protocol.

### Serial Line Interface Protocol

The *Serial Line Interface Protocol (SLIP)* is one of the simplest protocols used to connect two devices. The data octet stream is sent without any headers. Special octet values are used for control signals. An escape mechanism is used for control octets that might occur as part of the data stream. The SLIP protocol was developed by Rick Adamson for BSD-UNIX, and came into widespread use before there was an RFC describing it. When the RFC 1055 was written describing the SLIP protocol, it was based on existing UNIX implementations and was therefore called "A Nonstandard for Transmission of IP Datagrams for Low-Speed Serial Lines."

The original SLIP protocol did not support TCP/IP header compression. A later addition of the protocol called Compressed SLIP (CSLIP) has been implemented that provides for data compression. This protocol is described in RFC 1144 and is titled "Compressing TCP/IP Headers for Low-Speed Serial Links."

SLIP does not support protocol multiplexing and demultiplexing. This means that a SLIP connection cannot be used for transmitting different protocol traffic from multiple sessions between two computers.

SLIP is popularly used for dial-up connections to Internet hosts that provide SLIP connections. Figure 12.6 shows the TCP/IP connections over the SLIP protocol used by a RAS client.

### Point-to-Point Protocol

The *Point-to-Point Protocol (PPP)* overcomes the limitations of SLIP. PPP can be used for protocol multiplexing and demultiplexing. Like SLIP, PPP is popularly used for dial-up connections to Internet hosts. PPP also is used to provide point-to-point connections between routers. Figure 12.7 illustrates the uses of PPP.

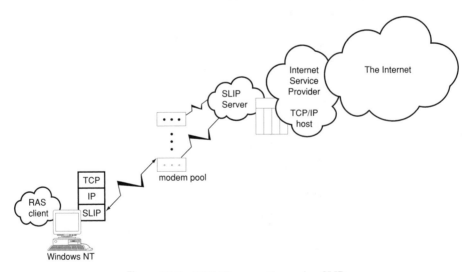

**Figure 12.6** TCP/IP connections using SLIP.

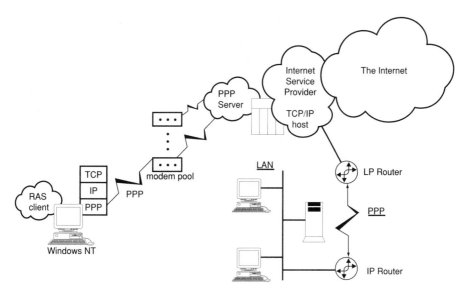

**Figure 12.7**  Uses of PPP.

Unlike SLIP, PPP provides a framing protocol that is based on the High Level Data Link Control (HDLC) protocol, and provides for compression and authentication. PPP is described by numerous RFCs, which indicates the importance of this protocol. These RFCs are listed as follows for your reference and further study:

- RFC 1598, PPP in X.25
- RFC 1570, PPP LCP Extensions (Updates RFC 1548)
- RFC 1552, The PPP Internetwork Packet Exchange Control Protocol (IPXCP)
- RFC 1549, PPP in HDLC Framing
- RFC 1548, The Point-to-Point Protocol (PPP)
- RFC 1547, Requirements for an Internet Standard Point-to-Point Protocol
- RFC 1378, The PPP AppleTalk Control Protocol (ATCP)
- RFC 1377, The PPP OSI Network Layer Control Protocol (OSINLCP)
- RFC 1376, The PPP DecNET Phase IV Control Protocol (DNCP)
- RFC 1334, PPP Authentication Protocols
- RFC 1333, PPP Link Quality Monitoring
- RFC 1332, The PPP Internet Protocol Control Protocol (IPCP)

Both SLIP and PPP are in widespread use. Over time, PPP is expected to become more widely used than SLIP.

### Microsoft RAS Protocol

The *Microsoft RAS Protocol* is a proprietary protocol that uses NetBIOS for RAS connections. Microsoft RAS requires RAS clients to use the NetBEUI protocol. The RAS server acts as a gateway for other protocols such as IPX and TCP/IP. Microsoft RAS is only supported on Windows 3.1, Windows for Workgroups, MS-DOS, and LAN Manager clients.

## Installing RAS Server

Starting with Windows NT Server 5, RAS services are also referred to as Dial Up Server. RAS server installation varies depending on the network protocols that you have installed. If you intend to use IPX or TCP/IP with RAS, you must install and configure these protocols before installing RAS. The following discussion assumes that you have already installed and configured the TCP/IP protocol. Also, the ensuing discussion focuses on the TCP/IP protocol configuration. Configuration of the IPX protocol, although simple, is beyond the scope of this book.

Before installing RAS, ensure that you have the appropriate modem, multiport, X.25 smart card, or ISDN card connected to the RAS server.

Although the procedure in this section describes setting up the RAS server, you can use this procedure as a guideline for configuring RAS clients as well. To install the RAS software, perform the following steps:

1. Log on as Administrator user to the Windows NT server.

2. Start the Network option in the Control Panel. You should see the Network dialog box. In the Network dialog box, choose the Services tab.

   In the Network Services tab, choose the Add button to invoke the Select Network Service dialog box (see Figure 12.8).

   In the Select Network Service dialog box, select Dial-Up Server and then click the OK button.

   Enter the path for the distribution files, if prompted, and click the Continue button. You should see a status of the files as they are copied to the server computer.

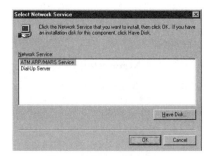

**Figure 12.8**   Select Network service dialog box.

The Dial-Up Server service should be added to the Select Network Services dialog box. Click OK.

Close any dialog boxes that were opened in this procedure.

## Configuring RAS to Use LAN Protocols

If the LAN protocols, such as NetBEUI and TCP/IP, are installed at the LAN server, they are enabled for RAS use when the RAS server service is installed. If the network protocols are installed after RAS is installed, or if you want to change the RAS configuration for an already installed protocol, you must explicitly configure these protocols for RAS usage.

The following sections describe the procedure for configuring the LAN protocols.

### Configuring RAS

You can use the following procedure for configuring the Dial-Up Server:

1. Log on as Administrator and start the Network option in the Control Panel.

2. From the Network dialog box, select the Services tab and choose Dial-Up Server. Click on the Properties button. You should see the Dial-Up Server Properties dialog box (see Figure 12.9).

3. Select the Security tab, if it is not already selected. In the Authentication and Encryption Settings section, select the encryption method to use:

   ■ Select the Allow Any Authentication Including Clear Text option button to support any authentication the RAS client uses. This option is useful if you have different types of RAS clients. This is the least secure of all the options, however, because it includes support for the Password Authentication Protocol (PAP). PAP uses plain-text password authentication and isn't an especially secure authentication protocol. PAP is useful if you have different types of RAS clients, and for supporting third-party clients that do work with PAP only.

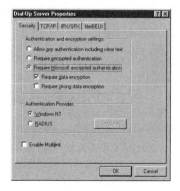

**Figure 12.9**  Dial-Up Server Properties dialog box.

Other authentication protocols supported by the Allow Any Authentication Including Clear Text option are CHAP, MD5-CHAP, DES, and SPAP. Briefly, *CHAP* is the Challenge Handshake Authentication Protocol used by RAS clients for its speed, simplicity, and small code size. Microsoft's CHAP implementation is based on the Message Digest 5 (MD5) encryption. The *DES* is the Data Encryption Standard designed by the National Bureau of Standards (NBS). The *SPAP* is the Shiva Password Authentication Protocol implemented by Shiva, Inc. Use of SPAP provides compatibility with Shiva clients. Unlike PAP, SPAP does not send the clear-text password and is therefore more secure than PAP.

- Select the Require Encrypted Authentication option to support any authentication used by the RAS client except the Password Authentication Protocol (PAP).

- Select the Require Microsoft Encrypted Authentication option to permit authentication using Microsoft's CHAP only.

- Select the Require Data Encryption option if all data sent on the RAS link is to be encrypted. If you want a stronger data encryption, you should also select the Require Strong Data Encryption option.

4. Select the Enable Multilink check box to activate the Windows NT Multilink option. Multilink lets you increase your remote-access bandwidth by using two or more communications links for a single connection.

5. In the Authentication Provider section, you can select either Windows NT or the Internet standard RADIUS (Remote Authentication Dial-In User Service) authentication. If you select the RADIUS authentication, you can select the Configure button to specify the RADIUS servers (see Figure 12.10). Use this dialog box to add the RADIUS search in the desired search order.

**Figure 12.10** RADIUS Server Configuration dialog box.

6. Select the TCP/IP tab to configure TCP/IP settings for the Dial-Up Server (see Figure 12.11). If RAS clients need to run TCP/IP applications that use the Windows Sockets interface over TCP/IP, you must configure the RAS server to use TCP/IP. The RAS server computer must have TCP/IP installed and configured on it so that it can be a TCP/IP host on the LAN that it connects to. In addition, the RAS server must also be configured to supply IP addresses to RAS clients. RAS clients that use TCP/IP require unique IP addresses. If the client does not have an IP address already assigned to it when it connects with the RAS server, the RAS server assigns an IP address to the RAS client. You can also configure the RAS server to use DHCP to assign IP addressing information for remote clients. The IP addresses assigned by the RAS server to the RAS clients must be valid to access the local subnet to which the RAS server is connected.

7. Select the Entire Network option if you want the RAS TCP/IP clients to access the entire network. This is the default choice.

8. Select the This Computer Only option if you want the RAS TCP/IP clients to access this RAS computer only. You may want to select this option to limit access to the network.

9. Select Allocate Network Address Automatically to assign the remote TCP/IP client addresses option if you have a DHCP server that will be used for allocating IP addresses.

10. If you are not using a DHCP server, you can alternatively select Use Static Address Pool to configure the IP addresses to be allocated to RAS clients. Use the Address and Mask fields to enter the range of IP addresses that will be used. The Range and Number of Addresses for Clients fields are automatically computed.

**Figure 12.11**   TCP/IP Protocol configuration for Dial-Up Server.

11. If remote RAS clients are configured with an IP address, you can enable the Allow Remote Clients to Request a Predetermined IP Address Option. The predetermined IP address used by the client must be compatible with the subnet that the RAS server connects to, or this could cause IP routing to get confused on the network.

12. Choose OK in the RAS Server TCP/IP Configuration dialog box, and in successive dialog boxes after completing any additional configuration steps.

Restart the RAS computer for the changes to take effect.

### Starting Remote Access Services

After restarting the Remote Access Server, you must verify whether the Remote Access Server Service is running. You can verify whether this service is running by using the System Service Management in the Administrative Tools program group. If the Dial-Up Server service is marked as a Manual start-up service, you have to start the Dial-Up service manually, every time the Dial-Up Server is restarted.

To ensure that the Dial-Up service starts automatically every time the Dial-Up Server is restarted, double-click Dial-Up Server Service in the service list and set the Startup Type to Automatic (see Figure 12.12).

## Administering RAS

Use the following four programs to configure, control, monitor, and update Windows NT Dial-Up Service:

■ Remote Access Admin (located in the Administrative Tools program group): Used to perform remote access administration.

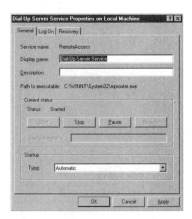

**Figure 12.12**   Dial-Up Server Service configuration.

- Dial-Up Monitor (located in Control Panel): Used to set dial-up preferences; view dial-up connections; and monitor transmit, receive, error, and carrier detect signals.

- Dial-Up Networking (located in the Accessories program group): Used to add phone book entries to make RAS calls.

- Directory Management (NT Version 5 or later) or User Manager for Domains (NT Version 4 or earlier): Used to configure which users have dial-in permissions and what level of callback security is configured for each dial-in user.

### Using the Remote Access Admin

The following is a guided tour that explains the features and capabilities of the Remote Access Admin program.

1. Log on as an Administrator user to the RAS server.

2. Select Programs in the Start menu and choose Administrative Tools. Select Routing and Remote Access Administrator.

   You should see the Routing and RAS Admin screen (see Figure 12.13).

3. To manage other RAS servers on another domain, choose Server, View Domain. You can directly enter the name of the RAS server to administer by typing its UNC name (\\computername). (By entering the Domain Name, you can get a list of all RAS servers in the domain.)

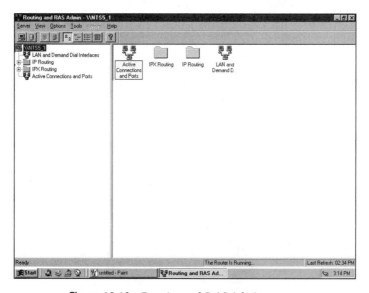

**Figure 12.13**  Routing and RAS Admin screen.

4. In the Routing and RAS Admin window, click Active Connections and Ports. The right pane shows the RAS clients that are connected to your router as well as the currently available RAS lines.

5. Right-click a user to show the status of the connection, or expand the user entry and right-click a device to get its status. You should see the Communication Ports dialog box. If a port is in use, you will see the user name and the time the user started using it.

6. You can send messages to any users by right-clicking on the user, and selecting Send Message or Send To All. You can disconnect a user's session by choosing the Disconnect User option.

7. To examine the Status of the RAS line, right-click and select Status (see Figure 12.14).

8. You can use the information in the dialog box for troubleshooting purposes. To reset the statistics counters, click the Reset button.

### Setting User Dial-In Permission

You can set dial-in permissions using Directory Management. The following is an outline of the procedure for performing this task:

1. Log on as an Administrator user.

2. Select Start, Programs, Administrative Tools, Directory Management.

3. Double-click on Microsoft Directory Service Manager.

4. Double-click on the domain name of the user account whose dial-in permission you want to configure.

5. Double-click on the Users folder to see a list of users on the right side panel.

6. Right-click on the user name whose dial-in property you want to change.

7. Select Properties. You should see the property sheet for the user (see Figure 12.15).

8. Select the Dial-in tab (see Figure 12.16).

**Figure 12.14**  Sample status for a RAS line.

**Figure 12.15** User property sheet.

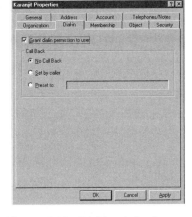

**Figure 12.16** Dial-in tab for the user.

9. Check the checkbox labeled Grant Dialin Permission to User.

10. Select the callback option. *Callback* refers to the feature in which the RAS server, upon receiving a connection from a remote user, terminates it and calls the user back at a specified number. This reduces the risk of security attacks. The default is No Call Back, which disables the callback feature for the selected user. If the Set by Caller option is selected, the server will prompt the user for a callback number. If the Preset To option is selected, the server will call the remote user at the fixed number specified in the field next to it.

11. After setting permissions, select OK.

12. Exit the Directory Management program.

### Using the Dial-Up Networking Program

The following is a guided tour that explains the features and capabilities of the Dial-Up Networking program:

1. Log on as Administrator user to the Windows NT server acting as the RAS server.

2. Start the Dial-Up Networking program from the Accessories folder. If the phonebook is empty, you see a message informing you accordingly. Choose OK to add a phone entry.

   You should see the New Phonebook Entry Wizard screen.

3. In the field labeled Name the new phonebook entry, type the name of the server, host, or organization that is to be called. This entry is used for ease of identification. Click Next.

4. In the next screen (see Figure 12.17), check any of the options that apply to your connection and click Next. If you are connecting to the Internet, see the section "Configuring Remote Access for Internet Use," later in this chapter.

   The third option, The Non-Windows NT Server..., alerts the New Phonebook Entry Wizard to prompt you for logon and TCP/IP information later in the setup process.

5. In the next screen (see Figure 12.18), select the modem or network adapter.

6. In the next screen (see Figure 12.19) enter the phone number to call. Click the Alternates button to enter additional phone numbers. If the first phone number does not succeed, the other phone numbers are tried in the order in which they are listed.

   Enable the Use Telephony Dialing Properties check box if you want to use dialing properties defined in the Control Panel Telephony application.

   Click Next after you finish configuring phone number options.

7. If you checked the third box in step 4 (The Non-Windows NT Server...), you will see four more screens asking you about the serial line protocol, the logon process, the IP address, and DNS and WINS server addresses. Skip to step 10 if you didn't check the third box.

8. In the next screen, enter the IP address required for the remote network. Check with your access provider before you enter an IP address here. Internet servers commonly are configured to assign IP addresses to connecting customers. If the server will supply your computer with an IP address, let the IP address default to 0.0.0.0. As the screen points out, don't choose the same address as your network adapter.

   Click Next.

9. In the next screen, enter the IP addresses of a DNS server and/or a WINS server for the connection (see Figure 12.20). Consult with your access provider. If the server will provide you with DNS server and WINS server addresses, enter 0.0.0.0 for each of these fields. Click Next.

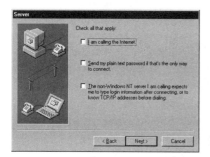

Figure 12.17   Add New Phonebook Wizard Server option.

Figure 12.18   Set modem or network adapter screen.

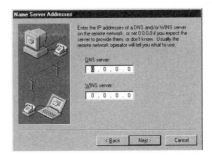

**Figure 12.19**  Setting the Phone Number screen.

**Figure 12.20**  Entering your DNS/WINS server addresses.

10. In the next screen, click on Finish to complete the phonebook entry.

11. After you add your first entry, you see the Dial-Up Networking screen (see Figure 12.21). This is the screen that appears when you start the Dial-Up Networking application.

    Click on the down arrow beside the Phonebook entry to dial drop-down list to display phonebook entries.

12. To add additional phone entries, choose the New button and follow the procedure for adding phone entries as outlined in the previous steps.

13. The Dialing from drop-down list specifies a dialing location. The dialing location defines dialing properties you'll need to dial from a specific location. You can edit location information by clicking on the Location button and invoking the Location Settings dialog box. To add or remove a location, click on Location list in the Location Settings dialog box (see Figure 12.22). The Location Settings dialog box is designed to let you specify a dialing prefix and suffix. You also can use the Control Panel Telephony application to create and edit dialing locations. The Telephony application offers additional configuration options and a more comprehensive user interface.

14. To dial using an entry, double-click on the entry in the entry list of the Dial-Up Networking screen, or select the entry and then choose the Dial button (refer to Figure 12.21).

    To hang up a connection, choose the Close button.

    For additional options, click the More button (see Figure 12.23).

15. Choose the Edit Entry and modem properties option to invoke the Edit Phonebook Entry dialog box (see Figure 12.24).

    The five tabs of the Edit Phonebook Entry dialog box provide configuration options for the phonebook entry, as follows:

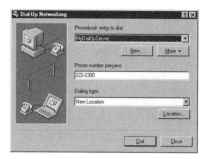

**Figure 12.21** The Dial-Up Networking dialog box.

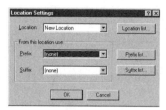

**Figure 12.22** Location Settings dialog box.

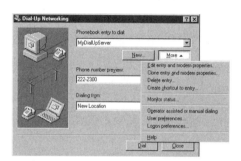

**Figure 12.23** Additional options in the Dial-Up Networking dialog box.

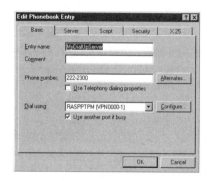

**Figure 12.24** The Edit Phonebook Entry dialog box.

■ The Basic tab defines basic characteristics of the entry, such as the entry name, phone number, and modem. You also can enable or disable Telephony dialing properties and enter an optional comment.

■ The Server tab enables and disables network protocols and software compression. The TCP/IP Settings button invokes the PPP TCP/IP Settings dialog box (see Figure 12.25).

■ The Script tab lets you define a script to run after dialing (see Figure 12.26). You can call for a terminal window to appear after dialing. Click on the Before dialing button to run a script or pop-up a terminal window before dialing.

■ The Security tab lets you define authentication and encryption options for the connection. The options are similar to those provided in the Network Configuration dialog box.

■ The X.25 tab provides settings for an X.25 connection (see Figure 12.27).

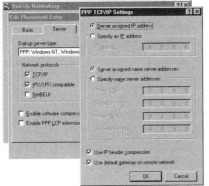

**Figure 12.25**  PPP TCP/IP Settings.

**Figure 12.26**  The Edit Phonebook Entry Script tab.

16. Select Clone Entry and Modem Properties (refer to Figure 12.23) if you want to copy a phonebook entry, make minor modifications to it, and save the copy as a new phonebook entry.

Select Monitor Status (refer to Figure 12.23) to access the Dial-Up Networking Monitor (described in the next section).

The User Preferences and Logon Preferences options in the More button menu (refer to Figure 12.23) enable you to specify preferences for the remote access session. The subsequent User Preferences and Logon Preferences dialog boxes are markedly similar. The Logon Preferences dialog box controls preferences that take effect if you enable the Logon Using Dial-Up Networking check box at the Windows NT Ctrl+Alt+Del Logon prompt. The Logon Preferences option doesn't appear unless you are logged on as Administrator. The User Preferences dialog box enables you to control preferences that are specific to the current user. The Preferences dialog boxes each have four tabs, as follows:

- The Dialing tab specifies the number of redial attempts, the seconds between redial attempts, and the idle seconds before hanging up. The User Preferences has an additional option called Enable Auto-Dial by Location. Auto-dial is a Windows NT feature that will maintain an association between a Dial-Up Networking entry and a network address. In other words, if Windows NT encounters a reference to a file that can be accessed only through a dial-up connection (such as a shortcut to a file on another PC), NT will attempt to make the Dial-Up connection automatically. In Figure 12.28, auto-dial is enabled at the current location.

**Auto-dial and Remote Access Auto-dial Manager Service**

You can't use auto-dial unless the Remote Access Auto-dial Manager service is running. Check the System Service Management in the Administrative Tools program group and make sure Remote Access Auto-dial Manager is started.

**Figure 12.27** The Edit Phonebook Entry X.25 tab.

**Figure 12.28** User Preferences Dialing tab.

- The Callback tab defines Callback properties for the connection (see Figure 12.29). If Callback is enabled for your account, you can place a call to the server and the server will immediately call you back to make the connection. This reduces the phone charges for the remote client. The Callback tab specifies how your system should respond if the server offers the callback option.

- The Appearance tab specifies a number of display preferences pertaining to the phonebook entry (see Figure 12.30). The Logon Preferences Appearance tab offers additional options for editing the phonebook and location during logon.

- The Phonebook tab specifies the active phonebook (see Figure 12.31). Dial-Up Networking entries are stored in a phonebook (actually, a `*.pbk` file). The default phonebook is the system phonebook, but you can create a personal phonebook of dial-up entries that are separate from the system-wide dial-up entries. The first time you select the My Personal Phonebook option button in the User Preferences Phonebook tab, Windows NT creates a personal phonebook file using the first eight characters of your user name and the `.pbk` extension. If you select OK, your personal phonebook becomes the active phonebook. The name of the active phonebook (if it's different from the system phonebook) appears in the title bar of the main Dial-Up Networking screen. You also can select the This Alternate Phonebook option button in the Phonebook tab and click on the Browse button to browse for a phonebook file. (The Logon Preferences Phonebook tab does not offer the personal phonebook option.)

17. After you add to and change the phonebook entries, exit the Dial-Up Networking dialog box.

**Figure 12.29** The User Preferences Callback tab.

**Figure 12.30** The User Preferences Appearance tab.

## Configuring Remote Access for Internet Use

Before you can use RAS to make a connection to the Internet through an Internet Service Provider (ISP), you must create and configure a phonebook entry in the Dial-Up Networking program to call an Internet Access Provider.

The settings for your Dial-Up Networking Internet connection will depend on your service provider's configuration. Your access provider should supply you with the information you need to set up the connection. Your provider may not have a ready-made recipe for connecting to the server via Windows NT Remote Access Service; if not, you may need to customize your Internet setup based on your provider's exact configuration requirements. If you can't get direct information about Windows NT setup from your service provider, you can glean most of the necessary settings from your provider's Windows 9x setup instructions.

Before you set up a phonebook entry for Internet access, ask your service provider to answer the following questions:

- Does the server require logon information after connecting?
- Does the server assign an IP address, or should you predefine an IP address for your PC?
- What are the IP addresses of DNS or WINS servers used by the Internet account?
- What type(s) of password authentication does the Internet server support?
- What type(s) of data compression does the Internet server support?

## Configuring RAS as a Router

A RAS server that is configured with IPX or IP can act as a static IPX or IP router. Static routers do not participate in dynamic routing update exchanges as normal routers do, and can route only between the networks they are connected to. This section discusses the RAS IP routers.

**Figure 12.31**    The User Preferences Phonebook tab.

### RAS TCP/IP Router

The static routing capability enables RAS to forward TCP/IP messages between RAS clients and TCP/IP hosts on the network. The IP routing is limited to the networks to which the RAS server directly connects.

Figure 12.32 shows an example of static IP routing in which the RAS TCP/IP client is running a Windows Sockets application such as an FTP client to access FTP servers on the network.

The IP router component on a RAS server does not forward the b-node broadcast requests sent by the RAS clients to the address 255.255.255.255 (limited broadcast) by RAS clients.

### Configuring RAS IP Router for Using the Internet

You could use the RAS IP router to provide routing between a simple LAN and the Internet over a dedicated PPP account provided by your Internet Access Provider.

Figure 12.33 illustrates a small LAN using the RAS server as an IP router. The default gateway IP address of the TCP/IP clients must be configured to the IP address of the RAS IP router.

Additionally, you must configure two value entries in the RAS server's Registry. The first Registry value entry to configure is the `DisableOtherSrcPackets`. This value entry is of data type `REG_DWORD` and must be created under the following key:

    HKEY_LOCAL_MACHINE\SYSTEM\CurrentControlSet\Services\RasArp\Parameters

If the value entry does not exist, its default value is `0`, which means that the IP packets sent by the RAS server will have the IP address of the RAS server as the source address. For the RAS to be used as a router, packets originating from a TCP/IP node on the LAN must have their IP address in the IP header. Therefore, you must create the value entry `DisableOtherSrcPackets` and set its value to `1`.

If the subnet that you have is of the same network class as your Internet access provider, you must add the `PriorityBasedOnSubNetwork` value entry of data type `REG_DWORD` under the following key:

    HKEY_LOCAL_MACHINE\SYSTEM\CurrentControlSet\Services\RasMan\PPP\IPCP

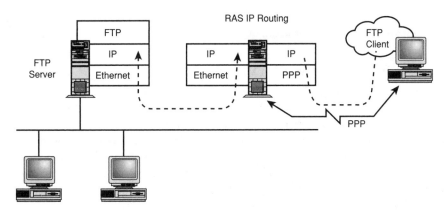

**Figure 12.32**  RAS Server IP Routing.

If the `PriorityBasedOnSubNetwork` value entry does not exist, it has a default value of 0. You must create the `PriorityBasedOnSubNetwork` value entry and set its value to 1.

Normally, if the RAS connection and the LAN adapter have the same network number in their IP address, and the Use Default Gateway On Remote Network option in the PPP TCP/IP Settings dialog box is checked (refer to Figure 12.25), all IP packets are sent to the RAS connection. This means that if the network adapter has an IP address of 132.156.190.12 and the RAS connection has an IP address of 132.156.195.2, RAS sends all packets destined for 132.156.*.* to the RAS connection because the network number 132.156.0.0 is the same for the RAS connection and the network adapter. If the `PriorityBasedOnSubNetwork` value entry is set to 1, RAS will send the 132.156.190.* packets to the network adapter and the 132.156.195.* packets to the RAS connection, assuming that a subnet of 255.255.255.0 is being used.

In addition to the previous steps, additional configuration must be done by your Internet Service Provider (ISP). For example, the ISP must have assigned a subnet to use and define routing entries on their network.

# Overview of the Point-to-Point Tunneling Protocol (PPTP)

The Point-to-Point Tunneling Protocol (PPTP) enables remote clients to connect to private servers over TCP/IP-based networks. PPTP provides a secure communications channel between PPTP clients and PPTP servers on both corporate and public networks, including the Internet and other public TCP/IP based networks. PPTP enables remote users to dial into local Internet Service Providers (ISPs) and connect via the Internet to a remote private server connected to the Internet.

Although it is run over TCP/IP networks, PPTP supports networking protocols, IP, IPX, and NetBEUI. Since PPTP encapsulates IP, IPX or NetBEUI protocols inside of

IP packets, remote users can still access systems running these protocols or use applications that may be network protocol dependent.

## Virtual Private Networks (VPNs)

PPTP makes use of Virtual Private Networks (VPNs), which provide a connection between two remote computers in different locations. The connection between these two computers, referred to as a *tunnel*, must maintain security and privacy and can take place over a public or private network using a PPTP device. Although VPN refers to a virtual connection between computers, Microsoft refers to the device used to create the virtual connection as a VPN. When you are installing or configuring PPTP on Windows NT or Windows 9x, you will actually be configuring VPNs, which are PPTP devices.

## Installing the Point-to-Point Tunneling Protocol

The installation of PPTP is comprised of installing the PPTP network protocol and configuring Virtual Private Network devices. Setup and configuration are similar to those sections that have been covered in the Remote Access Services section of this chapter.

PPTP is automatically installed for Windows NT version 5 when TCP/IP is installed. If for some reason PPTP is not installed, perform the following steps:

1. Log on as Administrator user to the Windows NT Server.

2. Start the Network option in the Control Panel. You should see the Network dialog box. In the Network dialog box, choose the Protocols tab.

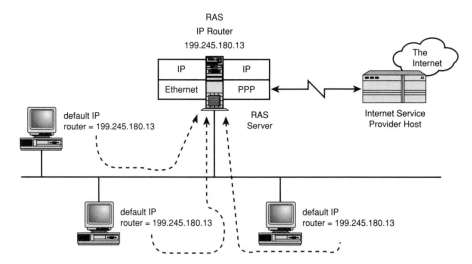

**Figure 12.33**   Small LAN connected to the Internet using a RAS IP router.

3. In the Network Protocols tab, click the Add button to invoke the Select Network Protocol dialog box.

4. In the Select Network Protocol dialog box, select Point-to-Point Tunneling Protocol.

5. If prompted, enter the path for the distribution files and click the Continue button.

6. You should see a status of the files as they are copied to the server computer. After the files are copied, select the Point to Point Tunneling Protocol option in the Protocols tab and select Properties (see Figure 12.34).

7. Select the number of Virtual Private Networks by clicking on the down arrow. The number of Virtual Private Networks is the number of VPN connections you want your server to support simultaneously. Windows NT Server can support up to 255 Virtual Private Networks. You can also use this screen to reserve the number of VPNs used exclusively for dial-out, dial-in, and routing.

## Installing and Configuring PPTP Clients

Windows NT Server, Windows NT Workstation, and Windows 9x can be used as PPTP clients. Each of these clients uses a Virtual Private Networking device to connect to the PPTP server. The Setup for each is similar to the setup for the Dial-Up Networking Client. The following sections review the installation of PPTP clients on Windows NT Server, Windows NT Workstation, and Windows 9x.

### Installing PPTP on a Windows NT System

The installation of PPTP on a Windows NT system is composed of installing the PPTP network protocol and configuring Virtual Private Network devices. Setup and configuration are similar to those sections that have been covered in the Remote Access Services section of this chapter.

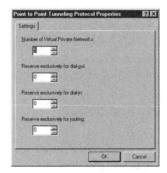

**Figure 12.34**   PPTP Configuration.

To install the PPTP software and configure the VPN devices, see the "Installing the Point-to-Point Tunneling Protocol" section earlier in this chapter.

### Configuring PPTP on a Windows NT System

The most common method of connecting to a private network using PPTP is through the Internet. In order to use this method, the PPTP client must have two entries configured in the phonebook; one for the Internet through the Internet Service Provider and one for the PPTP server that will be connected using the Internet connection. The steps to create phonebook entries, and set up a connection to the Internet were covered earlier in the chapter.

To configure a phonebook entry for a PPTP connection perform the following steps:

1. Log on to the Windows NT system.

2. Start the Dial-Up Networking program from the Accessories folder. If the phonebook is empty, you see a message informing you accordingly. Choose OK to add a phonebook entry.

   You should see the New Phonebook Entry Wizard screen.

3. In the Name the New Phonebook Entry field, type the name of the server that is to be called. Click on Next.

4. In the next screen, check the option to Connect to the Internet.

5. In the next screen, enter the TCP/IP address of the server to connect. For configuring and establishing a connection to the PPTP server, the address of the server is required, not the server's phone number.

6. Click on Next after you finish configuring PPTP server's TCP/IP address.

7. After configuring your connection to the Internet Service Provider and your connection to the PPTP server, you are ready to connect to the PPTP server. Using Dial-Up Networking, dial and connect to the Internet via your Internet Service Provider and across the Internet. You should have two Dial-Up Networking dialog boxes for your connections.

After the connection has been established to the PPTP server, you will no longer be able to gain access to the Internet through the ISP. Internet access will only be possible during the PPTP session, if the remote network permits access to the Internet.

A Windows NT Workstation is installed exactly as a Windows NT Server.

### Installing PPTP on a Windows 95 System

Windows 95 also supports PPTP as a client. With the latest release of Dial-Up Networking, PPTP is an available option for Remote Access. You must download version 1.2 or greater of the Dial-Up Networking software for Windows 95 in order to install and configure PPTP.

This section assumes that Dial-Up Networking version 1.2 or greater has already been installed on the Windows 95 system and that a connection has already been created for connecting to the Internet Service Provider.

To configure the VPN device and use PPTP on the Windows 95 system, perform the following steps:

1. From the Start menu, select Programs, Accessories, and then click Dial-Up Networking.

2. Click Make New Connection. The Make New Connection Wizard appears.

3. Type the name of the server in the Type a Name for the Computer You Are Dialing box.

4. Select Microsoft VPN Adapter in the Select a Modem box. Click Next.

5. Type the name or IP address of the PPTP server in the Host Name or IP Address box. Click Next and then Finish. An icon for connecting to the server is created in the Dial-Up Networking folder.

6. Double-click the icon in the Dial-Up Networking folder to connect to your ISP.

7. Double-click the PPTP Server Icon in the Dial-Up Networking folder to connect to the PPTP server. Enter the user name and password to connect to the remote server. You will now have two connections established, one to the ISP and one to the PPTP server.

After the connection has been established to the PPTP server, you will no longer be able to gain access to the Internet. Internet access will only be possible during the PPTP session, if the remote network allows access to the Internet.

As with Remote Access for other communication devices, the Remote Access Admin Administrator tool is used to monitor connections. Please refer to the topic discussed earlier in the chapter for Remote Access Admin.

# Installing and Configuring L2TP

With the release of Windows NT version 5, another protocol called the Layer 2 Tunneling Protocol that can be used for building VPNs has become available. L2TP has been submitted as an Internet Engineering Draft proposal and is expected to replace PPTP.

The installation and configuration of L2TP is similar to PPTP. The following is an outline of the steps:

1. Log on as Administrator user to the Windows NT Server.

2. Start the Network option in the Control Panel. You should see the Network dialog box. In the Network dialog box, choose the Protocols tab.

3. On the Protocols tab, click the Add button to invoke the Select Network Protocol dialog box.

4. In the Select Network Protocol dialog box, select Layer 2 Tunneling Protocol.

5. If prompted, enter the path for the distribution files and click the Continue button.

6. You should see the Layer 2 Tunneling Protocol added to the list of protocols on the Protocols tab. Click the Properties button to display the Layer 2 Tunneling Protocol Properties dialog box (see Figure 12.35).

7. Select the number of Virtual Private Networks by clicking on the down arrow. The number of Virtual Private Networks is the number of VPN connections you want your server to support simultaneously. Windows NT Server can support up to 255 Virtual Private Networks. You can also use this screen to reserve the number of VPNs used exclusively for dial-out, dial-in and routing.

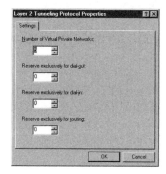

**Figure 12.35**   L2TP Configuration.

# Network File System Protocol Support for Microsoft Networks

**N**ETWORK FILE SYSTEM (NFS) IS A FILE service protocol originally developed by
SUN Microsystems and licensed to a large number of vendors. NFS allows a computer
on which the NFS server software is running to export its file systems to other clients.
*Exporting* a file system means that it is made available to clients on a variety of different operating system platforms, including Windows NT, as long as they are running
the NFS client software.

Because NFS runs on many different operating system platforms, it can be used to
share files between diverse platforms. NFS is particularly useful for integrating
Windows NT with UNIX platforms.

This chapter introduces you to the concept of NFS, its operation, and an example
of configuring NFS services for Windows NT.

## Understanding NFS

Figure 13.1 shows that the NFS server is exporting the /users directory. This exported directory can be accessed simultaneously by clients running different operating
systems.

Each NFS client views the file system exported by the NFS server in the environment of the client's native file system. For example, a Windows NT NFS client will
access the exported file system through a network drive letter assignment, and a
UNIX NFS client will see the exported file system as being linked to its local file
system.

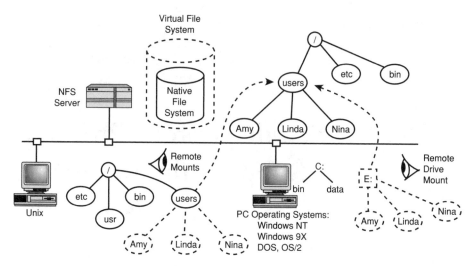

**Figure 13.1**   Using NFS.

# How Is NFS Different from SMB?

Microsoft networks use a file system-sharing protocol called *SMB* that is discussed in Chapter 2, "TCP/IP Protocols Infrastructure for Windows Networks." The SMB protocol provides file sharing and is similar in many ways to the NFS protocol. So why would you want to use NFS instead of using SMB?

In a pure Microsoft network, SMB services are already implemented, and there is little justification for using NFS as the file-sharing protocol. However, in a heterogeneous network with many different platforms from different vendors, NFS can be used to provide integration between the platforms by sharing the file systems on diverse computers. Because network data is often shared as files, NFS can provide a powerful means of integration.

It should also be pointed out the SMB protocol has been implemented on many UNIX systems. For example, the Samba software implements the SMB protocol on many UNIX systems. However, SMB is not nearly as widespread on diverse computers as is NFS.

## NFS Versions

NFS consists of a number of protocols that act together to implement a transparent file system. NFS was developed by SUN Microsystems in the early 1980s and has been licensed to over 200 vendors. The NFS protocol is documented in RFC 1094 on the NFS: Network File System Protocol specification.

NFS was originally designed in a Local Area Network (LAN) context. Although it can be used over a Wide Area Network (WAN), there are several characteristics of NFS that are not suited for the lower transmission bandwidth and unpredictable and longer delays associated with WANs. Another protocol called the Andrew File System (AFS) has been designed by researchers at Carnegie Mellon University. AFS is available as a product from Transarc Corporation but does not have the widespread acceptance that NFS enjoys.

The original NFS protocol as documented in RFC 1094 was designed to use UDP as the transport protocol. The UDP transport protocol was used in NFS versions 1 and 2. The use of UDP is optimized for LANs but has some disadvantages when used on WANs. NFS version 2 supported TCP but there was an overhead associated with using TCP because its use was not optimized. In UDP, the checksum for checking errors in the UDP packet is optional. Although the UDP checksum is optional, it is highly recommended when running NFS on a network that is not very reliable, such as running SLIP (Serial Line Interface Protocol) on unshielded twisted pair wiring.

More recent advances in NFS version 3 permit NFS to run on top of TCP. NFS version 3 is designed to run on TCP and is better suited for WAN usage, which is more error prone and has a wide variation in time delays. NFS version 3 removed the arbitrary 8 KB transfer limit of NFS version 2.

NFS version 3 is required by *Web NFS*, a new protocol that enables Web browsers to access NFS servers. NFS version 3 is documented in RFC 1813 on NFS Version 3 Protocol Specification.

## NFS Protocols

At the Session layer of the OSI model, NFS uses the Remote Procedure Call (RPC) protocol. There exists a number of RPC protocols that are quite different from each other; yet they are all called RPC. NFS's RPC is often called Sun-RPC to distinguish it from other RPC protocols, such as Microsoft's RPC, which is an implementation of DCE's (Distributed Computing Environment) RPC. RPC enables NFS services at the server to be accessed using the "procedure call" paradigm familiar to programmers. RPC provides a high-level access to NFS services without getting involved with details of communication protocols. Programmers who use RPC do not have to be communications experts to use the networking services that can be accessed using RPC. The Sun-RPC protocol is documented in RFC 1057 on RPC: Remote Procedure Call Protocol specification version 2.

At the Presentation layer of the OSI model, NFS uses the External Data Representation (XDR) protocol. The XDR provides a uniform way of representing data. For example, number data is represented using 2's complement notation and if a system uses a different number representation, conversion is done by XDR. The XDR protocol is documented in RFC 1832 on XDR: External Data Representation Standard.

At the Application layer of the OSI model, NFS uses the Network File System (NFS) protocol. The NFS protocol provides services such as writing to a file, creating a file, reading a file, and so on at the NFS server. The Application layer also consists of a number of support protocols for NFS, such as the mount and portmapper protocols. The *mount* protocol implements the NFS mounting procedure, and the *portmapper* provides clients that need access to a service with the port number for the service. When a client mounts an NFS file system, that remote file system becomes accessible to the NFS client.

The portmapper uses the well-known UDP port number 111. An NFS client wishing to access a particular service sends a request to the UDP port number 111. Server programs that wish to provide a service must register with the portmapper. Upon receiving a request for a registered service, the portmapper responds with the port number of the service to which the requests should be sent.

Figure 13.2 shows the different NFS protocols. At the Data Link and Physical layers of the OSI, NFS supports the wide variety of technologies that are available. At the Network layer, NFS uses IP. At the Transport layer NFS uses UDP or TCP. When NFS is used over UDP, it is highly recommended that the optional UDP checksum be used.

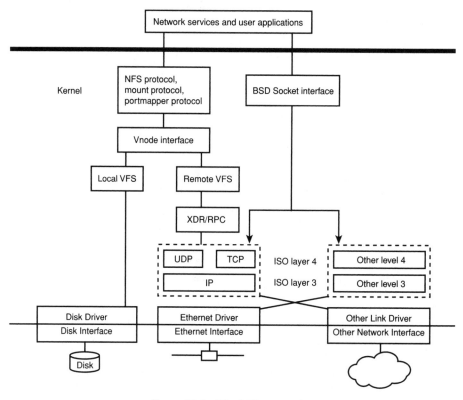

**Figure 13.2** The NFS protocols.

## NFS Remote Procedure Calls

The NFS communication between client and server uses the Remote Procedure Call model. NFS implements 18 remote procedure calls. The software code for these 18 procedures resides at the NFS server. The NFS procedures are used by NFS clients to access the network file services implemented by the NFS server. An NFS client accesses these procedures through the RPC mechanism.

The RPC protocol contains a program number and a procedure number. The program number identifies the service being accessed. For example, the NFS service has a program number of 100003. Within the program there are 18 procedures that are numbered from 0 to 17. For instance, the procedure number 6 deals with reading of a file. An NFS client that must read a file sends an RPC request that contains the program number of 100003 and procedure number of 6 (see Figure 13.3). Other parameters for the read operation will also have to be supplied in the NFS client's RPC request packet.

The RPC request also specifies the version number of the program that should provide the service. All programs that advertise their services have a version number. The version number allows a graceful way of enabling old and new versions of a program service to coexist. This enables existing NFS clients that use the older service to be supported, while newer NFS clients can access the newer (and hopefully better) version of the program.

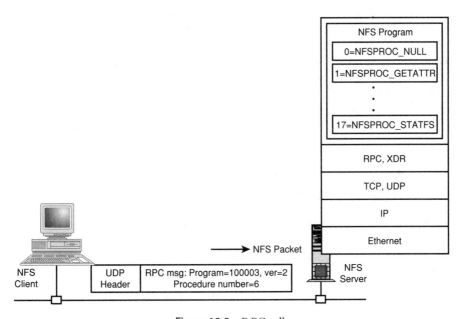

**Figure 13.3** RPC call.

Table 13.1 lists the different procedure numbers for the NFS program, and a brief description of their meanings. The NFSPROC_NULL, procedure 0, is described as a Do Nothing procedure. Procedure number 0, in all programs, "does nothing." Actually, it does a bit more than "nothing": If an RPC request is sent to procedure number 0, the procedure number simply returns the request back to the sender. In other words, procedure number 0 acts as a simple "echo" service. Many NFS clients use this "echo" feature as the basis for providing a diagnostic utility called nfsping. nfsping does what the name suggests. When the host name or IP address is supplied as a parameter to the nfsping utility, nfsping sends an echo request to procedure number 0 for the NFS program, and awaits a reply. The following is the syntax for using nfsping:

```
nfsping hostname
```

If the NFS service is active at the host, a reply is received; otherwise, you can conclude that the service is not available or the host is unreachable.

### Web NFS

The Web NFS protocol is designed to enable Web browsers to access NFS servers across the Internet. The Web NFS protocol requires the use of NFS version 3, which supports TCP connections, and it uses public handles.

In NFS, a *handle* is an internal data structure that is created by the NFS server when a mount request is made using the mount NFS protocol. The mount NFS protocol relies on RPC for communication between NFS client and server. The handle is returned when the mount daemon (UNIX term for an independent process) running at the NFS server mounts the requested file system. The mounting process involves verifying whether the mount request is permitted for the user, and initializing data structures with information about accessing the requested file system. The returned handle is then used in all subsequent operations for accessing the file system.

A *public* handle is a specially reserved file system handle that is used as an initial file system handle by Web browsers. The use of a public handle makes it possible for a Web browser to access a file system at an NFS server without having to issue an NFS mount command.

Figure 13.4 shows the use of Web NFS. The Web NFS server listens on TCP port 2049 for requests from Web clients.

The Web NFS protocols are documented in RFC 2054 on WebNFS Client Specification and RFC 2055 on WebNFS Server Specification.

# Implementing NFS

There are a number of implementations of NFS that run on Windows 9x and Windows NT platforms, such as ChameleonNFS and HummingbirdNFS. This chapter discusses NetManage's ChameleonNFS.

Table 13.1  **NFS Remote Procedure Call (RPC) numbers**

| Procedure number | NFS procedure | Description |
|---|---|---|
| 0 | NFSPROC_NULL | Does "nothing"; diagnostic check |
| 1 | NFSPROC_GETATTR | Gets attributes of file/directory, such as owner and group owner permissions |
| 2 | NFSPROC_SETATTR | Sets the attributes of a file/directory, such as owner and group owner permissions |
| 3 | NFSPROC_ROOT | Now obsolete; handled by the mount protocol |
| 4 | NFSPROC_LOOKUP | Obtains a file handle to a file in a specific directory |
| 5 | NFSPROC_READLINK | Reads contents of a symbolic link |
| 6 | NFSPROC_READ | Reads from a file |
| 7 | NFSPROC_WRITECACHE | Used in NFS version 3 to write to cache |
| 8 | NFSPPROC_WRITE | Writes to a file |
| 9 | NFSPROC_CREATE | Creates a file |
| 10 | NFSPROC_REMOVE | Removes a directory entry from a directory |
| 11 | NFSPROC_RENAME | Renames a file |
| 12 | NFSPROC_LINK | Creates a hard link to a file |
| 13 | NFSPROC_SYMLINK | Creates a symbolic link to a file |
| 14 | NFSPROC_MKDIR | Creates a directory |
| 15 | NFSPROC_RMDIR | Removes a directory |
| 16 | NFSPROC_READDIR | Reads a directory |
| 17 | NFSPROC_STATFS | Gets the file system attributes |

# ChameleonNFS

ChameleonNFS is manufactured by NetManage and is an application suite that provides other services such as e-mail, messaging, collaboration, host access, browsing, gopher clients, file and print sharing, and so on. ChameleonNFS provides an NFS client and an NFS server. Both NFS client and NFS server can run on a Windows 9x or Windows NT computer that is configured with TCP/IP.

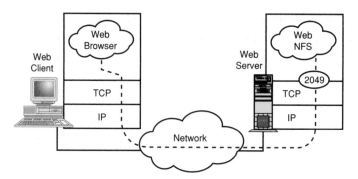

**Figure 13.4** Web NFS.

### Installing ChameleonNFS

ChameleonNFS comes on a CD-ROM distribution media, as does most Windows software. Prior to installing ChameleonNFS, you should install and configure TCP/IP on the system. If you are using Windows 9x, you can use the ChameleonNFS TCP/IP stack or the Microsoft TCP/IP stack. It is suggested, however, that you use the Microsoft TCP/IP stack, which is a 32-bit stack, whereas the ChameleonNFS TCP/IP stack has some 16-bit aspects to the code. For Windows NT, you should use the TCP/IP stack that comes with Windows NT; there is no TCP/IP stack for Windows NT from NetManage.

The installation procedure is similar to that for most Windows applications. After inserting the CD, the installation program runs. You are prompted for the key code and serial number that come with the product. The key code and serial number uniquely stamps the ChameleonNFS software installed on your system. The rest of the procedure involves a series of mouse clicks as you respond to the choices displayed on the screen. The system needs to be restarted before you can use ChameleonNFS.

### Configuring ChameleonNFS

After you install ChameleonNFS, you must configure the NFS client and the NFS server. Typically, you would install the NFS server on a special server machine and the NFS client on the Windows client machines. However, you can install both NFS client and NFS server on the same machine.

### Configuring the NFS Client Authenticator

All mount requests from a Windows computer are first authenticated using the PCN-FSD service. The *PCNFSD service* is an NFS daemon (process) that runs on the NFS server. The purpose of this service is to authenticate a username and password before attempting to mount a network drive. The PCNFSD service authenticates the username and password to a user account on the NFS server. The details of how this mapping is to be performed is part of the configuration at the NFS server. For example, you can map all user accounts specified by NFS clients to a common user account on the NFS server; or you can provide a table of user account mappings from the NFS clients to the user accounts on the NFS server; or you can specify that the user accounts from the NFS clients map to the same name user account on the NFS server.

The NFS server software comes with instructions on how to install PCNFSD on the server. On UNIX systems, the source code for the PCNFSD is usually included along with the script to compile the program and produce an executable binary program that must be run on the NFS server.

Usually the PCNFSD service runs on the server from which you mount the disk. However, if PCNFSD is not running on the server being mounted, you need to specify a central authentication server running PCNFSD to authenticate the mount request. You can do this by using the NFS Config program in ChameleonNFS.

To configure the NFS authentication in the NFS client use the following steps:

1. Log on to the Windows computer. On a Windows NT computer log on as an Administrator user.

2. Open the Control Panel (Start, Settings, Control Panel).

3. If ChameleonNFS was installed correctly, you will see the NFS Config icon.

4. Double-click on the NFS Config icon. You will see the NFS Config dialog box (see Figure 13.5).

5. If PCNFSD is being used to provide the authentication, you can set the Username field to the System Login Name. Alternatively, you can specify a special username of "nobody." The user account nobody maps to a special user account on the NFS server with limited access. The nobody account essentially acts as a guest account for NFS clients that do not specify authentication. When the user account nobody is specified, the PCNFSD authentication is not being used.

6. If the PCNFSD is not running on the NFS server whose file system is being mounted, you can specify the authenticator's IP address or host name in the Authenticator field.

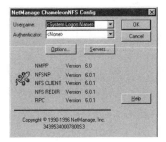

**Figure 13.5** NFS Configuration.

7. If you click on the Options button, you will see the options that can be set for the Windows client (see Figure 13.6). You can use this screen to set the Read and Write buffer sizes and the default umask value. The umask value is used on the NFS server to set default permissions for the files that are created on the NFS server.

### Configuring the NFS Server

If you are using ChameleonNFS as an NFS server, you must perform additional configuration. The following is an outline of the NFS server configuration:

1. Log on to the Windows computer. On a Windows NT computer, log on as an Administrator user.

2. Start the NFS Server. The NFS Server is installed in the Chameleon File & Print program group.

3. If this is the first time you have started the NFS server, you will see the NFS Server screen (see Figure 13.7).

4. Although the NFS server is running, there are initially no directories that are exported. You must therefore select the directories on the NFS server that must be exported for use by other NFS clients. To do this, click Exports on the menu bar. You should see the NFS Server Exports screen (see Figure 13.8). Exporting a directory using NFS is similar to sharing a directory in a Windows network, with the difference that NFS protocols are used to perform sharing and accessing the shared directory.

5. Highlight the directory to be exported and click the Add button. Figure 13.9 shows that the directory /c/kalpa is being exported. The drive letters C:, D:, and so on, are represented as /c and /d. Thus to export the entire C: drive on the NFS server you would use /c.

**Figure 13.6** NFS Options.

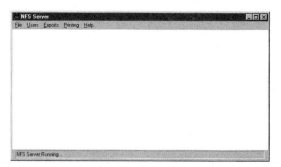

**Figure 13.7** NFS Server screen.

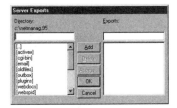 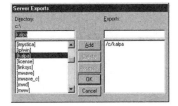

**Figure 13.8**   NFS Server Exports screen.     **Figure 13.9**   Sample directory being exported.

6. Next, you can specify the users who have access to the exported directory. If you do not specifically restrict users, all users can potentially access the directory. You can use this feature to restrict access to the exported directory. Highlight the directory that has been exported in the Exports list, and click the Access button. You should see the Directory screen (see Figure 13.10).

7. Highlight the user that appears on the user list and select the Add button to add that user to the access list (see Figure 13.11). You can add only those users that your server knows about by defining the users through the Users option in the menu bar. The following section, "Defining NFS Server Users," discusses how to define users.

8. Add other directories to the exports list as desired, and optionally restrict access to the directory.

9. Select OK to save your changes.

### Defining NFS Server Users

In order to restrict access to a directory for a user, that user must be defined on the NFS server. You can do this by using the following procedure:

1. Log on to the Windows computer. On a Windows NT computer, log on as an Administrator user.

2. Start the NFS Server. The NFS Server is installed in the Chameleon File & Print program group.

3. Select Users from the menu bar. You should see the Server Users screen (see Figure 13.12).

4. You can specify the local user account that a remote user maps to. You do this by specifying the local user and password for the Windows computer on which NFS is running. You specify the remote user account that maps to the local user account. Remote users have a UID (user identification) and a GID (group identification) associated with them. *UID* and *GID* values are 16-bit number values that identify user and group accounts on UNIX systems. Because of the initial NFS implementation on UNIX systems, you encounter UID and GID values in NFS. You can optionally specify the remote host on which the UID and GID

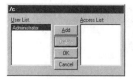

**Figure 13.10** Restricting access to an export-ed directory.  **Figure 13.11** Adding users to the access list.

values are specified. If the remote host value is not specified, the UID and GID values could exist on any remote host. After specifying the required values, select Add.

5. When you are done adding to the users list, select Save to save your changes.

6. Next, select Cancel to exit the Server Users screen.

### Using the NFS Client

To mount an exported file system from a Windows computer, you create a drive mapping to the exported NFS directory. This procedure is similar to mapping a drive on a file server such as a Windows NT server or a NetWare server. You can create a drive mapping from Windows Explorer or by right-clicking the My Computer icon on the desktop and selecting Map Network Drive.

Figure 13.13 shows the screen for mapping a network drive from an NFS client. Enter the path name to map to, using the following notation:

```
\\hostname/path
```

For *hostname*, substitute the IP address or valid hostname. Use the NFS–style syntax for pathname. For example, to mount a directory called C:\SHARED on host 199.245.180.102, you would use the following syntax:

```
\\199.245.180.102/c/shared
```

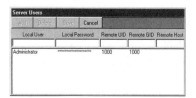

**Figure 13.12** Server users screen.

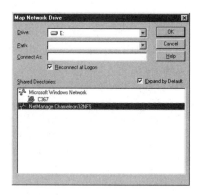

**Figure 13.13** Mapping a network drive screen.

# TCP/IP Mail Services for Microsoft Networks

M AIL SERVICES IS PERHAPS THE MOST widely used application on the Internet. Traditionally, mail services have been hosted on UNIX computers. However, mail services can also be hosted on Windows NT computers. In a pure Microsoft–based network it may be advantageous to host mail services on Windows NT computers because of the network administrator's familiarity with the system.

Several protocols for mail services are available, but the most widely used is Simple Mail Transfer Protocol (SMTP). Because of the large number of mobile and workstation users on the Internet, other support protocols such as POP3 (Post Office version 3) and IMAP4 (Internet Message Access Protocol version 4) have also been developed.

Many Microsoft networks use Microsoft Exchange as their internal mail services application. Microsoft Exchange uses a proprietary mail services protocol and has a provision for a gateway for Internet mail. Mail gateways that convert from a proprietary mail protocol to the Internet's SMTP mail protocol are called SMTP gateways.

## Simple Mail Transfer Protocol (SMTP)

SMTP allows ASCII text messages to be sent to mailboxes on TCP/IP hosts that have been configured with mail services. Figure 14.1 shows a mail session that uses SMTP. A user wishing to send mail interacts with the local mail system through the User Agent (UA) component of the mail system. The mail is deposited in a local mail outgoing mailbox. A sender-SMTP process periodically polls the outgoing box and when it finds a mail message in the box, it establishes a TCP connection on port 25 with the destination host to which mail is to be sent. The Receiver-SMTP process at the destination host accepts the connection, and the mail message is sent on that connection. The Receiver-SMTP process deposits the mail message in the destination mailbox on the destination host. If there is no mailbox with the specified name on the destination host, a mail message is sent to the originator, indicating that the mailbox does not exist. The sender-SMTP and receiver-SMTP processes that are responsible for the transfer of mail are called Message Transfer Agents (MTAs).

Mail addresses that are used in SMTP follow the RFC 822 standard. The mail headers are often referred to as *822 headers*. An example of an 822 address follows:

`KSS@SHIVA.COM`

The text string before the @ symbol specifies the mailbox name, and the text string after it specifies the hostname. If the mailbox name contains special characters such as %, the mailbox name contains a special encoding that is used by mail gateways. In the mail address of `KSS@SHIVA.COM`, the text string `KSS` is the name of the mailbox on host `SHIVA.COM`.

If you wish to send non-text messages using SMTP, you can encode the message as a text message by using the `UUENCODE` utility that is available on many systems. The receiver will have to decode the encoded message using a utility called `UUDECODE`. Another way of sending non-text messages is to use the MIME protocol. MIME (Multipurpose Internet Mail Extensions) is described in RFCs 1896, 2045, 2046, and 2049. MIME is used to describe different content types such as plain text, richly formatted text, image, audio, video, HTML documents, and so on (see Figure 14.2).

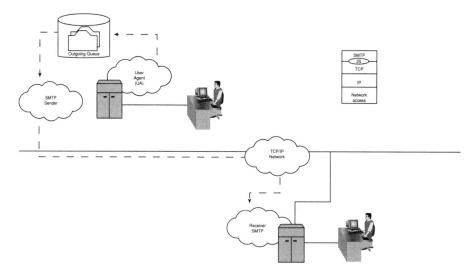

**Figure 14.1** SMTP user session.

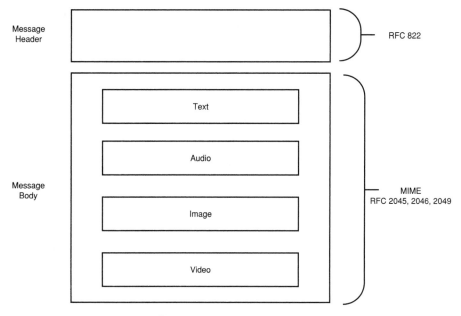

**Figure 14.2** MIME message.

MIME message bodies can have nested contents, and MIME user agents can select among alternative representations of contents. For example, if a dumb terminal that does not have the capability to display an audio/video message is used, it can display the text portion of this message. Another useful feature of MIME is that it can use a pointer to reference data that is stored elsewhere. For example, the pointer can refer to a document on an FTP site. This saves having to include the document in every mail message that is sent out on a mail distribution list. Only users who are interested in the document on the FTP site need retrieve this document.

The mail messages are sent using SMTP commands. Tables 14.1 and 14.2 show the SMTP sender and receiver commands for a minimum implementation. All SMTP commands are four letters long. The SMTP receiver is typically a mail server and responds to SMTP commands with three digit status codes that have the following syntax:

`DDD   Text message`

`DDD` is the three-digit status code.

Figure 14.3 shows an SMTP session using some of these commands. Notice that in this example, mail is being sent from the user `kss@scs.psi.com`, identified by the MAIL command.

The mail is being sent to `jones@scs.psi.com` and `bob@ltree.psi.com`. Note that the mailbox `bob@ltree.psi.com` does not exist, so an error message (`550` status code) is returned to indicate that there is no such user. The mail server responds to all other commands with a status code of `250`.

SMTP–related standards documents are described in Table 14.3.

Table 14.1 **SMTP Sender (Client) Commands for a Minimal Implementation**

| Command | Meaning |
|---|---|
| HELO *sender* | Connection request from a sender-SMTP. |
| MAIL FROM: *fromaddr* | This command is used to initiate a mail transaction in which the mail data is delivered to one or more mailboxes. |
| RCPT TO: *sendto* | This command is used to identify an individual recipient of the mail data. Multiple recipients are specified by multiple use of this command. |
| DATA | The receiver treats the lines following the command as mail data from the sender. The mail data is terminated by a line containing only a period, which is the character sequence <CRLF>.<CRLF>. |
| QUIT | This command specifies that the receiver must send an OK reply, and then close the connection. |
| RESET | This command specifies that the current mail transaction is to be aborted. |
| NOOP | This is a "no operation" command. It specifies no action other than that the receiver send an OK reply. Can be used as a diagnostic aid to check whether the receiver responds with an OK reply. |

Table 14.2 **Example SMTP Receiver (Mail Server) Commands**

| Command | Meaning |
|---|---|
| 250 | Requested mail action okay, completed. |
| 251 | User not local; will forward to <*forward-path*>. |
| 450 | Requested mail action not taken: mailbox unavailable. For example, mailbox is busy. |
| 550 | Requested action not taken: mailbox unavailable. |
| 451 | Requested action aborted: error in processing. |
| 551 | User not local; please try <*forward-path*>. |
| 452 | Requested action not taken: insufficient system storage. |
| 552 | Requested mail action aborted: exceeded storage allocation. |
| 553 | Requested action not taken: mailbox name not allowed. For example, mailbox syntax may be incorrect. |
| 354 | Start mail input; end with <CRLF>.<CRLF>. |
| 554 | Transaction failed. |
| 521 | Incoming mail not accepted. |

**Example SMTP Session**

```
S:   HELO machine
R:   HELO machine,  Pleased to meet you

S:   MAIL FROM:   kss@scs.psi.com
R:   250 OK

S:   RCPT To:        jones@scs.psi.com
R:   250 OK

S:   RCPT To:        bob@ltree.psi.com  }  User bob does not have a
R:   550 No such user here                  mailbox at ltree.psi.com

S:   RCPT To:        john@ltree.psi.com
R:   250 OK

S:   DATA
R:   354 Start mail input; end with <CRLF>.<CRLF>
S:   message text
S:   message text
S:   message text_etc.
S:   <CRLF>.<CRLF>
R:   250 OK
```

**R** = SMTP receiver
**S** = SMTP sender

**Figure 14.3**  Example SMTP session showing SMTP commands.

Table 14.3  **SMTP–Related Standard RFCs**

| Protocol | Name | Status | RFC# | STD# |
|----------|------|--------|------|------|
| SMTP | Simple Mail Transfer Protocol | Rec | 821 | 10 |
| SMTP-SIZE | SMTP Service Ext for Message Size | Rec | 1870 | 10 |
| SMTP-EXT | SMTP Service Extensions | Rec | 1869 | 10 |
| MAIL | Format of Electronic Mail Messages | Rec | 822 | 11 |

# Post Office Protocol Version 3 (POP3)

SMTP expects the destination host—the mail server—receiving the mail to be online. Otherwise, a TCP connection could not be established with the destination host. For this reason, it is not practical to establish an SMTP session with a desktop for receiving mail, because desktop workstations are often turned off at the end of the day.

In many network environments, SMTP mail is received by an SMTP host that is always active on the network (see Figure 14.4). This SMTP host provides a mail drop service. Workstations interact with the SMTP host and retrieve messages using a client/server mail protocol, such as POP3 (Post Office Protocol, Version 3), described in RFC 1939. POP3 uses the TCP transport protocol and the POP3 server listens on TCP port number 110.

Note that although POP3 is used to download messages from the server, SMTP is still used to forward messages from the workstation user to its SMTP mail server.

Tables 14.4, 14.5, and 14.6 list the POP3 commands and replies based on the RFC 1939 specification. Although the USER and PASS commands (see Table 14.5) are listed as optional commands in RFC 1939, most POP3 implementations support these commands. The USER and PASS commands can be regarded as optional because they can be replaced by the MD5 (Message Digest version 5) authentication method used in the APOP command.

Figure 14.5 shows a sample interaction between a POP3 client and POP server that uses some of the commands listed in Tables 14.4 through 14.6.

This sample POP3 session shows that the POP3 session initially enters into a *connection state*. In the connection state the TCP connection with the POP3 server is established. Next, the POP3 session enters into the *authorization state*. In this state, the user must provide a username and password to be authenticated by the POP3 server.

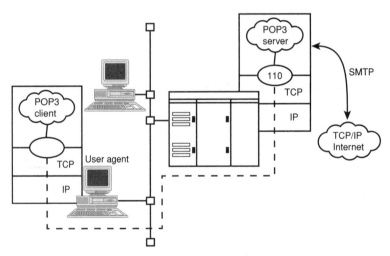

- **Message Transfer Agent (MTA) is run on a computer with more resources than that available to the workstation**
  - Offers a "maildrop" service to smaller nodes, such as workstations

- **POP3 provides dynamic access to maildrop server**

Figure 14.4   POP3 client/server.

Table 14.4  **Required POP3 Commands**

| Command | Meaning |
| --- | --- |
| STAT | Used to specify a positive response consisting of +OK followed by a single space, the number of messages in the maildrop, a single space, and the size of the maildrop in octets. Sample response: +OK *msgid size*. |
| LIST [*msg*] | When a message number is specified, it returns the scan listing for the message, such as its message number and size. When no message number is specified, a positive response is returned and then the response goes multiline, in which each line contains a scan listing of all messages waiting at the mailbox. |
| RETR *msg* | Used to retrieve a list of messages waiting for the user mailbox at the POP3 server. The POP3 server issues an initial positive response +OK, and then the response given is multiline. After the initial +OK, the POP3 server sends the multiline message corresponding to the specified message number. If a message cannot be found, the -ERR response is returned. |
| DELE *msg* | Marks the specified message as deleted. |
| NOOP | No Operation. The POP3 server does nothing, it merely replies with a positive response: +OK. Can be used as a diagnostic to check whether the POP3 connection is okay. |
| RSET | Unmarks any messages marked as deleted by the POP3 server. The POP3 server then replies with a positive response: +OK. Example response might be +OK maildrop has 3 messages (430 octets). |
| QUIT | The POP3 server removes all messages marked as deleted from the maildrop and replies as to the status of this operation: +OK or -ERR. The POP3 server releases any exclusive-access lock on the maildrop and closes the TCP connection. |

After the user has been authorized, the POP3 session enters the *transaction state*. In the transaction state, a number of commands such as STAT, LIST, RETR, DELE, RSET, and so on, can be issued. In Figure 14.5, the POP3 client issues a STAT command and the server returns the number of messages with a total size (1729 octets) of these messages. The POP3 client then uses the LIST command to ask for a list of all the messages. The POP3 server returns the message numbers for each message and its corresponding size. The client then issues the RETR commands and specifies each message identifier that is to be downloaded. Depending on the setting at the POP3 client, the POP3 client may issue a DELE command to delete a message that has been retrieved.

### Authentication in POP3

In earlier POP3 implementations, the username and password authentication information is sent as clear text and is susceptible to compromise. This means that someone examining the POP3 packet trace can discover the username and password combination. In POP3, as specified in RFC 1939, however, an alternative, more secure authentication method based on MD5 can be used.

Table 14.5  **Optional POP3 Commands**

| Command | Meaning |
| --- | --- |
| USER *name* | Used to specify the name string to identify a mailbox. |
| PASS *string* | Specifies a server/mailbox-specific password for the username. |
| TOP *msg n* | The POP3 server sends an +OK response, then the headers of the specified message, *msg*; then a blank line followed by *n* lines in the indicated message body. If the number of lines requested by the POP3 client is greater than the number of lines in the message body, the POP3 server sends the entire message. |
| UIDL [*msg*] | Used to return a unique identifier listing (UIDL) for the message. The POP3 server sends an +OK response with a line containing information for that message. This line is called a *unique-id listing* for that message. If no argument was given and the POP3 server issues a positive response, +OK, then the response goes multiline. After the initial +OK, for each message in the maildrop, the POP3 server responds with a line containing information for that message. A unique identifier listing consists of the message-number of the message, followed by a single space and the unique-id of the message. |
| APOP *name digest* | The *name* is a string that identifies the mailbox, and *digest* is the MD5 (Message Digest version 5) digest string. This is used to provide an alternate authentication method to the normal USER/PASS exchange, which is sent as clear text. The APOP authentication-method provides for both origin authentication and replay protection. More important, with APOP, the password is not sent in the clear over the network. |

Table 14.6  **POP3 Server Replies**

| Command | Meaning |
| --- | --- |
| +OK | Command was executed correctly |
| -ERR | Command execution resulted in error |

After the messages have been downloaded, the POP3 session enters the *update state*. In the update state, the POP3 client issues a QUIT command to close the connection. Both a POP3 client and a POP3 server may then update their internal states to reflect the new count of messages in their respective mail boxes. The TCP connection is then closed.

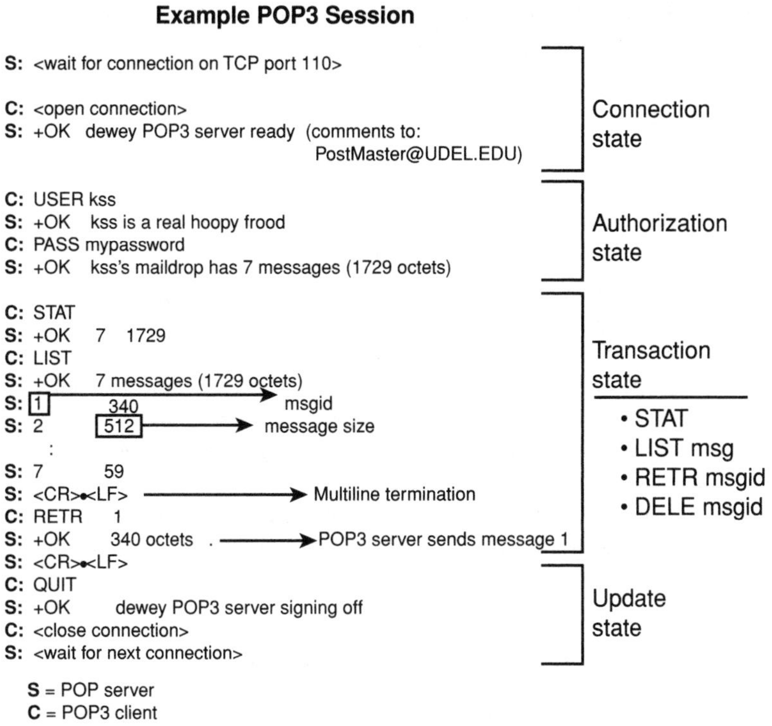

**Example POP3 Session**

```
S: <wait for connection on TCP port 110>

C: <open connection>
S: +OK   dewey POP3 server ready  (comments to:
                              PostMaster@UDEL.EDU)

C: USER kss
S: +OK   kss is a real hoopy frood
C: PASS mypassword
S: +OK   kss's maildrop has 7 messages (1729 octets)

C: STAT
S: +OK    7   1729
C: LIST
S: +OK    7 messages (1729 octets)
S: 1      340            ─────────► msgid
S: 2      512  ──────────► message size
      :
S: 7      59
S: <CR><LF>  ─────────────► Multiline termination
C: RETR    1
S: +OK       340 octets  . ───────► POP3 server sends message 1
S: <CR><LF>
C: QUIT
S: +OK        dewey POP3 server signing off
C: <close connection>
S: <wait for next connection>
```

```
                    ┐
                    │  Connection
                    │  state
                    ┘
                    ┐
                    │  Authorization
                    │  state
                    ┘
                    ┐
                    │  Transaction
                    │  state
                    ├─────────────
                    │   • STAT
                    │   • LIST msg
                    │   • RETR msgid
                    │   • DELE msgid
                    ┘
                    ┐
                    │  Update
                    │  state
                    ┘
```

   **S** = POP server
   **C** = POP3 client

Figure 14.5   POP3 sample session.

# Internet Message Access Protocol, Rev 4 (IMAP4)

Although POP3 has served well as a client/server protocol for workstations to download their email messages, it has a number of weaknesses, such as the fact that the mail must be downloaded to the workstation before it can be manipulated. It does not permit the direct manipulation of mail messages at the server. For this reason, IMAP4 has been proposed as a replacement to POP3.

IMAP4 allows a client/server protocol designed to access and manipulate electronic mail messages on a server. This protocol permits manipulation of remote message folders, called *mailboxes*, in a way that is functionally equivalent to local mailboxes. IMAP4 also provides the capability for an offline client to resynchronize its mailboxes with the server.

IMAP4 client features include the following:

■ Accessing and manipulating portions of email messages on a server without downloading them

■ Reviewing messages and attachments without downloading them

- Downloading all messages for offline operation
- Resynchronizing local mailboxes with those at the server

IMAP4 provides operations such as the following:

- Creating, deleting, and renaming mailboxes
- Checking for new messages
- Permanently removing messages from mailboxes
- Setting and clearing flags indicating status of messages
- Recognition of RFC-822 headers and parsing of MIME–encoded messages
- Searching and selective fetching of message attributes, texts, and portions thereof

Messages in IMAP4 are accessed by the use of numbers. These numbers are either message sequence numbers or unique identifiers. IMAP4 supports a single server. A mechanism for accessing configuration information to support multiple IMAP4 servers is also being considered.

Like POP3, IMAP4 does not specify a means of posting mail. This function is handled by a mail transfer protocol such as SMTP. Figure 14.6 shows the client/server interaction for IMAP4.

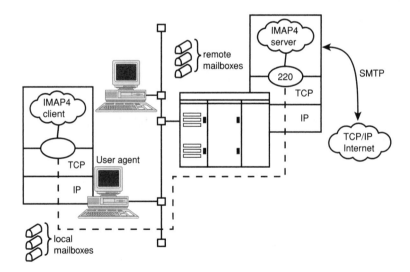

- **Message Transfer Agent (MTA) is run on a computer with more resources than that available to the workstation**
  - Offers a "maildrop" service to smaller nodes, such as workstations

- **POP3 provides dynamic access to maildrop server**

Figure 14.6   IMAP4 client/server.

The behavior of IMAP4 can be described in terms of a state diagram (see Figure 14.7). As Figure 14.7 illustrates, IMAP4 can be in one of four states. Most IMAP4 commands are valid only in a particular state. A protocol error is generated if an IMAP4 client attempts a command in an inappropriate state. The following IMAP4 states are defined:

- **Non-authenticated state.** In the *non-authenticated state*, the IMAP4 client supplies authentication credentials. Most commands will not be permitted unless the client has been authenticated. This state is entered when a connection starts unless the connection has been pre-authenticated.

- **Authenticated state.** In the *authenticated state*, the client is authenticated and must select a mailbox. This must be done before commands that affect messages are permitted. This state is entered when a pre-authenticated connection starts, or when acceptable authentication credentials have been provided. If an error is made in selecting a mailbox, this state is re-entered so that another mailbox can be selected.

- **Selected state.** The *selected state* is entered after a valid mailbox has been successfully selected.

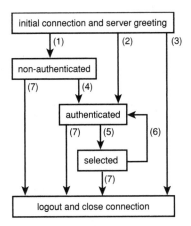

(1) connection without pre-authentication (OK greeting)
(2) pre-authenticated connection (PREAUTH greeting)
(3) rejected connection (BYE greeting)
(4) successful LOGIN or AUTHENTICATE command
(5) successful SELECT or EXAMINE command
(6) CLOSE command, or failed SELECT or EXAMINE command
(7) LOGOUT command, server shutdown, or connection closed

**Figure 14.7** IMAP4 state diagram.

■ **Logout state.** In the *logout state*, the connection is terminated, and the IMAP4 server closes the connection. This state can be entered as a result of a client request or by a server decision.

IMAP4 is the subject of a great deal of interest among messaging vendors. Table 14.7 describes the IMAP4–related RFCs.

# Mail Services Implementation in Windows NT

The Microsoft Resource Kit for Windows NT comes with a mail services implementation. At the moment of this writing, the mail services in Microsoft Resource Kit for Windows NT Server version 4 has only been tested; the Microsoft Resource Kit for Windows NT 5 has not been released. The mail services in Microsoft Resource Kit for Windows NT version 4 works fine with Windows NT Server version 5.

In addition to the Microsoft Resource Kit for Windows NT, there are a number of third-party products such as NetManage's mail services for Windows NT.

## Mail Services in Microsoft Resource Kit for Windows NT

The Windows NT security provides a high level of security, both for individual users and for Windows NT–based networks. However, Mail Server supports only the clear text password authentication of POP3 and does not support the APOP command that provides encrypted authentication. *Clear text* passwords are sent over the network in readable (clear) format and are not encrypted. If network security is a concern, administrators should use caution when using the Microsoft Mail Server utility.

The following sections discuss the capabilities of the Resource Kit mail service components.

Table 14.7 **IMAP4–Related RFCs**

| RFC# | Status | RFC Title |
|------|--------|-----------|
| 2095 | PS | IMAP/POP AUTHorize Extension for Simple Challenge/Response |
| 2088 | PS | IMAP4 non-synchronizing literals |
| 2087 | PS | IMAP4 QUOTA extension |
| 2086 | PS | IMAP4 ACL extension |
| 2061 | I | IMAP4 COMPATIBILITY WITH IMAP2BIS |
| 2060 | PS | INTERNET MESSAGE ACCESS PROTOCOL — VERSION 4rev1 |
| 1733 | I | DISTRIBUTED ELECTRONIC MAIL MODELS IN IMAP4 |
| 1732 | I | IMAP4 COMPATIBILITY WITH IMAP2 AND IMAP2BIS |
| 1731 | PS | IMAP4 Authentication mechanisms |

### Overview of Mail Services in Microsoft Resource Kit for Windows NT

The Mail Server program is implemented by `Mailsrv.exe` and is a basic SMTP (Simple Mail Transport Protocol) and POP3 (Post Office Protocol) service for Windows NT Server. `Mailsrv.exe` supports Internet-based mail clients and is completely separate from the Microsoft Mail program.

The intermediate files required by Mail Server and the mailboxes are all spooled on the Windows NT server that is running the service. They are kept in special spool files in the SPOOL subdirectory where the Mail Server is installed. The spooled mail can be accessed through a public-domain or commercial POP3 client. Mail Server automatically creates a mail folder with secured permissions the first time the user's account receives mail or the first time the user checks their mail via a POP client.

### Installation of Mail Services from Microsoft Resource Kit for Windows NT

Because Mail Server is integrated with the local account database for Windows NT, it must be installed on a local NTFS (Windows NT File System) drive. The installation will fail if you attempt to use a network or non-NTFS drive for your spool directory.

The Mailsrv installation requirements are as follows:

- The spool directory must be on a local drive.
- This local drive must be formatted NTFS.
- The NT system should be installed on an NTFS drive.

The Mail Server installation program (INSTALL.EXE) adds Mail Server and the supporting services to the Service Controller and starts Mail Server.

The following outlines the procedure for installing mail services from the Microsoft Resource Kit for Windows NT:

1. Log on to the Windows NT computer as an Administrator user.
2. Insert the Resource Kit CD in the CD-ROM drive. You will see the initial screen for installing the resource kit.
3. Select the option to install the Resource Kit.
4. Accept the license agreement.
5. Enter your name and organization, and confirm this information when asked.
6. Click OK to accept the default folder to install the Resource Kit or select an alternate folder.
7. You can select the Typical installation, which installs most of the common components, or Custom/Specific installation, which you can use to select the specific components that you want to install. The mail services are installed in either situation.
8. If you selected Custom/Specific, you will see a list of components. At the very least, you should check the Internet and TCP/IP components and continue with the installation.

9. You will see a status of files copied and a message that the installation is complete.

10. Exit the installation program. You are now ready to configure the mail services.

11. A new program folder called Resource Kit should be installed under the Programs folder.

12. To install the mail services, select Programs, Resource Kit, Internet Utls, Install Mail Service.

13. You will see a choice to install or deinstall the mail service components on to the system. Select the install option.

14. You will see a choice for selecting the directory where you want the mail service components to be installed. You can accept the default value or enter your own directory of choice.

15. Click OK and confirm the creation of the mail service directory if so prompted.

16. Restart the computer and log on as Administrator user.

17. Check the services that are running to see if the SMTP server and POP3 server have started. You can do this by selecting Programs, Administrative Tools, System Service Management. Figure 14.8 shows the SMTP and POP3 services are started automatically when the system starts. Also, the DNS server must be configured with an A (address) record as well as an MX (mail exchange) record for the mail server.

When the Mail Server program runs, it registers the following services that can be viewed using the System Service Management:

- **SMTP Server.** Responsible for receiving/sending SMTP mail.
- **POP3 Server.** Responsible for POP2/POP3 clients and requests.

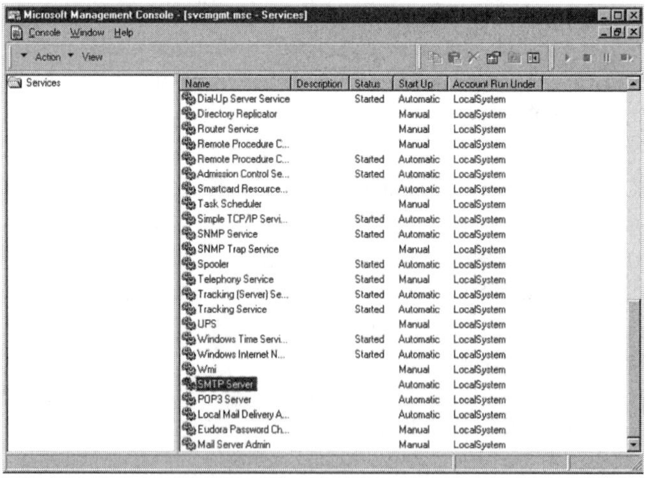

**Figure 14.8** SMTP and POP3 services running on Windows NT.

- **Local Mail Delivery Agent.** Responsible for delivery of local mail.
- **Eudora Password Change Server.** Responsible for Eudora password change requests. By default, the Eudora Password Change Server service is not enabled because it allows password changes based on unencrypted requests. To enable this service, go into the System Service Management and change the service's state to enabled.
- **Mail Server Admin.** An administration program that is not fully operational in the current release of Mail Server.

### Mail-Server-Specific Registry Entries

Installation of Mail Server creates specific registry entries under the following key:

```
HKEY_LOCAL_MACHINE\System\CurrentControlSet\Services\MailSrv
```

The parameter values (see Figure 14.9) under this key include the following:

- **Mail Directory.** The top of the mail directory hierarchy.
- **Logging Level.** This specifies flags indicating how much information to place in the event log.
- **SMTP Retry.** This specifies the retry interval in seconds for outbound SMTP messages.
- **Local Retry.** This specifies the retry interval in seconds for local messages.
- **SMTP Gateway.** This specifies the gateway to use for all SMTP mail (no DNS resolving is done).
- **Inbound Transforms.** This specifies the rules that are applied to addresses coming in.
- **Outbound Transforms.** This specifies the rules that are applied to addresses going out.
- **Aliases.** This specifies one alias per line. Multiple alias lines can be listed. Aliases are completely dynamic. The key name corresponds to the incoming name, and the key value is the alias it should be transformed into. Two examples are placed in the Registry entry during installation: one for Postmaster, which is required and must not be deleted, and one for `MAILER_DAEMON`.

There are additionally the following dependent Registry entries under the `HKEY_LOCAL_MACHINE\System\CurrentControlSet\Services\Tcpip` that are used in the transformation rules:

- **Domain.** Used by the `$(Domain)` token as the system's domain.
- **DhcpDomain.** If above `Domain` key is invalid, this key is queried for the `$(Domain)` value. One of these two keys must contain valid information.
- **Hostname.** Used by the `$(Me)` token as the computer's name.
- **NameServer.** IP addresses of the DNS servers to be used for name resolution.
- **DhcpNameServer.** IP address of the DNS servers to be used for name resolution.

**Figure 14.9**   Mail Server Registry Keys.

### Mail Server Transform Rules

*Transforms* are rules applied to addresses coming in and going out on Mail Server. Their primary purpose is to allow domain owners to mask out the computer names (hostnames) and/or domain names within the domain.

Inbound transforms and outbound transforms are each of type `REG_MULTI_SZ`. Each line in the `MULTI_SZ` is a transform, and is searched in the order of its appearance. If a rule matches, it is applied, and the search is completed. If no rules are matched, the address remains unchanged.

Each transform takes the following format:

*pattern > transformed pattern*

Consider the following pattern, which may appear as part of the transformation rule:

`$1@$2`

If an email address `kss@mic.com` is supplied, it is tokenized as follows:

`$1 = kss`
`$2 = mic.com`

If the previous pattern was `$1@$2.bitnet` and the email address was `kss@siyan.bitnet`, then the email address will be tokenized as follows:

`$1 = kss`
`$2 = siyan`

Consider the following transform:

`$1@$2.bitnet > $1%$2.bitnet@bitnetgateway.org`

The previous email address of `kss@siyan.bitnet` would be translated as follows:
`Tokenized email address components:`

`$1 = kss`
`$2 = siyan`

The transformation will result in the following address:

`kss%siyan.bitnet@bitnetgateway.org`

Without the `%` symbol there would be two occurrences of the `@` symbol and this would be an invalid email address. Therefore the first `@` symbol is set to the special symbol `%`, in order to make it a valid email address.

In addition to the `$1` and `$2` symbols used to tokenize the email address, the following special tokens are recognized:

| | |
|---|---|
| $(Me) | corresponds to `hostname.domain` |
| $(Hostname) | corresponds to `hostname` |
| $(Domain) | corresponds to `domain` |

When Mail Server initializes it creates these tokens by querying specific keys in the registry. The `$(Domain)` key is read from the registry entry:

`HKEY_LOCAL_MACHINE\System\CurrentControlSet\Services\Tcpip\Parameters\`
`Domain`

If that entry does not exist, Mail Server tries to obtain a value for `$(Domain)` by querying the following Registry entry:

`HKEY_LOCAL_MACHINE\System\CurrentControlSet\Services\Tcpip\Parameters\`
`DhcpDomain`

The `$(Hostname)` is obtained from the following Registry key:

`HKEY_LOCAL_MACHINE\System\CurrentControlSet\Services\Tcpip\Parameters\`
`Hostname`

You should ensure that one of the above keys exists. If not, the Mail Server services will fail when initializing. If the Registry entries do not contain the correct information for the Mail Server, do not use the special tokens in your transforms.

Some additional examples of using the transformation rules will help make their application clearer. Consider the situation in which the administrator of Mail Server on the Internet wants to set up several inbound transforms so Mail Server recognizes that several different domains all correspond to the local machine:

`$1@kinetics.com > $1`
`$1@siyan.com > $1`

If Mail Server received mail for `kss@kinetics.com`, it would be transformed into mail for `kss` and queued for local delivery. If it received mail for `kss@siyan.com` it would also be transformed into `kss` and queued for local delivery. However, if `Mailsrv` received mail for `kss@rama.kinetics.com`, it would then use the outbound transforms and queue the mail for remote delivery. This is because the Mail Server would think that this is for a remote machine since no rule was matched.

So, if you want to ensure that all mail to any hostname on the `kinetics.com` domain was routed for local delivery, we could create the following inbound transforms:

```
$1@kinetics.com > $1
$1@$2.kinetics.com > $1
```

All mail destined for `kinetics.com` would be queued for local delivery. `$1` would represent the local account name. `$2` would represent any prefix to the domain name `kinetics.com`. In the example of email address `kss@rama.kinetics.com`, `$2` would be set to "`rama`" and the email address would be transformed to the local user account of `kss` for local delivery. If no local account is found by the name represented by `$1`, Mail Server will attempt to send an undeliverable mail message.

You could also accomplish the previous using the following special tokens. Assuming `$(Domain)` is equal to `kinetics.com`, this could be set up as follows:

```
$1@$(Domain) > $1
$1@$2.$(Domain) > $1
```

If `$(Domain)` is `kinetics.com`, then all mail for any host at `kinetics.com` would be queued for local delivery. You should ensure that the information in the special `$(Domain)` token is valid for the above transformation rules to work.

Consider another example that involves the outbound transforms rule. You might want to set up an outbound transforms so that the outbound mail has a different return address. Consider the following outbound transforms rule:

```
$1@$(Me) > $1@kinetics.com
$1@$(Hostname) > $1@kinetics.com
$1@$2.bitnet > $1%$2.bitnet@bitnetgateway.org
```

If the return email address is `kss@nts.kinetics.com`, on computer `nts` there would be a match with the first rule, where `$1` is set to `kss` and `$(Me)` matches `nts.kinetics.com`. The return address will be transformed to `kss@kinetics.com`.

If the return email address is `kss@nts` on computer `nts` there would be a match with the second rule, where `$1` is set to `kss` and `$(Hostname)` matches `nts`. The return address will be transformed to `kss@kinetics.com`.

If the return email address is `kss@siyan.bitnet`, there would be a match with the third rule, where `$1` is set to `kss` and `$2` is set to `siyan`. The return address will be transformed to `kss%siyan.bitnet@bitnetgateway.org`.

### Creating Email Accounts for Mail Server

Mail Server is integrated into the machine's local account database. To set up a new email account, you must create a local account for the user via User Manager. A domain user account cannot be used for the purposes of a Mail Server email account. For instance, Mail Server cannot deliver mail to a username like `DOMAIN\user1`. Instead, you must create a local user account named `user1`.

The mailbox for a user will be created by Mail Server the first time a valid local user checks for mail or receives mail. The mailbox will have secured permissions and can only be accessed by the user.

## Internet Mail Clients for Windows

There are a variety of email client packages for Windows 9x and Windows NT workstations such as PC Eudora, Zmail, Netscape Navigator, and Microsoft mail.

The user interfaces to these User Agent programs and their configuration procedures are different, although they provide comparable features. Regardless of the email client package, the following information needs to be configured for the email client:

- SMTP server
- POP3 server
- IMAP4 server
- User name and password on mail server

The SMTP server is set to the domain name or IP address of the server used for sending the email. The email client packages use SMTP for sending mail.

The POP3 server is set to the domain name or IP address of the server used as a maildrop server for receiving email for users. The email client packages use POP3 for receiving mail. Usually, the SMTP server is the same as the POP3 server.

The IMAP4 server is set to the domain name or IP address of the server used as an IMAP4 server. This needs to be set only if the email client supports IMAP4 and you are planning on using IMAP4. For example, the latest versions of Zmail and Netscape Communicator support the IMAP4 protocol.

The username and password are for the local user account on the mail server.

### Password Settings for Mail Account

You should ensure that the account flag User Must Change Password at Next Logon is not set when a user checks the mail for an account. If set, this flag will cause an error when the user tries to retrieve mail from a mailbox.

# Diagnostic Tools for Microsoft TCP/IP Networks

T HIS CHAPTER DISCUSSES SEVERAL DIAGNOSTIC TOOLS that are useful in troubleshooting Microsoft TCP/IP networks. These diagnostic tools ship with the
Windows operating system and include tools for testing the ability to reach hosts on
the network, examining the address resolution tables, and testing the path to a specific
destination. Other tools give statistical information on the network and protocols used
on the network.

## Using ICMP and PING for Troubleshooting

One of the most widely used tools for troubleshooting is the PING tool. *PING* is an
acronym that stands for Packet InterNet Groper. The PING tools send a message of a
certain size to another TCP/IP node. The destination node returns the message as a
reply. If the message does not come back, you can deduce that the network or host is
down or the packet was lost in transmission. The PING tool usually repeats the test a
certain number of times. You can also set up the PING tool to send packets continuously. The PING tool that ships with Windows NT is a command-line tool.

### PING and the Internet Control Message Protocol (ICMP)

The PING tool actually uses the Internet Control Message Protocol (ICMP). ICMP is
a versatile protocol that is used to report error conditions and information about the

network. ICMP defines many different types of messages dealing with troubleshooting and reporting problems with protocol or network operation. The PING tool uses two of the message types for ICMP: Echo Request (message type = 8) and Echo Reply (message type = 0). The PING tool sends an Echo Request packet to the destination host, and the destination host replies with an ICMP Echo Reply packet.

ICMP is implemented as part of the IP module modules (see Figure 15.1), and as per the RFCs is required to be implemented in all IP. In terms of protocol layering, however, ICMP sits on top of IP (see Figure 15.2). In other words, ICMP is encapsulated by an IP header. This fact is significant because it allows the ICMP message encapsulated by an IP header to be routed through IP routers. An IP router can only forward IP Datagrams. This means that ICMP messages (and also PING messages) can traverse arbitrarily complex networks connected by IP routers.

Figure 15.3 shows how the PING utility might be used. This figure shows the situation where PING can be used to test the ability to reach local and remote hosts—which can be Windows computers or any computer that is configured with TCP/IP. In Figure 15.3, host B is local to host A, and host C is remote from host A. The ICMP messages sent between A and C are treated as normal IP datagrams by the intervening routers and do not get any special consideration. If ICMP messages get lost, no attempt is made to re-send the ICMP message.

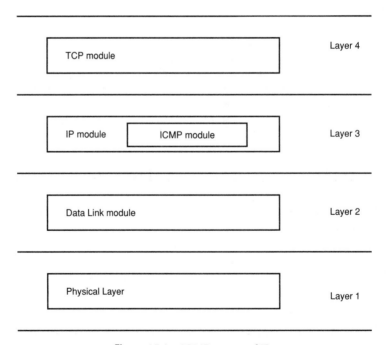

**Figure 15.1** ICMP as part of IP.

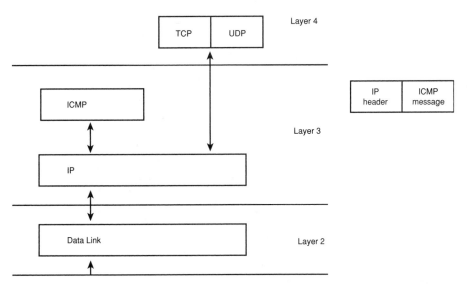

**Figure 15.2**  ICMP layered on IP.

The PING utility is used to generate the ICMP Echo Request message. The IP module running on the destination node responds to ICMP messages automatically. There is no need to run any special software on destination nodes to generate the ICMP Echo Reply. This means that all IP nodes on an internet are capable of responding to ICMP Echo Request messages generated by the PING utility.

There is no standard for the options and capabilities provided by the PING utility, although most implementations provide similar services. The actual syntax for invoking the PING utility is operating system-dependent, although similarities do exist in many operating systems, especially between the Windows NT and UNIX operating systems. Most operating system implementations provide a command-line version of the PING utility that is appropriately called *ping*, although graphical implementations may also be available. Most implementations of the PING utility give an estimated round-trip delay measured in seconds and statistics about datagram loss. There are also a number of options that are available with some implementations of the PING utility. For example, you can use options to send various sizes of data in each ICMP Echo Request message, and control the time interval between the sending of Echo Requests. In Windows NT, the time interval is a second between the sending of Echo Requests unless you use the option to ping continuously until interrupted (option-t). If the option is used to ping continuously, Windows NT sends Echo Requests as fast as it can. This can cause a substantial amount of network traffic, which could slow the network. Some PING utilities allow you to send different IP options, such as the IP source route option, which can be used to control the path taken by the ICMP message.

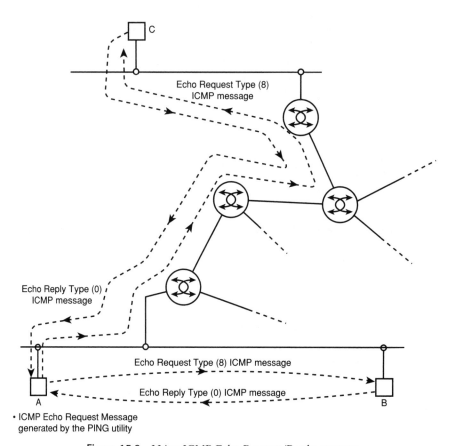

**Figure 15.3**   Using ICMP Echo Request/Reply messages.

The format of the ICMP Echo Request and Echo Reply messages are shown in Figure 15.4.

The Type field has a value of 8 for Echo Request and a value of 0 for Echo Reply. The Code field is set to 0 for both Echo Request and Echo Reply message types. The Checksum field is common to all ICMP message types and has been described earlier.

The Identifier and Sequence Number fields are used to identify the ICMP Echo Request and Echo Reply messages uniquely so that they can be properly matched. Matching is necessary because the IP network makes no guarantees that the ICMP Echo Reply messages will be sent in the correct order.

The Data field is provided so that arbitrarily sized messages can be sent. This is very useful in testing the capacity of a network to carry large Datagrams. For example, a router or host may properly handle small-sized Datagrams but not large datagrams. By using PING to send large data fields, this problem can be detected.

The Echo Reply message sends the same data that was received from the Echo Request.

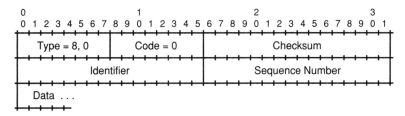

**Figure 15.4**  ICMP Echo Request/Reply format.

## Using PING

The PING tool is available on both Windows NT and Windows 9x. The PING syntax is described next:

```
PING [-t] [-a] [-n count] [-l length] [-f] [-I ttl]
[-v tos] [-r count] [-s count] [[-j computer-list] ¦
[-k computer-list]] [-w timeout] destination-list
```

| Argument | Description |
| --- | --- |
| -t | Pings repeatedly until interrupted. |
| -a | Displays the name of the computer, given the IP address, when pinging. |
| -n count | The number of times to ping the computer; the default is 4. |
| -l length | The number of bytes to send to the computer being pinged. The default is 32 bytes. |
| -f | Instructs gateways on the way to the computer not to fragment the data packet. |
| -I ttl | Sets the Time To Live field to the value ttl. |
| -v tos | Sets the Type Of Service field to the value tos. |
| -r count | Displays the route taken by the ping data. count can be between 1 and 9 routers. |
| -s count | The timestamp for the number of hops specified by count. |
| -j computer-list | Utilizes the computer-list to specify packet routes. Successive computers can be separated by transitional gateways. |
| -k computer-list | Utilizes the computer-list to specify packet routes. Successive computers cannot be separated by transitional gateways. |
| -w timeout | A timeout interval specified in milliseconds. |
| destination-list | A list of computers to ping. |

The simplest way to use PING is to specify the hostname or the IP address of the destination host as an argument to PING. For example, to ping a host with an IP address of 199.245.180.10, you would use the following command:

```
PING 199.245.180.10
```

Figure 15.5 shows the result of using this PING command. As can be seen by this command, the default size of the message is 32 bytes and the PING is repeated four times.

If you want to change the message size, you can do so using the -l option. A message size of 8192 bytes is usually larger than the MTU (Maximum Transmission Unit) size of most common networks. If you specify a large message size, you can force IP datagram fragmentation to occur on the network. The destination host is required to put the IP datagram fragments back in the original order in a process that is called IP datagram reassembly. Using a large message size can be used to test whether the destination host is handling datagram reassembly correctly. For example, to ping with the message size of 8192 bytes, you can use the following:

```
PING -l 8192 199.245.180.10
```

To ping a host for a specified number of times, use the -n option. For example, to ping a host 10 times, you can use the following:

```
PING -n 10 199.245.180.10
```

To ping repeatedly until interrupted manually, you can use the -t option:

```
PING -t 199.245.180.10
```

Figure 15.6 shows an example of a ping test where the -l and -n options are combined, using this command:

```
PING -l 8192 -n 10 199.245.180.10
```

Because of the large message size, IP datagram fragmentation occurred on this test network that had an MTU size of 1500 bytes. It is interesting to note that although the first ping test failed, the remaining nine tests succeeded. The failure of the first ping test reported as Request timed out. Upon troubleshooting the cause of the timeout using a protocol analyzer such as the Netmon tool (discussed in Chapter 6, "TCP/IP Protocol Traces"), it was detected that the request timeout was caused by an IP datagram fragment being lost in transmission.

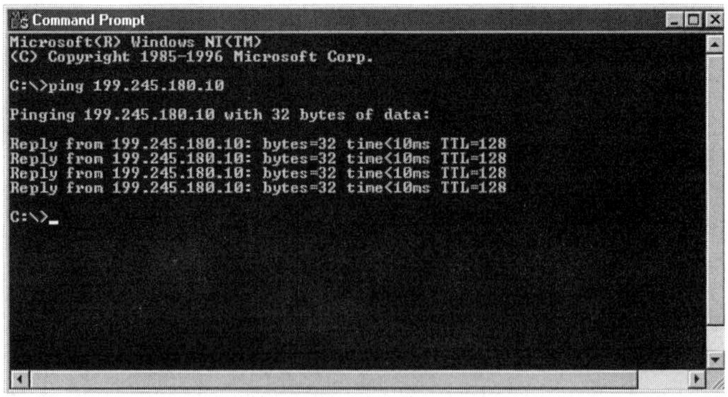

**Figure 15.5**   Using the simple form of PING.

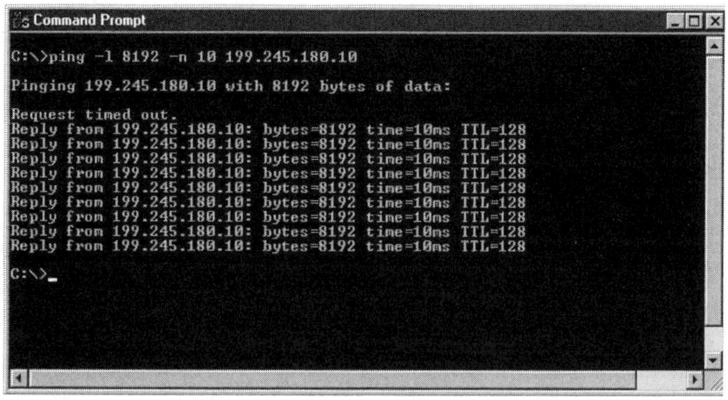

**Figure 15.6**   PING with *-1* and *-n* option.

To verify whether fragmentation is required you can use the -f option, which sets the Don't Fragment (DF) flag in the header of the IP packet that encapsulates the ICMP message. Setting the DF flag is an instruction to routers along the path not to fragment the datagram. If a router is unable to forward an IP datagram because its DF flag is set, the router discards the datagram and sends an ICMP message (Type 3, Code 4) back saying that fragmentation was needed but Don't Fragment was set. Typically, DF is set by diskless workstations that need to download their system image using the Trivial File Transfer Protocol (TFTP). Figure 15.7 shows the results of using the -f option with a large MTU size. Note that the message returned says Packet needs to be fragmented but DF set.

The -j and -k options specify loose and strict source routing. These options are used to specify a list of addresses of routers that must be visited by a packet. This can be used to force a packet to go along a certain path. The *loose source routing* (-j) requires only that the packet visit the specified routers along the path. Between any two routers that are specified using the loose source routing option, there can be other intervening routers. The strict source routing (-k) requires all messages to traverse the specified routers in the order listed. There can be no intervening routers between any two routers specified in the list.

The -I option is used to change the Time To Live (TTL) field value of the IP packet that encapsulates the ICMP message. This can be used to control how long the message lives on the network. Each router is required to decrease the TTL value by at least 1 second. When the TTL field value reaches 0, the datagram is discarded and an ICMP message (Type 11) is sent back saying that the TTL field expired. The PING utility takes TTL field values from 1 to 255 seconds.

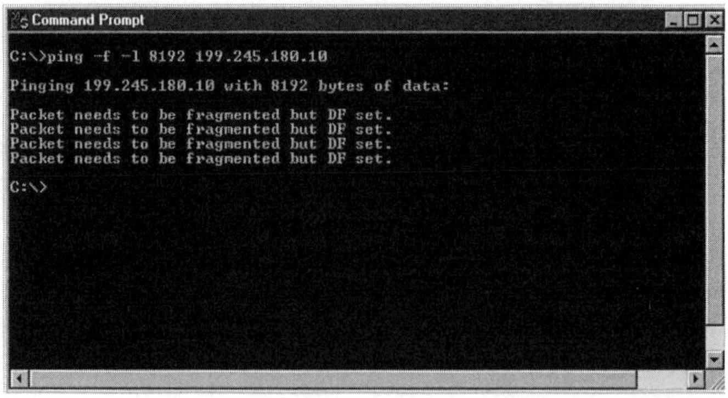

Figure 15.7 PING with -l and -f option.

# Microsoft's Implementation of Traceroute (TRACERT)

The Traceroute program originated under UNIX but has been ported to Windows (NT and 9x) where it is called TRACERT. TRACERT is used to trace the route followed by IP Datagrams to reach a specified destination.

TRACERT works by sending ICMP messages with an expanding scope of TTL values (see Figure 15.8). For example, TRACERT first sends an ICMP message with a TTL value set to 1. The first router that sees this message decreases it by 1; that is, TTL becomes 0. When TTL becomes 0, the router discards the message and sends an ICMP message (Type 11) back to the sender, the TRACERT program, saying that the TTL field expired. From the IP address of the sender of this message, the TRACERT correctly deduces the identity of the first hop router. A number of messages are sent for a given TTL value. From this, TRACERT determines the minimum, maximum, and average times to the router. The TRACERT then repeats the test with a TTL value of 2. Next, it repeats the test with a TTL value of 3, and so on, until a message is sent back from the target host specified in the TRACERT command. If a message is not returned after a certain number of hops, TRACERT will timeout. You then have knowledge of which routers were reachable. TRACERT also uses reverse DNS queries, where possible, to report symbolic names of routers. If reverse DNS query is not set up for the router addresses, these are reported by their IP addresses only.

**TRACERT May Not Work with Some Routers**

You should be aware that some routers can be configured to drop packets sent by commands such as TRACERT; in this case the hop information will not appear in TRACERT's output. Also note that routers can be configured not to send TTL expiration messages.

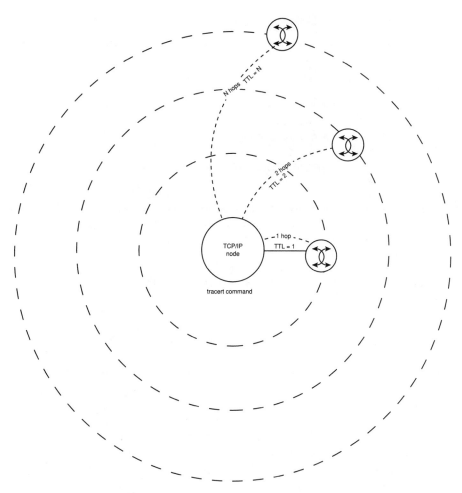

**Figure 15.8**   Operation of TRACERT.

The TRACERT program has the following syntax, described in the table:

```
TRACERT [-d] [-h maximum_hops] [-j computer-list]
[-w timeout] target_name
```

| Argument | Description |
| --- | --- |
| -d | Does not convert the IP addresses of computers between the local computer and *target_name* into computer names. |
| -h *maximum_hops* | The maximum number of hops between the local computer and *target_name*. |
| -j *computer-list* | Specifies loose source route along *computer-list*. |

*continues*

| Argument | Description |
|----------|-------------|
| -w *timeout* | Waits the specified number of milliseconds before timing out. |
| *target_name* | The remote computer to locate. |

The following is a sample output from the TRACERT program:

```
C:\> TRACERT FTP.MICROSOFT.COM
132 ms 138 ms 144 ms gw1.iquest.net [198.70.144.10]
176 ms 166 ms 169 ms li.mci.net [204.70.41.5]
316 ms 237 ms 201 ms fin2.mci.net [204.70.3.65]
170 ms 175 ms 160 ms core.mci.net [204.70.1.82]
225 ms 222 ms 221 ms seabr1-gw.nwnet.net [192.147.179.5]
250 ms 240 ms 252 ms msoft-t3-gw.nwnet.net [198.104.192.9]
230 ms 242 ms 238 ms ftp.microsoft.com [196.105.232.1]
Trace complete.
```

# Using the Address Resolution Protocol (ARP) Tool

The ARP command tool is used for examining and changing the values in the ARP cache table. The ARP cache table contains the bindings between hardware addresses and IP addresses. In a broadcast network such as Ethernet, Token Ring, or FDDI, the hardware (MAC) address of the TCP/IP node to be contacted is discovered based on its IP address. This is done by using the ARP request broadcast; and the reply to this broadcast, called the ARP reply, contains the hardware address of the node to be contacted. The hardware address and IP address pair discovered via ARP is cached in memory for a period of time called the ARP cache timeout. The ARP tool can be used to display the contents of the ARP cache, add entries, or change entries.

The ARP command displays the current mapping of MAC (physical adapter) addresses to IP addresses. The ARP command can also verify whether your IP protocol stack is properly bound to your adapter, and whether you can view other devices on your network. If the IP protocol module is not properly bound to the network adapter, the ARP cache table will be empty. ARP will not display an entry for the current adapter; you must use IPCONFIG -all to view the MAC address of your current adapter.

Following is the syntax of the ARP command, described in the table:

```
ARP -a [inet_addr] [-N [if_addr]]
ARP -d -g in_addr [if_addr]
ARP -s in_addr ether_addr [if_addr]
```

**IPCONFIG Problems and Versions**

If IP is not working properly, IPCONFIG will not show any TCP/IP related information. On Win9x machines, you would use the GUI utility WINIPCFG. Windows NT comes with a similar GUI in the Resource Kit, called WNTIPCFG.

**Argument  Description**

-a          Displays current entries in the ARP cache. By default, all IP addresses
            other than the current adapter are displayed. If an *inet_addr* value is
            provided after -a, the entry for only that adapter is displayed.

-g          Same as -a.

*inet_addr* Specify an IP address here, in the familiar xxx.xxx.xxx.xxx notation,
            in which xxx can be any value from 0 to 255.

-N          Displays the ARP entries for the network interface specified by
            *if_addr*.

*if_addr*   Short for interface address. This is used if you have multiple adapters
            in your system, and you need to view or modify the ARP cache for a
            particular adapter. If this is left blank, the first available interface will
            be used.

-d          Deletes the specified entry.

-s          Adds an entry in the ARP cache to associate the IP address *inet_addr*
            with the MAC address *ether_addr*.

*ether_addr* The MAC address. The physical address is entered as HH-HH-HH-
            HH-HH-HH, where H is a hexadecimal value from 0 to F. Each net-
            work adapter will have a burned-in address from the factory (the
            UAA or Universally Administered Address) that can be overridden in
            the Control Panel with an address of your choosing (LAA, or Locally
            Administered Address). This can be the address of a token-ring net-
            work adapter. The parameter *ether_addr* was probably used for histor-
            ical reasons; Ethernet technology and IP technology have a closely
            linked history.

IPCONFIG will list the MAC addresses for all physical adapters on your system,
including the modem if you are connected to an IP network. Moreover, PINGing an IP
address on your LAN will automatically add it to the ARP cache of your default adapter.

To display all the entries in the ARP cache table, use the -a option:

```
C:\> arp y a
Interface: 199.245.180.101 on Interface 1
Internet Address      Physical Address      Type
199.245.180.1         00-00-c0-7a-2d-5c     dynamic
199.245.180.10        00-00-c0-dd-14-5c     dynamic
```

The Type of entries is listed as dynamic because they are timed out.

If you want to see an entry for a specific IP address, list that address as part of the
command:

```
C:\> arp
 -a 199.245.180.1
Interface: 199.245.180.101 on Interface 1
Internet Address      Physical Address      Type
199.245.180.1         00-00-c0-7a-2d-5c     dynamic
```

An ARP cache table is maintained for every network interface on a multihomed machine. The ARP command, by default, only reports the cache table for the first network adapter. If you want to display the ARP cache table for other network adapters, you can use the -N option and specify the MAC address of the interface. For example, you can use the following to see the ARP cache table on interface 00–00-C0-E0-DF-34.

```
arp -a -n 00-00-C0-E0-DF-34
```

To delete an ARP cache table entry you can use the -d option and specify the IP address for the entry to be deleted:

Why would you want to delete an ARP cache table entry? You may want to do this if the ARP cache table has become corrupt because of duplicate IP address problems. In this case the corrupt entry can be manually deleted.

As part of manually fixing problems of corrupt entries in the ARP cache table, you may want to add additional entries. You can do this using the -s option. For example, if you want to manually add an entry for 199.245.180.3 that is bound to an interface address of 00-00-C0-BA-DE-FA you can use the following command:

```
arp-s 199.245.180.3 00-00-C0-BA-DE-FA
```

Entries added using the -s option are static entries and are not timed out. For example, if you were to reexamine the ARP cache table after the previous command, it might look like the following:

```
C:\> arp -a
Interface: 199.245.180.101 on Interface 1
Internet Address    Physical Address    Type
199.245.180.1       00-00-c0-7a-2d-5c   dynamic
199.245.180.3       00-00-c0-ba-de-fa   static
199.245.180.10      00-00-c0-dd-14-5c   dynamic
```

# Displaying Network Connections and Statistics with *NETSTAT*

The NETSTAT command is used to display the current TCP/IP network connections and protocol statistics. The syntax of the NETSTAT command is as follows:

```
NETSTAT [-a] [-e] [-n] [-s] [-p protocol] [-r] [interval]
```

| Argument | Description |
| --- | --- |
| -a | Displays connections and listening ports. |
| -e | Displays Ethernet statistics. May be combined with the -s option for more options. |
| -n | Displays addresses and port numbers. |
| -s | Displays per *protocol* statistics. Used in conjunction with the -p option, you can ask for a subset of the default (TCP, UDP, ICMP, and IP). |
| -p *protocol* | Displays connections for the *protocol* specified (tcp or udp). If the -s option is used in conjunction with this parameter, *protocol* may be tcp, udp, icmp, or ip. |

`-r`             Displays the contents of the routing table.

*interval*       Redisplays selected statistics, pausing between each display. In order to stop the redisplay, press Ctrl+C. If *interval* is omitted, information is displayed only once.

The following is an example of using the NETSTAT command:

```
C:\> NETSTAT
Active Connections
   Proto  Local Address          Foreign Address         State
   TCP    ntsrvr:1025            localhost:1026          ESTABLISHED
   TCP    ntsrvr:1026            localhost:1025          ESTABLISHED
   TCP    ntsrvr:1108            199.245.180.10:telnet   ESTABLISHED
```

NETSTAT reports the following protocol and connection information for each session:

- **Proto.** This is the transport protocol type (TCP, UDP) over which the session is established.
- **Local Address.** This is the local endpoint address of the session. This is the name or IP address of the local computer, and the local port number used by the local end of the connection.
- **Foreign Address.** This is the remote endpoint address of the session. This is the name or IP address of the remote computer, and the remote port number used by the remote end of the connection.
- **State.** This shows the state of the TCP connection. The possible values of the state include the following: ESTABLISHED, CLOSED, CLOSE-WAIT, FIN_WAIT_1, FIN_WAIT_2, LAST_ACK, LISTEN, SYN_RECEIVED, SYN_SEND, and TIMED_WAIT. These states are the state that a TCP session can be in. Figure 15.9 shows the state diagram for a TCP session. The details of the TCP operation are described in this author's book, *Inside TCP/IP*, from New Riders Publishing.

The following are examples of the uses of NETSTAT.

If you want to see the results in numeric rather than symbolic name format, you can use the -n option. The previous NETSTAT information, obtained by using the -n option, is displayed as follows:

```
C:\> NETSTAT -N
Active Connections
   Proto  Local Address          Foreign Address         State
   TCP    127.0.0.1:1025         127.0.0.1:1026          ESTABLISHED
   TCP    127.0.0.1:1026         127.0.0.1:1025          ESTABLISHED
   TCP    199.245.180.101:139    199.245.180.1:1033      ESTABLISHED
```

The -a option gives detailed information on the statistics:

```
C:\> NETSTAT -A
Active Connections
   Proto  Local Address          Foreign Address         State
   TCP    ntsrvr:1025            localhost:1026          ESTABLISHED
```

```
TCP    ntsrvr:1026           localhost:1025        ESTABLISHED
TCP    ntsrvr:nbsession      LTREE1:1033           ESTABLISHED
UDP    ntsrvr:135            *:*
UDP    ntsrvr:nbname         *:*
UDP    ntsrvr:nbdatagram     *:*
```

The -e option displays Ethernet statistics:

```
C:\> NETSTAT -E
Interface Statistics
                           Received          Sent
Bytes                      1169462           209901
Unicast packets            286               340
Non-unicast packets        235               192
Discards                   0                 0
Errors                     0                 0
Unknown protocols          11300
```

The -e option can be used to discover errors caused by a faulty network card.

The -s option gives statistics for each of the protocols: IP, ICMP, TCP, and UDP. Because the display reports on problems and error conditions, you can use this to detect problem conditions with the network. Of particular note are the values of error counters such as Received Header Errors, Received Address Errors, and so on.

```
C:\> NETSTAT -s
IP Statistics
  Packets Received                    = 489
  Received Header Errors              = 0
  Received Address Errors             = 0
  Datagrams Forwarded                 = 0
  Unknown Protocols Received          = 0
  Received Packets Discarded          = 0
  Received Packets Delivered          = 444
  Output Requests                     = 431
  Routing Discards                    = 0
  Discarded Output Packets            = 0
  Output Packet No Route              = 0
  Reassembly Required                 = 54
  Reassembly Successful               = 9
  Reassembly Failures                 = 0
  Datagrams Successfully Fragmented   = 20
  Datagrams Failing Fragmentation     = 8
  Fragments Created                   = 120

ICMP Statistics
                          Received      Sent
  Messages                86            115
  Errors                  0             0
  Destination Unreachable 12            0
```

```
Time Exceeded            0          0
Parameter Problems       0          0
Source Quenchs           0          0
Redirects                0          0
Echos                    0          115
Echo Replies             74         0
Timestamps               0          0
Timestamp Replies        0          0
Address Masks            0          0
Address Mask Replies     0          0

TCP Statistics

Active Opens                 = 3
Passive Opens                = 9
Failed Connection Attempts   = 0
Reset Connections            = 1
Current Connections          = 3
Segments Received            = 133
Segments Sent                = 110
Segments Retransmitted       = 0

UDP Statistics
Datagrams Received   = 225
No Ports             = 86
Receive Errors       = 0
Datagrams Sent       = 206
```

In the previous display output, the `ICMP Destination Unreachable` count of 12 might indicate a network reachability problem or some host may be down. The `Datagrams Failing Fragmentation` count of 8 indicates a problem with the fragmentation of some IP Datagrams.

The -r option is particularly useful for solving routing related problems because it displays the routing table:

```
C:\> NETSTAT -S
Active Routes:
Network Address   Netmask           Gateway Address  Interface        Metric
127.0.0.0         255.0.0.0         127.0.0.1        127.0.0.1        1
199.245.180.0     255.255.255.0     199.245.180.101  199.245.180.101  1
199.245.180.101   255.255.255.255   127.0.0.1        127.0.0.1        1
199.245.180.255   255.255.255.255   199.245.180.101  199.245.180.101  1
224.0.0.0         224.0.0.0         199.245.180.101  199.245.180.101  1
255.255.255.255   255.255.255.255   199.245.180.101  199.245.180.101  1
```

```
Route Table
Active Connections
  Proto  Local Address        Foreign Address       State
  TCP    ntsrvr:1025          localhost:1026        ESTABLISHED
  TCP    ntsrvr:1026          localhost:1025        ESTABLISHED
  TCP    ntsrvr:nbsession     LTREE1:1034           ESTABLISHED
```

As can be seen in the preceding example, the -r option also displays the active connections.

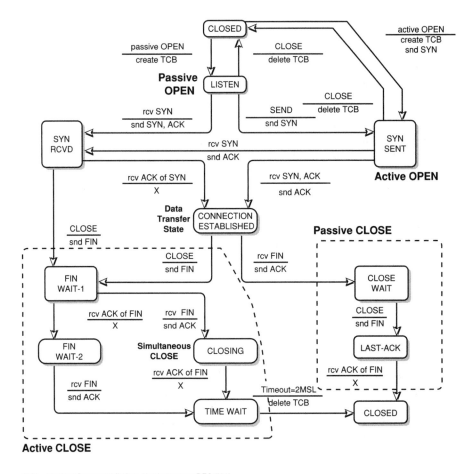

**MSL**= Maxium Segment Lifetime (2 minutes per RFC 793)

**TCB** = Transmission Control Buffer (contains state information on the TCP end point)

**Figure 15.9**   TCP/IP state diagram.

# Displaying TCP/IP Statistics and Connections with *NBTSTAT*

The NBTSTAT displays TCP/IP statistics and current connections using NetBIOS over TCP/IP (NBT), if TCP/IP has been installed. The syntax is as follows:

```
NBTSTAT [-a remotename] [-A IP address] [-c] [-n] [-R] [-r]
[-S] [-s] [interval]
```

| Argument | Description |
|---|---|
| -a *remotename* | Displays a remote computer's name table by name. |
| -A *IP address* | Displays a remote computer's name table by IP address. |
| -c | Displays the contents and IP addresses of the local computer's NetBIOS name cache. |
| -n | Displays the local NetBIOS names. |
| -R | Reloads the LMHOSTS file after deleting the names from the NetBIOS name cache. |
| -r | Displays the name resolution statistics for Windows networking name resolution. On an NT system configured to use WINS, this argument lists the number of NetBIOS names resolved and registered by broadcast or by WINS. |
| -S | Displays all client and server sessions, with remote systems listed by their IP addresses. |
| -s | Displays all client and server sessions. Using the local HOSTS file, attempts to convert the remote system's IP address to a host name. |
| *interval* | Redisplays some statistics, stopping for a couple of seconds between each display. To stop, press Ctrl+C. If *interval* is omitted, NBTSTAT lists the configuration information one time. |

For example, the -r option is very useful for displaying the name resolution statistics for Windows networking, such as the number of name resolutions occurring by each type of name resolution method:

```
C:\> NBTSTAT -r
NetBIOS Names Resolution and Registration Statistics
-------------------------------------------------
Resolved By Broadcast     = 1
Resolved By Name Server   = 0
Registered By Broadcast   = 13
Registered By Name Server = 0

NetBIOS Names Resolved By Broadcast
-------------------------------------------
    LTREE1          <00>
```

The -n option is used to list all local NetBIOS names:

```
C:\> NBTSTAT -n
Node IpAddress: [199.245.180.101]
Scope Id: []

NetBIOS Local Name Table
    Name                Type        Status
-----------------------------------------------
    NTSRVR        <20>  UNIQUE      Registered
    NTSRVR        <00>  UNIQUE      Registered
    NTDOMAIN      <00>  GROUP       Registered
    NTDOMAIN      <1C>  GROUP       Registered
    NTDOMAIN      <1B>  UNIQUE      Registered
    NTSRVR        <03>  UNIQUE      Registered
    INet~Services <1C>  GROUP       Registered
    IS~NTSRVR......<00> UNIQUE      Registered
    NTDOMAIN      <1E>  GROUP       Registered
    NTDOMAIN      <1D>  UNIQUE      Registered
    ..__MSBROWSE__.<01> GROUP       Registered
    ADMINISTRATOR <03>  UNIQUE      Registered
```

The NetBIOS name types are described in Chapter 9, "TCP/IP Name Resolution Using WINS."

The -s option is used to display the NetBIOS connection table:

```
C:\> NBTSTAT -s NetBIOS Connection Table

Local Name            State     In/Out   Remote Host     Input   Output
-------------------------------------------------------------------------
NTSRVR                Connected  In      199.245.180.1   582B    470B
NTSRVR      <03>      Listening
ADMINISTRATOR <03>    Listening
```

# Index

# X–Z

# New Riders Professional Library

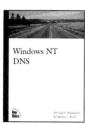

## Windows NT DNS

By Michael Masterson &
Herman L. Knief
1st Edition Summer 1998
325 pages, $29.99
ISBN 1-56205-943-2

Have you ever opened a Windows NT book looking for detailed information about DNS only to discover that it doesn't even begin to scratch the surface? DNS is probably one of the most complicated subjects for NT administrators, and there are few books on the market that really address it in detail. This book answers your most complex DNS questions, focusing on the implementation of the Domain Name Service within Windows NT, treating it thoroughly from the viewpoint of an experienced Windows NT professional. Many detailed, real-world examples illustrate further the understanding of the material throughout. The book covers the details of how DNS functions within NT, then explores specific interactions with critical network components. Finally, proven procedures to design and set up DNS are demonstrated. You'll also find coverage of related topics, such as maintenance, security, and troubleshooting.

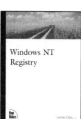

## Windows NT Registry

By Sandra Osborne
1st Edition Summer 1998
500 pages, $29.99
ISBN 1-56205-941-6

The NT Registry can be a very powerful tool for those capable of using it wisely. Unfortunately, there is very little information regarding the NT Registry, due to Microsoft's insistence that their source code be kept secret. If you're looking to optimize your use of the registry, you're usually forced to search the web for bits of information. This book is your resource. It covers critical issues and settings used for configuring network protocols, including NWLink, PTP, TCP/IP and DHCP. This book approaches the material from a unique point of view, discussing the problems related to a particular component, and then discussing settings, which are the actual changes necessary for implementing robust solutions. There is also a comprehensive reference of registry settings and commands making this the perfect addition to your technical bookshelf.

## Exchange Server Implementation and Administration

By Excell Data Corporation
1st Edition Fall 1998
450 pages, $29.99
ISBN 1-56205-931-9

If you're interested in connectivity and maintenance issues for Exchange Server, then this book is for you. Exchange's power lies in its ability to be connected to multiple email subsystems to create a "universal email backbone." It's not unusual to have several different and complex systems all connected via email gateways, including Lotus Notes or cc:Mail, Microsoft Mail, legacy mainframe systems, and Internet mail. This book covers all of the problems and issues associated with getting an integrated system running smoothly, and addresses troubleshooting and diagnosis of email problems, with an eye towards prevention and best practices.

## Windows NT Performance Monitoring

By Mark Edmead
1st Edition Fall 1998
400 pages, $29.99
ISBN 1-56205-942-4

Performance monitoring is a little like preventative medicine for the administrator: no one enjoys a checkup, but it's a good thing to do on a regular basis. This book helps you focus on the critical aspects of improving the performance of your NT system, showing you how to monitor the system, implement benchmarking, and tune your network. The book is organized by resource components, which makes it easy to use as a reference tool.

## SQL Server System Administration

By Sean Baird, Chris Miller et al.
1st Edition Fall 1998
400 pages, $29.99
1-56205-955-6

How often does your SQL Server go down during the day when everyone wants to access the data? Do you spend most of your time being a "report monkey" for your co-workers and bosses? *SQL Server System Administration* helps you keep data consistently available to your users. This book omits the introductory information. The authors don't spend time explaining queries and how they work. Instead they focus on the information that you can't get anywhere else, like how to choose the correct replication topology and achieve high availability of information.

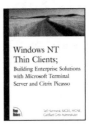

## Windows NT Thin Clients
*Building Enterprise Solutions with Microsoft Terminal Server & Citrix Picasso*

By Ted Harwood
1st Edition Winter 1998
500 pages, $29.99
ISBN 1-56205-944-0

It's no surprise that most administration headaches revolve around integration with other networks and clients. This book addresses these types of real-world issues on a case-by-case basis, giving tools and advice on solving each problem. If you use Citrix Picasso in your heterogeneous networking environment, this book is for you. The author also offers the real nuts and bolts of thin client administration on multiple systems, covering such relevant issues as installation, configuration, network connection, management, and application distribution.

## Windows NT Technical Support

By Brendan McTague & George Neal
1st Edition Winter 1998
300 pages, $29.99
ISBN 1-56205-927-0

Well, you did it. You finally migrated your Enterprise network to Windows NT. Now what you need is a methodology, a logical way you can rigorously approach any problem, whether it's server or workstation related, and quickly get to its root. That's what we asked Brendan and George, part of the group responsible for supporting Swiss Bank's worldwide NT enterprise, to put together for you. These guys have to support thousands of users on three continents—so they understand what technical support is. So why don't you read through their methodology, practice it on several of the sample work tickets included in the book, then go out and try it yourself?

## Windows NT Security

By Richard Puckett
1st Edition Winter 1998
600 pages, $29.99
ISBN 1-56205-945-9

Swiss cheese. That's what some people say Windows NT security is like. And they may be right, because they only know what the NT documentation says about implementing security. Who has the time to research alternatives, play around with the features, service packs, hot fixes and add-on tools, and figure out what makes NT rock solid? Well, Richard Puckett does. He's been researching Windows NT Security for the University of Virginia for a while now, and he's got pretty good news. He's going to show you how to make NT secure in your environment, and we mean really secure.

## Windows NT Administration Handbook

By Eric Svetcov
1st Edition Winter 1998
400 pages, $29.99
ISBN 1-56205-946-7

Administering a Windows NT network is kind of like trying to herd cats—an impossible task characterized by constant motion, exhausting labor and lots of hairballs. Author Eric Svetcov knows all about it - he's administered NT networks for some of the fastest growing companies around Silicon Valley. So we asked Eric to put together a concise manual of best practices, a book of tools and ideas that other administrators can turn to again and again in administering their own NT networks. Eric's experience shines through as he shares his secrets for administering users, for getting domain and groups set up quickly and for troubleshooting the thorniest NT problems. Daily, weekly and monthly task lists help organize routine tasks and preventative maintenance.

## MCSE Core Essential Reference

By Matthew Shepker
1st Edition Fall 1998
500 pages, $19.99
ISBN 0-7357-0006-0

You're sitting in the first session of your Networking Essentials class and the instructor starts talking about "*RAS*" and you have no idea what that means. You think about raising your hand to ask about *RAS*, but you reconsider—you'd feel pretty foolish asking a question in front of all these people. You turn to your handy *MCSE Core Essential Reference* and find a quick summary on *Remote Access Services*. Question answered. It's a couple months later and you're taking your Networking Essentials exam the next day. You're reviewing practice tests and you keep forgetting the maximum lengths for the various commonly used cable types. Once again, you turn to the *MCSE Core Essential Reference* and find a table on cables, including all of the characteristics you need to memorize in order to pass the test.

## Lotus Notes & Domino Essential Reference

By Dave Hatter & Tim Bankes
1st Edition Winter 1998
500 pages, $19.99
ISBN 0-7357-0007-9

You're in a bind because you've been asked to design and program a new database in Notes for an important client that will keep track of and itemize a myriad of inventory and shipping data. The client wants a user-friendly interface, without sacrificing speed or functionality. You are experienced (and could develop this app in your sleep), but feel that you need to take your talents to the next level. You need something to facilitate your creative and technical abilities, something to perfect your programming skills. Your answer is waiting for you: *Lotus Notes and Domino Essential Reference.* It's compact and simply designed. It's loaded with information. All of the objects, classes, functions and methods are listed. It shows you the object hierarchy and the overlaying relationship between each one. It's perfect for you. Problem solved.

## Linux System Administration

By James T. Dennis
1st Edition Winter 1998
450 pages, $29.99
ISBN 1-56205-934-3

As an administrator, you probably feel that most of your time and energy is spent in endless firefighting. If your network has become a fragile quilt of temporary patches and workarounds, then this book is for you. For example, have you had trouble sending or receiving your email lately? Are you looking for a way to keep your network running smoothly with enhanced performance? Are your users always hankering for more storage, more services, and more speed? *Linux System Administration* advises you on the many intricacies of maintaining a secure, stable system. In this definitive work, the author addresses all the issues related to system administration from adding users and managing files permission to internet services and Web hosting to recovery planning and security. This book fulfills the need for expert advice that will ensure a trouble-free Linux environment.

## Domino System Administration

By Rob Kirkland
1st Edition Winter 1998
500 pages, $29.99
ISBN 1-56205-948-3

Your boss has just announced that you will be upgrading to the newest version of Notes and Domino when it ships. As a Premium Lotus Business Partner, Lotus has offered a substantial price break to keep your company away from Microsoft's Exchange Server. How are you supposed to get this new system installed, configured, and rolled out to all of your end users? You understand how Lotus Notes works — you've been administering it for years. What you need is a concise, practical explanation about the new features, and how to make some of the advanced stuff really work. You need answers and solutions from someone who's been in the trenches; someone like you, who has worked with the product for years, and understands what it is you need to know. *Domino System Administration* is the answer — the first book on Domino that attacks the technology at the professional level, with practical, hands-on assistance to get Domino running in your organization.